Mentor Texts

Teaching Writing Through Children's Literature, K–6

Stenhouse Publishers
Portland, Maine

Lynne R. Dorfman & Rose Cappelli

Foreword by Linda Hoyt

Stenhouse Publishers
www.stenhouse.com

Credits
Pages 27, 92, 127, 142, 184–185, 253: CRAB MOON. Text Copyright © 2000 Ruth Horowitz. Illustrations Copyright © 2000 Kate Kiesler. Reproduced by permission of the Publisher, Candlewick Press, Somerville, MA.
Pages 120, 146: From WIDGET © 2001 by Lyn Rossiter McFarland. Reprinted by permission of Macmillan Publishing Group, LLC d/b/a Farrar, Straus, and Giroux Books for Young Readers. All Rights Reserved.
Page 258: Illustration by Laura Huliska-Beith from THE RECESS QUEEN by Alexis O'Neill. Scholastic Inc./Scholastic Press. Illustration copyright © 2002 by Laura Huliska-Beith. Used by permission.

Library of Congress Cataloging-in-Publication Data
Names: Dorfman, Lynne R., 1952– editor. | Cappelli, Rose, 1950– author.
Title: Mentor texts : teaching writing through children's literature, k–6 / Lynne R. Dorfman and Rose Cappelli.
Description: Second edition. | Portland, Maine : Stenhouse Publishers, 2017.
    Identifiers: LCCN 2016050295 (print) | LCCN 2017017104 (ebook) | ISBN 9781625311320 (ebook) | ISBN 9781625311313 (paperback)
Subjects: LCSH: Language arts (Elementary) | Children's literature—Study and teaching (Elementary)—Activity programs. | English language—Composition and exercises—Study and teaching (Elementary)
Classification: LCC LB1576 (ebook) | LCC LB1576 .D657 2017 (print) | DDC 372.6/044—dc23
LC record available at https://lccn.loc.gov/2016050295

Photographs by Rose Cappelli and Ralph Abbott
Cover photo by Rose Cappelli
Cover design, interior design, and typesetting by Martha Drury

Manufactured in the United States of America

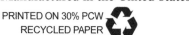
PRINTED ON 30% PCW
RECYCLED PAPER

23 22 21 20 19 18 17   9 8 7 6 5 4 3 2 1

To our mentors,
professional as well as personal,
who have taught us the secrets of living,
writing, and teaching

Contents

Foreword

*We all need mentors in our lives—those knowledgeable others who help us learn
how to be teachers, mothers, musicians, artists, athletes—who help us do what
we could not do before on our own.*

—Lynne Dorfman and Rose Cappelli

This second edition of Rose Cappelli and Lynne Dorfman's *Mentor Texts* brings
special insights about the use of mentor texts to lift student writing. While reading, I became completely hooked when Lynne and Rose described a classroom
writing experience: "Their words rushed and gushed in rivers and whispered in
silver streams, and the air was filled with writing by students who believed they
were writers." What a magical writing moment in a classroom! Who wouldn't
want experiences like that for their students?

Lynne and Rose open a deeply personal window into their work with children and take readers on a journey filled with richly detailed classroom experiences. The authors demonstrate the power of teaching children to lean in
closely and investigate the ideas, the craft, and the language of mentor texts.
The thoughtfully organized chapters reveal a plethora of ways to motivate,
extend, and develop written and linguistic proficiency for learners of all ages.

The compelling power of this resource resides in the way mentors are
linked to careful scaffolding that is designed to support and extend thinking,
help writers experiment in their writer's notebooks, and develop fully executed
writing projects. Throughout, Lynne and Rose hold steadfast to their mission:
not just to teach a book but to lift writers with strategic, transferable thinking.
The tips are practical, carefully executed, and often accompanied by student
artifacts. In all cases, the authors hold true to their belief that "a reflective
writer is one who understands the whys and hows of writing and can transfer
strategies to future writing situations."

I also love the way Lynne and Rose focus on important elements of craft
such as syntax, endings, conventions, and grammar. By recasting these conventions as craft elements and then focusing on them through investigations of

mentor texts, modeled writing, and shared writing, the authors help writers redefine the role of conventions. How exciting for writers to adjust their linguistic lenses and learn to perceive conventions as helpful tools, rather than as simple functions of correctness. As Lynne and Rose say, "When you study parts of speech through the use of mentor texts, eventually it spills over into the students' own writing. Students become mentors for each other during peer conferences and shared readings."

You'll see that the authors have expanded on some of the most popular features of the first edition of *Mentor Texts*. They have again included the Your Turn lessons, which have been so effective for teachers, and added even more. I love these lessons because they contextualize the learning so effectively. They've also kept the powerful Treasure Chest of Books, updated and kept current in this second edition. The Treasure Chest, a true wealth of possibility, is a resource you won't want to leave on the shelf. It belongs on your desk, where you can easily tap into its bounty on a daily basis.

Mentor Texts is like having a literature expert and master teacher at your side all year long. Enjoy it, mark it up, and make it your friend. You and your students will be energized and motivated as you savor richly constructed mentor texts and connect them to amazing writing opportunities. Happy writing!

Linda Hoyt

Author of *Interactive Read-Alouds*,
Explorations in Nonfiction Writing,
and *Conventions and Craft*

Acknowledgments

Many people have acted as mentors in our professional lives, helping to inform our thinking and shape the beliefs that guide our teaching. Some of them are personal friends and supportive colleagues with whom we interact on a regular basis. Others are people we have listened to at conferences and whose work we have read extensively. Both groups have left a lasting impression in our minds and hearts, and have provided us with insights, gentle nudges, and words of encouragement.

Regie Routman, Shelley Harwayne, and Linda Hoyt provided invaluable guidance through their written words as well as through personal conversations. Shelley helped us see the power of the anecdote in a professional book such as this. Regie showed us the power of a peer response group for feedback on clarity and purpose. Linda became a model for our presentation work and always offered us words of encouragement. Other authors such as Katie Wood Ray, Donald Graves, Ralph Fletcher, Barry Lane, Lucy Calkins, Stacey Shubitz, Kelly Gallagher, Clare Landrigan, and Tammy Mulligan have influenced our teaching and our personal writing. Their voices are inside our heads, and as we wrote, they spoke to us. We believe you will hear them, too.

Thank you to literacy consultant Sue Mowery for your friendship and your enthusiasm as our biggest fan. Over the years your work provided a model for taking risks and trying things that we never thought were possible. Thank you, Bill Mowery, for your insight in bringing us together as a collaborative team. Our love of children's picture books was greatly fostered by friend and colleague Nancy McElwee. Thank you, Nancy. We think we finally have more picture books than you do!

Thank you to everyone involved with the Pennsylvania Writing and Literature Project at West Chester University, especially former director Dr. Robert H. Weiss and current director Dr. Mary Buckelew. Our participation in the institutes and courses brought to life the idea of teacher as writer. The ideas shared in those writing communities challenged us to reflect on our teaching practices. Our ideas for this book originally developed through our facilitation of Writing and Children's Literature, a graduate course we have offered every summer. This course was instrumental in bringing us together to share our thinking as we grew and changed. Our collaboration each summer produced the seeds of the ideas presented in this book. We'd like to thank teachers Teresa Moslak and Lorie Epperson for stepping into our roles as coordinators for this wonderful course. Through the years we have met a multitude of teachers from various districts as we present courses and inservices. Thank you all for trying out our ideas, giving us new ones, and sharing your classroom successes with us.

Our involvement in the Keystone State Reading Association has given us many opportunities to present our ideas at state conferences and local council events. We sincerely thank all the wonderful people in KSRA who have encouraged and supported us in our journey.

Several years ago we began meeting with Patti Sollenberger of Reading Matters to have conversations about picture books as avenues for helping students become more successful writers. As we sat around the table at the Reading Matters office, we all came to the realization that we had more to say. Thank you, Patti and Phil Sollenberger, for your support and the introduction to our Stenhouse editor.

We consider ourselves fortunate to be considered Stenhouse authors. Our editor, William Varner, gave us solid advice and provided the right information at the right time to empower us as writers. Thank you, Bill, for your support, your kind and thoughtful words, and your belief in our message. Thank you also to everyone else at Stenhouse who has had a hand in shaping our book, particularly Chris Downey, Jay Kilburn, and Grace Makley. Thank you to the copyeditor, Laurel Robinson, and designer, Martha Drury. Thank you, Chandra Lowe, for your enthusiastic support and wonderful organizational skills.

Finally, thank you to all the children's authors who write the amazing books that touch the lives of the students we teach. They are the mentors who stand beside us every day in our classrooms and enable us to create successful writers.

From Rose:

A few years ago I received a Christmas card from a friend and colleague. Along with the appropriate holiday sentiment were the words *Write the book*. I kept that card in my desk drawer, rereading it when doubts about my ability to finish this manuscript surfaced in my head. Somehow, it served as a reminder of the many people who supported, encouraged, and believed in this project. (Thanks, Joe.)

Thank you to all past and present teachers at Fern Hill Elementary School in the West Chester Area School District, West Chester, Pennsylvania, for welcoming me into your classrooms and working alongside me as we discovered more about the development of writing in young children and the possibilities they can achieve. A special thanks goes to Pat Aubry, Erin Bove, Patty Cleveland, Mary Jane Corabi, Stephanie Cullen, Sharon Dean, Shawn

Dzielawa, Heather Garvey, Connie Harker, Jeannine Langlois, Nicole Lockhart, Christine Miller, Joe Mulvey, Kim Parise, Sue Phifer, Peggy Ridgway, Heather Santry, and Linda Trembath with whom I worked most closely.

Thank you to Cheryl Ash and Sara Missett, former principals of Fern Hill Elementary, for your constant encouragement and belief in me. Thanks also to current principal Rebecca Eberly for your unending support. You are a true cheerleader!

Thank you, Lynne. Without your vision this book would never have been. I always eagerly anticipate our discussions and our work together. You have taught me how to keep looking forward.

Thank you to my family. To my sister, Margaret DeAngelis, for memories of reading aloud and for demonstrating the writerly life. Thank you to my children, Brian and Ann, for inspiration you never knew you gave. And, last but not least, thank you to my husband, Allan, whose love, support, and friendship sustain and fulfill me.

From Lynne:

I want to begin by thanking all the teachers and students of the Upper Moreland Intermediate School in the Upper Moreland School District, Hatboro, Pennsylvania. How lucky I am to have had your constant support and inspiration! A special thanks to Maribeth Batcho, Sue Coram, Dawn Costello, Mark Curtis, Marlajean Fay, Sandra Fedele, Kelly Gallagher, Teri Gearhart, Valerie Hawkins, Shelly Keller, Jen Kennedy, Brenda Krupp, Lisa Labow, Teresa Lombardi, Cathy McParland, Michelle Moore, Sue Powidzki, Kathy Randolph, Karen Drew Rhoads, and Barbara Wright for letting me try out so many Your Turn lessons, conduct writer's cafés, and refine the use of writer's notebook in your classes. A big thank-you to friend and colleague Bruce Bloome and his son Matthew Bloome. All I can say is, Bruce, I'm still waiting for your first picture book! Matthew, thanks for sharing all the wonderful children's books and your insightful discoveries.

My heartfelt thanks to my former principal Dr. Joseph Waters, colleague and friend. I loved working for you and hope to continue to engage in professional discussions. Thank you, Dr. Robert Milrod, for supporting my position as a writing coach and giving me opportunities to grow as a literacy leader. You are a good friend.

To Sister Anne Marie Burton, thank you for helping me develop writing stamina. Thanks to you and all the professors at Immaculata University who have touched my life and helped me challenge my thinking.

Thank you, Dave. You always said I should write. You nudged me through a master's thesis, supported me through a dissertation, and continued to urge me to publish. Thank you, Shinners family, for always believing in me and giving me the joy of having a wonderful goddaughter, Alexandra Paige. Alex, Brooke, and Caitlyn, you are always in my heart wherever I go.

Fran, I miss you every day. Thanks, Tom, for continuing to cheer me on. Mary, Janice, and Diane, you are my friends, colleagues, and the best of listeners. Thank you for always being there for me. Thank you, Diane and Willie, for your belief in my ability to write this book. And Ralph, you were so happy for me when I announced that Rose and I were going to create a second edition of this book.

Even though you are not here to read these words, thank you, "GaGa," for giving me all those wonderful memories so I would never run out of grandfather stories to write about in my writer's notebook. When I write about you, I feel as though you are still here with me.

Finally, a big thank-you to Rose. I could never have written this book without you, Rosie. Our collaboration in course work and as a writing team has been one of the best things that has ever happened to me. I have learned so much.

Introduction
to the Second Edition

Welcome to the new edition of *Mentor Texts: Teaching Writing Through Children's Literature, K–6.* During the past decade, we have continued to develop our thinking, revisiting the work of our tried-and-true mentors and learning from new mentors as well. These mentors include both children's and professional authors, teachers, and students. We have closely followed the work of Peter Johnston (2012) and Carol Dweck (2008), whose thinking provides new energy for writing workshop regardless of grade level. Like Peter Johnston, we see a writing community as a giant think tank. The rich discussions that center around the use of mentor texts and the attention to writing process engineer a growth mind-set built on hard work, persistence, and ongoing reflection. When students are willing to take risks and seek feedback, they can continue to grow as writers through practice and effort.

We have also read extensively about the importance of close reading from the work of Lehman and Roberts (2013) and Fisher and Frey (2014). Close reading occurs in writing workshop, too. As a student examines a mentor text, he chooses what he would like to lift and imitate in his own writing. Eventually, he revises in ways to make this craft, convention, or organizational structure something he will use again and again. Close reads in writing workshop provide the gentle nudges to move our students forward as writers so they may grow. By studying mentor texts and mentor authors, students become increasingly more sophisticated and better equipped to write in different forms and genres. They learn to vary their sentence lengths and patterns and produce texts that are largely satisfying for their target audiences.

What's New in This Edition
New Titles

In our first edition, we clearly defined what we mean by a *mentor text*. Although some teachers use the term *touchstone texts* to describe books that serve as models for students, we take a slightly different view. A touchstone can be a word such as *dog* to help a reader remember the sound of *d*. It can be a phrase such as "furrow followed free" from *The Rime of the Ancient Mariner* to remember alliteration. It can be a book that uses one word to organize a story such as *Suddenly!* by Colin McNaughton (1998). To us, a touchstone text is remembered for a specific purpose. Throughout this book, you will find many titles that can be used to teach a particular skill or strategy. Some books may be touchstone texts, but you will discover other titles that are used over and over. These books serve as our mentor texts—books that we know well and love deeply. In this edition, we have included new titles within the chapters and in the updated Treasure Chest. Just as a librarian examines her collection at the end of a school year to remove titles that have lost their appeal or are simply outdated, classroom teachers examine their set of mentor texts to determine whether new titles may serve their students in a better way. Sometimes this is a random discovery—you may realize you are returning to a new read-aloud in student conferences for several different purposes. We offer many titles for you to explore in the hopes that you will make your own decisions about which mentor texts will best serve the needs and purposes of you and your students. We have tried to include new titles that will help students find themselves in the characters, settings, and problems. We believe it is important for students to clearly identify with the texts we return to again and again.

New Sections Within Chapters

In every chapter, we've added new thinking to the discussions of the big ideas. But in some chapters we have added whole new sections. Here's a quick reference:

- Chapter 1—The Student as Writer
- Chapter 3—Using Classroom Conversations to Discover the Inside Story
- Chapter 4—Dipping into Dialogue; Moving from Here to There
- Chapter 5—Transitioning to the Middle; Building a Narrative
- Chapter 6—Alphabet, Numbers, Colors, and More!
- Chapter 8—Sentence Fluency: The Ebb and Flow of Language
- Chapter 9—Improving Sentences with Participial Phrases
- Chapter 10—A Journey Through a Mentor Text

New Your Turn Lessons

Each chapter contains additional Your Turn Lessons to provide practice for both teacher and student. The lessons are a good fit for the study of mentor texts, always linking with quality literature and moving to the production of student text through the gradual release of responsibility model. They are teacher friendly and student tested, helping teachers develop young writers who are both problem solvers and decision makers.

Think About It—Talk About It—Write About It

At the end of each chapter, we have provided questions that can engage you in self-reflection and conversations about writing with trusted colleagues. We hope some of this thinking finds its way into writer's notebooks, professional development opportunities, and thinking that occurs before, during, and after conferences with students. It is through our study of writing, our reading of professional books, our close reading of mentor texts, and our conferences with students that we begin to internalize what we have learned. Through reflection and conversations with others about writing, we discover what works in our classrooms and what we might try. It's the teacher that makes the difference. There is no scripted program that can meet the needs of every student in the classroom. It is up to us to take charge of our writing workshop—to be writers ourselves and to be the biggest cheerleaders for our young writers. We invite you to imagine the possibilities!

Chapter 1

Reinventing the Writer with Mentor Texts

With you as a guide, and literature as the landscape, you can open young writers'
eyes to the full range of possibilities before them.

—Ralph Fletcher and JoAnn Portalupi, *Writing Workshop: The Essential Guide*

What Are Mentor Texts?

Patricia and Emily MacLachlan's book *Painting the Wind* tells the story of a young boy who loves to paint the water and sky and special places on his island home. But one thing he has never been able to do is paint the wind. The boy eagerly awaits the long days of summer when his friends, the painters, will return. They are his mentors—his teachers who willingly share their craft. The boy sets his easel alongside each one and learns how to paint flowers and faces and still lifes. One day he accompanies the landscape artist to the beach. The artist paints his dog, Meatball, running along the beach with his ears flying in the wind. The boy, feeling the wind on his face, begins to paint the bent trees. Later, the two view their paintings as they hang side by side, and the artist points out to the boy that he has accomplished what he has longed to do—he has painted the wind. The boy responds, "He is right. On my island, surrounded by water and light, I have done what I could not do before. I have painted the wind."

We all need mentors in our lives—those knowledgeable others who help us learn how to be teachers, mothers, musicians, artists, athletes—who help us do what we could not do before on our own. So, too, do our young writers need mentors. Although it is impossible to have our students open their notebooks and write alongside Cynthia Rylant or Jane Yolen just as the boy was able to paint alongside the island artists, we can bring the literature of those authors and many others into our classroom communities to serve as mentors. Writing mentors are for everyone—teachers as well as students. Katie Wood Ray (2002) describes the importance of feeling the presence of authors in our classrooms as we go about our daily teaching of writing:

> *I often think that when I watch a really good teacher of writing, it's almost like there are life-size cardboard cutouts of authors all around the room. Jane Yolen is standing up by the chalkboard and Eloise Greenfield is just by the door to welcome students as they enter . . . With a room full of authors to help us, teaching writing doesn't have to be so lonely.* (150)

Mentor texts are pieces of literature that we can return to again and again as we help our young writers learn how to do what they may not yet be able to do on their own. We believe a mentor text is a book that offers myriad possibilities for our students and for ourselves as writers. Katie Wood Ray (2002) tells us, "As we develop teaching relationships with authors and their work, we will find that certain texts seem to surface as very important to teaching. These are texts that are just full of curriculum potential" (147). Mentor texts are books that are well loved by the teacher and known inside and out, backward and forward. Sometimes they have been used so often that they can be rendered almost without looking at the pages. They have been revisited many times to help students examine an unusual sentence structure, find the poetry in prose, connect with their own memories, think about how a setting creates a mood, or find the places where an author shows instead of tells. In other words, they become our coaches and our partners as we bring the joy of writing to our students. And we, as teachers of writing, will never be alone again if we have mentor texts stored in our classrooms. Mentor texts serve as snapshots into the future. They help students envision the kind of writer they can become; they help teachers move the whole writer, rather than each individual piece of writing, forward. Writers can imitate the mentor text and continue to find new ways to grow. In other words, mentor texts help students and teachers continually reinvent themselves as writers.

The "fingerprints" of the authors' craft found in mentor texts often become our own. Mentor texts are as comfortable as a worn pair of blue jeans. Their familiarity allows us to concentrate on writing skills and strategies—we know the text that well. They ignite the writer's imagination and determination to create high-quality text that mirrors the mentor text in many ways. Mentor texts help writers notice things about an author's work that is not like anything they might have done before and empower them to try something new.

Often students, and sometimes even teachers, think that it is not okay—that it is almost cheating—to borrow an idea from or imitate the writing style of an author. But this is how we learn to walk, to talk, to do almost anything: we imitate what we see others doing. The important thing to remember here is to find stellar literature that will inspire students to "copy" the author's style, focus, or organization. Mary Oliver talks about how we learn everything by imitation. She advises us that on our writing journey, imitation should be encouraged in order to learn something well instead of "partially and haphazardly" (1994, 13). Peter J. Lancia (1997) calls this imitation *literary borrowing*. He goes on to say that literature was a most effective model for writing in his classroom.

> *The literature-rich environment in combination with an interactive workshop enabled this mentorship to blossom. The children made natural connections between their reading and writing through their daily interactions with books as well as their conversations with fellow authors.* (475)

Mentor texts serve to show, not just tell, students how to write well. They, along with the teacher, provide wonderful examples that help students grow into successful writers through supportive partnerships. Allison Marchetti and Rebekah O'Dell (2015), authors of *Writing with Mentors: How to Reach Every Writer in the Room Using Current, Engaging Mentor Texts*, explain:

> *Mentor texts . . . have become the single most important element of our writing instruction. We used mentor texts sparingly in the beginning—mainly to introduce students to a new genre of writing or to*

illustrate a specific skill—but our dalliance with these texts and the authors behind them quickly turned into a full-on love affair when we realized all that they enable . . . Mentor texts enable all of us—teachers and students alike—to do far more than we could ever do on our own. (3)

We couldn't agree more!

Choosing a Mentor Text

How do you go about choosing a mentor text? The first criterion is that you must connect with the book and love it. You might be drawn to the subject matter, the author, the illustrations, or the genre. Then you'll want to look through the book to find examples of author's craft such as powerful language, effective repetition, predictable patterns, use of imagery, or rhythm and rhyme. Next, think about how the book serves your students' needs and connects with your curriculum. Is this a book that your students could relate to and/or read alone or with a partner? Does it provide examples of the kind of writing you want from your students? Can it be revisited often for multiple purposes, providing opportunities for lessons across the traits of writing? In choosing mentor texts, it is always good to have a balance of genres such as fiction, nonfiction, memoir, and poetry. Wordless picture books and graphic novels can help today's young writers move forward, too. In addition, teachers should choose some texts for cultural diversity, for high engagement, and for demonstrating lessons for living in a social world. Choosing a mentor text is in many ways a personal decision.

Any piece of writing can serve as a mentor whether it is found in a book, a newspaper, a magazine, or a teacher's notebook. As Matt Glover (2014) explains, "Teachers can also act as mentors by sharing their own writing. Additionally, students can become the mentor when teachers, or the students themselves, share student writing" (57). It is our hope that the titles and the teacher and student samples we offer as mentor texts will provide a foundation for you to build on. For a more detailed look at choosing a mentor text, see the introduction to Chapter 10.

Introducing Mentor Texts

We firmly believe that young writers should be introduced to mentor texts first as readers. They need to hear and appreciate the story and characters as well as the rhythms, words, and message. Only then can they return to a well-loved book and examine it through the eyes of a writer. We teach students to read like writers when we use mentor texts in our classrooms. When teachers bring literature to serve as mentor texts into the writing workshop, they demonstrate the power of the reading-writing connection. Shelley Harwayne (2005) reminds us of how that works:

Writers take their reading very seriously. When they read, they discover topics for their own writing. They become interested in new genres and formats. They study authors' techniques to learn how to improve their own writing. They develop mentor relationships with their favorite writers, aspiring to be more like them. (121)

That is what we do with mentor texts. We introduce them as read-alouds, appreciating and responding to them as readers. Then, we revisit them through the eyes of a writer. It is with these writing eyes that we use mentor texts to help us (teachers and students) set goals over the course of the year.

Shelley Harwayne (1992) talks about her visits to reading and writing workshops. On the back of the clipboard, she carries is a line she borrowed from a magazine: *I wonder if I can do that.* She tells the young writers she works with that "those words remind me that it's okay to be jealous of the books I read. It's okay to fall in love with a writer and try to do what that writer has done." Sometimes this happens quite unexpectedly, as was the case one afternoon as Rose worked in a first-grade classroom. She had just shared the book *Barn Savers* by Linda Oatman High. This book is about a boy who helps his father dismantle an old barn and save the parts for reuse in building new barns and houses. It is filled with rich language used in interesting ways. The students were discussing what they liked or disliked about the book, and Rose asked them to think about the words. Chase's hand shot up immediately. "I didn't like all the chicken words," he commented. Because Rose wasn't quite sure what he meant by *chicken words*, they returned to the text for some examples. Sure enough, there were several places where the author referred to chickens:

Papa plops the tools in the trough, and dust floats like chicken feed.

Darkness falls soft and silent like chicken feathers around the barn.

Then Becky pointed out that perhaps the author used the *chicken words* because chickens live on farms and the book is about barns, which you mostly find on farms. Rose and the children then noticed that there were other references to things that were farm-like:

Finally, the darkness fades to dawn, and the sun rolls before us like a wagon wheel.

I stack and stack, and the sun sinks low in the sky like a sleepy, red-faced farmer.

Could these first graders be on to something? Rose observed that as usual, Becky had been writing about her soccer game in her journal that day. "Becky," she said, "what exactly about your soccer game were you writing in your journal today?" Becky explained that she had been writing about the goal she scored and how far she kicked the ball. "So," Rose continued, "if you were to compare how far you kicked the ball to something else in sports, then you would be doing what Linda Oatman High did."

Brian chimed in, "I know! A home run goes really far. You could say you kicked the ball as far as a home-run hit." It was an unplanned, teachable moment. Without really understanding similes, this first grader had noticed a particular craft and was able to copy it—to do what she could not do before. *Barn Savers* was becoming a mentor text in that first-grade classroom.

These first graders were engaged in a close read—returning to the text several times for a specific purpose to understand what the author was doing and what effect it had on the reader. To do this, students need to read like writers. That is, they need to slow down and look at how individual words, sentences, and paragraphs work to convey meaning to the reader. For student writers, this close read enables them to "carefully and analytically read texts to identify the key features to be imitated in their versions of that kind of text. That means students need to engage in such reading with an eye aimed specifically at identifying features of craft and structure, something not likely to happen when students read without any or much explicit guidance" (Shanahan 2014,10).

It is not only the craft of writing that we learn from our mentor texts. We also learn that they are places from which writers gather ideas. Many authors write about names. Kevin Henkes writes about the joy and sadness of having a unique name in his book *Chrysanthemum*. Lois Lowry echoes these sentiments in *Gooney Bird Greene*, as does Patricia MacLachlan in *Journey*. In *House on Mango Street*, Sandra Cisneros writes a series of vignettes that describe what it is like to grow up Latino. Lynne used the vignette "My Name" as a read-aloud in a fourth-grade classroom. She encouraged the students to share what they knew about their own names. After reading it aloud, Lynne displayed the text with a document camera. The students read it with her, taking turns, and then as a choral reading. She wanted them to internalize the cadence of the text and understand the power of the words. She suggested that they, too, could write about their name just like Sandra Cisneros did. Here is one example:

My Name
by Beatrice
My name is Beatrice.
My boy name would be Robert Bruce.
I don't like my name for I could not
Spell it until third grade.
I only like one part about it—
I was named after a princess!
If it were up to me my name would be Bridget.
My Native American name would be Little Creek,
A nickname from my Indian Club.

And so I go by my middle name;
It has a pretty ring,
So my family and friends call me Grace.

Rose used a chapter from Lois Lowry's *Gooney Bird Greene* to inspire a group of second graders to think about their names. Zoey wrote this in her journal:

> I got my name for three reasons: Zoe from Sesame Street, because my grandma didn't want another J (my sister's name is Jaz), and because no matter what my name was Jaz would call me Zoe. Zoe was spelled with no "y" but my mom added it.

Mentor texts help students find ideas and breathe courage into their writing by helping them take risks and think outside their "writing box." In conferences, teachers collaborate with mentor texts to help their students solve problems with drafting and revision. Mentor texts are the "benchmarks." As mentor texts become part of the writing community, they inspire students and teachers to set goals that will help them continually reinvent themselves as writers.

Picture books make great mentor texts because they can be read and reread many times within the course of a school year. Students can easily hunt through them to find the craft idea they are hoping to imitate. Furthermore, these books provide examples in every genre, are culturally diverse, and serve as a model for the kinds of texts we want our students to imitate. They are a manageable size and help students understand that length is not always a criterion for good writing. In addition, picture books are rich in wonderful illustrations that layer the text and pull in our more reluctant readers and writers. Although most of our mentor texts are picture books, you will find that we sometimes use excerpts from chapter books and young adult literature. They add another layer to the use of literature as mentor texts. Additionally, song lyrics, newspaper and magazine articles, comic strip series, video clips, student samples, and even blog posts can serve as mentor texts.

The Teacher as Writer

Central to our beliefs about how to help students become successful writers is our understanding that a teacher of writing must be a teacher who writes. "Teacher as writer" drives everything else we do in writing workshop. Like the hub of a giant wheel, it helps us connect the spokes of all our other teaching practices. In fact, teacher as writer is the core belief we must articulate to our students, our colleagues, and ourselves. We do this by allowing our beliefs to guide us in our daily teaching practices. Spandel (2005) addresses the importance of teacher as writer:

> *Almost nothing does more to sustain a culture of writing than a teacher who writes with students, thereby underscoring the importance of*

writing, and also allowing students to see the process—one writer's version of it—as it unfolds. (42–43)

The benefits of "teacher as writer" are far-reaching. When teachers share and model with their own writing, they stand with their students as members of the writing community and as fellow writers instead of as "the writing teacher." The writing community needs a teacher who is willing to take risks in the composing process and face the same peaks and valleys that his or her students do. When teachers take the responsibility for providing the high-quality support our students need to move forward as writers, we commit ourselves to leading a writerly life.

Writing for our students is part of the explicit instruction that we do for them. It allows us to make our thinking visible—to explain the thinking behind the choices we make as they watch us draft and revise. We have established ourselves as part of the writing community, so when we model in front of the students and get stuck, they help us get unstuck, freely offering suggestions for revision. This offering of suggestions then also becomes part of the explicit instruction as teachers decide whether they will use the suggestions. We constantly model what we do as writers.

Bruce Morgan (2005) models writing by gathering his students in the "Oval Office," where he sits in a comfortable chair with all the materials he needs: chart paper, markers, and picture books. He gathers his writers together because he believes it strengthens the writing community and it helps him monitor students' engagement and attentiveness. Morgan does this daily so that students can observe him thinking aloud as he models with his writing. He talks about his writing process—the things that are going right, the things that are going wrong, and where he's stuck. During this time, Morgan expects his students to listen with both ears so that they can, in turn, try to approximate what he is modeling. He asks his students for their help because their responses help him assess their understanding. It also raises students to a conscious understanding that they, too, are writers.

When we write ourselves, it helps us engage in the same struggles as our young writers and the same problem-solving strategies we want them to use. It helps us be more fluid and flexible through experimentation with specific targeted skills and strategies for specific writing situations. Therefore, it becomes easier to help our students in teacher/student conferences. In other words, it would be difficult to teach someone how to swim if you didn't do it yourself. Trying it out yourself makes you privy to all the little secrets of the craft. You can more easily find the places where your students need help and make appropriate suggestions to them. Perhaps most important of all, when we write regularly in our writer's notebook and in front of our students, we sit down to confer from the perspective of a writer. In other words, the conference is writer to writer, not teacher to student. Although at first it may not appear to be very different, in truth, it makes all the difference in the world. When teachers make suggestions to students, there may be little discussion. The students think they must make the change to satisfy the teachers and get a "good grade." When students see teachers as fellow writers, they are more open to explaining their thinking in greater detail or to reaching a compromise.

Additionally, writing will help us provide clear guidelines of what we expect from our students. We need to believe that students can do better and can use the strategies that we offer them. We should not be afraid to show them things that we think may be just beyond their reach. According to Russian psychologist Lev Vygotsky (1978), children learn best when they are in the "zone of proximal development" and can work in collaboration with a more knowledgeable other (teacher, student, and/or mentor text) to help them reach their full potential. Through modeling and shared and guided experiences, they will eventually be able to try out new strategies and skills on their own.

Writing for ourselves and for our students will help improve our own confidence, competence, and self-esteem. We improve in writing because we write. Although writing in front of our students is the best model, allowing us to teach more effectively in less time, sometimes we need to take smaller steps toward that goal. Lynne is very comfortable writing on her feet, but Rose found that she had more confidence when she did a little planning first. With practice, she discovered that jotting down some short notes or engaging in oral rehearsal before the actual lesson helped her write in front of her students with ease. Now when the teachable moment arises, she is more comfortable writing without rehearsal. You may be fearful about writing in front of your students because you think your models aren't good enough. You will find, however, that your students will applaud your efforts, and even if by chance they create some better pieces of writing than those you've modeled, that means your teaching was successful! According to Regie Routman (2005), "If you have never written in front of your students before, take the plunge: They will appreciate your risk taking, and you will have a much clearer idea of what you are actually asking them to do" (25).

When we write our own memoirs, poems, and essays and share them with our students, we learn to enjoy writing, and at the same time, we become more real to our students. Morgan (2005) writes, "We write to capture our lives, and that's what our students need to see us model" (62). Writing will inspire our students, develop a classroom synergy, spark curiosity, and create passion for writing. We join our students as a player in the classroom writing community instead of standing apart as a spectator. Vicki Spandel (2005) reminds us, "Writing comes from who we are; modeling must begin with sharing ourselves and what interests *us* . . . . Let them see who we are first, and how that translates into what we write" (81).

To treat our students like genuine authors, respect their abilities, and understand their struggles, we need to write so that we can call ourselves "author." Because we are part of the writing community, our writing efforts should be included in hallway and classroom bulletin board publications and as part of classroom writing anthologies. Our writer's notebook should always be available to record our thoughts and observations. Writing for our students and for ourselves continually immerses us in the fundamentals of the writing craft and process.

So, if you are feeling a little afraid or even if you do not like to write, take a deep breath and purchase a writer's notebook. Write about the things that are happening all around you. Read professional books like this one to let other people's thinking into your mind and into your heart. The Your Turn lessons in this book are for everyone, including you, the teacher. Try them out on your own to build confidence before you write in front of your students. And read the experts, the children's authors themselves, to find interesting sentence structures, powerful leads, vivid language, useful scaffolds, and ways to play with time. Not only will you see your own writing improve, but you will notice that your students' writing is improving, too. If we truly want to have a writing workshop where all children are encouraged to find their own writing voices, we must first find our own.

The Student as Writer

A student writer is part of a larger community. He needs to feel safe when he puts his writing out into the world. Clearly, norms must be established that the community honors. Central to "rules to live by" is the idea that a writer is never personally criticized—only the writing, and only in the spirit of moving the writer forward. Student writers must understand that they are not alone and that writing is not a solitary act. Indeed, they must be able to listen attentively and let the thinking of the community be something they consider and learn from. Noticing problem-solving strategies and appropriating those strategies in writing workshop will be a key factor to success and growth in writing.

Student writers also come to realize that mentor texts and mentor authors support their journey. They learn to "listen in" to the rhythm of the words—the symphony the authors create for those who listen, note, and imitate. They begin to realize they are never alone, even while they are planning and creating their first drafts.

Several years ago Rose was working with some second graders while filming *Writing with Mentors*. While conferring with one student, Rose remarked on how the young writer, Brianna, had used a particular strategy to build content in her description. Rose asked Brianna why she had chosen that particular strategy. Brianna replied, "Well, that's what Alice and Linda do." Although Rose was not familiar with all of the students in the class, she was fairly sure there were no Alices or Lindas. She quickly realized that Brianna was referring to Alice Shertle and Linda Oatman High, two authors whose works the students were studying. To Brianna, these were fellow writers and friends who were part of her writing community.

When students enter school, their heads are filled with stories to share. Most of them see themselves as writers even if they can write only with scribbles and drawings. As these students get older, some of them lose their writing identity. They are fearful to pick up their pencils and write. Cries of "I don't have anything to write about!" are heard in almost every grade. So the question is, "What has happened to these young writers to convince them that they do not possess the skills and tools to write about what they are thinking, feeling, or wondering?" Teachers can make a conscious effort to reconnect students with their writing identity. An easy strategy is to use the word *writer* to refer to each student in writing workshop. Even during a conference a teacher might say, "So writer to writer, what kind of ending do you think fits best with this story?"

Another way to help students view themselves as writers is to let them own the writing process—the whole process, including being resources for each other. In other words, we must teach our student writers how to take the lead in a conference and how to offer praise and polish to their peers. Students need to have a handle on their likes and dislikes, strengths and needs, and goals for themselves. They need to have a vision for where they are heading and where they might possibly be by the end of a school year. In *The CAFE Book: Engaging All Students in Daily Literacy Assessment*, Gail Boushey and Joan Moser (2009) discuss the importance of helping students establish a reader identity. Students make goal setting visible by posting their name on a bulletin board under the area of reading they are working on. Gail and Joan encourage teachers to share with students what they as teachers have discovered about the student's reading strengths and needs through focused observation and assessments "so that over time they will assume responsibility for their goals and learning" (42). We think the same holds true for helping students establish their writing identity. In the beginning during conferences, we may have to point out to students what it is they do well or need help with, but in time they will begin to internalize more about what it means to be a good writer and where they are in that journey—they will begin to create a writing identity and a vision of how they can grow.

To see themselves as writers, students need choice, opportunities to collaborate, venues for real-world publishing, and time for reflection. Writing workshop should be about engagement, not compliance. Student writers need voice, variety, and vision. In addition to the mentor authors whose work they read and study, students must also see their own work as essential to moving their writing community forward.

How Mentor Texts Fit into the Curriculum

Ralph Fletcher and JoAnn Portalupi (2001) describe the writing workshop as a place where students acquire the necessary skills for writing, develop a feel for the power and purpose of writing, and have the opportunity to see themselves as writers. From Fletcher, as well as others such as Donald Graves, Lucy Calkins, and Katie Wood Ray, we have learned about the essentials of creating a writing workshop environment. We have learned how to use purposeful language as we present focused mini-lessons and offer suggestions to our growing writers. Powerful writing comes from students having the opportunity to choose their writing topics and lots of time to put words on paper. It comes from specific feedback that helps them reflect on what they have done well and the direction in which they need to go to move their writing forward.

It is important to help students become strategic learners. To do this, teachers should make the strategy visible to the students. How can we become strategic teachers? We point out how authors use the strategy during read-alouds, literature circles, or even content-area discussions. We name the strategy up front, and we model it. For example, we might say something like this to our student authors:

> **"** We have been working on how an author reveals his character to his readers, and I want to show you how I use this knowledge as I write. **"**

Teachers should model the strategy they hope to eventually see their students use in their own writing as many times as necessary and find examples of mentor texts where the author's purpose for using the strategy is clear. It is also important to mention that only a small section of text is needed to model the strategy. Therefore, returning to a mentor text does not mean the entire picture book or chapter of a novel needs to be reread. Nonfiction texts should also be used as early as the primary grades so that students can start to understand the strategies needed for writing in this mode.

Traditionally, the format for the writing workshop has included a short, focused mini-lesson. This short lesson is an opportunity for the teacher to demonstrate a particular skill or strategy and for students to try it out briefly in a supported environment. It is followed by a sustained period of time in which students work on individual projects or confer with their teacher or peers. The workshop ends with a sharing session in which students can read the work they have done that day in small or whole groups. Fletcher and Portalupi (2001) compare this format to the busy atmosphere of an industrial arts class in which students are all working on individual projects. Occasionally, the teacher will pull the students together to demonstrate the use of a particular technique. Most often, the teacher roams about the room offering encouragement and suggestions, or conferring individually with a student on the use of a technique.

Because the majority of time in the workshop should be devoted to students' writing, the mini-lesson must of necessity be just that: highly focused and short. A technique or strategy is demonstrated, and students have the opportunity to try it out with support. Sometimes this model presents enough information and practice for students to apply the technique in the work they are doing that day. If the technique doesn't lend itself to direct application to their independent writing that day, they can store it away for use later. But for many students, this short lesson isn't enough.

Using Your Turn Lessons

Sometimes students need extended time to really try out a technique before it can become part of their repertoire of strategies. In our work in classrooms, we have found that the mini-lesson format does not always provide enough time for students to understand the strategy and make it their own. The demonstrations, as well as the shared and guided experiences, need to be expanded before students engage in independent writing. If students have the opportunity to experiment or to play around with the technique offered by the lesson, often collaboratively with teacher guidance, they get a feel for how it will fit into the context of their own writing. Here mentor texts play a key role. Their rich, distinctive features enable student writers to say, "I see what he [the author] is doing and why he's doing it. I can try this, too." During these times, the workshop might look and feel more like a laboratory. Everybody is experimenting with the same thing—perhaps not in the same way or in the same context but working toward the same result. Like true experimentation, it takes time for students to study something in depth. The writing they produce may or may not become a finished piece, but because students have had the opportunity to delve a little more deeply, they may be more likely to remember the technique when they need it. This is the format we refer to as the Your Turn lesson. The Your Turn lessons described throughout the book are not specific to any grade level. They can be adapted for use with all students. They are not intended as recipes. Rather, they serve as guides to help all teachers try out writing experiences to grow as writers themselves and to lower their level of concern about writing with their students.

The Your Turn lessons incorporate a gradual release of responsibility model: a demonstration of the strategy, a shared and/or guided experience in which students can learn and practice together, and then an opportunity to try the strategy or technique on their own. During the demonstration, the teacher is in control, modeling and engaging in explicit teaching. In shared and guided experiences, students take on some of the responsibility, with the teacher there to offer help and encouragement as needed. Regie Routman (2005) explains it this way:

> *In shared writing, the teacher and students compose collaboratively, the teacher acting as expert and scribe for her apprentices as she demonstrates, guides, and negotiates the creation of meaningful text, focusing on the craft of writing as well as the conventions . . . Shared writing is the context in which the students gain the skills and confidence to "have a go" on their own, with guidance.* (83, 84)

Shared writing experiences can be conducted with the whole group, in small groups, or in pairs. This is probably the most important part of the lesson, because it is by trying things out collaboratively and with guidance that true learning takes place. Particularly for our struggling writers and English language learners, the shared writing experience provides a valuable scaffold for more practice before the performance. Routman goes on:

> *One of the most powerful aspects of shared writing (or reading) is that it is here that many students begin to figure out how written language works. Much of that learning occurs through the collaborative opportunities and social interactions that take place, not just through our explicit teaching.* (84)

In guided writing experiences, students take on even more responsibility, as they are most often working alone but still receiving help as needed from the teacher during conferences. Although there are some differences between shared and guided writing, the goal is the same: to provide the opportunity students need to try out a skill or strategy with support. For this reason, we include them together in the Your Turn lessons. The important thing to remember is that this step is crucial to all learning. Sometimes we need to have several shared or guided experiences before we move on to independent work. Don't worry if you can't finish a Your Turn lesson in one day. If your students need more practice, it might extend over several days. Just make sure they are doing some kind of writing (shared, guided, independent) every day. We can't expect students to understand what we want them to do by simply demonstrating. They need opportunities to experiment, try things out, and play with language with our guidance to build the confidence they need to write independently. This part of the gradual-release-of-responsibility model is what helps all students achieve success.

When we make use of the Your Turn format, we isolate one skill or strategy to better understand how to use that skill as we write our own pieces. Sometimes, we choose to isolate a skill or strategy because we are introducing it to a majority of students in our class. Sometimes we choose a strategy because it is important to the mode of writing we are talking about and trying out. We need to provide authentic reading experiences (mentor texts) first, and then model the target strategy with our own writing, making sure our students have an opportunity to try it out in shared or guided writing. Therefore, the Your Turn lessons are for everybody—teachers as well as students. Your Turn lessons will help classroom teachers become writing teachers who write.

Reflection Time in Your Turn Lessons

Unlike the traditional mini-lesson format, the Your Turn lessons provided at the end of each chapter in this book build in time for reflection. Students are encouraged to notice things about their writing and to ask questions about how a particular strategy, craft, or organizational format worked for them—how it improved their writing. They have the opportunity to stand back and think about their writing through the eyes of a writer. Writing involves creating text and critiquing what was created. Reflection gives students the thinking time they need to envision other possibilities for a strategy. When teachers simply tell or feed students information, they don't own it or remember it. Students need to try something out several times and then ask themselves how it worked and how they could use it again. This kind of thinking will lift the quality of the writing and will move the writer forward, not just the individual piece of writing.

The reflection component is an integral part of the Your Turn lesson design. Although we know it is tempting to omit this part because of the ever-increasing curricular demands on our time, we believe that in the end it will save teachers precious time. It is important to slow down the process and help students become aware of themselves as writers. How did the use of the strategy or skill work for them? How did it improve their piece? How will they revise the use of the strategy or add their own personal touch? A reflective writer is one who understands the whys and hows of writing and can transfer strategies to future writing situations. Therefore, teachers will not find it necessary to reteach the same skills and strategies over and over to the majority of their students. Reflection also helps students and teachers during writing conferences. The reflective writer comes prepared with key questions for focused revision work, instead of handing a piece of writing to the teacher with the idea that she will fix it. Reflection, the most powerful form of revision, reaches far into the future. It helps our writers imagine and create even before their pencils ride across the pages of their notebooks, trotting out their thoughts. Like the young boy in *Painting the Wind* who needed the painter of landscapes to point out to him what he was finally able to do, students need opportunities to help them understand what it is that they can do well, and what it is that they still cannot yet do on their own.

Writing takes time. As Katie Wood Ray and Lester Laminack (2001) tell us, "There is no quick, easy way to get to good writing instruction, no one place we can go to find out all we need to know. That may, in fact, be one essential characteristic of being a good teacher of writing—that you have to love the learning journey" (120). To that we might add, you have to *live* the journey as well, learning along with your students as you write and reflect together every day.

Our Hope for This Book

In creating this book, we draw on our experiences as teachers of writing and lovers of children's literature. In addition to our work with students, we have had the privilege of working with many teachers through the Pennsylvania Writing and Literature Project at West Chester University and in schools and workshops throughout the country. We've noticed that teachers are at various levels in their understanding of how to teach writing. Some teachers have simply assigned it as class work and/or homework. Some teachers have tried to offer explanations or strategies based on how writing was taught to them. We have helped these teachers reach another level, putting into practice a vision for writing workshop that includes the partnership of the teacher as writer and mentor texts to provide rich models of high-quality writing. Peter Lancia (1997) writes about just such a model:

> *In a classroom where students have the opportunity to interact with books and authors every day and to practice writing in an environment built on support and encouragement, authorship becomes real as they imitate their role models and write their own stories. Literature inspires, influences, and instructs young writers by providing examples needed for effective learning.* (475)

Furthermore, we have demonstrated to teachers how their students can become more independent if they are taught to read like writers, recognizing that mentor texts can show them how to take their writing to new limits. We have encouraged teachers to take time for reflection, helping students understand how they are growing as writers. Finally, we have taught our colleagues how to reexamine their classroom libraries and personal collections of children's literature with new eyes, looking for mentor texts that can provide a host of lessons for teaching the traits of writing. It is our hope that through this book we can share these ideas with you, helping you discover the authors and literature that will serve as experts for your classroom—experts who will help reinvent you and your students as writers.

Think About It—Talk About It—Write About It

- How do you feel about yourself as a writer? Why do you write? What do you like to write about?
- What do you know about your students as writers? How have you discovered these truths? How does it drive your instruction?
- What goal(s) do you have for yourself as a writer? Make a list and create a plan.

Chapter 2

Digging for Treasure: Discovering Personal Stories by Connecting with Literature

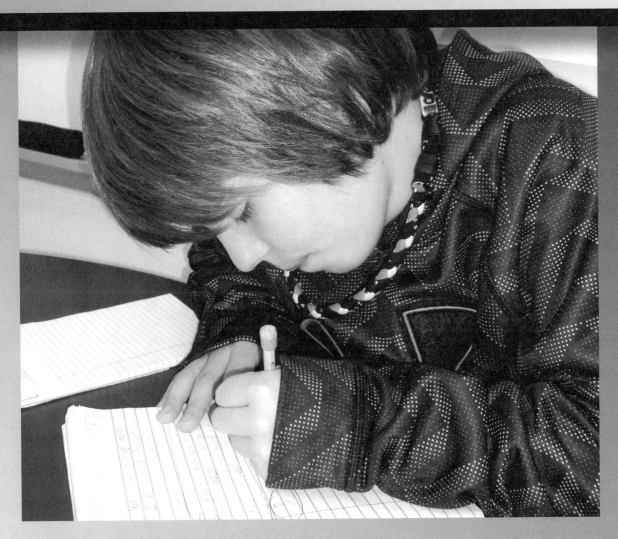

Literature triggers thoughts, unlocks memories, and helps children realize they have something important and interesting to say. We want children to remember the powerful memories they often forget when they sit down for writing time.

—Shelley Harwayne, *Lasting Impressions*

If literature is to become an essential part of the writing workshop, it must first become part of the classroom community. Before we teach students how to read and think about literature through the eyes of a writer, we must show them how to make meaningful connections to the story. Students should always be introduced to a new book first as a reader. They need to get beyond the content before they can focus on the craft of writing the story. Students need to let the story take them to a new place, introduce them to new friends, or help them understand some aspect of their world. Ellin Keene and Susan Zimmerman (1997) taught us the importance of making connections to deepen comprehension. These connections can also help children unearth a treasure chest of memories that will provide them with topics for writing in the writing workshop. When students connect to literature on a personal level, they can begin to see that they have similar experiences or feelings. This allows them to understand that the everyday occurrences in their lives have meaning and are worth sharing. Of course, to enable them to do this we must choose books that represent our students in many ways—where they live (city, suburbs, country), who they are (cultural beliefs and values), and what they enjoy doing or dream about doing. According to Shubitz (2016), "All students deserve to read mirror books, in which they see themselves, and window books, in which they learn about others" (5). When young writers are encouraged to tell the stories of their lives and are helped to think those stories are important, it won't be long before they are eagerly writing them. This is the power of the read-aloud and the first job of the mentor text. The books that our students connect with on many levels are the books they fall in love with and want to return to for many reasons. These are the books that become mentors for our writers.

Welcoming Responses to Read-Alouds

Because students have different backgrounds and experiences, their responses and the connections they make to a book will vary. *Fireflies!* by Julie Brinckloe tells the story of a young boy who catches a jar full of fireflies with his friends on a summer evening. Eventually he realizes that, to save the fireflies, he must let them go. One student might connect to this book by thinking of a similar experience catching fireflies, another might be reminded of a summer evening game of flashlight tag with a group of friends, and yet another might connect to that feeling you get when you think you might have done something wrong. By allowing students to share their personal connections to read-alouds in whole-group discussions, we create a reservoir of new meanings from which our students can discover topics to write about. Harwayne (1992) reminds us that we must carefully choose the texts we use to help students find topics for writing. We need to choose texts that are "rich, enticing, and full of flavor" to evoke a variety of personal responses among our students. Books rich in stories about families, children, animals, and special places, to name a few, are the kinds of books we should introduce to our students as read-alouds. In addition to being the kinds of books students can easily relate to, they provide models of the type of writing we expect our students to do. When literature becomes a part of the classroom community, when books are shared throughout the day and across the curriculum, it will naturally spill over into the writing workshop.

There is no one way to respond to a book, and reactions can trigger all sorts of memories and go in different directions. For instance, hearing Jane Yolen's *Owl Moon* read aloud might elicit the connection "I saw an owl in the zoo." Children might also take an insignificant part of a story and tie it to something they know. "My sister has red boots like Lilly's" does little to help connect with the feelings and situations that are important to comprehending *Lilly's Purple Plastic Purse* by Kevin Henkes, but it may help a young writer unearth a topic for writing. Upon hearing the same story, other children might think about an important teacher or perhaps a time they felt bad about something they did. These memories triggered by the books we read aloud to our students are the topics we hope they return to when it is time to write.

Filling Our Treasure Chests

Writers should always have a place where they can record their writing ideas so they are not lost when it comes time for writing workshop. For younger students this may be in the form of pictures, short phrases on sticky notes, or lists that they keep inside a writing folder or perhaps a daily journal. Teachers can help by creating lists on chart paper through a shared writing experience and posting them in a writing center so they can be revisited often. As students get older, writer's notebooks become their treasure chests. They write their observations, anecdotes, connections to literature, and discoveries about authors' craft. They write the tiny stories that record the history of their lives. Lists also find their way into the writer's notebook and can be collected in one place, perhaps the back, for easy reference when needed for finding a new writing topic. By dating each page and giving the entry a generic title, student writers can find threads of topics that are important to them. Revisiting a writer's notebook, for example, and finding several pages about a best friend or a beloved pet may help a student know that he or she has enough interest in that topic to write a longer piece—a poem, a narrative, a friendly letter. Returning to a writer's notebook builds confidence in all writers, especially those students who struggle with writing or who opt out whenever possible.

Books such as Jane Yolen's *Owl Moon*, Eve Bunting's *The Wednesday Surprise*, Lauren Castillo's *Nana in the City*, or Matt de la Peña's *Last Stop on Market Street* tell stories about times spent with special people. Connections with books such as these could evolve into a class list of "happy times" or "special people" and include such things as visiting Grandma, rediscovering your neighborhood, or going hiking with Dad. From these general lists writers can narrow their topic further so that it becomes more specific and personal.

Sensory images are powerful tools for evoking memories. *Night in the Country* by Cynthia Rylant is about the sounds heard outside on a quiet night. Connections to this book might lead to lists such as "The Sounds of Christmas" or "Things That Go Bump in the Night." Richard Paul Evans demonstrates how smells can call up a childhood memory with vivid detail in *The Christmas Box*.

> I remember once, in grade school, we made Christmas ornaments by poking whole cloves into an orange. I can remember how wonderful it smelled for the entire season. I can still smell it. And then there is the smell of perfumed candles, and the hot wassail or creamy cocoa on a cold day. And the pungent smell of wet leather boots after my brothers and I had gone sledding. The smells of Christmas are the smells of childhood.

After using this excerpt in her class, Lynne's students buzzed about all the gifts they had ever made for important people in their lives. They remembered the smell of peanut butter on their hands as they made birdfeeder gifts. Some talked about the smells of the holiday season such as the wreaths, Christmas trees, buttery sugar cookies baking in their grandma's oven, the clean smell of the air after a first snow, and scented pine candles. Together, Lynne and her students listed the smells of the holiday season on the board. Some students created individual lists in their writer's notebooks and expanded their thinking to include other senses or other holidays. Later, they returned to these lists to compose poetry and stories from the memories called to mind by the imagery found there.

Even though *The Christmas Box* is not a children's book, it demonstrates how teachers can bring the books they are reading into the writing workshop. Read-alouds do not always have to be whole books. They can be one or several passages from a chapter of a more lengthy text, including those intended for older audiences, as well as excerpts from magazines, newspapers, catalogs, and travel guides. When teachers share the things they have been reading for pleasure with their classes, they demonstrate that they, too, are readers. Being a reader is a necessary ingredient to becoming a confident and successful writer. As our reading world expands, so does our writing world.

Some books such as *Imogene's Antlers* by David Small, *George Shrinks* by William Joyce, *The Day the Crayons Quit* by Drew Daywalt, or *Matthew A.B.C.* by Peter Catalanotto show how possibilities for writing might occur simply by asking "What if." In one fifth-grade classroom, Rose guided the students in brainstorming familiar settings where a "What if" story could happen. They started with places common to their experience—school, home, shopping mall—but she also encouraged them to think about places that might be unique to their individual experiences. For example, if they played baseball, they might list the baseball field, or the dance studio if they were taking dance lessons. One student listed a local animal shelter run by the Society for the Prevention of Cruelty to Animals, a place she visits often. (See Figures 2.1, 2.2, and 2.3.)

Grace   5-C

<u>House</u>   SPCA

• What if you walked into your house and you fell into a giant black hole.

• What if you ran in your house for dinner but instead of having steak, your Mom + Dad gave you an alive cow.

• What if you walk into the SPCA and they were giving out a free pet of your choice.

✓ • What if you just adopted a dog from the SPCA (It was a girl). When you got in the car it gave birth.

<u>Go Surfing</u>   <u>Camping</u>

• What if you went surfing and an animated seahorse come up to you.

• What if you went surfing and then got stung by a Jelly fish and a sting Ray at the same time on the same day.

✓ • What if you went camping and a grizly bear came into your tent and snuggled with you.

• What if you went camping and your tent flew into the lake with you in it.

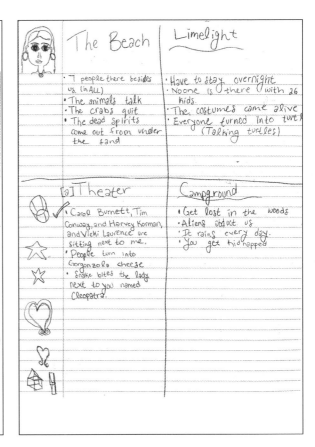

The Beach   Limelight

• 7 people there besides us (in ALL)
• The animals talk
• The crabs quit
• The dead spirits come out from under the sand

• Have to stay overnight
• Noone is there with 26 kids.
• The costumes came alive
• Everyone turned into turtl (Talking turtles)

[a]Theater   Campground

✓ • Carol Burnett, Tim Conway, and Harvey Korman, and Vicki Laurence are sitting next to me.
• People turn into Gorgonzola cheese
• Snake bites the lady next to you named Cleopatra.

• Get lost in the woods
• Aliens abduct us
• It rains every day.
• You get kidnapped

What if... I went to Limelight for rehersal, and I had to stay overnight?

Plot
• Show up for practice
• Practice is over
• Huge blizzard going on
• Try to figure out what to do
• Play theater games
• Look for snacks/dinner
• Get younger kids to sleep
• Wake up
• Parents are there!

Yay!

The end.

By: Louise Siing

Figure 2.1 *(top left)* Grace, a fifth grader, brainstorms settings for a "What if" story.

Figure 2.2 *(top right)* Louise's brainstorming for a "What if" story.

Figure 2.3 *(left)* Louise's plan for a "What if" story taken from the brainstormed list.

Rose reminded the students that the "What if" did not necessarily have to lead to a fantasy story but that they might find it easier to write around something based in reality. A good mentor text for this is *Happy Like Soccer* by Maribeth Boelts. In this book, Sierra plays soccer every Saturday, but her aunt can never attend her games because she works. (What if you never had a family member attend one of your soccer games?) Authors often have one foot in reality and the other in fiction. In other words, they might start with a personal experience and expand it into a story. (See the Your Turn lesson at the end of this chapter.)

Writing treasures are often unearthed in the way a book is introduced. In *Crab Moon* by Ruth Horowitz, a young boy named Daniel experiences the spawning of hundreds of horseshoe crabs in the middle of the night. In the morning, he finds a marooned crab and helps free it. Although not all children who hear this story have had that exact same treasured experience, they can be led to connect to it and find their own similar treasures in the way the read-aloud is introduced.

One fall Rose was working with a group of first graders on digging for those treasured moments of their lives. The children each had an outline of a treasure chest inside their writing journals. As stories were read aloud and thoughts were shared in conversation, Rose encouraged the children to use sticky notes to jot down ideas or experiences in the form of a few words or a small picture. They placed the notes on the treasure chest so they could use them to write about later. On one particular afternoon, Rose introduced the class to *Crab Moon*. During the previous weekend, the Northeast had experienced a spectacular meteor shower—one of those extraordinary events that happens once or twice in a lifetime. Rose knew that many of the children had awakened in the darkness of the early morning hours to experience the meteors just as Daniel's mother in *Crab Moon* had awakened him to watch the crabs lay their eggs. In her introduction to the read-aloud, she asked the children whether they had ever gotten up in the middle of the night or very early in the morning to see or do something special. Of course there was much excited talk about getting up to see the meteors, what they had looked like, how many they had seen, and how long they had stayed up. But the conversation went beyond this event as other memories were triggered. One child recalled getting up very early to go fishing with her grandfather. Another child talked about starting the long drive to their vacation spot so early that it was still dark. By beginning to introduce the story in this way, the children's connections for the stories they could write were not limited to the scope of Daniel's experience in *Crab Moon*. Rose didn't want these young writers to lose their tiny treasures of time, so they took a few minutes to jot them down on sticky notes and add them to their treasure chests of writing ideas.

Next, Rose asked them to think about how they felt during those times they had recorded on their treasure chests. Helping children connect to the feelings of the characters in the books we read aloud, rather than just the events of the story, can help foster new connections and unearth even more writing treasures. The students then had the opportunity to talk with partners about their recorded events and the feelings connected to them.

As Rose prepared to read *Crab Moon* aloud, she told her students that the story was about a boy named Daniel who gets up in the middle of the night to see something special. She asked them to think about what he might be feeling as they listened. She wanted the children to connect with Daniel's feelings not only to deepen their comprehension of the story but also to extend this understanding to their writing lives. Together they isolated three parts of the story to identify Daniel's feelings and discussed how the author's words helped them do it.

Surprise:
The path felt cool under Daniel's feet. As the beam of their flashlight swept the beach, he drew a sharp breath.

Excited:
In the morning, Daniel raced back to the beach. The tide was low now. The crabs were gone. Curly black seaweed was strewn on the sand, like streamers left over from a party.

Afraid:
He carefully lifted the crab. As her body left the ground, her claws started to snap. Daniel put her down fast. Then he took a deep breath and reached for her again.

Figure 2.4 *(left)*
Jessica writes about a time she felt nervous.

Figure 2.5 *(right)*
Jessica's expanded piece.

Next, they created a web of these feelings. The children were then invited to record on a small slip of paper a time when they, too, felt surprised, excited, or afraid. Some continued the idea they had originally added to their treasure chest about the meteor shower or fishing outing, but for others it may have been a new experience they recalled as the read-aloud and the talk surrounding it took them deeper into recalling the moments of their lives. Their treasure chest of writing topics was becoming richer. On subsequent days during writing workshop, many children returned to these recorded moments and extended their thoughts into a small, focused piece. (See Figures 2.4 and 2.5.)

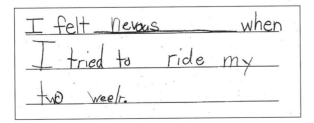

An Angel for Solomon Singer by Cynthia Rylant is the story of a lonely, elderly man who lives in a New York hotel for men. He wishes for the wheat fields of Indiana where he once lived, and for other things that would help him be more content with where he lives now. He never wishes for these things out loud, but he gradually finds the contentment he seeks. At first, it seems that it might be difficult for a young child to connect with a book like this, but again, we can plant the seed for a deeper connection in the way we introduce a book. When Rose reads this book aloud to young children for the purpose of connecting for understanding and digging for writing treasures, her introduction goes something like this:

> **"** Think about celebrating your birthday. Think about how after the candles on the cake are lit, everyone sings 'Happy Birthday' and then you get to blow out the candles. Before you blow them out, you make a wish, but you don't say it out loud. In this book, a man named Solomon Singer makes wishes. They are called dreams, and he never says them out loud. Think about how some of his wishes come true and how maybe some of your wishes come true. **"**

Such an introduction often leads to talk about secret wishes, but just as often it might lead to connections to birthdays. Through conversation children can be led to thinking about why a certain birthday was special. Was it the place, the people, the wishes that came true? This thinking not only will help students understand the book on a deeper level but also can provide the writing treasures that may find their way into a writer's notebook. *An Angel for Solomon Singer* is a book that can be returned to again and again for discussion to deepen comprehension as well as to help young writers unearth more writing treasures such as the special people in their lives, favorite places, hopes for the future, and home.

Book illustrations are another way for young writers to discover writing treasures by connecting with the feelings or actions of the character. In the wordless book *Wave*, Suzy Lee brings us into the world of a young girl spending a day at the beach and playing with the ocean waves. Through the illustrations, we can see the range of emotions the girl experiences—wonder, fear, courage, joy, and defiance. Writers can list similar times they experienced these emotions and then draw or write about them. In *Chalk* by Bill Thomson, another wordless picture book, children's drawings of butterflies, dinosaurs, and rain come to life. It will draw students into a fantasy and allow them to connect with the emotions of the main characters evoked through the illustrations. Peter Catalanotto is a master at evoking thoughts and feelings through the images he creates. *Emily's Art* is the story of a young girl whose spirit is crushed when her artwork is judged by its content instead of by its creativity. The judge of the art contest is about to award Emily the prize because of her wonderful detail and use of color, but the teacher tells her that the painting is of a dog, not a rabbit.

> "A DOG??!!" screeched the judge. "I was attacked by a dog once! Nasty thing ripped my favorite dress! UUUUGHH! I hate dogs!"
>
> Emily's heart twisted.

In the powerful illustration that accompanies this text, we see Emily with her head down. She appears to be almost invisible, as the background of the painting shows through her. If we allow children to linger on the illustrations during a read-aloud, returning to them for conversation after the final words are read, or perhaps even the next day in writing workshop, we can help them make the connections that will lead to meaningful writing. In this case, they might have experienced something that made their "heart twist" just as Emily's did. The best books for reading aloud are those that can be returned to for many purposes throughout the day and especially in the writing workshop.

The Memory String by Eve Bunting is an excellent source for digging up the writing treasures of older primary or intermediate children. In this story, a young girl, Laura, is having difficulty adjusting to having a stepmother. She has a memory string of buttons, each of which represents a piece of her family's history. The most precious of these buttons belonged to her mother, who has died. When the string breaks and a button is lost, Laura's new stepmother, Jane, is there to comfort her as her mother would have. But it just isn't the same. Although not all children can relate to having a stepparent or a parent who has passed away, a deeper understanding of the feelings and actions of the characters can be brought about by the talk we create in our book introduction. An introduction to *The Memory String* might go something like this:

> 66 Have you ever had to find room for someone or something new in your life? 99
>
> or
>
> 66 Did you ever say something to someone deliberately to hurt him or her and then wish you hadn't? 99
>
> or
>
> 66 Did you ever have the feeling of being 'choked up'? 99

After the teacher poses a probing question, students can take a few minutes to do a quick-write in their writer's notebooks before having a group discussion. These entries can then be returned to later as possible topics for an expanded piece of writing. Teachers could also create the list of memories that each button in the memory string represented for the main character, Laura, about her mother. Students could then be encouraged to do the same in their writer's notebooks. Lynne chose her mother to model a set of memories before she asked her students to try it out for themselves:

Memory String for Mom
reading the Cat in the Hat
coloring in coloring books when I was home sick
walking with my sisters and me to the library
eating at Barson's restaurant
teaching me how to drive
shopping at Gimbels for college clothes

Money ✱ *Yard Sale* by Eve Bunting is another good choice that will evoke conver-sations, questions, and emotions. In this story, Callie watches her family's pos-sessions being sold at a yard sale. The reader quickly discovers that this yard sale is a little different. It includes not only items the family no longer has use for but also items the family can no longer keep because of money problems. The read-aloud will lead students to turn and talk about reasons for moving to a new home, leaving friends behind and making new ones, giving up prized pos-sessions, and what is really important to a family.

In Sharon Dennis Wyeth's *Something Beautiful,* ✗ a little girl takes us on a journey that reveals the ugliness that exists in her world. When her teacher talks about the word *beautiful* in school, she writes in her notebook:

> Beautiful! I think it means: something that when you have it, your heart is happy.

She searches through her neighborhood and finds that everyone has "something beautiful," like the smooth worry stone that Mr. Sims keeps in his pocket, the tasty fried-fish sandwiches that Miss Delphine serves up, or Jamaal's new shoes. In the author's note, Wyeth reveals that as a young child she asked her mother for something beautiful to take away some of the ugliness of her world. Her mother gave her one of her wedding presents—a small pitcher—that the author still keeps next to her bed. Like the author, we all have memories tied to objects, places, and people. We all have our own treasure chest of "something beauti-fuls" and need only the help of a good book and a good writing teacher to unearth them. After reading this book with a group of fourth graders, Lynne wrote the following notebook entry:

> *Memphis, my wonderful tri-colored Welsh Corgi, is my something beautiful. He always has been a cuddle-bug since he was little. I love the way he jumps up on the couch and throws himself against me so I can wrap my arm around him while I watch the morning news and sip my tea. He loves his walks and helps me get some exercise. I think without him I would weigh at least ten pounds heavier! I love his company. Every day he is there waiting for me at the big picture window as I drive onto the driveway and burst through the door with my big ton of books.*

*Whenever I'm away I start to miss his snuggles and cuddles, my silly
Corgi with one ear up and one ear down—Mr. Personality Plus!*

After sharing her entry, Lynne asked the students to make a quick list of
the things they considered a something beautiful in their lives and then turn and
talk with their partner. She reminded them of the definition of *beautiful* that the
little girl in Wyeth's book wrote in her notebook. The students were asked to
choose one thing from their list and create a notebook entry about it. They were
also told they could draw a picture to go along with their entry. (See Figure 2.6.)
For some students, drawing helps trigger ideas and details about those ideas.
For others, it is a culminating activity. The power of the read-aloud, combined
with the teacher model, inspired all the students to find the words to write about
their something beautiful. Celina, a fourth grader, remembered her mother:

★ Memories

I hugged my bear as tears of sorrow crept down my cheeks. I remembered
all the stories she had told and all the cookies we had baked. But most of
all, I remembered her smile. I could still feel the mushy cookie dough in
between my fingers as I shaped it like soft clay into perfect round pieces. I
remembered all the lovely dresses she wore, and all the giggles we had
playing games in the Giggle Berry Fair held inside at Peddler's Village. I just
couldn't stand the thought of my mother being buried. I turned to face the
pillow and I cried and cried until I felt I had no tears left.

Figure 2.6
"Something Beautiful"
notebook entry by
Kelliann, grade four.

After hearing books like *The Memory String* or Mem Fox's *Wilfrid Gordon McDonald Partridge*, students are often inspired to bring in objects from home that represent stories from their lives. In Paul Fleischman's *The Matchbox Diary*, a great-grandfather shares memories with his great-granddaughter by talking about the matchboxes housed in a cigar box. Each box holds a small treasure that captures a memory, such as the sunflower seeds that helped him mark the days it took to cross the ocean from Italy to New York. The objects and the matchboxes are like pages in his diary. Students can then make real treasure boxes full of tangible things—a soccer trophy, a hair ribbon, a shiny pebble—that will help them discover those tiny treasures of time that are so important to their writing. A good read-aloud for introducing children to the idea of writing around an object is *Aunt Flossie's Hats (and Crab Cakes Later)* by Elizabeth Fitzgerald Howard. In this book, two young girls visit Aunt Flossie every Sunday. Aunt Flossie has a trunk full of hats, each with its own story, which she never tires of telling. Rose sometimes has children bring in a favorite hat in preparation for this read-aloud. She contributes an old straw beach hat and tells the story of how one day she was sitting in her backyard, totally engrossed in a book, when she suddenly felt something tugging at her hat. In an instant, it seemed, the hat was lifted from her head and dropped to the ground several yards away. She peered cautiously and noticed a small bird pecking at a loose piece of the straw. She then encourages the children to share the stories connected with their hats. At first, there are often those superficial connections, such as, "Well, it's just my baseball hat!" But with some guided questioning, children can find the stories behind them. After reading and discussing the stories behind Aunt Flossie's hats, the children are asked to think about the places or the people that their hat may remind them of. Before long, talk about the day the team won their first game and everyone threw their hats up in the air or the time the coach gave everyone a special "big league" wool hat on picture day fill the classroom. These are the almost-forgotten treasures of time that become the seeds of writing projects.

Some authors use photographs to reveal their treasured moments in time. In *My Rotten Redheaded Older Brother*, Patricia Polacco skillfully includes pictures of her and her brother inside the front and back covers of the book. We see them as children on their grandmother's farm in front of the garden, happily celebrating birthdays, and engaged in playful poses across various settings. The stories behind these photographs are the stories the author tells in the book. Polacco uses a similar technique in *My Ol' Man*. In the pictures included on the end pages in this book, we meet the characters whose thoughts, feelings, and stories she poignantly brings to life. Photographs also play a major role in *Journey* by Patricia MacLachlan as the main character, Journey, searches for answers to his life in the photographs taken by his grandfather. Books such as these can inspire students to bring in photographs and tell the stories behind the pictures. Lynne models this technique with a set of pictures all taken at the stable where she once worked as a riding coach. It was the middle of January, and Lynne was on top of the manure pile with one of her students, attempting to flatten it by using a pitchfork to spread the manure. A parent snapped photos of the riding students making snowballs in the courtyard and firing them at Lynne and Jody, the student. Lynne ended up falling over backward into the manure pile and disappearing from view. After she shared her story, she encouraged her students to ask her more questions about what had happened—the who, what, where, when, and why behind it. Later during writing workshop, Lynne drafted the story and shared it the next day. Before long, some of the students were tucking photos inside their notebooks and using them to spark story ideas.

In the first-grade classrooms that Rose visits, she often lingers on the displays brought in by the "student of the week." Many of the displays contain photographs used to introduce family members or pets. Rose often engages the student in a guided conversation, leading him or her to tell the story behind a picture in the display—the who, what, when, where, and why behind it—to bring to mind rich detail. She then encourages the student to jot down the memory, often in the form of a short phrase, in his or her writing folder, journal, or notebook. The story behind the picture becomes a writing treasure to which the young writer can return during writing workshop.

When using photos as a vehicle for finding writing topics, it is important to model for students that the story must be theirs, not one told to them by someone else such as their parents or grandparents. For elementary classrooms, taking these stories through the entire writing process to publication is a worthwhile project. Stories with photos are often read and reread by the wider school community when hung in the hallways or classrooms.

As in *An Angel for Solomon Singer*, read-alouds can also help children uncover the memories connected with special places. In *All the Places to Love* by Patricia MacLachlan, we read of a small boy who is thinking about the places he loves best on the farm where he lives.

> What I saw first were all the places to love: The valley, The river falling down over rocks, The hilltop where the blueberries grew.

In My Momma's Kitchen by Jerdine Nolen explores different happenings that all take place in the kitchen. As the narrator explains, "Seems like everything good that happens in my house happens in my momma's kitchen." We can encourage young authors to dig up writing treasures associated with the special places in their lives: a vacation spot, a secret hiding place, a favorite park. The Your Turn lesson at the end of this chapter describes a technique that involves sketching and conversation to encourage young writers to dig up the stories connected to special places.

An Outdoor Writer's Café

Finding topics for writing can be difficult, especially as spring arrives and students begin to think about summer vacation, Little League games, and weekends at the shore. State testing takes a great deal of energy from both students and teachers. One year Lynne thought it was time to renew her students' love and enthusiasm for writing, and she thought a writer's café would be the perfect way to do it. She talked with a fifth-grade class about her ideas for an outdoor writer's café. They had been working on a poetry cycle and using scaffolds to create poems. The weather promised to be unusually warm for April, so Lynne wanted to take advantage of it. "Tomorrow we're going to do exactly what writers do. We are taking our notebooks and pencils and going outside for about forty minutes. I want you to write about the things you see, smell, hear, taste, and feel. I am going to ask you to write from at least four different vantage points. Don't stay in one spot for too long. And the first time we go outside, I don't want you to talk with anyone—not even your teacher or me. Just write. Don't evaluate whether or not the stuff you are writing is good or bad. Just write it down. Don't let any ideas escape. Capture them in the white-lined pages of your writer's notebook. But first, today I want to share a picture book titled *Right Outside My Window* by Mary Ann Hoberman."

Lynne gathered the students and read. She asked the students to turn and talk about things they might notice outside the windows of their classroom. As the students talked, she reminded them to think about everyday things in extraordinary ways. Lynne looked at her students' faces and knew she had captured their interest. She listened in while Rachel described the jungle gym as "lonely" and Jason talked about the playground as a "home" to many kids and adults. After five minutes of writerly talk, Lynne said, "Let's go outside for a quick tour today and think about possible topics for writing and where we might want to be to observe those things." Outside, Lynne modeled her writing by talking out loud as she wrote. "Here I'm going to take some notes about the school." She wrote these observations and shared them with the class:

> shiny windows
> squares neatly stacked
> brown brick rectangles
> sun reflected on windows
> empty slides and basketball courts
> yellow school buses waiting to take kids home

Then she turned her attention to the church and its steeple:

> slender steeple
> whiter than clouds
> a simple cross

a strong message
keep the faith

She asked the students to suggest topics. Steven said he could write about the basketball that had been left outside. "I could be the ball. I'd feel lonely and forgotten." Some students chose the pine trees, or the slender, young trees with delicate pink blooms, or the light post in the church parking lot, or the baseball diamond. Lynne was satisfied that they would find lots of things to write about. "Now remember, sometimes a poem will just spill onto the page. Other times, you may need to make a quick sketch and/or write down some words, phrases, and sentences. There's no right or wrong way to do this. We all have our own writing process that works best for us."

When they returned to the classroom, Lynne wrote her notes on the board. Then she created a draft of two poems from the notes she had made. The following poem is about the school.

> *Shiny-clean windows,*
> *squares neatly stacked*
> *while brown brick rectangles*
> *march along like a Cub Scout troop.*
>
> *But inside, cold and silent,*
> *as empty as the slides and*
> *basketball courts on Friday afternoons*
> *when children leave on yellow school buses . . .*
>
> *Looking out the shiny-clean*
> *windows of the school bus*
> *and dreaming of home-run hits*
> *and pedal-fast bike rides*
> *and sleepy Saturday-Sunday*
> *mornings when alarm clocks*
> *are strangely silent.*

Lynne encouraged the students to talk about her poem. They noticed that some of the things she added to her poem did not appear in the original list. "That's exactly what you will do. You'll come up with something you never imagined before. That's because you'll be doing what writers do: noticing little details that other people miss."

The next afternoon the class took their notebooks and went outside to write for forty minutes. Their teacher wrote, too. Lynne wrote. Everybody was writing. When a third-grade class came out to play kickball, the game just became another topic to write about. Here are Amber's notes from her notebook, untouched:

I'm brown and hard and smooth and fell off of my father and alone in the grass.
—branch

I smell beautiful with a soft top and a strong stem and green leaves.
—flower

People leave footprints on me
And when rain comes,
I turn into mud
And dry in the sun.
—dirt

I'm dying for water, some of me is green and
some of me is brown, some of me is soft and some is rough.
—grass

Kurt wrote about the empty baseball diamond that borders the playground behind the school and imagined the following poem from his notes:

The Pitch

The sun beats down on us
As the whole world waits, silent
For the one final pitch.
The dust tumbles as
I bend my legs in the shape
Of a crooked nine.
The crowd hollers as
The red and white ball flies through
The open-aired field.

Maria observed the pine trees and wrote several poems about them. This was a class favorite:

Pine

Pine tree.
Sweet pine scents filling the air,
Not like the other trees that stand empty and bare.
Lined with prickles on every side,
By a school and a church standing tall and wide.
Overgrown grass all in its middle,
Green needles dropping little by little.
Pine tree.

The kids were amazing! Barbara (their teacher) and Lynne were speechless. They wrote and wrote, and when it was time to go back inside, they came in slowly, as if a film had been set at slow motion to notice every detail. They kept stopping to kneel down to write one last thought. They scanned the field, the playground, the sky . . . hungry for more. When Lynne asked if anyone wanted to share, the students took turns coming to the podium to read notes and poetry. Their words rushed and gushed in rivers and whispered in silver streams, and the air was filled with writing by students who believed they were writers. When their teacher (who is quite fond of mathematics) announced that she had several poems to share, they listened eagerly and burst out in enthusiastic applause when she was finished. Lynne had to pull herself away to go to her next class, and as she left, the students were still sharing their writing.

Sometimes a writer needs a change of scenery to help generate ideas. A walk through the school or a walk in the playground or neighborhood might just do the trick. In *Ideas Are All Around*, Philip Stead takes us outdoors on a walk in his neighborhood and reveals how he gathers ideas for writing. He tells us he is a writer by trade—that it is his job to come up with ideas for writing—but that even published writers can get stuck sometimes. We see his thinking and imaginings from what he sees and hears as he walks with his dog. Stead uses real photographs and extends his thinking in drawings. Encouraging students to write or sketch in their notebooks, or maybe even take photos during an outdoor adventure, will help them capture moments to remember and write about.

Shelley Harwayne (1992) captures the value of response to literature as a resource for writing topics: "Literature helped recreate very powerful moments for students, those that they often forget when they sit down at their school desks for writing time" (79). One of the techniques she describes is using sticky notes on which children record their responses. These notes can be posted, honored, and shared and then added to a notebook or treasure chest of writing ideas. We have used this technique many times with various sizes of sticky notes. When very small sticky notes are used, children may respond with just a word or a short phrase. Later, during writing workshop, they can return to it and extend their thinking—as Harwayne (1992) says, they can "write to get to the bottom of it." Although responses often lead to the writing of personal narratives from the unearthed memories, students sometimes try out other formats: poetry, persuasive pieces, letters, even recipes. *Mud* by Mary Lyn Ray is a delightful book that describes the "season" of mud—when winter is waning, the earth is defrosting, and mud is overflowing. After reading this, Rose asked a group of second graders to respond on a small sticky note. Sarah wrote "mud pies." As we shared responses, she told about making mud pies with her sister and brother in the hollow of a large tree in their backyard. A few days later she drew the tree in her writer's notebook, along with a recipe for making mud pies. (See Figure 2.7.)

Figure 2.7
Sarah's notebook entry is a recipe for making mud pies (grade two).

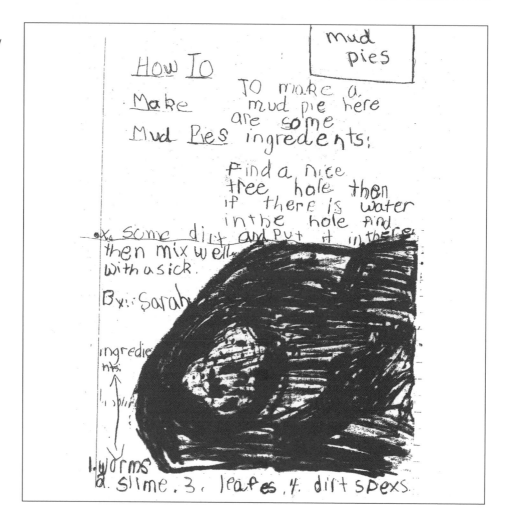

Carol Gay (1976), in writing about the importance of reading aloud to children, reminds us of the inescapable link this practice has to the development of writing:

> *Reading aloud is inseparably linked with learning to write. If elementary school teachers fail to read aloud to their students often, regularly, and for reasonably long periods of time, those students are going to be severely handicapped in learning to write.* (87)

The read-aloud is an important part of writing workshop and establishing a community of writers. Through careful selection of high-quality literature as mentor texts rich in experiences that are both personal and magical, we can provide our student authors with a treasure chest of opportunities to find writing topics. As Carol Gay says, "Only by hearing good literature can a child come to realize what it is and to understand what writing has to offer him—an opportunity to describe, define, and perhaps understand his world" (93).

Think About It—Talk About It—Write About It

- Choose one of your favorite classroom read-alouds. How do you introduce it to your students so that all (or at least most) of them can make meaningful connections?
- How do you share books across the day (outside of reading/writing workshop)? What is the value of doing this?
- What books (excerpts, leads, endings, descriptions) have you used or could you use from your personal reading to help students see you as a reader? Make a list in your writer's notebook. How can you extend this experience to help them see you as a writer?
- Consider Carol Gay's quote: "Only by hearing good literature can a child come to realize what it is and to understand what writing has to offer him—an opportunity to describe, define, and perhaps understand his world" (93). What meaning does this quote hold for you? Do you agree? Why or why not? Reflect in your writer's notebook using words and/or drawings.

Drawing and Talking to Find Topics

Through sketching and conversation, writers dig up memories connected with objects or events from a special place. Variations of this lesson are endless: the setting could be a backyard, a park, the playground, a vacation spot, a field trip, and so on. Try this out on your own so that you have a model to share with your students.

Hook: Read from *Right Outside My Window* by Mary Ann Hoberman, *In My Momma's Kitchen* by Jerdine Nolen, or *All the Places to Love* by Patricia MacLachlan. Through whole-group conversation invite students to make connections to events that happen in a special place. Be sure to participate in the discussion and share your own connections.

Purpose: *Writers, just like some authors tell stories about things that happened in a special place, today we will learn how to use a familiar setting to help dig up memories and find topics and stories for our writing.*

Brainstorm: Ask students to create a list of favorite or familiar places such as their backyard, the playground, or a vacation spot. Have them turn and talk with a partner to share their lists and add or revise as needed. Ask students to circle or star one place they would like to sketch and write about.

Model: Distribute a strip of plain drawing paper (approximately 6 by 24 inches) to each student. Instruct them to fold back approximately one-third of the strip. Share the sketch you have prepared, thinking aloud and talking about each object or relating small stories that you are reminded of as you explain your drawing. Ask students to sketch their place on the two-thirds portion of the strip. You may have to demonstrate what a sketch is so that students don't spend too much time on the drawing.

> *Writers, close your eyes and think about the place and the experiences you have had there. Think about the objects in this place. Sketch this place on the long part of your strip. Remember that this is only a sketch and that a sketch takes only a few minutes.*

Allow students some time to sketch and then ask them to talk and share.

> *Now turn to your partner and talk about the different things in your sketch. Tell the stories that you remember when you think about or talk about each part of your sketch.*

Continue to model by choosing one object that evoked a special memory or a story. Sketch this again on the small folded part of the paper strip, this time elaborating and adding more detail.

This tree in my backyard has many special memories attached to it, but one thing I remember is the time I watched a robin build a nest for her eggs, then take care of the babies and teach them how to fly. So on this part of the strip I'm going to zoom in on that tree and add the detail of the robin's nest.

Invite students to do the same.

Think about the one thing in your sketch you had the most to talk to your partner about. Zoom in on that and sketch it again on the small part of your strip. Add as many details as you can. You can list words or short phrases that come to mind as you sketch.

Shared/Guided Writing: Talk to the students about your detailed sketch. Model for them how you might jot down words or phrases that you can use. Then begin to draft your piece. Invite students to do the same.

Turn and talk again with your neighbor about your detailed drawing. As you talk, create a list of words or phrases that describe your object or memory. Share your list with your partner.

Circulate and listen in, often asking clarifying questions to guide the thinking.

Independent Writing: Invite students to write a small story or notebook entry on the memory from the sketch.

Reflection: Invite students to reflect on the strategy.

Did the sketching help you focus your thoughts? How?

When could you use this strategy?

Students can first share in pairs and then share ideas with the whole group. After they've reflected on the strategy, ask students to reread their writing and think about the things that they do well as a writer. What revisions could they make? Some students might choose to continue to work on their piece during subsequent workshops.

Finding Topics from a Memory Chain

A memory chain is a prewriting experience to help writers find topics and ideas to write about. It is a wonderful strategy to use when students are experiencing writer's block. A memory chain is a collection of ideas that are sometimes related and sometimes unrelated. It is a menu that helps a writer make good choices for a writing piece.

Hook: *Small Beauties* by Elvira Woodruff is an excellent book to demonstrate to writers how objects can spark memories. Talk about how different objects in the book remind Darcy of things she experienced in Ireland and helped her family remember. Options: *Night Tree* by Eve Bunting and *Bigmama's* by Donald Crews.

Purpose: *Writers, sometimes objects or words can remind us of things that happened to us or things we wonder about, just like Rosie is reminded about the lake. Today I'm going to show you how to create a memory chain. When you are having difficulty finding a topic for writing, a memory chain can help you unlock some ideas.*

Brainstorm: Together with the class, brainstorm objects in the room, words, ideas, seasons, or holidays that could be a starting point for a memory chain. For example, *bulletin board, desk, flag, playground, window, winter, Thanksgiving*, and so on.

Model: Choose one of the words from the brainstormed list and write it on the board or overhead. Continue to think aloud, recording ideas that are generated as a stream of consciousness. Here is an example from Rose's notebook:

> *snow*
> → *blizzard at the farm*
> → *ice skating on the pond*
> → *ice skating at Italian Lake*
> → *the whip—skating over my finger*
> → *hot chocolate at Christina's house*
> → *Daddy making hot chocolate before school*

Try to make your memory chain as long as you can so you have lots of ideas to choose from. Then go back to the list and circle one idea that you think you could write about today. Orally tell the story, or write the story on chart paper.

Shared/Guided Writing: Ask students to choose a word and try out the technique in their writer's notebooks. Sometimes it is interesting to have the class all start with the same word and then see how many different ideas can come from it. After students have completed their chains, have them share with a partner. Partners can give feedback on what story they would like to hear more about. They can then circle those ideas and tell their stories to each other, providing oral rehearsal.

Independent Writing: Invite students to complete a notebook entry on the memory they circled.

Reflection: This strategy can work very well but can also hit a dead end—it all depends on where the ideas take you. Try it out several times, and begin this part of the lesson discussing with students how the strategy has worked for you. Then ask students to share their ideas on how the strategy worked for them.

How did the strategy work for you?

When would you use it again?

What changes would you make?

Your Turn Lesson 3

Finding Topics and Using Senses to Create First Memories

First memories of an event, a place, or even a person are usually vivid because they are associated with several senses and have strong emotional appeal. They offer young writers an array of starter topics. Students can use them as writer's notebook entries, eventually finding seeds of ideas for narratives, poems, and even informational pieces.

Hook: Read *Hello Ocean* by Pam Muñoz Ryan. Discuss how Ryan awakens the senses in her readers and helps them visualize the seashore—its sounds, smells, and sights, and the feel of the sand. (Another option is *Crab Moon* by Ruth Horowitz.) Create a web of ideas organized around the senses. Refer to the text for specific language. Ask your students the following questions:

> *How did the mentor text inspire you?*
>
> *What words and images from the text stayed with you?*

Note: Geographical location may be important to think about here for first-memory topics. Lynne used books about the seashore because most of her students vacation at the New Jersey shores. If your students live in Arizona or New Mexico, you might use books by Byrd Baylor.

Purpose: *Writers, often we can recall with extraordinary detail and powerful feelings the people, places, and events of our first impressions—our first memories. They are etched in our hearts and our minds, and when we begin to write about them, our words often spill onto the page. Today I will show you how to use your senses to create a first memory for your writer's notebook.*

Brainstorm: Together with the class create a list of possible first memories. Some examples may be learning to ride a bike, sledding down a hill, riding a horse, surfing or Boogie boarding, watching a sunrise or a sunset, and seeing the ocean for the first time.

Model: Choose one of the ideas from the brainstormed list and create a first memory with strong appeal to the senses. Lynne's example:

> *I am standing on the beach and curling my toes into the warm, grainy sand. My grandparents stand on each side of me and hold a hand tightly. They know I want to run toward the water. I close my eyes and breathe the salty air into my lungs. When I gaze out onto the blue-meets-blue horizon, I catch a glimpse of a gull floating high above me. I think to myself, I wish I could be that*

gull and never leave here. *The waves roll in and out, in and out . . . a pulsating rhythm that beats like my heart. It reminds me of life itself. I watch the water stain the sand a dark beige color. The foamy fingers waltz out again to continue their dance from the sea to the shore. My grandparents smile at me, and I cry out to them and the whole world, "It's so beautiful . . . it's so very beautiful!" I catch my breath as the wonder of it all wraps around me like a warm blanket.*

Shared/Guided Writing: Students note the appeal to the senses used in the teacher's model and think about its effectiveness. Ask students to choose an idea from the list and try writing about it in their writer's notebooks. Some students may need to start with a prewriting experience such as a graphic organizer that makes use of the senses. Circulate to encourage, ask questions, and give feedback. Students may share with a partner or in small response groups, noting powerful words and phrases that appeal to the senses.

Independent Writing: Invite students to complete a first draft from their notebook entry or to choose a new topic and write another notebook entry.

Reflection: Students examine their first-memory piece. During individual conferences, whole-group discussion, or partner sharing, they can guide their thinking with the following questions:

How did the use of the senses strengthen your writing?

What writing strategies did you use to help the reader "be there" with you?

What other first memories could you write about?

Your Turn Lesson 4

Every Picture Tells a Story

Whereas some authors write personal narratives from photographs that spark memories, others use pictures or artifacts to create fictional accounts. This lesson will show your students how to create stories from pictures. To prepare for this lesson, collect pictures from magazines or newspapers that are rich in detail and that might inspire places, characters, or events for stories.

Hook: Introduce the use of photographs to reveal moments in time by reading *Journey* by Patricia MacLachlan or *My Rotten Redheaded Older Brother* by Patricia Polacco. Options: *Finding Winnie: The True Story of the World's Most Famous Bear* by Lindsay Mattick and *Teammates* by Peter Golenbock. These books use photographs of real people to tell their story.

Purpose: *Sometimes authors build stories around pictures or photographs. Sometimes the stories are personal memories sparked by connections made to the photographs. Sometimes the pictures provide the ideas for settings, characters, or events for fictional stories. Today I will show you how to build a story around a picture.*

Brainstorm: Choose a picture from a magazine and display it with a document camera. Ask students to think about the characters, setting, problems, story events, and so on that the picture makes them think about. Elicit as many ideas as possible and make a web on a chart or whiteboard. This brainstorming can be repeated for several pictures. An alternative for older students is to place a picture at the center of a piece of chart paper. Create several of these charts and display them around the room. Students can do a "gallery walk" (walk around the room looking at the pictures as they would in an art museum) and jot down ideas for characters, setting, events, and so forth.

Model: Begin to map out or outline a story idea by choosing from the list of brainstormed suggestions. Use thinking aloud to let your students in on how you chose the ideas—how you think of the things that might work best for you. Your outline can be written on a prepared story map outline or simply listed.

Characters:

Setting:

Problem or Goal:

Events:

Resolution:

Ending:

Talk through your story, demonstrating how it might sound when you start to compose.

Shared/Guided Writing: Create another outline or story map from the brainstormed list, using a shared writing format. Invite students to tell the story orally. Students can also work in pairs to create story outlines that can be posted.

Independent Writing: Ask students to begin a story in their notebooks. They can choose to write one of the stories that the class already outlined, or they may want to choose a new picture and begin to jot down a new set of possibilities. Offering students several choices can help differentiate among those who may still need more guidance and those who are ready to try it on their own.

Reflection: Using pictures to create stories involves lots of thinking and decision making. Your class may want or need to spend several days working with this strategy. Encourage your students to find pictures that spark ideas. These can be put in a writing center or kept inside a notebook. Remember to focus on the strategy by guiding discussion around the following points:

How did the pictures help you think of story ideas?

Did any of the pictures spark connections and lead to writing personal narratives?

What type of pictures work best?

Did the sharing of ideas help? How?

Did the pictures spark ideas that led to revisions on previous work?

When might you use this strategy again?

Developing a "What If" Story

Many authors talk about the power of the "What if" as a way to explore story ideas. Since children have a natural curiosity about the world, they seem to ask this question almost constantly. Although simply keeping a list of the "What if" questions they come up with is a place to start, helping students harness that curiosity may make for some interesting story ideas.

Hook: Return to books such as *The Day the Crayons Quit* by Drew Daywalt or *Matthew A.B.C.* by Peter Catalanotto and share with students that the ideas for these books came from asking "What if." Drew Daywalt saw a box of crayons on his desk one day, noticed that they were used unevenly, and wondered, *What if these crayons could talk? What would they say?* In the case of *Matthew A.B.C.*, Catalanotto asked himself, *What if everyone in a class were named Matthew?* You could also share books like *Imogene's Antlers* by David Small, *A Bad Case of Stripes* by David Shannon, or *Chalk* by Bill Thomson and ask students to guess what the "What if" behind these books might be.

Purpose: *Writers, today I'm going to show you how to discover and map out a story idea by asking "What if."*

Brainstorm: Together with the students, brainstorm and chart a list of places they are familiar with. This list might include home, school, backyard, the play-ground, the park, a zoo, and so on. Choose one of the places and create a list of "What if" scenarios. For example, for "school" you might say something like, "What if you came to school one day and . . ." Model your thinking aloud and chart your answers. Here's one we created:

> What if you came to school one day and . . .
> all the classroom chairs were gone.
> all the books in the library were missing.
> the classrooms were all mixed up in different places.
> your teacher had been transformed into a dinosaur.
> it snowed so hard you had to stay overnight.

Model: Choose a scenario and create a map of events for the story. This could be charted as bullet points to develop an understanding of plot (character has a problem and attempts to solve it). Share your thinking about the events you include or decide to discard. Allow the students to help you when you are stuck. Here is our example for "What if you came to school one day and all the classroom chairs were gone?"

- The teacher calls the office to report the problem.
- No extra chairs are available until tomorrow.
- Kids gather on the meeting rug.

- The kids get tired of sitting on the rug and kneel at their desks.
- Their knees get tired so they stand.
- One student has an idea.
- He or she goes to the gym and brings a cart filled with balls.
- Students balance on balls for the rest of the day.

Shared/Guided Writing: Return to the brainstormed list, add any suggestions, and choose one to plot with the entire class. Older students can follow along in their writer's notebook and even add their own variations. If students need additional practice, have them work in partnerships to brainstorm questions for another place and map one out.

Independent Writing: Encourage students to think about "What if" scenarios and create a list in their writer's notebook that can be used to create narratives throughout the year. They could return to the shared experiences and write the story.

Reflection: *How did a "What if" structure help you think of ideas for writing a narrative?*

Could you use this structure to write an informational piece or a poem?

Can you find another book whose idea may have come from the author asking "What if"?

How did it go? Was it easy or hard to think of the events for your "What if" story?

Chapter 3

What Are You Really Writing About? Discovering the Inside Story

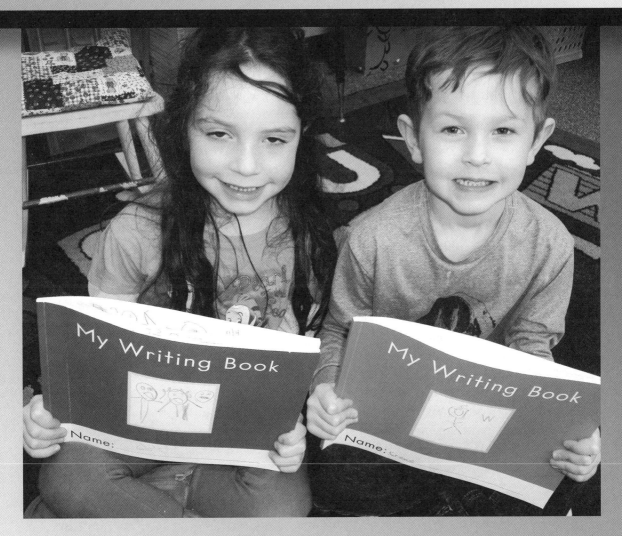

Good writing will come from finding fresh new things to say about a topic and from knowing how to write about the topic in different ways for different audiences.

—Katie Wood Ray, *Wondrous Words*

Exploring Writing Territories

Where do writers find their story seeds—the kernels of rich ideas that can grow and blossom into narratives, poems, letters, and articles? In looking closely at the works of authors, we can often begin to find evidence of what Nancie Atwell (1998) refers to as writing territories, the treasure chests of their hearts and minds where they store precious memories about people, places, events, and objects. Cynthia Rylant, for instance, grew up in the hills of West Virginia with her mother and grandparents. Her extended family of aunts, uncles, and countless cousins played an important role in her life and served as a territory from which she could farm the ideas for books such as *When I Was Young in the Mountains, The Relatives Came,* and *Night in the Country,* among others. In *Best Wishes* (1992), Rylant says that as she was growing up, she liked to roam around the town where she lived. This wandering gave her the opportunity to meet many people, watch what they did, and listen to the kinds of conversations they had with one another. It helped her begin to develop her "people" territory. Rylant also met many animals as she roamed, such as a big dog named Mudge, who eventually became a central character in the Henry and Mudge books. We can find other evidence of her "animals" territory in books such as *The Great Gracie Chase, Dog Heaven, Cat Heaven,* and *Gooseberry Park.*

Sometimes authors include a note in the front or back of the book. This section has value for young writers, often revealing the seed of an idea that was plucked from a larger territory. Judy Schachner is another author, like Cynthia Rylant, whose territories include family and pets, writing territories young authors can easily relate to. Schachner's Siamese cats are the subjects of *The Grannyman, Skippyjon Jones,* and *Bits and Pieces.* In the afterword of *Mr. Emerson's Cook,* Schachner provides some background information on Ralph Waldo Emerson and explains that her great-grandmother Ann, the main character in the book, actually worked as a domestic in the Emerson home. *Mr. Emerson's Cook* is based on stories passed down to Schachner from her father. In *Yo, Vikings!* we learn of how an authentic Viking ship found its way into the Schachners' backyard. This story is found in the background information provided about Vikings in the author's note, as well as in the information on the dust jacket (another good source of information about the origin of story ideas).

As in *Yo, Vikings!* sometimes the story comes from one specific event that the author experienced. In *Butterfly Tree,* Sandra Markle reveals in the author's note that the story stemmed from an experience she had one autumn afternoon as she observed a migrating flock of monarchs settle for the night. Sometimes this one event happens over and over again as in *In a Village by the Sea* by Muon Van. Here the author helps us gain insight into a way of life in a different culture. *In a Village by the Sea* tells the story of a family waiting for a father to return from a fishing trip just as Vietnamese families have done for centuries. Sometimes the story idea is a compilation of many experiences. In the author's note to *The Raft,* Jim LaMarche explains that the story comes from bits and pieces of his boyhood summers—time spent with his grandmother, a raft he found, the power of drawing.

Lynne usually begins her discussion of writing territories by talking about authors such as Allen Say, Patricia Polacco, Gary Paulsen, and Eve Bunting. These authors are interesting to upper elementary and middle school students because they deal with themes the students find interesting, such as friendship, courage, divorce, death, separation, and family traditions. Students read biographical excerpts about these authors on Internet websites, in newspaper book reviews, and in dedications and about-the-author information in books, as well as in the author's notes previously mentioned. In *Bat Loves the Night* by author/zoologist Nicola Davies, the reader learns that the author enjoys being out under the stars and watching bats. As a matter of fact, she happens to live in a cottage with pipistrelle bats (the subject of the book) residing in the roof. Lynne talks to her students about how heavily the writer draws from personal experiences—the people, the places, the events, and the objects that bring about an emotional response and clear, crisp memories. If we are alert to discovering the inside stories (the stories that only the authors know and can write) in the writing territories of the authors we introduce in the classroom, we can help our students identify their own writing territories and the stories that are contained within them.

Students Discover Their Territories

Once students are familiar with the concept of a writing territory, they can more easily begin to explore their own. In a fourth-grade classroom, early in the school year, Lynne wrote her list of writing territories on a chart. However you choose to record your thinking, it is important that the students see your brainstorming process. Although Lynne had saved countless lists of writing territories, she demonstrated the writing of the list as if it were being written for the first time. The list she created looked something like this:

[handwritten annotation: ① Brainstorm Territories]

special events	Girl Scouts	The first time I . . .
relatives	surprises	best friends
grandfather	trouble!	bullies
parents	sisters	sad times
holidays	teachers	happy times
summer fun	animals	hairdos
horses	Christmas	sports
pets	school tales	car stories
church and synagogue	embarrassing moments	angry times
		when I was afraid

Next, Lynne asked her fourth-grade students which territories they thought they could write about. Most students included friends, school, holidays, pets,

[handwritten annotation: ② Kids decide which ones they can write about.]

and animals as writing territories. For this particular list, they also added vacations, parties, and times they needed to be brave. Todd volunteered, "How about weather? My big German shepherd turns into a chicken during a thunderstorm." That created a ripple effect, and the class buzzed with talk about weather stories.

Marie asked, "What about family traditions?"

"Do you mean traditions that revolve around holidays?" Lynne questioned.

Marie explained that she was thinking about the Irish dancing that her grandmother had passed on to family members. It took on a special meaning when the class learned that Marie had lost her grandmother the year before. Lynne clarified, "Two territories for Marie could be 'grandmother' and 'family traditions.'" She helped her students understand that the territory "relatives" can be listed as well as a separate territory for one or two special relatives. In addition, certain holidays having special traditions and celebrations can be listed separately. Sometimes the same story seed can arise from two or three different territories, as did the Irish dancing story for Marie. The point is, it's not the territories themselves that are important, but the use of them as trigger words that spark the memories for the inside stories. Lynne talked about "horses" as one of her writing territories to show her students that territories can lend themselves to persuasive and informational writing as well. She talked about creating an essay on how to prepare a horse for competition or why horseback riding is a great sport for children. Finally, Lynne's students listed their territories in the back of their notebooks where they could refer to them often and add to their list as the year progressed.

A territory can spark a notebook entry, a prewriting experience, a drawing or graphic organizer, a poem, or a first draft. The notion of having many, many stories about a territory is important for students to reflect on. They need to know that they don't have to tell *everything* about their grandfather in one piece of writing. With this understanding in place, students can eliminate the practice of writing "bed-to-bed" stories or writing five to ten pages or more about a single topic with no real direction. Once students understand the difference between a territory and a specific topic, they can understand that every piece will have a point or sharp focus. The writer knows why his or her piece is memorable or important and can effectively communicate the purpose to the readers.

Moving from a Territory to a Specific Topic

Of course, the hard part begins once a territory is chosen. For Lynne, a huge territory is her maternal grandfather. To help the students visualize the depth and breadth of a writing territory, she wheels a cart containing a set of World Book encyclopedias into the classroom. She hands the books out to the students so they can feel the weight of the books and examine the number of pages. She explains to her students that she could write a set of *A* to *Z* encyclopedias about her grandfather because he was her friend, her confidant, and her hero. "What shall I write about him today?" she muses. "Should it be the story of how he took my Raggedy Ann doll to work every day? What about the Easter when he brought home three live chicks? Or maybe it should take the form of a poem about our walk in the woods and the rescue of a fir tree I named Little Pocono." Lynne models how she narrows her territory using an inverted triangle to help her zoom in on the one story, poem, or essay she plans to write today during writing workshop. She thinks aloud in the form of a continuum from general (territory) to most specific (topic) while recording her thinking on an inverted triangle on a chart.

> *Writers, today I've chosen my grandfather as the territory I'd like to explore. As I'm looking through my writer's notebook, I see that I have many holiday entries that include thoughts about him. We spent every Easter together. Now I'm remembering one special Easter when Grandpa made me very happy but made my grandma very unhappy. He came home with a cardboard box containing three small chicks—one dyed blue, one dyed red, and one dyed pink.*

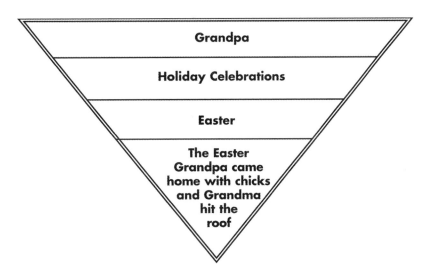

Without revealing any more information, Lynne asks the students if they would want to hear the entire story. By doing this, she demonstrates the importance of writing for a target audience and understanding what they would like to read or learn more about.

One of the Your Turn lessons at the end of this chapter models the use of the inverted triangle. This graphic organizer can be placed on chart paper and laminated so that both the teacher and the students can use it over and over. By hanging it in a writing center and encouraging students to take turns using it on a daily basis, teachers can help young writers quickly internalize the process for this strategy. An additional advantage is the sharing of ideas. Writers who are having difficulty identifying their territories can begin to make connections to similar experiences that arise from the territories of their peers. Students can also begin to recognize that similar territories, for example, "summer vacations," can yield a wealth of stories.

It is important for students to understand that a writing territory is far too large to tackle. Often, it takes two or three steps to lead us from a vast territory to a specific writing topic we can handle. Eve Bunting's *Night Tree* isn't about all the events of Christmas Eve, but rather about one special event where Luke's family goes into the forest and chooses a tree to decorate with goodies for all the wild animals. What a great example for students who want to write about a special holiday! They can use Eve Bunting's story as an example of how to shrink their topic to a manageable size.

Nicola Davies, in her book *One Tiny Turtle,* includes a foreword that explains to the reader how she narrowed her topic:

> ### About Turtles
> *Sea turtles are related to tortoises and terrapins. They are all reptiles. Sea turtles are great wanderers, traveling thousands of miles each year, often far from land. This makes them difficult to study. So scientists are only just beginning to find out about their mysterious lives. There are seven species of sea turtles. This book is about the loggerhead turtle. Loggerheads live in seas all over the world.*

This foreword can easily be represented in an inverted triangle as an example for young writers on how to narrow a topic in a work of nonfiction.

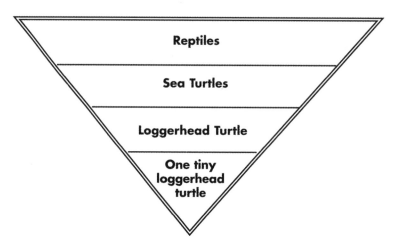

Usually, a territory can be voiced in one or two words, whereas the specific topic of a writing piece is written as one complete thought. A specific topic is something a writer can wrap his or her arms around. It is a topic that enables a writer to complete a high-quality first draft within one or several workshop settings.

Heart Mapping to Find Writing Topics

Georgia Heard (2016) talks about helping writers find topics for poems. She tells them that poets write from their hearts about the things they care deeply about. She shares with them that her poems come from the memories she has of her family, of growing up in Virginia, and of the people she meets as she travels. To help them understand this, Heard asks the students to make maps of their hearts. Heard has found that this visual display of the important people, places, and memories in these young writers' lives helps them write with depth and feeling. In our work with writers, especially our youngest writers who may still be struggling with spelling, we have used the technique of heart mapping as an alternative to listing writing territories.

In some of the primary classes Rose works with, writing workshop often takes the form of journal writing. Students write about themselves in small bound notebooks. These young writers often struggle with finding topics for their entries. Using "safe words" (words they know how to spell or are comfortable with), they write lists of things they like or tell about something they did or somewhere they went in one sentence.

> I love my mom and dad.
> I like sal [school].
> I like poomrn [Pokemon].
> I like me.
> I like my tegr [teacher].
> I went too my ferid hous. [I went to my friend's house.]

In trying to help these writers better understand the concept of territories and discover the small moments within their territories, Rose uses the technique of heart mapping. Eileen Spinelli's *The Best Story* is a great mentor text to illustrate the importance of finding topics that you know about and care about. As the young writer in the book shares her writing, her family members make suggestions to improve it. The problem is, the suggestions are ones that the young writer doesn't care about or know about, so she ends up with a story that is not hers and doesn't make sense. Finally, her mother tells her to write from her heart, and she does.

In one particular first-grade class, early in September, Rose gathered the students together on the rug to introduce them to journal writing. She explained that a journal is a place where you can write about things that happen to you, people and places that are important to you, or things you might wonder about. She told them that because writing comes from one's mind and one's heart, she would show them how to make maps of their hearts so that they would always have something to write about. Rose then shared her heart map—a simple outline of a heart shape divided into sections. Each section had an illustration, sometimes accompanied by labels, of places in her heart where her writing stories come from: her family; her yellow Lab, Casey; vacation spots; her backyard; and music. Some of the sections were intentionally left blank. She wanted these young writers to understand that they could return to their heart maps and add ideas as new places opened up to them. Perhaps later in the year they would start to play baseball or take dance lessons. These big ideas could then become places where many stories could be found. Before the students made their own heart maps, Rose engaged them in conversation and sharing until she was sure they all had some ideas. This scaffolding is described in the Your Turn lesson at the end of the chapter.

The following day, Rose demonstrated how to find a story from a place in their heart maps. She returned to her map and looked at the section with the picture of her yellow Lab, Casey. "I have lots of stories about Casey," she explained. "I remember when Casey was a puppy, she used to dump all of her toys out of the basket until they were all over the room, and then she would play with the basket. One time she ran in circles in the backyard trying to catch a bee, and one time she locked herself in the bathroom for a whole day. I think that's the story I want to write about today: the time Casey locked herself in the bathroom." Rose went on to describe the story in great detail—how the bathroom was really just a powder room and she thought Casey went in to poke around in the trash can and accidentally knocked the door closed as she was trying to turn around. She described how she couldn't find Casey when she came home from school that day but could hear a muffled whimpering from somewhere in the house. Rose wrote in front of the students, but she wrote only as much as she thought they might be able to write from a story like that. She wanted to give them a model for their own writing so that they could say to themselves, *I think I can do that!*

> *One day Casey locked herself in the bathroom. She jumped and she scratched at the door. She couldn't get out. Poor Casey was so scared!*

Rose then asked the students to pick a place on their heart maps where they thought they had a story that they might like to write about, share that idea with a partner, then write it in their journals. (See Figure 3.1 for an example of a heart map.)

During sharing time, Mark showed the picture of a hermit crab on his heart map and shared his entry. "My friend has a hermit crab," he read.

"Can you tell me a little more about the hermit crab?" Rose probed. "Is there something about this hermit crab that caught your attention or something that happened with it when you went to visit?"

Mark replied, "Well, he lives in a cage, and he drinks water from a sponge."

Rose nudged, "Tell me more."

Mark thought for a moment, then said, "Sometimes he's a little scary. One time I saw his big, huge claw come out of the shell, and he started to climb up the side of the cage, and I thought he might get out and jump on me!"

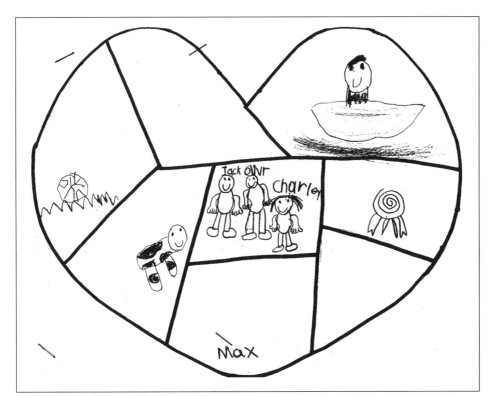

Figure 3.1
Max's heart map (grade one).

Figure 3.2
Peter's heart map (grade five).

"Aha!" Rose exclaimed. "There's your story!"

Sometimes students need a little more guidance to find their inside story. In this case, Mark learned that he could let his readers know much more than just the fact that his friend had a hermit crab. He could make the point that sometimes the hermit crab is a little scary.

Of course heart maps can be used with students in all grade levels. Older students can draw their maps freehand instead of using a template. They also tend to use words in addition to pictures. (See Figure 3.2.)

Another way to help students explore topics for writing is to let them create a neighborhood map. We encourage students to sketch with pencils first and label important places such as a library, a corner deli, a church, or a park. Older students can do cutaways to continue to label the insides of some of the places—including their own home. *Blizzard* by John Rocco is a great mentor text with a map showing a young

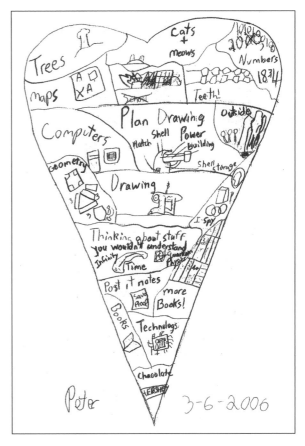

boy's journey from his home through his neighborhood on his way to get groceries during a snowstorm. Included in the map are captions that mark the things he stops to do along the way. Each one could be a small writing moment or be part of a longer narrative. As students revisit their neighborhood maps, they can add captions or speech bubbles. (See the Your Turn lesson at the end of this chapter.) Another possibility is to allow your students time to imagine their neighborhood maps in different seasons or times of the year, during activities, events, holiday gatherings, and celebrations. Even the landscape of the community changes throughout the year. Returning to neighborhood maps, heart maps, or territories honors those students who are more comfortable with sketching or drawing than writing. It allows them to revise by adding details and ideas to their drawings. For reluctant writers, you can make the connection between revision in drawing and revision in writing. This will help those writers become more confident and develop a deeper understanding of the writing process. (See Figures 3.3 and 3.4.)

Figure 3.3
Figure 3.4
Third-grade maps.

The conversations surrounding the heart maps, neighborhood maps, territory lists, and triangles are as important as these organizers themselves. You can move among the students, conducting roving conferences, or hold guided conversations in front of the whole class. In this way, you are helping your young writers discover the stories they want to tell as well as the reasons for telling them—topic and point.

The Point Versus the Topic

As literature is introduced throughout the day, consider taking a few moments to pause and guide students in thinking not just about the topic but also about the point that is being made. What is the author's purpose for writing this piece? What thoughts or images did he or she think should linger on the reader's mind long after the book was finished? Arthur Howard's *When I Was Five* tells the story of a young boy, Jeremy, who is looking back on the things he enjoyed as a five-year-old. Although he has many different favorite things now that he is six, Mark remains his best friend. With simple language and colorful illustrations, Howard helps young readers discover the point of his writing—that although many things in life change, there is comfort in knowing that some things remain the same. The last line crystallizes the point: "Some things never change."

Sometimes the point can be found in the title, as in *Chameleons Are Cool* by Martin Jenkins, *Bear and Squirrel Are Friends* by Deb Pilutti, *Red Is Best* by Kathy Stinson, or *I Wanna New Room* by Karen Kaufman Orloff. Many students are familiar with the Elephant and Piggy books such as *Waiting Is Not Easy!* and the Pigeon books such as *Don't Let the Pigeon Drive the Bus!* by Mo Willems. The books in these series are all great examples of making a point. Helping students discover the point of an author's work means young writers will begin to understand the importance of making a point in their own writing and the many ways in which it can be expressed.

Closely connected to point is the idea of point of view. Books such as *The True Story of the Three Little Pigs!* by Jon Scieszka, *Hey, Little Ant* by Phillip and Hannah Hoose, and *Voices in the Park* by Anthony Browne help students understand that a story can be told from many sides. In *Spoon* by Amy Krouse Rosenthal, the main character (Spoon) laments over how life is better for his friends Fork, Knife, and Chopsticks. About halfway through the book, the reader is introduced to a different perspective: Fork, Knife, and Chopsticks think it is Spoon who has the better life. Krouse Rosenthal does the same thing in *Exclamation Mark*. In this story, the exclamation mark feels he doesn't fit in with all the periods (even though a period is a part of him). In the end, the question mark helps him discover how great it is to be an exclamation mark.

[handwritten marginal note: POV]

Some books such as *Sierra* and *Heartland* (both by Diane Siebert), *My Light* by Molly Bang, and *Atlantic* by G. Brian Karas are written from the point of view of an inanimate object, bringing a certain intrigue to the reading of the text. Portalupi and Fletcher (2001) call this technique "writing through a mask."

[handwritten marginal note: Point of view from Objects]

Even our youngest writers can understand this technique. In one kindergarten classroom, the teacher, Shelly Keller, shared *Atlantic* with her students. Since they were writing nonfiction books on the topic of their choice, she suggested they try to write in the voice of the animal or object. Grace wrote in the voice of snow. (See Figures 3.5a–3.5e.)

Figures 3.5a Grace's story, "Snow"

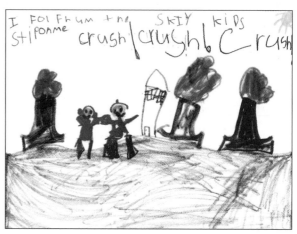

Figure 3.5b I fall from the sky. Kids step on me. Crunch! Crunch! Crunch!

Figure 3.5c I get made out of a storm. Snow is beautiful!

Figure 3.5d I was born in the cold.

Figure 3.5e I am as cold as ice. When I fall, you are as cold as ice!

At the end of Chapter 6, you will find a Your Turn lesson designed to help students understand how to write in the persona of another.

Using Classroom Conversations to Discover the Inside Story

We should never underestimate the power of talk in the writing workshop to help young writers discover their inside story. Throughout the book, you will notice that we often refer to teachers conducting guided conversations in front of the whole group or asking their students to "turn and talk" with a partner. Discussion partners especially play an important role in the writing workshop. Partnering gives all students a chance to be heard and encourages 100 percent participation. In addition, when students share ideas, they learn to appreciate the rich diversity of thinking in the writing community. Students monitor their own thinking to make sure they are on the right track and often find new ideas—unexpected treasures—triggered by their partners' ideas and questions.

In *Stella Tells Her Story*, a book useful to both students and teachers, author Janiel Wagstaff takes us into a second-grade classroom to watch the writing process unfold through the eyes of Stella, the main character. Talk and partner sharing play a prominent role in helping all the students get started on their narratives. As Wagstaff explains in the end pages, "She [Stella] was influenced by an idea she heard another student sharing, which often happens when teachers allow children time to scaffold their writing through talking" (31).

This process of oral rehearsal provides each writer with an authentic audience—giving them a purpose for their writing and increasing engagement through the immediacy of feedback. It's that extra charge that gets writers going and helps sustain them through the first draft. It's not possible for us as teachers to listen to every child's idea before he or she starts writing. When too many children are sharing individually in whole group, attention wanders and ideas are lost. Sharing orally in partners gets our students writing more quickly. This process—talking before writing—creates opportunities to ask questions, share mentor texts, exchange ideas, and form partnerships.

Sometimes writers get stuck and need a little help from their peers. In *Bear Has a Story to Tell* by Philip C. Stead, Bear has waited all winter to tell his story. In the spring, he is reunited with his friends, but finds he has forgotten the story. With some suggestions from Duck, Mole, Mouse, and Frog, the story unfolds. This idea of rich collaboration is important for another reason. When students get together to talk about their stories and share their thinking as writers, they get to know the other students in their classrooms as writers, too. Later, when peer conferences are introduced into writing workshop, students readily recognize the power of collaboration with their writing community, not just the person who is sitting next to them or their best friend.

Another must-have book for your collection is *Ralph Tells a Story* by Abby Hanlon. In this narrative, Ralph's frustration with writing and finding a story to tell turns to joy when he realizes, through an oral rehearsal share, that he does have a story, even though it is a small one (about an inchworm). The excitement of his writing community is shared with us through speech bubbles, and they ask questions to help Ralph tell more. Don't miss the end pages in this book—empty writing pages in the beginning and titles of books Ralph wrote in the end.

To discover the inside story, writers must begin by finding those treasures locked away in their hearts and minds that might make good topics for writing. Big ideas, or territories, need to be reduced to very specific topics. Authors must be able to wrap their arms around their topics and hold on tight. They must be able to discover what it is they really want to say about the topics—the stories that only they know and can tell. With this in mind, they write with clarity and purpose. Their points are not mysteries to the reader. Mentor texts can serve as wonderful models to young writers as they begin to understand how to sharpen their focus and make their points.

Think About It—Talk About It—Write About It

- How will you help students narrow a writing topic to a sharp focus? What ideas from this chapter would work for your students? What other ideas do you have for helping students find a focus?
- What mentor texts do you/will you use to help students understand what it means to have a point to their writing regardless of genre?
- How do you foster collaborative conversations in your classroom?
- What are your writing territories? Make a list in your writer's notebook. What are the writing territories of your students? Why is it important to know both?

Your Turn Lesson 1

Using an Inverted Triangle to Find a Specific Writing Topic

Hook: Read *When I Was Five* by Arthur Howard, *I'm in Charge of Celebrations* by Byrd Baylor, or any other personal narratives that invite students to think about territories for writing such as weather/storms, relatives, friends, or school.

Purpose: *When you are trying to find a topic to write about, sometimes it is easier to start with a big idea and work to make it smaller and smaller until suddenly, there it is—the "inside story," the one only you know and can write. It's like starting with a slab of marble or block of wood and chipping away until your sculpture is revealed to your audience. Today, writers, I'm going to show you how to start with a writing territory and find your specific topic by using an inverted triangle.*

Brainstorm: Think about the big ideas—your writing territories—and the seeds of ideas you might be able to use to grow stories, poems, letters, and essays around a specific topic. Revisit your list of territories and add new ideas you might have after hearing *One Lucky Girl*. (Students typically add weather or storms.)

Model: An inverted triangle is a useful graphic organizer to help you refocus your camera lens from wide angle and zoom in on a specific subject. After reading Lyon's story, here is a possible example:

Follow with a few more examples. From *Night at the Fair* by Donald Crews, here is another model:

Shared/Guided Writing: Students try out the inverted triangle to take a territory and find a specific writing topic. Students share one of their efforts that led them to a suitable topic. Make sure that the students have not stopped at the "general" topic but have moved to a specific statement to flesh out the "inside" story about their writing topic. The statement can help the writer focus on both topic and point (the point is why the author wrote the piece or what is most important or memorable about this topic). Ask students to talk about their point if they end up with only a topic statement. Here, you may have to model on chart paper or on the board with two or more examples from your territories list.

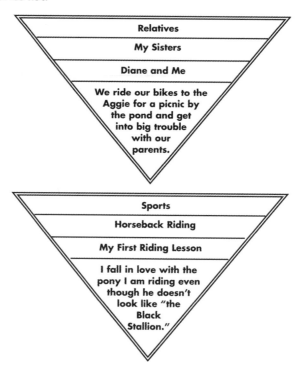

Continue to practice on the laminated chart paper each day where one student places his or her information in the spaces of the inverted triangle. Each student writes with a transparency pen that can be washed away the next day. The chart should be placed in a writing center or on a bulletin board where it is accessible to all students.

Independent Writing: Students can continue to use inverted triangles to narrow a territory to a specific topic across different modes. When they have found an appropriate topic, from one of their inverted triangles, invite students to create a first draft, notebook entry, or prewriting experience for the specific topic they wish to develop during workshop time.

Reflection: After completing a notebook entry or first draft for a poem, a letter, a narrative, or an essay, allow time for students to "turn and talk" about the use of the inverted triangle to find a specific writing topic or about how the laminated chart paper containing new examples each day helped them find new topics or create specific topics for writing.

How did the use of the inverted triangle help you narrow your topic?

How could the use of an inverted triangle help you when you get "lost" (you have wandered off topic and are unsure of where your writing is headed) in the middle of writing a piece?

Did you discover a new writing idea from the use of this strategy?

Your Turn Lesson 2

Creating a Heart Map

Hook: Return to any personal narrative read-alouds you have used in the classroom, and talk about where the author might have gotten the idea for the story. Encourage your writers to think in terms of "big ideas"—family, school, and so on. *When I Was Little: A Four-Year-Old's Memoir of Her Youth* by Jamie Lee Curtis works well to help primary students understand writing territories. Students can easily identify many writing territories for the child in the book, such as people she knows, family, things she likes to do, and school. Options: *Goin' Someplace Special* by Patricia McKissack, *In My Momma's Kitchen* by Jerdine Nolen, and *Song and Dance Man* by Karen Ackerman.

Purpose: *Sometimes it's hard to think about something to write about. This happens to all writers. It's important to remember that writing comes from your mind and your heart. Today I will show you how to make a heart map. A heart map is a way to remember what is in your mind and your heart so that you'll always have something to write about.*

Brainstorm: Think aloud about the big ideas that are in your mind and your heart that might give you lots of stories to write about—family, school, a hobby, and so on. Quickly relate some stories within those categories. It is important to demonstrate that these are big ideas, not small moments of time that capture a single event. Ask the students to share some of the things they might put on their heart maps. These ideas can be listed on the board or simply shared orally.

Model: Share your own heart map. You can either have this created ahead of time or quickly sketch it in front of the students. At this point, the heart map does not have to be completely filled in. Choose a section and relate a small story that comes from it. Write a short entry on the board or overhead.

Shared/Guided Writing: Invite one or two students to the front of the room to share their ideas in a guided conversation. If they start to relate single-event stories—for example, if they say something like, "One day my brother and my dad and I caught ten fish"—ask them if they have any other stories about their brother or dad. Lead them to the understanding that the place they might put on their heart map for these stories would be a place for family. Questions such as the following can help guide their thinking:

> *Who are the special people in your life?*
> *Do you have any pets?*
> *Are there any places where you go that hold special memories for you?*
> *When you are at home, where do you spend most of your time?*
> *What are the things that you like to do?*

Again, ask students to quietly think about some of the things they might include on their heart maps, and then ask them to turn and share with a partner. Encourage students to ask questions as you did in the guided conversation to help their partner formulate ideas.

Independent Writing: Allow time for students to create their own heart maps. We have found that with young writers it is easier to provide a heart template, but students can certainly draw the heart outline on their own. When the heart maps are completed, ask students to think of a small story from one of the areas on their heart map, turn to a partner and share, and then write a short entry in their journals or notebooks.

Reflection: After students share their entries with partners or in small groups, ask them to think about how the heart map they created can help them think of things to write about. Questions such as the following can help guide their thinking:

How can a heart map help you find a writing topic?

What will you write about next?

What are some stories you have about _____? (Choose a section from the map.)

Did listening to others share their heart maps give you ideas for yours?

Note: For very young children, the above lesson can be split and taught over two days. On the first day, just have the students create the heart map. On the second day, demonstrate how to choose a story from a section on the map and write it.

Your Turn Lesson 3

Creating a Hand Map

In *Writing as a Road to Self-Discovery*, Barry Lane describes the use of a hand map as a prewriting technique to help writers bring memories to a conscious level. We have adapted this technique for use with students.

Hook: Find a favorite personal narrative that has a deep emotional effect on your target grade level. The first chapter of *Charlotte's Web* by E. B. White works well for intermediate grade levels (three to six). Students can easily name Fern's emotions and/or character traits that are revealed through her dialogue and actions. Options: *Crab Moon* by Ruth Horowitz; *Shortcut* by Donald Crews; *Fireflies!* by Julie Brinckloe; and "Mrs. Buell" in *Hey World, Here I Am!* by Jean Little.

Purpose: *Do you remember when we read* Fireflies!*? What was the character feeling at the beginning of the story? How did he feel when he realized the fireflies would die if he didn't release them? What was he feeling at the end of the story? [List the emotions on the board as the students name them.] Can you see how much of this story depends on the emotions of the main character and how they change during the telling of it? When we are trying to write about specific topics, sometimes it is easier to find an important topic—something you really want to write about—if you start with an emotion or one of your character traits. Today I am going to model how to use a hand map to find a specific topic.*

Brainstorm: In whole group, students make a list of emotions after they have had a chance to "turn and talk" with a partner. This list can become part of a writing binder or a writer's notebook entry. At some point, create a list of character traits. A hand map can use emotions or character traits or a combination of both. It is probably easiest to start with the emotions.

Model: Share your own hand map with your students. (See the model for the hand map in Figure 3.6 that Lynne shares with her students.) Start with basic emotions such as anger, fear, sadness, happiness, and excitement. Place one on each finger after tracing your hand on the board or on chart paper with fingers spread wide apart. From each finger, extend lines to connect to examples of times you felt that way. Try to think of one example for each emotion, but tell students that they can concentrate on one at a time or move around. Hand maps are writers' tools like thesauruses and dictionaries and should be returned to often to add ideas or to use an idea to explore a writing topic. Finally, choose an example from your hand map and write it in your writer's notebook.

This notebook entry came from Lynne's hand map where the emotion "happiness" led her to think about Saturday breakfasts. Each entry in her notebook is always dated and has a title to help her know what it is about.

No more than one entry is written on each page. This format saves time when a writer is searching through his or her notebooks to find common threads or entries about certain topics.

> *September 24, 2005*
>
> *<u>Special Saturday Breakfasts</u>*
>
> *I loved Saturdays because Mom made special breakfasts. My favorite was when she made perfect pancakes—round, golden brown, light, fluffy, and filled with fresh blueberries. I loved to watch the pat of butter slip-slide its way down the stack onto my plate. I drizzled maple syrup on the top and added more as I ate. Yummy! My sisters, mom, and dad always shared this breakfast together. Maybe that's why the food tasted so good!*

Shared/Guided Writing: For this particular lesson, students create a "whole group" hand map, choosing from the list of emotions and/or character traits and volunteering ideas that are stated as complete thoughts. It is important to insist that students work in phrases or complete sentences when they create their own hand maps.

Examples:

scared—We drove home from the shore late one night during a bad storm.
happy—My parents finally let me get a puppy!
nervous—first time I played a solo in a school concert

While students are creating the group hand map, they should have their own hand maps in front of them. If they hear a good example for an emotion that applies to them, they can add it to their map. Continue to have students work on hand maps and share in small groups while you circulate around the room to observe, ask questions, and offer suggestions.

Independent Writing: Have students pick one description (example) from their hand map and write a short entry about it in their writer's notebook or begin to draft. They can return to their hand map to choose a different example if the first one does not work. Teachers should work on their own hand maps for the next several sessions, modeling that they are not finished in one sitting and that the maps should be reviewed and added to throughout the year. Students can create more than one hand map, especially to try out different emotions and character traits.

Reflection: Students examine their writer's notebook entries, work-in-progress folders, and portfolio pieces to find examples that started with seeds of ideas from their hand map(s).

How effective is your hand map as a tool for finding a specific writing topic?

What kinds of writing seem to spring from your hand maps?

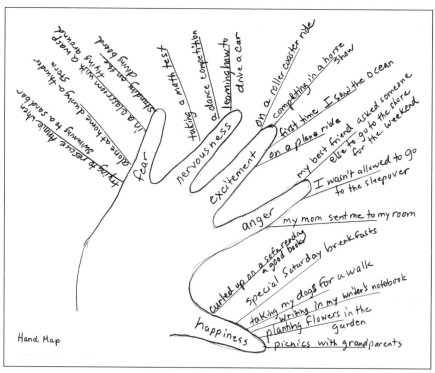

Figure 3.6 Lynne's model of a hand map.

Creating a Neighborhood Map

Hook: Return to *Blizzard* by John Rocco to share the map of the boy's journey to the store. Share the author's note that reveals that this story is based on an actual experience that happened when he was ten. Encourage students to think about what such a walk would look like in their neighborhood (it doesn't have to be a winter walk). Ask them to compare and contrast their neighborhood with his. Options: *Nana in the City* by Lauren Castillo, *All the Places to Love* by Patricia MacLachlan, and *Last Stop on Market Street* by Matt de la Peña.

Purpose: *Sometimes writing begins with drawing. Today I will show you one way to find ideas for writing by creating and labeling a neighborhood map.*

Brainstorm: Students can turn and talk with a partner about the places they visit in their neighborhood. List ideas on an anchor chart as children share (swim club, supermarket, nail salon, church, school, police station, doctor's office). If students are having difficulty with this task, ask them to turn and talk about their school, their home, a mall, or a playground/park.

Model: Share your neighborhood map. You can either have this created or partially created ahead of time or quickly sketch it in front of the students. Talk about some of the places and add labels, captions, and/or speech bubbles. The captions and speech bubbles could capture conversations, emotions,

Figure 3.7
Lynne's neighborhood map.

thoughtshots (the thoughts of the character), descriptions of objects or people, and events that occurred at that place. Choose one place that serves as a springboard for a story and begin to write.

> *I spent most Tuesdays and Thursdays attending Hebrew school at the Jewish Community Center across from my elementary school. Usually, my father appeared to pick me up during the winter months when it grew dark early. Usually . . .*
> *This December evening I stood and waited for a small eternity. I trotted to Thouron Avenue, then back again to the side entrance to the community center. I grew cold and frightened as I realized Dad was not coming. Finally, I took off down Gilbert Street, shivering at strange shadows and the sounds of barking dogs. Without stopping to look, I sprinted across Durham Street, up the steps, and onto the stoop of my house. When Mom opened the door, I rushed into her arms, sniffling and sobbing. I could hardly speak, but I was safe. I was home.*

Shared/Guided Writing: Display a map of the school and ask students to help you label it (if it's not already labeled) and begin to talk about possibilities for a story. What happened in the cafeteria this week? What was going on during gym class? What happened on the playground? After jotting down a few ideas from the students, have them help you decide on one to write about.

Independent Writing: Ask students to create their own maps of their neighborhood (or house, mall, and so on). Encourage them to add labels and captions. Ask them to choose one place on their map that has a story to tell. Give them time to turn and talk with one or several partners. Encourage partners to ask questions to clarify and extend thinking. Give students time to write their story.

Reflection: Students can turn and talk in whole or small group about how their maps helped them find and tell a story. The following questions can guide their thinking:

> *What helped you find your story—the sketches, the captions, the speech bubbles, or a combination of some or all of them?*
>
> *How did the partner sharing of the map help you choose your story?*
>
> *Will your map offer other opportunities to write? Will you return to your map in the future?*

Note: This lesson can be taught over two days. Maps can be created on the first day. Begin the next day with the partner sharing of the maps before students begin to write.

Your Turn Lesson 5　Finding the Point of Your Story

Many books are written about the same topic or theme but make a different point. By demonstrating this to students, they understand that the point is what they are really writing about—the inside story.

Hook:　Return to four or five mentor texts around a theme or topic that have been used as read-alouds. Make sure they all make a different point. Share them quickly as picture walks, helping students recall what each story was about. Here is an example of a text set built around friendship.

> *Virgil and Owen* by Paulette Bogan
> *Across the Alley* by Richard Michelson
> *Super Jumbo* by Fred Koehler
> *The Recess Queen* by Alexis O'Neill
> *Peach and Blue* by Sarah S. Kilborne

Ask the students what all of the books have in common. In this case, they are all about friendship.

Purpose:　*Writers, today we are going to think about big ideas we call themes or topics to help us write the inside story—what you know and can bring to a text, what you care about and want to zoom in on. Even though these books are all about friendship, they all tell a different story and have a different message or point.*

Brainstorm:　Divide your class into small groups and give them a text set around a particular topic or theme. Ask each group to explore the books and come up with a common theme or topic. If you need help with titles, ask your librarian for help. Some common topics might be dogs, holidays, family, houses, or pets. You could also include themes such as love, cooperation, self-discovery, loss, or courage. Students can record their ideas on an anchor chart. After the groups are finished, review the chart and ask them to think about additional topics or themes that could be added (such as change, machines, occupations, and celebrations).

Model:　With the set of friendship books, determine the message or point for each one and create a web or anchor chart to record them. Here are some examples:

> *Virgil and Owen*—Friends should be shared.
> *Super Jumbo*—A day is always better when shared with a friend.
> *Across the Alley*—Friends can teach each other something new.
> *The Recess Queen*—You never know where or when you are going to find a new friend.
> *Peach and Blue*—Friends can help each other appreciate different things.

Continue to add to the chart or web with your own personal experiences (finding a new friend, dealing with the loss of a friend, staying in touch with a faraway friend). Choose one of the points or messages and orally create a story or the skeleton of a story. For example, *My story is going to be about two girls who do everything together but one can't ride a bike because she is scared she will fall. Her friend takes her to a grassy backyard and encourages her to try. She teaches her to keep her balance by looking straight ahead. Soon her friend is riding, and now they can ride their bikes together.*

Shared/Guided: Ask groups to return to their text set and consider what point or message is in each story. They can draw a web or chart the ideas and continue to add to them based on their own experiences. Share in whole group. The charts can be posted. Ask students to suggest one topic and pick a point that the whole class could write or orally plan a story around.

For younger students, take one text set and chart it together in whole group. Then choose one point and develop the story.

Independent Writing: Ask students to begin an entry based on one of the suggested topics or themes with a specific point.

Reflection: *How did you choose your topic or theme?*

What did you include in your story to help you get your point across to your reader?

What kind of graphic organizer could you use in the future when you are deciding what your inside story is?

Why is the point important to a story?

Chapter 4

When Writers Use a Magnifying Lens

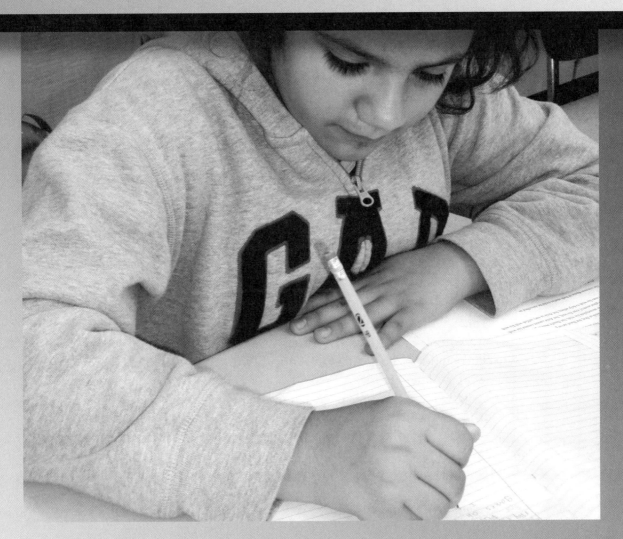

When we write, our entire lives are like a stretch of mountains and we can choose where to dwell.

—Barry Lane, *After THE END*

In *Nature Spy*, authors Shelley Rotner and Ken Kreisler help us understand that when we look closely at things in nature, we notice many more interesting details, such as patterns in leaves, a turtle's shell, or the center of a sunflower. It's like putting something under a magnifying lens: we focus in on something small to make it big and bring out all the details. It's the same thing when we write. We need to help our students bring their writing in closer so that we can see all the fine details that make it big. To do this, students need to be the first reader of their work and develop their writer's ear. Reading out loud as well as silently is almost a must and applies to writers of all ages. It's the way writers start to internalize the music of their words. In *Close Writing: Developing Purposeful Writers in Grades 2–6*, Paula Bourque explains, "First, students must develop a habit of regularly reading their writing. . . . Changing behavior takes a conscious effort, and we cannot change what we are not aware of" (33).

Slowing Down Time in Writing

What we should point out to children is the need to develop their ideas first—the content—by writing about small moments of time. Schuster (2003) tells us always to put content first and second when we respond to student writing. After all, content is the most important writing characteristic. When high-quality ideas are developed, readers can visualize, make connections, use their senses, and dream the possibilities. To "take a reader's breath away," we must first start with specificity. We must encourage young writers to uncover the real story they want to tell as they write and stop telling us what we already know or can easily find out about. They must put their writing under a magnifying lens and look for those small moments that can be enlarged to take their readers there, wherever that might be.

Young writers struggle to create a movie in their readers' minds whether they are writing in the narrative, persuasive, or informational modes. They often hurry through the text they are creating for their readers, and it looks like good writing—after all, isn't it two or three or even four pages long? But when we read it, we are disappointed. Often it reads like an agenda or a time schedule, moving from event to event in a blurring whir that leaves us scratching our heads and wondering what the piece is really about. As readers, we can't make any connections or form any pictures. The writing is a list (sometimes a very long list, but a list nevertheless). Does the following piece of writing sound familiar?

> I went to the aquarium with my class. I was really happy we were going on a field trip because I am going to be a scientist one day and study ocean animals.
>
> We saw lots of fish. I saw a hammerhead shark. Then I saw beluga whales. Next we went to see tropical fish. They were neat and all different colors and sizes. We were hungry so we had lunch. I had a peanut butter sandwich and an apple. My mom didn't pack anything to drink so I had to

use the water fountain. Then I had to use the bathroom because I drank so much water. We saw some seals. Then we saw some manta rays. They were cool. Then Tommy and Jimmy started fighting. My teacher said it was time to go back to the bus. We bought some souvenirs. I bought a candy bar because I was still hungry.

The bus trip was long. We sang songs. Tommy fell asleep. My teacher looked sleepy, but she stayed awake because she has to. I needed to use the bathroom as soon as we got back. It was almost time to go home, so my teacher read us a book about whales and then the bell rang and school was over. It was a pretty good day.

—third grader (November)

We need to find mentor texts that we can use to show students how an author slows down a moment in time to look at an important event, examine a feeling, or reveal a character. We need to slow our writers down. If you look back at this young writer's piece, can you find a place where he could linger and put a small moment under a magnifying lens? Perhaps it is where he chooses to talk about tropical fish. He says manta rays are cool. Maybe this spot is ideal. Elementary school children write just like they do everything else—quickly. They live in a fast world, packed with schedules, video games with action figures, outdoor sports. They need to learn to slow their writing down at a special place. An author does this by taking a "small moment" (Calkins 2003) and putting it under a magnifying lens to enlarge it, just the way scientists use microscopes and magnifying lenses to look at something very small and make it much bigger so they can observe all the details.

The details are essential to good writing. Specificity is what makes it interesting for the writer to write, and it's also what moves the reader (Fletcher 1993). Slow scenes usually include longer passages built with such things as dialogue, sensory details, anecdotes, and other strategies from an author's craft. Sometimes authors add the thoughts of a character. Barry Lane (2016) calls this strategy a thoughtshot. We find the places in the text that help slow down a moment in time and point them out as examples of powerful sentences, giving a piece both clarity and depth. In *Mice and Beans* by Pam Muñoz Ryan, Rosa María remembers that she has forgotten to fill the piñata. However, when the children break the piñata and the candy spills, we hear her thoughts: "'How could that be?' Rosa María puzzled. 'I must have filled it without even realizing!'"

In *Tiger of the Snows*, Robert Burleigh uses italics to set off the thoughts of the main character, Tenzing Norgay. Tenzing's monologue with the mountain shows his thinking as he becomes the young man who eventually realizes his dream of climbing Mount Everest.

Mountain,
Mountain
I cast my small shadow against your eternal skyscape.

Sometimes authors don't use the exact words of the character's thinking but just tell us what they thought, as Bottner and Kruglik do in *Wallace's Lists*: "Wallace awoke to the sound of rain plinking on his window. He thought that on such a dreary day he might like to share some nice onion soup with Albert."

Dipping into Dialogue

The use of dialogue is an essential element of story. Sometimes authors present the characters' talk in speech bubbles or italics. Other times authors rely on standard conventions using quotation marks, commas, and appropriate indenting.

Authors use dialogue to open up a scene, adding interest and details. We often learn more about the characters from what they say, how they say it, or what others say about them. In *Sugarbush Spring*, Marsha Wilson Chall intersperses description with dialogue as the little girl waits for the sap to turn into syrup. We can feel her anticipation and excitement in her words:

> Already the sugarhouse smells like pancakes. "Is it syrup yet?" I ask Jim. "Too soon," he says, and taps the thermometer. "Should be two hundred nineteen degrees. Seven degrees to go." I keep my eye on that thermometer: two hundred fifteen . . . two hundred sixteen . . . The bubbles creep higher, swelling to the top of the pan. "There she blows!" I yell.

As the main character in Sharon Dennis Wyeth's *Something Beautiful* roams the neighborhood in search of *her* something beautiful, she enters into many conversations with those she meets about *their* something beautiful.

How much more interesting it is to the reader to hear the words and conversations of the characters! In Mo Willems's pigeon books, dialogue is the story told through a series of speech bubbles. Willems uses a conversational tone—words such as *C'mon* and *Y'know*, fragments, and variation in print— to make the dialogue sound real. Some authors use dialogue as a thread to pull the reader through the story. For example, in *Butterfly Tree* by Sandra Markle, the dialogue between mother and daughter is written in italics. The dialogue is used to pique curiosity and sustain interest. This strategy keeps the reader waiting and allows the author to make sure he or she is not giving away too much too soon. Markle also uses dialogue in this book to create a satisfying ending:

> I'll always remember seeing the monarchs too, I say, and that we saw them together.

In *Happy Like Soccer*, Maribeth Boelts advances her story through splashes of dialogue between the main character, Sierra, and her auntie or between Sierra and her coach. This dialogue helps bring the characters to life.

Sometimes dialogue is strategically placed in the most important part of the story. In *Shortcut* by Donald Crews, dialogue creates drama focusing on the most important event in the story: the unexpected freight train. In *Nana in the City*, Lauren Castillo creates dialogue for a late-night scene between the grandson and his nana. The boy reveals to his grandmother, for the first time, his fear of the city. The dialogue also reveals how Nana solves the problem. She has stayed up all night knitting a red cape.

"For you to wear on our walk today," she said.

Dialogue brings the story full circle when the grandson wraps his cape around Nana:

"This will keep you brave," I tell her.

In that one moment and with that one line of dialogue, the reader understands how the boy has solved his problem, too. He no longer has to worry about his nana living in the city. The cape will keep her safe.

Sometimes authors use dialogue as a way to offer an explanation or add information. In *Toad Weather* by Sandra Markle, Mama helps the reader and her daughter, Ally, learn more about nature through dialogue.

"Rainy days are perfect for earthworms," Mama says. "Their skin has to stay wet for them to live."

"Over a few weeks each spring," Mama says, "when it's perfect toad weather—like tonight—they head to water to mate and lay their eggs."

In both *Over and Under the Snow* and *Up in the Garden and Down in the Dirt*, Kate Messner uses this same technique: dialogue to offer an explanation. However, in *Up in the Garden and Down in the Dirt*, dialogue is also used to give a direction and express emotion.

Types or sentences

"Give them a drink," Nana says. *(direction)*

"Rain shower!" Nana turns the hose on me! "Eeeee!" *(expressing delight)*

When discussing the effective use of dialogue with students, however, it is important to help them realize the reasons authors use it, and that even though a conversation can serve to add interest and details, too much dialogue may make the piece tedious or difficult to understand. Dialogue should be sprinkled in the same way we season our food with salt. We don't open the top of the shaker and pour it on. Rather, we sprinkle just enough to bring out the flavor without masking the taste. (See the Your Turn lesson at the end of this chapter.)

Descriptions: Digging Deeper

Readers are a lot like scientists. They like to "study" the events, feelings, and actions of characters, lingering a little longer to make connections and visualize in their minds. That's what good readers do. They can't do it without the help of the author. Fletcher (1993) tells us that Donald Murray calls readers "bottom feeders" who like to gobble up all the details like scavengers on the oceans' floors. We need to provide them with descriptions of our setting, characters, and even important objects by both telling and showing them.

Setting is an important element of story. However, our young writers often fail to do more than sum up the setting in one word. Robert Burleigh describes the dramatic landscape of the moon in *One Giant Leap* with color, strong verbs and adjectives, and a unique simile:

> The moon!
> It is gray, it is brown, it is blue-edged.
> Its billion-year-old landscape is cracked and scarred,
> Its surface gouged and cratered and pitted with tiny holes,
> Like a battlefield from some ancient war.

Burleigh could have stopped after the first line, but then his readers would not be able to see the moon from the perspective of the astronauts. In *Miss Moore Thought Otherwise: How Anne Carroll Created Libraries for Children*, Jan Pinborough describes the new Children's Room in the New York Public Library: "Hundreds of new children's books in many languages waited within reach. And beneath every window, a cozy window seat waited for children to curl up in it."

Characters, another important element of story, can be brought to life through physical descriptions—like looking at a photograph. Judy Schachner opens *The Grannyman* with a description of her main character—the old cat:

> Simon was a very old cat.
>
> With the exception of his nose, most of his parts had stopped working long ago. He was blind and deaf, and his bones creaked as he climbed up and down the stairs.

In *A Book for Black-Eyed Susan* by Judy Young, Cora's baby sister is described like this: "As Cora softly stroked the tassel of yellow hair on her sister's head, the baby opened her eyes. They were pitch-black." In this same book, Judy Young helps us learn how we can offer a description of character through emotion. After Cora's mother dies, we understand the extent of Pa's grief through the author's words:

> Pa sat leaning against the wagon wheel, his head in his hands.
> Something was wrong . . .

When Pa lifted his head, the lantern light fell across his face. Tears rolled down his cheeks. All he could do was shake his head and pull Cora tight to his chest.

In *The Tree in the Courtyard: Looking Through Anne Frank's Window*, Jeff Gottesfeld reveals something about Anne Frank by describing something she loved to do. "When they visited the factory, she would play by the canal or write by the kitchen window. She wrote for hours. Even when her father called her, she wrote." Authors can use descriptions of a sport, free time, or a hobby as a way of providing insight into a character's personality—what he or she values.

The story in Kevin Henkes's *Lilly's Purple Plastic Purse* revolves around Lilly's obsession with the things (particularly the purse) she bought on a shopping trip with her grammy. Students can visualize the purse and its contents by the descriptions Henkes provides:

> She had a brand new purple plastic purse that played a jaunty tune when it was opened . . . And the purse played such nice music, not to mention how excellent it was for storing school supplies.

Robert Burleigh also builds content around an object—the spacecraft that landed on the moon—in his book *One Giant Leap*:

> The Eagle is like a gold-speckled bug falling out of the sky—
> Its odd-shaped body plastered with many boxes,
> Its outer walls thinner than human skin.
> The spacecraft's spindly legs poke out as it rides on its back.

One technique Burleigh uses here to make the description clear to the reader is to take the unknown (the *Eagle*) and compare it to the known (a bug, human skin).

Patricia and Emily MacLachlan describe the work of the still-life painter in *Painting the Wind* with a list: "She painted until dawn—the peppermint plant in the window, the glass bowl of tulips, their green stems crisscrossing in water." Writers often describe specific time periods as Jan Pinborough does in *Miss Moore Thought Otherwise: How Anne Carroll Moore Created Libraries for Children*:

> In the 1870s many people thought a girl should stay inside and do quiet things such as sewing and embroidery.
> But Annie thought otherwise. She preferred taking wild toboggan rides from the cemetery all the way down past Main Street, or bouncing along in Father's buggy to the sound of Pocahontas's clip-clopping hooves.

It is important to give students opportunities to practice writing rich descriptions of people, places, animals, and objects. After all, description is found in every type of writing.

[handwritten margin note: Description with list of examples]

Appealing to the Senses

Description also helps students understand how to be more specific since they are writing about just one thing. But they don't have to stop with simply describing what they see. Writers use all the senses to give us a concrete, physical experience. The act of reading and comprehending what we read is fairly abstract. If we want our readers to remember what they've read, to linger over passages where they can close their eyes and imagine what it would be like, how they would feel, what they would do, what they *will* do, then we must provide them with details to give them this concrete experience to balance with the abstract act of thinking about and comprehending text. In Chapter 2, we discuss the use of strong sensory images to help writers unearth memories for writing topics. Appealing to the senses is also a powerful way to add details to writing, bringing the reader in closer. In *Up North at the Cabin*, Marsha Wilson Chall uses specific sensory details to help anchor images in our minds, where they linger long after we have closed the book. Maybe she closed her eyes and imagined the scene through her senses:

> Grandma serves up my sunnies with fried potatoes and corn-on-the-cob.
> We eat at a long table on the screen porch, sitting next to one another
> on the same side so we can all watch the loons dance down the sun.

Can't you just taste the delicious meal and imagine the butter from the corn on the cob dripping down your chin? Do you feel the hardness of the bench or the warmth of the sun on your face? Can you hear the soft flutter of the loons as you watch them lightly splash down on the lake as the sun slowly sinks from view?

Jane Yolen masterfully uses the senses to add details to her description of an outing of a father and child in *Owl Moon*. Through her words, we see the brightness of the moon reflected in the whiteness of the snow; we hear the song of the train whistle and the crunching of the snow; we feel the cold air and furry wetness of the child's scarf. These details bring us in closer and make us feel as if we are there.

In *Twilight Comes Twice*, Ralph Fletcher helps us experience the dawn by appealing to our senses:

> Walking at dawn is a special kind of walk . . .
> The air is still moist from the cool of the night and your own skin feels
> all tingly clean . . .
> Outside the bakery the smell of doughnuts makes your stomach rumble
> and growl.

By lingering on these passages as we read these mentor texts aloud, we can begin to help our students understand the importance of using the senses to add details to their writing. A wonderful mentor text that we often use to introduce use of the senses to students is *Hello Ocean*. In this rhyming text, Pam Muñoz Ryan describes the ocean through each of the five senses. After students are familiar with the book, we might return to it to record the images on a visualization chart such as in the following:

step 1 from mentor Text

I see	amber seaweed
	speckled sand
	bubbly waves
	glistening tide pools
I hear	rushing water
	boats
	screak of gulls
I feel	a wet embrace
	tickling tide
	squishy, sandy, soggy ground
I smell	salty wind
	suntan lotion
	reeky fish
	musty shells
I taste	tears
	sandy grains

② step 2

The next step would be to brainstorm some familiar places common to all the students, such as the school cafeteria, the playground, or even the classroom, and fill in a visualization chart together. Sometimes we add an additional box for thoughts and emotions. This adds another layer to the details. The students can then use the chart to describe the place either orally or in a shared writing experience. Finally, the students can try it out on their own.

It is important to show students that authors use specific words to describe the things they experience through their senses. For example, Pam Muñoz Ryan talks about "speckled" sand and "musty" shells. It is also important to remember that some young writers need lots of modeling and chances to work together before they are ready to venture out on their own. Rose remembers working with a second grader who was very excited to try using a visualization chart to help him describe one of his favorite summer hangouts, the community swimming pool. Within minutes of getting started, Ryan raised his hand signaling that he was finished. "That was easy!" he said. "Listen: I see the water. I hear the water. I feel the water. I smell the water. I taste the water." With a little more encouragement, Rose helped Ryan add the specifics he needed to extend his thinking and help bring the swimming pool in close to his readers.

Using Anecdotes to Reveal Details

Another way to help students add details to their writing is through the use of anecdotes, or short accounts of an incident. Anecdotes can be used to reveal something about a character or an event, or simply to add interesting or entertaining information to a piece of writing. In *My Brother Martin: A Sister Remembers Growing Up with the Rev. Dr. Martin Luther King Jr.*, Christine King Farris uses anecdotes to help her readers envision what her brother Martin was like as a child. We read about how Martin, Christine, and their younger brother, Alfred, enjoyed playing pranks as children. In the afterword of the book, the author tells us that she wanted to share some true and funny stories about Martin's earlier life so that her readers could get to know him as a regular boy growing up. Through the use of anecdote, Farris adds the details that bring us closer to Martin Luther King Jr.

Mother to Tigers by George Ella Lyon tells the story of Helen Martini, the Bronx Zoo's first woman keeper, who initially raised baby tigers in her apartment. An anecdote about the tigers jumping into the tub reveals their mischievous side:

> Once, washing clothes in the bath, Helen heard Raniganj crying. His head was caught behind a pipe. While she ran to the rescue, Rajpur and Dacca discovered the tub. Crouch . . . leap . . . splash! Tigers love water.

In another anecdote from this book, Lyon reveals how determined Martini was to achieve her goal of starting a nursery at the zoo. These small stories add details that make the characters seem more real.

A true mentor text for anecdotes is *Talkin' About Bessie: The Story of Aviator Elizabeth Coleman* by Nikki Grimes. The fictionalized-but-based-on-fact story tells the life of Bessie Coleman through the memories of twenty mourners who have gathered after her death to honor her. They represent people from all aspects of her life, and their anecdotes about her reveal the true Bessie Coleman—her struggles and successes, her shortcomings and her strengths, her hopes and dreams. In the following example, we find Willie Coleman telling the mourners that Bessie was quite a storyteller:

> My sister-in-law shoulda been a writer since her was always tellin' tales. Enhancin' the truth was her specialty. Drummin' up publicity, she called it. Hear her tell it, she was bosom buddies with the Red Baron, had flown a German sea plane, and was near 'bout born with wings. Told the *New York Times* she went to France with the Red Cross during the war, and that she had one of them brigade officers teach her how to fly. Now, you tell me if that ain't stretching the truth!

In a fifth-grade class, the students were working on hero essays to write to an audience other than the classroom teacher. These essays were about people the students knew very well, and they were going to mail their essays to their intended audience when they were finished. Lynne talked with them about how anecdotes could add some interesting or humorous content to their writing while revealing character traits or quirks about their subjects. After sharing many examples from mentor texts, Lynne shared an anecdote about her grandfather:

> *When I was little, my grandfather taught me how to swim. I remember the time we were at Sailor's Lake. The water felt cold even though it was the middle of July. Grandpa put his strong arms under me and told me to paddle with my arms and kick with my legs.*
>
> *"Reach as far as you can, Lynnie," he told me. Grandpa showed me how he cupped his hands to pull through the water, keeping his fingers together. He practiced going under the water with me, too. We held hands and dunked our heads over and over again. One time, I took such a big gulp of air before going under that I made Grandpa laugh. Grandpa laughed so hard that he swallowed some of the lake water. He made me laugh, too. Suddenly, I wasn't afraid anymore! And before I knew it, I was swimming through the water on my own.*

She explained how adding this to her hero essay about her grandfather would demonstrate what a wonderful teacher he was and how he helped her work through her fears. She explained how powerful anecdotes are across the modes (narrative, persuasive, and informational). Later on in the year, Eleanor was writing a narrative about a bike-riding trip and included a humorous anecdote about her dad:

> When we arrived at the river, it was jam packed so we barely got a parking place. My daddy started to yell at a guy who opened his door and slammed it into our car. Mommy and I whimpered in the corner as Daddy and the guy had a shouting fight. Finally, Daddy won and when the guy left he gloated in triumph. "Did you see me? He was nothing compared to me!" And on and on about it. (You know how guys are . . . when they win something, they never stop talking about it!)

After students have the opportunity to try out a strategy such as using anecdotes to build content, they will try it out again when the strategy seems appropriate or necessary. It is important to revisit strategies and key Your Turn lessons so that students can embed the technique in their repertoire of writing strategies.

Moving from Here to There

In Dawn Costello's second-grade classroom, one young writer, Ben, was having difficulty deciding how to get himself from one place to the next in his personal narrative. Dawn returned to *Down the Road*, a mentor text the class had been studying for description. Together, they studied the part where Hetty is on her way from home to Mr. Birdie's store to buy eggs. In this book, the author, Alice Schertle, skillfully paints a picture of Hetty's journey from here to there:

> Then she continued down the road . . . through a meadow . . . across a stream . . . past a house or two . . . down a street . . . around a corner . . . up some steps . . . and into the cool shadows of Mr. Birdie's Emporium and Dry Goods store.

Dawn pointed out how the use of ellipses added to the understanding of how far Hetty had to travel all by herself. That was just enough for Ben to figure out how he could show getting from the place he was hurt to the hospital in his story (see Figure 4.1).

Figure 4.1
First page of Ben's story, where he used "moving from here to there" strategy.

I was in a small room with a blue toilet. The walls were white and a blue shower curtain hung from a gigantic pole. A brown mirror hong on the wall. That's where the worst day ever began.

It was silent. I was fainting. I fell to the ground. My mom heard a boom! My Dad put me in the car. we drove past about twenty houses, past large bildings, a park, and arrived at the hospital.

I was in a room with my mom.

In *Kitten's First Full Moon*, Kevin Henkes shows distance through the use of a dash and commas:

> So she chased it—
> down the sidewalk,
>   through the garden,
>   past the field,
>   and by the pond.

The way the print is placed on the page also helps the reader understand the distance. Both Henkes and Schertle string together prepositional phrases to show movement from here to there.

In *Happy Like Soccer*, Maribeth Boelts helps the reader understand how far Sierra must travel to get to and from her soccer games. Buried within this description, the author mentions an empty lot—key to understanding how the problem in this story will be solved:

> We weave past the empty lot and through my neighborhood and outside the city, where the buses don't run . . .
> After the game, we ride back home, into the city, through my neighborhood, past the empty lot, and right to the restaurant . . .

Sometimes students also need to be able to show passage of time to include only events that are important to the story. This will prevent the "bed-to-bed" scenario where every detail in the day is included. An essential strategy to use here is the use of transitional words and phrases placed in appropriate locations within the text. For example, *Crab Moon* by Ruth Horowitz begins with Daniel's family arriving at the seashore. To move to an event that takes place in the evening, the author begins with the phrase "That night . . . " After watching the horseshoe crabs mate, Daniel and his mom return to the house. We do not need to know the other events that may have happened that night, because they are not important to the story. The author moves us to the next day with another transitional phrase: "In the morning . . . " In *The Relatives Came*, Cynthia Rylant moves us from the beginning of the summer to the end through a description of grapes. In the beginning when they leave home, Rylant describes the grapes as "nearly purple enough to pick, but not quite." At the end of the story when they are traveling back to Virginia, they were thinking "about their dark purple grapes waiting at home." Lindsay Mattick uses a train's journey to show the passage of time in *Finding Winnie: The True Story of the World's Most Famous Bear*: "The train rolled right through dinner and over the sunset and around ten o'clock and into a nap and out the next day, until it stopped at a place called White River." The accompanying three-panel illustration helps the reader understand the movement in time from sunset through nighttime and into the next day. Mattick's use of the word *and* to connect prepositional phrases that describe time passing using only one sentence helps the reader understand how long the journey actually took. This sentence is a masterful way to show both distance and passage of time. The Your Turn lesson on examining details for a good fit at the end of this chapter explores how writers can use these techniques to leave out what is not important and yet show that time has passed.

Focusing on a Moment

Without elaboration, content becomes a mere list. Many of our young writers believe that adding details to a piece of writing is about adding a new idea. Although sometimes that may be true, more often teachers are really suggesting that their students go back into their stories and say something more about what is already on the page. Here is where mentor texts can help. In *The Dog Who Belonged to No One* by Amy Hest, the author adds details to further explain how the dog was helpful before continuing the story.

> The dog who belonged to no one tried hard to be helpful every day. When the baseballs of summer sailed into the woods, he found the baseballs. When the air turned cold and mittens were missing, he found the mittens.

In *Henny* by Elizabeth Rose Stanton, we learn about an unusual chicken who is different because she was born with arms. This difference causes Henny to have many worries, which the author elaborates on with examples. This passage also provides two good examples of the power of three:

> She worried about what to wear . . . . Long sleeves or short sleeves?
> Gloves or mittens? Buttons or zippers?
> She even worried about things she didn't quite understand—like tennis elbow, and hangnails, and whether she might need deodorant.

In *Each Kindness*, Jacqueline Woodson provides the kind of sophisticated elaboration we hope our students will eventually begin to use in their writing—adding a telling detail. To elaborate, we need to stop and say something more about what we have just said.

> We all stared at her.
> Her coat was open and the clothes beneath it looked old and ragged.
> Her shoes were spring shoes, not meant for the snow.
> A strap on one of them had broken.

If you examine this passage, you can see that Woodson is explaining why the children stared, but her description is so specific that we are left with an understanding that Maya is wearing hand-me-downs that are well used and perhaps should have been discarded long ago. She added that telling detail about the strap to the description of the shoes.

Once students have learned several strategies for developing the content of their writing, they can combine some or all of them to talk about one very important moment in time. Barry Lane (1993) talks about "exploding a moment" by using powerful tools such as snapshots, "thoughtshots," appealing to the senses, and lots of detail to write in slow motion. When we are finished modeling and guiding students with mentor texts, they can move to independence by returning to the picture book to try out a strategy without having us there.

Consider the picture books of Robert Burleigh. In *Home Run,* he introduces his main character, Babe Ruth, in the first several pages, setting us up for the small moment he places under his magnifying lens—a moment that lasts from the pitcher's windup to the home-run trot around the bases. How long would that moment take? Certainly no more than a few minutes, and yet, Burleigh slows the action for us so that we feel we are there, watching "the Babe" hit another home run. Consider only a piece of this beautifully written moment in time as Burleigh takes us to the ballpark to watch a legend:

> He watches the pitcher lean. Rotate. Rock back and forth. The leg wheels out. The arm whips over the head. Babe narrows his hunter-like gaze and strides into the pitch that is now only a tiny speck of whirling whiteness. This time. He swings big. His bat comes down and around. Powerfully. He swings "through the ball." Always "through the ball."

In his book *Flight,* Burleigh describes Charles Lindbergh's Atlantic crossing. He does not attempt to tell his reader about the entire life of Lindbergh, only the most important event in the aviator's life. We feel like we are crossing the Atlantic with him:

> He moves through the dense, curling fog, lit ghostly by the moon. He suddenly enters a huge stormcloud. The plane shimmers, moving up and down in the uniform blackness. He wonders: Can I fly above it? Slowly, he soars to 10,500 feet. Here it is clear, but very cold. He extends his arm outside the cockpit and feels "stinging pinpricks." He clicks on his small flashlight and peers out: Heavy ice has formed on the plane's wings. He cannot risk his instruments icing up. He points the Spirit of St. Louis back down. The wings quiver as they slice through the turbulent air. The fog continues, but now, at least, the air is warmer. The ice begins to melt and Lindbergh roars ahead.

Ruth Horowitz creates a "slow scene" at the end of the middle of her narrative *Crab Moon.* The scene begins when Daniel finds a horseshoe crab he believes may be dead and uses a piece of driftwood to nudge her. The author describes every detail as Daniel plucks up his courage to turn over the horse-shoe crab marooned on the beach and by doing so, saves her life. Horowitz would not have captured her readers' interest if she had simply written, "Daniel picked up the tail and turned the crab over." Through detailed description, the author slows down the action, placing us on the beach with Daniel:

> Daniel reached out one nervous finger. The tail felt stiff, but not sharp. He carefully lifted the crab. As her body left the ground, her claws started to snap. Daniel put her down fast. Then he took a deep breath and reached for her again. This time, he quickly turned the crab over, and gently set her down.

At the end of *A Taste of Blackberries*, Doris Buchanan Smith's powerful story, the main character returns to the blackberry patch to pick berries for his mother and for Jamie's mother. Jamie has died from an allergic reaction to bee stings, and his best friend is remembering him as he picks his way through the patch. Smith's words bring us right to the blackberry thicket, and we can see, feel, taste, and smell everything with the main character.

> I hunched and picked my way into the thickest place . . .
>   Steadily, steadily my baskets filled. My fingers were stained red-violet. I could smell bubbling blackberry pie already. I balanced berries one on another up and over the top until I was afraid I couldn't carry the baskets without spilling.
>   Then I took one plump berry between my thumb and forefinger. It was so full-to-popping that juice eased out onto my finger. I let the berry stay on my tongue a moment before I pressed it to the roof of my mouth and let the juice trickle down my throat.

Before beginning a unit of study on narratives in her fourth-grade classes, Lynne reads excerpts from previously shared read-alouds such as *Crab Moon* by Ruth Horowitz. When the students have found a topic and are ready to write, Lynne focuses their attention on the middle of these narratives to look for fast and slow action scenes. As the students discover the small moments that the authors have placed under their magnifying lenses, they turn and talk with a partner or small response group to try to understand what made the writing effective. They reread the passages from *A Taste of Blackberries* to find key strategies that helped the author slow down a moment in time. In whole-group sharing at the close of writing workshop, students discuss strategies from the various books Lynne has used and any other books they have read. Then Lynne charts these strategies so that the students can use them to create a slow scene and/or revise it during their next workshop time.

For teachers of upper elementary and middle school grades, an excellent reference is Barry Lane's *After THE END: Teaching and Learning Creative Revision.* An entire chapter is devoted to playing with time, a technique used by writers, play directors, photographers, artists, musicians, and cinematographers to create mood, rhythm, and strong emotion. The first thing a writing teacher needs to do is share these small moments that are expanded into larger moments in a text. Find three or four good examples and try it out yourself. Think about what strategies you used to develop one moment in time. Examine these moments for author's craft. How did you create a moment in time where the reader could climb in and walk around? Lynne's third and fourth graders listed these strategies:

- Show, don't tell
- Appeal to the senses
- Thinking of the character
- Dialogue
- Strong verbs
- Vivid adjectives
- Unexpected words (such as adjectives created by a string of words connected with hyphens such as *full-to-popping*)
- Striking color words
- Exact nouns
- Humor or another emotion
- Effective repetition
- Metaphor
- Simile
- Personification
- Alliteration
- Details
- Description of setting, character, or an important object
- Writing in the present tense
- Anecdotes

Instead of writing an entire story, ask your writers to brainstorm a list of small moments with you. Recently, we worked with teachers representing first grade through eighth grade in a graduate class for the Pennsylvania Writing and Literature Project. Together, we compiled the following list of possible scenarios for small moments that our students could choose to expand:

Things to write about!

- Flower girl/ring bearer walking down the church aisle
- Standing on the sidelines waiting to be picked for a game
- Trying to get rid of a bee that has entered the classroom
- Being called up to the stage to receive an award

- Waiting for the curtain to open as you stand on stage to perform
- Final lap of a race
- Seeing or holding your baby brother or sister for the first time
- Right before a bicycle or car crash
- Being stopped by a policeman
- The long walk to the principal's office
- The first-time stories (like jumping off a high dive)
- Agreeing to a dare
- Sitting in the dentist's chair
- Tryouts
- A surprise party
- Losing a tooth
- Plane takeoff or landing
- Walking into the classroom on the first day of school
- Finding money
- The moment you are caught doing something you are not supposed to be doing
- Seeing the tree on Christmas morning

Of course, we always share a small moment of ours first with the students. Lynne had her third graders think about what they do in the springtime and gave them some sentence stems to help them get started. They used "Spring makes me happy because . . ." and "Spring reminds me of . . ." Next, they created an idea splash on a big piece of chart or construction paper. The students drew a picture and labeled their small moment. Then they wrote words, phrases, and sentences around the picture to help them vividly recall that moment in time. Lynne's small moment was the first time she jumped a four-foot stone wall on a horse named Chances Are. Lynne drew her picture on the whiteboard and placed her words around it while she was thinking aloud. (See Figure 4.2.)

> *I remember thinking that the wall looked as big as the Hoover Dam! My heart was climbing up my throat, and my hands were so sweaty that they kept sliding all the way back the well-oiled reins to the buckle. I gripped the saddle with all my might and silently said a little prayer. Please don't let me fall off in front of all my friends! Then I leaned forward, grabbed some mane, and looked right between my horse's huge ears. Suddenly, he rocked back on his hind legs, and then we were flying! It was a small miracle. Somehow I managed to stay on. I was victorious!*

Lynne pointed out all the words and phrases she had written on the board.

> *Here I already have a wonderful simile that actually fits my story. Over here there are quite a few "show, don't tell" phrases. Can you tell me*

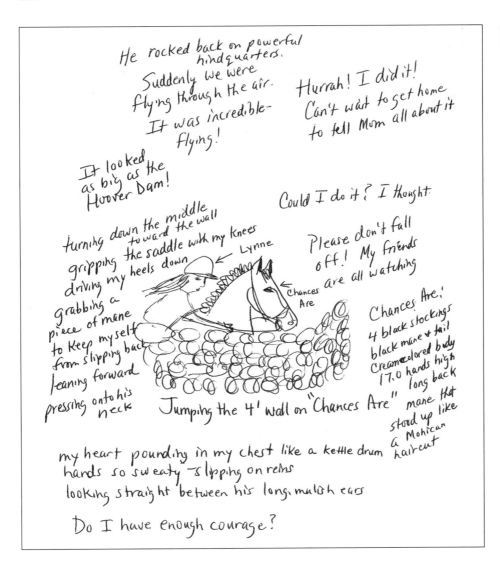

Figure 4.2
Lynne's idea splash.

what emotions I might be feeling? Let's look for strong verbs and exact nouns. I am ready to write. I know what the most important moment in my story is going to be and how to develop it.

When the students were finished discussing Lynne's model, they used large pieces of construction paper to plan their small moment. We do not have the students use this strategy every time, but it is especially helpful to struggling writers who need to draw and engage in more extensive prewriting to stay focused and develop their ideas. Once your students have created their idea splashes, they can begin to draft. You might give them a checklist of writers' strategies they can try out when they reach the revision stage. Be sure to ask some of your young authors whether you can have a copy as an exemplary model for your future classes. Here are some small moments that were expanded into larger moments:

Spring makes me happy because I can hurry outside on my driveway and play basketball, my favorite sport. I love the sound of the ball when it swooshes as it drops through the net. My arms grow tired and more tired as I dribble harder and faster. Then I shoot. The ball rolls around and around the rim like a moon orbiting a planet, almost in and then . . .
—Philip (grade three)

The line inched forward again. I had a don't-make-me-do-this look on my face. I squeezed my dad's hand (harder than I ever did before). I held back small tears. We were next. The cars moved up. We got on the middle car. I squeezed the handle bar. It took off faster and faster. Then, suddenly it stopped. "Oh, no!" I thought. The hill. It went higher and higher. I stuttered to Dad, "I'm really scared." He remarked, "Don't worry." The roller coaster came to the top. I held my breath (longer than I thought I could). Then, it burst forward. I came three inches off of the seat! The next hill, the next one . . . one after the other. CREEEEEEEEK! It came to a stop. The bar lifted and released us from this torture trap of a roller coaster. I stood up, stuttering and shaky-legged. Surprisingly, I had a do-it-again look smacked onto my face. I heard myself saying in a shaky voice, "That was fun."
—Kelley (grade five)

After the students have created several small-moment entries in their writer's notebooks, Lynne asks them to choose one and create a narrative with a beginning, a middle, and an end. The most important thing here is to be sure to include a small moment that has been placed under a magnifying lens so the reader can linger there with you. *The Yellow Ball* is a second grader's attempt to play with time. See Figure 4.3.

After reading *Up North at the Cabin*, Frank, a fifth-grade student, knew exactly what he wanted to write about in his writer's notebook that day. Author Marsha Wilson Chall describes the special moments at the cabin one by one with such precision that you feel as if you know the place. She has you convinced that you are there.

Up north at the cabin, I am a smart angler. Grandpa tries pink spinners, leeches, and dragonflies—but I know what fish like. I bait my hook with peanut-butter-and-worm sandwiches, then jig my line and wait.

Perhaps Frank was imitating Chall, and we believe that imitating the experts (the authors themselves) is exactly why we need to use mentor texts and revisit them often. At the very least, the picture book brought back a flood of memories and gave Frank a topic to write about in his notebook. The words seemed to spill out of him with an urgency of waters racing toward the falls—effortlessly, hungrily, and powerfully. This kind of first-draft writing happens for young writers only when they write about what they know, what they love, and

My mom and I were in the soothing, blue water playing with my most favorite yellow ball. We were having so much fun that we didn't even notice an enormous wave in back of us. When I turned around to get my ball I saw it, the enormous wave. I called my mom over. All we could say was AAAAAhh! It felt like my heart stopped beating. My face must have looked as white as my white bed sheets. The next moment it

turned ripe apple red from holding my breath. I was so scared I couldn't even move. When it started to tip, I started to fall! In my mind I was saying, "Good-bye, Ball." My mom and I were tumbling over each other.

I thought I was going to die before it was over! I came out of the ocean, and I must have taken a million breaths. I will be much more alert next time. And my favorite ball? The ocean still has it!

Figure 4.3 Billy's story "The Yellow Ball."

what is important to them. Frank wrote about one event, not an entire day or even an entire afternoon. Consider his small moment about fishing with his uncle. Notice his appeal to the senses, use of a sprinkle of dialogue, thought-shot, exact nouns (even a proper noun!), and vivid verbs.

> I am wearing my gold and blueberry-blue Scooby-Doo life jacket. "Hold on!" my uncle says as we leave the spring-boarded dock. As we start to pull away, the old gas motor smells like a thunderstorm that has just finished. I throw my grass-green and Crayola-purple jig into the water. All of a sudden . . . PLOP! My rod dips into the water like an Oreo when you dunk it into cotton-white milk. After battling hard, I win the battle that takes me a long five minutes. "Fifteen-and-a-half-inch flounder," I yell. So close, I think, but I'm proud about my first flounder that looks sunflower-yellow and dirt brown and smells like a skunk's spray.
> "Half an inch and he is almost a keeper!" my uncle yells back.

As part of a Your Turn lesson about exploding a small moment in time, Frank returned to his notebook to choose a small moment where he could practice this strategy. He chose his fishing story and was excited to share the place where he thought he could elaborate. Where do you think Frank needed to add more? What was the most exciting part in this story that he could expand for his readers to give them a better picture? Frank focused on this sentence: "After battling hard, I win the battle that takes me a long five minutes." In a conference with Lynne he explained how he battled with the fish and almost lost it. He recalled many vivid details that helped Lynne "be in the moment" with Frank, even though Lynne had to admit she had never gone fishing. By putting his writing under a magnifying lens (by closely reading), Frank was able to make this piece come to life.

> All of a sudden . . . PLOP! My rod dips into the water like an Oreo when you dunk it into cotton-white milk. My uncle and I watch our lines and the water. My hands are wet and clammy with anticipation. *If only I can bring home a fish today*, I think to myself. Hours pass . . . nothing. Then I feel a little tug. I wait. Yes, there it is again. Or is it just my imagination?
> Yes! There it is again! The line is bowed and I feel the tension as the fish (It must be a fish?) pulls hard to get away. I struggle to lift him up out of the water. I feel salty sweat stinging my eyes, but there is no hand free to brush the sweat away.
> My toes are smashed against the side of the boat and causing me great pain. Why did I take my sneakers off? I concentrate on the task at hand, my heart beat, beat, beating in my chest with excitement. All of a sudden, I yank the rod, and my prize is dangling in the air. The battle that takes me a long five minutes is definitely worth it!

In *Pictures of Hollis Woods*, Patricia Reilly Giff plays with moments of time by alternating her chapters about her main character, traveling from the past to the present. Each chapter about Hollis's past is written as an expanded moment that helps the reader visualize that moment—to feel as if Giff has magically transported us there. It is as if she is giving us the chance to be eyewitnesses to these important events that play in her main character's memory. She even calls these chapters written about past events "pictures." Consider how Giff has "exploded" this small moment in time:

> Like a miracle I caught my first fish that afternoon. Hooked it and watched the silver curve as it broke the surface of the water. It was a huge fish, and Steven said, "Bet you a buck you can't hold on to it."
>
> He was right there with the net, though, wanting me to get it, as I slipped on the rocks, feeling the water on my legs and then my back as I slid. I tried to get my balance with one hand, my feet going out from under me, not sure how deep the river was, wondering if my head would go under.
>
> Steven's arm was on my elbow then, holding me up, and the Old Man called, "You're all right, Hollis."
>
> My feet anchored into the sand then. I edged myself back, pulling on the rod, and then the fish was mine.

That is what writers do. They take moments in time and put them under a magnifying lens, examining every small detail for its worth, its importance to the whole. Each time we "explode a moment," we write small to write big. We write with the specificity we need to keep our audience's attention. We write with anecdotes, sensory details, thoughtshots, and dialogue. We write with rich description. We want our readers to continue reading. We want our words and pictures to linger on their minds long after they have finished reading. Teach your students how to look at people, places, objects, and events with a magnifying lens.

Think About It—Talk About It—Write About It

- How could you help your students develop the content of their stories?
- What difficulties have you noticed your students encountering with developing their ideas?
- What strategies are your students using successfully?
- Do you have students who could "lead the way" or teach their peers how to appeal to the senses or use description, dialogue, or elaboration to help build content effectively?
- Examine your writer's notebook to discover places where you can expand a small moment with a rich description, dialogue, anecdote, or thoughtshots. Write and revise to make your reader feel like he or she is in that moment with you.

Adding Details Through Questioning

Hook: Kevin Henkes's books provide excellent models of the importance of adding details to writing, especially for young writers. The hook used in this lesson is *Lilly's Purple Plastic Purse*. For the lesson to be effective, this book should be a familiar read-aloud. Return to it and read the first few pages, but leave out all the details.

> Lilly loved school.
> And, most of all, she loved her teacher, Mr. Slinger.
> At home Lilly pretended to be Mr. Slinger.
> One morning Lilly came to school especially happy.
> "Look, everyone. Look what I've got!"

By this time, students should be noticing that the book does not go like that. Acknowledge that they are indeed correct, that when you read it, you left out all the details. Reread the first sentence: *Lilly loved school*. Ask students what questions they have when they hear that sentence. What do they want to know right away? Ideally, they will say that they want to know what she loved about school. Then read the three sentences that follow and answer the question directly. Continue with the other sentences.

Purpose: *Writing without details leaves too many unanswered questions and makes writing fuzzy. Today I will show you how to ask questions as you write. Asking questions will help you think of the details to add to your writing so that it is clear to the reader.*

Brainstorm: Ask students to think about some things they've done recently, things they like to do, or perhaps places they've recently gone. For example, played soccer, went to art class, went to a friend's house. Ask students to jot down these ideas in their notebooks, or have them share orally and record some ideas on the board.

Model: Share some of your ideas about things you've recently one or places you've recently gone, pick one, and record the idea in one sentence on a chart or overhead. Here is Rose's example:

> *Writers, today I'd like to tell you about the walk I took with my dog, Casey, last night. So I'll write here: Last evening I took Casey for a walk.*

Ask students what questions they have. In this example, they asked what kind of dog Casey was, where she and Rose went, and what they saw. As each question is asked, answer it orally and add it to your writing. Tell students that by answering the questions they have, you are adding details to the story to make it clearer and more interesting. The story started above might end up something like this:

> *Last evening I took my yellow Labrador retriever, Casey, for a walk. We strolled all around the neighborhood, past houses and parked cars, for almost an hour. We saw children playing street hockey and riding bikes. Casey wanted to run after a squirrel she saw scamper by, but I held her tightly so she wouldn't run away.*

Shared/Guided Writing: Ask students to choose something from their brainstormed list and write it in one sentence in their notebooks as you first modeled. Invite one or two students to the front of the room for a guided conversation. Ask them to share their sentence; then share the questions you have. As the questions are answered, do some oral writing, demonstrating how these details, generated from the questions asked, could be added to the writing to make it clearer. Ask students to turn to a partner, share their sentence, and then ask their partner to share the questions they have. Have students return to their seats and add the details to the piece they began with the one sentence they wrote in their notebook. The details should be based on the questions asked by their partner.

Independent Writing: Students can return to a draft or published piece and look for places where they have questions. They can mark the places with a small colored dot or simply a check mark. Students add more details by answering their own questions. Older students can work with a partner to mark each other's drafts and ask questions. The goal here is to create writers who can ask their own questions as they write, adding details their readers want to know that would help make their writing clearer. Encourage them to ask more questions themselves, until their writing becomes as clear as possible. They can then share again with their partner and receive feedback.

Reflection: Ask writers to reflect on how the strategy worked for them. Make sure students understand that when questions arise, more details are probably needed.

> *How did your writing become clearer as questions were answered?*

> *How could you use this strategy when working with a partner or in a small group?*

> *How could you use this strategy when writing a research or opinion piece?*

Your Turn Lesson 2

Using Illustrations to Add Details

Sometimes writers are in a hurry to get from the beginning to the end and leave out all the details in the middle, or the events in the middle sound more like a list. The reader is left trying to imagine what happened from one point to the next. We can help students learn how to build content and add details to the events in a story by adding words to illustrations found in picture books.

Hook: Return to some favorite picture book read-alouds in which illustrations add details that are not found in the text. Suggestions include *Arthur's Pet Business* by Marc Brown; *One Day, The End: Short, Very Short, Shorter-Than-Ever Stories* by Rebecca Kai Dotlich; or *Shortcut* by Donald Crews. Choose some pages where specific details are found only in an illustration. Ask students to compare the illustration with the text and to think about the details that may be missing from the text. This Your Turn lesson is based on *Arthur's Pet Business*.

Purpose: *Writers, sometimes authors use illustrations only to add details to a story. When we write, we aren't always able to add illustrations, so important details must be added to the text. Today I'm going to show you how building content with details helps our readers better visualize what is happening in the stories we write.*

Brainstorm: Return to the picture used in the hook. Ask students to think about what is happening in the picture—what they see, what they think the character might be saying or thinking, what sounds the character might be hearing, and so on. Students can turn and talk with a partner and then share their responses in whole group. Try to elicit as many details as possible. As responses are shared, list them on a chart or whiteboard. In *Arthur's Pet Business*, Marc Brown shares how Arthur cares for Perky. Student responses to the illustration accompanying the text "Every day he brushed her" might include these:

> Arthur put Perky on a table.
> He is using a soft brush.
> There is dog lotion or perfume on the table.
> Arthur is smiling.
> Perky looks annoyed.
> Perky's eyebrows are frowning and one tooth is showing.

Continue charting responses to the other illustrations found on that page and/or the pages describing what Arthur did each day.

Model: Use the responses from the students and model how you could expand on the one sentence of text using details from the illustration. For the above example, you could write something like this:

> Every day he brushed her. *Arthur put Perky on a table so he could reach her easily. He got a soft dog brush and some special perfume that would make her smell wonderful. Carefully he began to brush the fur on her back.*
> *Arthur felt happy. He knew this brushing would help Perky feel special. But Perky was not happy. She frowned and growled until Arthur had to stop.*

Shared/Guided Writing: In whole group, use the charted responses from one of the other pictures to draft a short paragraph. Students could also work in pairs to write paragraphs from other charted responses, or look for other examples in books where details are found in illustrations and add them to the existing text.

Independent Writing: Ask students to look at a piece of writing where events may not be fully explained. Invite them to add details with words as if they were painting a picture. They can also work in pairs during peer conferencing to help each other identify places in their writing where the reader might need more detail to have a clear picture in their mind about what is happening.

Reflection: In whole group, ask students to reflect on how this strategy worked for them:

> *How did the illustrations help you imagine important details in the story? Did writing the details help you better understand the story? Might you have missed something if you hadn't taken the time to study the illustrations?*
>
> *Why is it important to add details to writing?*
>
> *Were you able to find spots in your writing that needed more detail for your reader?*
>
> *How might sketching help you find the details you need to add?*
>
> *When will you use this strategy again?*

Your Turn Lesson 3

Building Content Through Showing, Not Telling

Hook: Choose some mentor texts that show characters' emotions. One good choice is Roald Dahl's *The Witches*, in which the main character reacts with fear when he discovers that the nice ladies on the other side of the screen are really witches. Reread the chapter "The Meeting" and chart all the words that Dahl uses to show fear such as "My blood turned to ice. I began to shake all over." Options: *The Memory String* by Eve Bunting, *Lilly's Purple Plastic Purse* by Kevin Henkes, and *Crab Moon* by Ruth Horowitz.

Purpose: *Writing by telling alone is boring. Authors try to balance telling with showing. One of the easiest things that authors can show is emotions. Today we will find ways that reveal the emotions of our character through showing instead of telling just like Roald Dahl did.*

Brainstorm: Have students brainstorm a list of emotions that they could show, not tell. The list could include excitement, disappointment, anger, sadness, happiness, anxiety, frustration, surprise, loneliness, and joy, to name a few. Ask them to think about how nonverbal cues or actions could show these emotions in a piece of writing.

Model: Ask the students to imagine other ways in which Roald Dahl could have shown fear in the scene from *The Witches*. This list could include such things as hands shaking, an inability to speak, dry mouth, turning pale, goose bumps popping out, cold shivers, being rooted to the spot, knees knocking together, whimpering, and crying. Then choose another emotion and write a scene around it. Let the students guess what the emotion is. Have them come to the board and underline the words or phrases that helped show that emotion. Here is an example from Lynne's notebook that shows nervousness:

> Ryan <u>fumbled</u> with his shoelaces. He couldn't seem to tie them with his <u>shaking hands</u>. A <u>sickening feeling in his stomach</u> was creeping up into his throat. The big game today would decide who would be champions—state champions. Playing goalie wasn't ever easy. He knew if he wasn't at his best today, the team would probably lose. As he grabbed his jacket, he <u>shook his head to clear his mind</u>. His <u>legs felt like spaghetti noodles</u> as he <u>trudged down the steps while holding on to the banister</u>. "Bye, Mom," he <u>called out weakly</u>. "I'll see you later at the game." He <u>swallowed</u> hard and walked to the bus stop.

Shared/Guided Writing: Choose another emotion and have the class brainstorm a list of nonverbal cues or actions for it, and then create a scene around the emotion in a shared writing experience. It is best to choose something that centers on school so that the students can all join in. Stage the scenario in the cafeteria, nurse's office, classroom, or somewhere similar. Students could also work in pairs if you think they are ready.

Independent Writing: Ask the students to return to a previous story in their writing folder or an entry in their writer's notebook and revise the content to reveal an emotion by showing instead of telling. They could also start a new piece and try out the show, don't tell strategy to build content.

Reflection: Ask students to reflect on how this strategy worked for them.

> *How did adding details to show an emotion rather than just tell it make your writing better?*

> *What kinds of words help you show an emotion? (For instance, strong verbs can be used to show actions that indicate anger.)*

> *When is this strategy best used? Is it sometimes better to tell?*

Ask students to find other examples as they read independently where authors have used the show, don't tell strategy and copy them into their notebooks.

Your Turn Lesson 4

Building Content with Dialogue

This lesson is designed to help teachers and students find the perfect place(s) to add a splash of dialogue within a narrative. Dialogue is a key element of story along with character, setting, problem, and solution. This lesson is not about how to correctly punctuate conversation. We think students first need to understand that dialogue must be important to the text and not added simply to make a text longer.

Hook: Eve Bunting's *The Wednesday Surprise* provides an excellent model to teach students how to build content through effective dialogue that is sprinkled lightly throughout the text. After students are familiar with the book as a read-aloud, return to the text to display a few pages where dialogue is used. Examine the conversation between Grandma and her granddaughter, Anna, and the satisfying ending where dialogue plays a key role. You might choose to rewrite sections without the dialogue so that students can compare the versions and develop an understanding of how authors use dialogue to develop their content. Point out to students how dialogue can be used to reveal a character's name, reveal what the character is thinking or feeling, offer an explanation, ask a question (not necessarily responded to in dialogue), or give an example. What we want students to understand is that dialogue is almost never used as a filler; it must have a purpose. Options: *Nana in the City* or *The Troublemaker* by Lauren Castillo, *Thunder Cake* by Patricia Polacco, *Happy Like Soccer* by Maribeth Boelts, *Toad Weather* by Sandra Markle, and *Down the Road* by Alice Schertle.

Purpose: *Writers, when you are writing a story and thinking about story elements, you will need to think about dialogue and where it will help make your story more interesting to your readers. Today I am going to show you how to do that and challenge you to give it a try.*

Brainstorm: Together with your students think about some scenes and events where dialogue would naturally occur. If your students need some help, put them in small groups with some mentor texts in which dialogue is used, and ask them to think about possible events. Here are some examples: opening presents at a birthday party, saying good-bye to a friend, planting flowers with Mother, discovering something on a walk or bike ride, riding on the school bus, teaching someone a skill, shopping for clothes or shoes, or being sent to the principal's office.

Model: Choose an event from the brainstormed list and compose a short piece in front of the class. Don't worry if you are not including dialogue in the first draft (that might be better!). You can revise your piece, and students can see the difference between the two pieces. Here are our examples:

Example 1
I entered the principal's office with my stomach flipping and my heart beating fast. I had never been in trouble before. My best

friend, Jamie, did not seem to be nervous. He had been here many times. The principal asked us what happened in the cafeteria. I wasn't involved in the food fight, but I couldn't get the words out. Jamie admitted that he had thrown the first potato chip. He stood up for me so I wouldn't get into trouble. When I left, the principal closed the door. I wondered what would happen to Jamie.

Example 2
I entered the principal's office with my stomach flipping and my heart beating fast. "Wh-wh-wh-what's going to happen?" I whispered to Jamie. I had never been in trouble before. My best friend, Jamie, did not seem to be nervous.

"I'm an expert at this. Just follow my lead," Jamie said, giving me a whack on the back.

"What happened at lunch today?" the principal demanded. I wasn't involved in the food fight, but I couldn't get the words out. Jamie admitted that he had thrown the first potato chip. He stood up for me so I wouldn't get into trouble. When I left, the principal closed the door. I wondered what would happen to Jamie.

(Note: Model correctness by beginning on a new line every time a speaker changes. But don't dwell on this. It's something for another lesson.)

Shared/Guided Writing: Return to the brainstormed list, choose a different scene, and compose a shared experience as a whole group. If students need more practice, allow them to work with a partner to create another scene that uses dialogue effectively.

Independent Writing: Ask students to try to add dialogue in one or several places in a narrative they are working on or perhaps revisit a notebook entry where dialogue would naturally fit. Option: Students can also use a photograph, a calendar picture, or an illustration from a book to imagine a conversation between two characters.

Reflection: Ask students to think about how they might use dialogue to improve their narratives with the following questions:

Why do authors use dialogue?

How did the use of dialogue change your original piece?

Where would you use dialogue again? Where would it be appropriate and most effective?

Could you use dialogue in an informational piece? In a poem? In an opinion piece?

Your Turn Lesson 5

Examining Details for a Good Fit

This lesson is designed to show students how they can move through time in a story without writing the "bed-to-bed" version. Through our years of experience we have found that it is very difficult for students to tell a story without verbalizing every single thing that happens throughout the day. Students often like to write about something that happened on a weekend, vacation, or over a holiday and sometimes need to include key events from two or more consecutive days. Then they are really in a quandary. We hope this lesson can help you address this problem.

Hook: Choose some mentor texts that span the course of a day or more and that use transition words and phrases, and sometimes illustrations, to help the reader move through a meaningful sequence of events. A good choice is *Nana in the City* by Lauren Castillo because it is about an entire weekend that a young boy spends with his nana. Talk about the main events. Discuss the phrases Castillo uses to move the story forward such as "at night," "when I woke up in the morning," and "when it was time to leave." Options: *Each Kindness* by Jacqueline Woodson, *Crab Moon* by Ruth Horowitz, and *Down the Road* by Alice Schertle.

Purpose: *Writers, we have spent some time talking about building content. Today I'm going to show you how you can use transition words and phrases to capture the important events of your story.*

Brainstorm: Together with your students, brainstorm a list of words they are probably familiar with (*first, next, then, finally,* and so on). Ask students to work in small groups to examine some books for additional transitional phrases that help readers move through time. These might include *early that morning, later that day, in the afternoon, two weeks later, later in the year,* and others.

Model: In front of your students brainstorm a few topics you would like to write about and choose one. Start with a working title and put bullets in front of all the events, even minor ones, surrounding this occasion or topic. Don't be judgmental here—just list everything. Here's an example:

> Going to a show in Philadelphia
> - Had a great pancake breakfast
> - Went shopping for groceries
> - Walked the dogs
> - Made a salad for lunch
> - Planted spring flowers
> - Had dinner

- So excited to change into a new dress bought for this occasion
- Drove with friends to the city
- Saw murals on buildings
- Talked about our plans for summer vacation
- No parking to be found
- Finally parked eight blocks away
- Walked past an interesting shop
- It started to rain—no umbrellas
- Got to the theater soaking wet
- Had great seats in the center of the theater
- People next to us not happy because we were wet
- Bought a soda and chips at intermission
- Called home to check on the babysitter
- Got to sing our favorite songs from the show with the cast at closing
- Enjoyed the show even though hair and clothes were dripping wet

Begin to tell the story orally, including all the details that are listed. At the end, ask the class if all of that made sense and if all the events were necessary to the story and the point (the so-what). Ideally they will see that not every detail was needed and that the number of details slowed the story down too much. Have the class help you identify the key events to the story. Here are the events we identified:

- So excited to change into a new dress bought for this occasion
- Drove with friends to the city
- No parking to be found
- Finally parked eight blocks away
- It started to rain—no umbrellas
- Got to the theater soaking wet
- Had great seats in the center of the theater
- People next to us not happy because we were wet
- Enjoyed the show even though hair and clothes were dripping wet

Retell the story using some of the transition words identified in the brainstormed list.

Shared/Guided Writing: In this particular lesson, the modeling is interactive and naturally becomes a shared experience. Many of the students may be ready to write independently. If you think some of your students need additional practice, you can do a shared writing around a common topic such as a birthday party. Or, you could ask to use a student sample of a draft. Display it and ask for revision help to take out events and details that weigh the story down and are not necessary, replacing them with transition words or phrases to move the story forward.

Independent Writing: Ask students to return to a story they are working on and revise it to eliminate unimportant details and events. Ask them to add transition words that will move the story forward.

Reflection: *Were you able to easily identify the best place to begin your story?*

How did you use transition words to help you travel through time?

What transition words and phrases worked best for you?

Was this difficult or easy for you to do? Explain.

Chapter 5

Growing a Narrative from Beginning to End

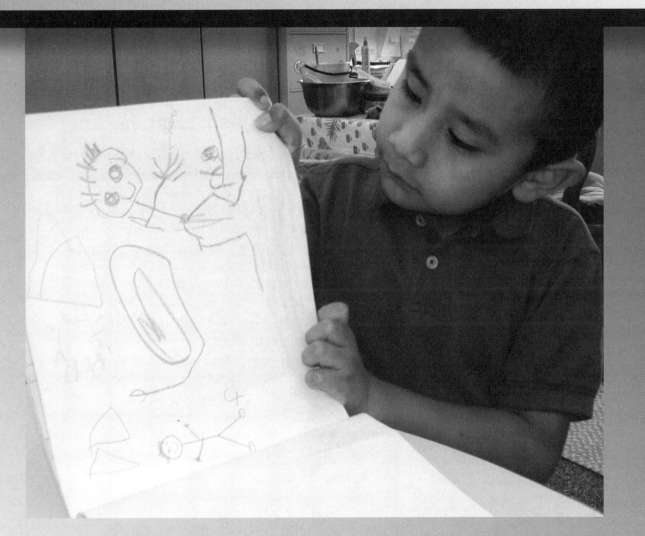

As a community of learners, we discovered how thick and tight the story line must be from its beginning all the way to its end.

—Pamela Murphy

Have you ever read the first page of a book to decide whether or not you want to keep reading? Are you one of those people who peeks at the ending to have a sense of what emotions you might be left with as you finish your reading? E. B. White used a provocative question written as dialogue to begin *Charlotte's Web*. "'Where's Papa going with that ax?' said Fern to her mother as they were setting the table for breakfast." What reader wouldn't want to continue? The ending of this well-known book leaves the reader with the warm feeling of friendship. "It is not often that someone comes along who is a true friend and a good writer. Charlotte was both."

Beginnings and endings are important parts of story writing and are tied together with threads woven throughout the middle in the same way that introductions of informational pieces are tied to their conclusions. Before students can begin to work on the beginnings and endings of their pieces, they must have internalized the scaffold of the narrative—the typical format of beginning, middle, and end.

Understanding and Controlling Narrative Time

Our students often struggle with writing stories because they don't know how to control time. They often don't know the best place to begin a story to get to the most important event that is going to happen in that story and do it justice. For example, students often begin their stories springing out of bed to the sound of an alarm clock ringing; or they use the ever-popular "One Saturday morning . . ." lead, even when their story is about something that happened later that afternoon or evening. By the time they get to the true focus of their story, they have lost stamina—they start writing lists or even omit chunks of important details. If students have the schema for a story structure and truly understand the focus of the story they want to tell, they can start making decisions about when and where it should begin. The importance of setting becomes clear as an integral element of the beginning. Because our students are often reading chapter books, they lose sight of the simple truth that in writing workshop they do not have the luxury of a year or more to write a "book." Besides, they lack the writing stamina to write an entire book. But we can teach them how to write a good story, one that has an enticing beginning, an interesting middle, and a satisfying ending. Picture books will show students the way. In only thirty-two pages, they tell a good story.

To help our students internalize the narrative scaffold and the literary elements of story—character, setting, problem/goal, plot, solution/resolution—we can provide a variety of mentor texts that clearly illustrate this concept. Books we continue to use over and over across grade levels include *Crab Moon* by Ruth Horowitz, *Fireflies!* by Julie Brinckloe, *Widget* by Lyn Rossiter McFarland, and *Shortcut* by Donald Crews.

In *Shortcut*, Donald Crews manages to tell a good story that takes place in a matter of minutes. The characters in this book are on their way home and decide to take a shortcut because it is getting dark. Unfortunately, the shortcut is on the train tracks, and a freight train is approaching. Crews makes effective use of repetition in his lead to set the reader up for the problem and how the story is going to unfold.

As he begins the middle of his text, he uses a brief description of the setting followed by quick, short sentences written in noun-verb fashion leading up to the most important moment—the moment when the children realize that a train is approaching. He again uses repetition effectively for the ending of the story to help the reader understand the magnitude of the children's feelings. Crews ends the story with a decision that was reached based on the poor choice made at the beginning: "We decided to take the shortcut home [Beginning]. . . . we didn't take the shortcut again [End]." *Shortcut* helps students understand that one small moment of time can be captured and told with excitement and strong emotion. Sometimes that's enough.

Julie Brinckloe's story *Fireflies!* spans an entire evening from dusk to bedtime. Brinckloe's main character is sitting at the dinner table looking out the window when he sees the fireflies beginning to flicker. He quickly joins his friends and catches lots of fireflies in a jar. In the end, he realizes that to save them he must set them free. This story is a great mentor text because it helps students understand the importance of writing a beginning that is not too far away in time from the most important event of the story. Students can easily see the logic of writing a story about catching fireflies when it is beginning to get dark outside. They clearly understand that starting this story at daybreak with the character springing from his bed would not be a good choice.

When we talk to students about how the authors of our mentor texts have told their stories, we can help them better understand where to begin their own stories and how to make good decisions about what to include and what to leave out. A good beginning leads to a more satisfying ending and, ultimately, to a better story.

When young students begin to write, their pieces are usually quite short—one or two sentences about something from their lives. For example, "I went to a birthday party" or "I helped my mom plant flowers." With lots of modeling, guided conversations, and supported peer talk, we can help young writers envision a structure to their life stories. We can help them see that the stories they share have a beginning, a middle, and an end, just like the stories they hear in the classroom.

Rose works collaboratively with the teachers in the kindergarten classes in her school during journal writing, a loosely structured writing workshop time. After the modeled lesson, Rose always invites students to come to the front of the room and talk about the idea they have for writing that day. Through guided conversation, she helps them add the important details that make their stories come alive. In the beginning of the year, the students typically use one sheet of paper in their journals during each writing time. Although many of the details that are unearthed during the conversation end up in the illustration, they aren't always included in the text. But as these young writers progress in their ability to form letters, stretch out the sounds in words, and become more confident in their ability to express themselves in writing, they are eager to add more details or to continue their stories over several days. To facilitate this development, the journals gradually give way to small books—three journal pages stapled together where students can record the moments of their lives with more elaboration. *Bunny Cakes* by Rosemary Wells is a true mentor text for the kindergartners Rose works with, helping them understand the different ways in which we write and the reasons we write, showing them the importance of details and word choice, and providing examples of word spacing and end marks. This book is also an excellent model for helping young writers understand how they can write a story with a beginning, a middle, and an end.

On one particular morning, Rose placed three blank journal pages on the whiteboard and then asked the students to gather on the rug. "Writers, let's think for a minute about the story of Max and Ruby in *Bunny Cakes*. What happened in the beginning of this story?" she asked them. As the children retold the beginning of the story, she pointed to the first blank journal page. She then asked them to tell the middle. As they came up with responses, she repeated their suggestions while pointing to the middle page. Finally, as she pointed to the last page, she asked them to tell how the story ended. Then she told them, "Today I'm going to show you how you can write a beginning, a middle, and an end just like Rosemary Wells did in *Bunny Cakes*." The lesson proceeded as Rose modeled a beginning, a middle, and an end with a story of her own.

Writers, one spring I planted beautiful daffodils in my backyard under an oak tree. The next spring the leaves came up, but there were no flowers. This happened again the next spring. I thought there might be something wrong with the bulbs, so I dug them up. I threw them away behind the shed where we throw grass clippings and weeds. Guess what? The next spring the daffodils bloomed—right in the place where I threw them!

This time, after telling the story while pointing to each blank page on the board, she also recorded it on the page.

One spring the daffodils under the oak tree did not bloom.	I dug them up. I threw them behind the shed.	The next spring my daffodils bloomed right where I threw them. What a great surprise I had that day!

She asked the students to think about their topic for writing that day and then invited Cassidy to come to the front of the room to tell her story about the time her friend got stuck in a tree. They first engaged in a guided conversation so

Rose could be sure Cassidy included all the details. When it seemed like Cassidy was stopping, Rose encouraged her to tell more by asking her, "Then what happened?" Next, Rose gave Cassidy one of the three-page books and asked her to orally tell the story again as Cassidy put her hand on each page, moving from the beginning to the middle to the end. Rose wanted them to understand that the story doesn't just stop after the first sentence—there is more to tell. Before the students returned to their tables to write, they turned to their partners and shared their ideas for the day's writing. Rose encouraged the students to ask their partners, "Then what happened?" to encourage them to tell more. (See Figures 5.1a–5.1c for Cassidy's completed story.)

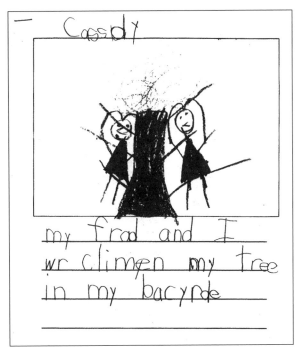

Figure 5.1a *(top right)*
Page 1 of Cassidy's story: "My friend and I were climbing my tree in my backyard."

Figure 5.1b *(bottom left)*
Page 2 of Cassidy's story: "She tried to get down. I put something underneath of her but when she turned to get down she scraped."

Figure 5.1c *(bottom right)*
Page 3 of Cassidy's story: "her knee getting out of the tree. My mom and her mom put a special bandage on her."

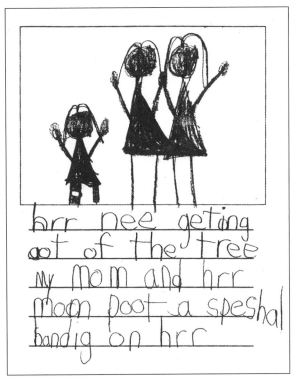

As students become more proficient at putting words to paper, they tend to write the infamous bed-to-bed stories. This kind of writing usually occurs at the end of first grade or the beginning of second grade. Students write everything that happens from sunup to sundown and sometimes continue into the next day. Now is the time to make use of the mentor text *Widget* by Lyn Rossiter McFarland. Widget is a stray dog that desperately needs a home. He finds a home with Mrs. Diggs, but she already has six cats. The strength of this story is that it has a clear beginning, middle, and end and is the perfect story map. Because it is written in simple language, young writers can imitate the structure. Traditionally, when a story is mapped, the beginning includes the characters, the setting, and the problem or goal. The middle describes how the character or characters attempt to solve the problem or reach the goal. Usually there is a series of events that contain both fast and slow action. We tell students they need to keep the reader waiting and not solve the problem too quickly. Otherwise, the story is over before it gets started and there is no excitement or adventure. The middle of the story builds to the most important event, where the goal is reached or the problem is solved. The ending ties everything together in a way that satisfies the reader and lets us know what the main character is thinking and/or feeling.

The hardest thing for elementary school students to learn how to do is write a satisfying ending. Very young students will often omit the ending of a story entirely, satisfied with writing "The End." They simply stop because they are tired of writing and don't know where their story is going or what they need to do to end their piece successfully. In *Widget*, McFarland has created a satisfying ending. She also has a page that is ideal for stopping and pretending that the book is over. "Everyone came. Mrs. Diggs was saved!" Sound like an ending? It certainly sounds that way to the students until you ask them to think about story maps.

"What was the problem the book presented?" Lynne asked her third graders.

Carly's hand shot up. "Widget was a stray and he needed a home."

Steven added, "And he couldn't stay because he was a dog and the cats didn't like dogs."

"I see," Lynne said. "So what is the most important thing the reader needs to know at the end of the story?"

Isabel replied, "Oh, I get it! If the story ends here, we don't know if Widget gets to stay."

Lynne continued, "That's right. That's why Lyn Rossiter McFarland didn't end her story here." When Lynne finished reading the book, a discussion followed about how the author uses dialogue to reveal what the main characters are thinking and feeling at the end of the story. Lynne talked about how the ending satisfies the reader because it relates to the beginning of the story and the problem of the main character.

Patches Lost and Found by Steven Kroll is another excellent mentor text that easily lends itself to story mapping and clearly illustrates how the ending must satisfy the reader. In this book, Jenny, who would much rather draw than write, is having difficulty coming up with a topic for her writing assignment. A second problem occurs when she arrives home and discovers that her guinea pig, Patches, is missing. Jenny makes several attempts to find Patches, all the while drawing pictures of where she thinks he might be or what might have happened to him. Eventually, Jenny's neighbor returns Patches. We can lead students to the understanding that if the story ended with finding Patches, they would still wonder if Jenny ever thought of a topic for her writing assignment. In the end, Jenny engages in a final action: she uses all the pictures she drew of what she thought might have happened to Patches to write an imagined story. *Patches Lost and Found* is also an excellent example for students of how they can use pictures to plan out a story.

Wordless books are one resource you can use to help your students internalize a story map and get practice in telling a story from beginning to end. When using wordless books it is helpful to have students go through the book first, verbalizing what they notice on each page. Older students can jot ideas in a notebook. Go through the book again and ask students to help you tell the story orally. As they go along, they may have to revise what they have already said. This process can contribute to internalizing the story structure. The next step is to chart a basic story map: characters, setting, problem or goal, events (climax), resolution. Finally, invite your students to help you write the story for the pictures. Giving students lots of opportunities to discuss their ideas with a partner helps to sustain energy and ensure more participation. Unless an idea that is offered does not make any sense or really cannot fit into the flow of the story, take it. Remember, there are many ways to interpret pictures and tell a story. It may not be the story that is in your head, but it will be the one created by your class. Excellent choices for this activity are *The Farmer and the Clown* by Marla Frazee, *Tuesday* by David Wiesner, or *The Lion and the Mouse* by Jerry Pinkney.

Once students begin to internalize the flow of a story—a beginning that introduces the characters and setting and perhaps describes the problem or goal of the main character; a middle where attempts are made to reach the goal, solve the problem, or describe the experience; and an ending that leaves the reader satisfied—then they can begin to think about the many different ways that authors choose to begin and end the stories they write.

Beginnings

For all writers, the lead—the first sentence, the first paragraph, or the first several paragraphs that begin the story—is absolutely crucial. E. B. White wrote more than a dozen leads for *Charlotte's Web* before he settled on a question written in dialogue form. His entire first chapter captivates the reader as Fern engages in a mental battle—a heated debate with her father—to save the runt, Wilbur, one of the story's main characters. The common ingredients of a good beginning are creating the mood by establishing the setting; information about the main character that reveals his or her hopes, thoughts, and feelings; and at least a hint of the problem, goal, or direction of the story. It's like receiving an invitation to a party that gives some information to help you know what to expect (for example, a swim party: bring your bathing suit and a towel). Revisiting mentor texts can provide students with examples of well-crafted beginnings that they can try out with their own stories.

Some authors begin their books by painting a picture of the setting in the reader's mind. Some of our favorites are *Owl Moon* by Jane Yolen, *Butterfly Tree* by Sandra Markle, and *Fletcher and the Falling Leaves* by Julia Rawlinson. Nicola Davies begins her book *The Promise* with a description of setting, describing the city as an unpleasant place to live: "Nothing grew. Everything was broken. No one ever smiled." We know immediately how the character is feeling through the words Davies chooses to use to describe the setting: *mean, hard, ugly*. Her similes also help establish a feeling tone of sadness.

The beginning is also a writer's chance to create a mood through the description of the setting. Consider these two beginnings that create a feeling of loneliness:

> Alejandro's small adobe house stood beside a lonely desert road. Beside the house stood a well, and a windmill to pump water from the well. Water for Alejandro and his only companion, a burro. It was a lonely place, and Alejandro welcomed any who stopped by to refresh themselves at the well. But visitors were few, and after they left, Alejandro felt lonelier than before.
> (from *Alejandro's Gift* by Richard E. Albert)

> Amber lived on a mountain so high, it poked through the clouds like a needle stuck in down. Trees bristled on it like porcupine quills. And the air made you giddy—it was that clear. Still, for all that soaring beauty, Amber was lonesome. For mountain people lived scattered far from one another.
> (from *Amber on the Mountain* by Tony Johnston)

Students can imitate these beginnings—first, in their writer's notebooks—or they can simply try them out. Lynne often begins by asking her students to make a list of settings. Then she asks them to choose a setting and try to describe it through their senses, keeping in mind the mood they wish to create. Often she returns to *Amber on the Mountain* because it is a mentor text and the children are familiar with it. Sometimes it is easier for students to start with Tony Johnston's beginning, placing Amber in a different setting, rather than composing one from scratch. Jessica, a fourth grader, chose to put Amber on an island:

> Amber lived on an island so small it stood in the deep-dark sea like a lost whale. Palm trees tangled on it like monkey tails. And the coconuts made

you giddy—they were that delightful. Still, for all the spectacular sights, one thing put Amber in her darkest mood. There were few hut-like houses near hers—less friends, more tears.

Some students will return to a previously written piece and revise their beginnings to add a description of setting that also creates mood. This strategy of using the author's syntax is described in detail in Your Turn Lesson 1 at the end of Chapter 9.

Often authors begin a book with a description of the main character. In Chapter 4, we examined how Judy Schachner opens with a physical description of her main character in *The Grannyman*. Sometimes they talk about the characters' likes, dislikes, or traits. In *Amazing Grace*, Mary Hoffman opens with a description of what her main character loves:

> Grace was a girl who loved stories. She didn't mind if they were read to her or told to her or made up in her own head. She didn't care if they were in books or movies or out of Nana's long memory. Grace just loved stories.

In *The Recess Queen* by Alexis O'Neill, the main character is described through a trait:

> Mean Jean was Recess Queen and nobody said any different. Nobody swung until Mean Jean swung. Nobody kicked until Mean Jean kicked. Nobody bounced until Mean Jean bounced.

Another book that uses this same technique is Don Tate's *Poet: The Remarkable Story of George Moses Horton*.

> GEORGE LOVED WORDS. He wanted to learn how to read, but he was enslaved . . .
>
> But that didn't stop George from admiring the language that was all around him . . .
>
> George was determined to learn how to read.

Sometimes an author even begins with what other people say about the characters, as Jerry Spinelli does in *Maniac Magee*:

> They say Maniac Magee was born in a dump. They say his stomach was a cereal box and his heart a sofa spring.
>
> They say he kept an eight-inch cockroach on a leash and that rats stood guard over him while he slept. They say if you knew he was coming and you sprinkled salt on the ground and he ran over it, within two or three blocks he would be as slow as everybody else.
>
> They say.

Introducing Characters Through Settings

Many times the character description is woven into a description of setting. One good example for primary students can be found in *Widget*:

> Widget was a little stray dog. He had no home. He had no friends . . . He saw a house at the end of the road. There was a door just his size. He peeked inside. He saw six cats, six warm beds, and six bowls of hot food.

Pat Mora combines a description of setting with a description of how her main character is feeling in *Tomás and the Library Lady*:

> It was midnight. The light of the full moon followed the tired old car. Tomás was tired too. Hot and tired. He missed his own bed, in his own house in Texas.

In a third-grade classroom, Lynne spoke to the students about doing just that: creating a good beginning for an informational piece or a narrative by placing the main character in a familiar setting. Lynne returned to *Widget* and *Tomás and the Library Lady* to open her discussion with the students on how they might combine a description of character and setting. The students examined other books they had used that year such as Cynthia Rylant's *The Great Gracie Chase* and *Mr. George Baker* by Amy Hest. The students shared their discoveries in whole group, and then Lynne modeled for the students by first placing the people she knew the best in a setting where she could clearly see them. "I would place my dad," she explained, "in the yard pushing the lawn mower or planting bushes and trees. I can see him now in his Bermuda shorts and sneakers, his long skinny legs with his calf muscles bulging. If I close my eyes, I see my grandma in her kitchen with her fingers deep in a doughy mixture. She's dressed just like Mrs. Cleaver in *Leave It to Beaver*—a string of pearls around her neck, a tailored dress, and a pair of low heels. But my mom— I see her sitting somewhere else." She asked the students to try to visualize the setting and the description of her mother as she wrote:

> *Long, slender fingers with perfectly manicured ruby-red nails rest on the ivory keys. They press down gently and the beautiful music, "Lara's Theme" from* Doctor Zhivago, *spills out into the air. I smile at her, and her blue eyes twinkle as she tosses her golden brown hair from her face. I snuggle next to her on the bench, trying to understand the language of the black notes on the page. She smells squeaky clean like Ivory soap. She sighs and stands up, her red-checkered apron still wrapped around her middle. She squeezes me and I squeeze back. She's perfectly perfect. She's my mom.*

The students' responses when Lynne finished clearly indicated that they could see her with her mother at the piano. Together, they discussed how Lynne had used words to effectively help them visualize the scene. Lynne also told them that she had written the scene in the present tense because this strategy often helps her be there in the moment. She gave them the option of writing in past or present tense but told them to make sure they chose a character they knew almost as well as they knew themselves—mother, father, grandfather, grandmother, or caregiver. Together they listed some possible settings for their special person such as the garden, a golf course, at the computer, shopping at the mall, the kitchen, the living room, the bedroom, and the supermarket. Many of the children decided to use their mom. As you can see from Figures 5.2 and 5.3, Lynne's modeling served as an integral part of the lesson.

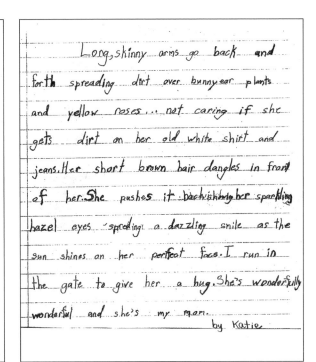

We dive through the shining blue-green water as she puts on sunblock and takes off her sandals. We splash her, and she dives in to get us back. She hides under the blue-green water, and finally we see her blond hair swishing in the water like a waving hand. I wave back at it. She tags me. I'm it! I stare into her pickle-green eyes and ask if I can have a dolphin ride. She smiles and nods slowly at me. I hold onto her back as, we dive in. She's extraordinarily extraordinary, and she's my mommy.

by Alexis

Figure 5.2 Alex's beginning paragraph for a piece about her mom.

Long, skinny arms go back and forth spreading dirt over bunny ear plants and yellow roses... not caring if she gets dirt on her old white shirt and jeans. Her short brown hair dangles in front of her. She pushes it back with her sparkling hazel eyes spreading a dazzling smile as the sun shines on her perfect face. I run in the gate to give her a hug. She's wonderfully wonderful and she's my mom.

by Katie.

Figure 5.3 Katie's beginning paragraph for a piece about her mom.

Other mentor texts that can be used to show students how authors create beginnings where characters are introduced through the setting are *Granddaddy's Turn: A Journey to the Ballot Box* by Michael S. Bandy and Eric Stein, *Yard Sale* by Eve Bunting, and *Ellen's Broom* by Kelly Starling Lyons.

Weather Leads: A Good Place to Start

Probably the best way to help students develop a beginning when they are having trouble getting started is by describing the weather. They hear people talking about the weather all the time. A description of weather will use strong verbs and striking adjectives. It's easy to make a leap and create a simile or metaphor or even use personification. Besides, it helps students show, not tell, the time of day or season. Additionally, use of vivid color words and appeal to the senses help build a strong beginning. Consider these examples from mentor texts we use with our students:

Snow drifted through the streets and now that it was dusk, Christmas trees glittered in the windows.
(from *Too Many Tamales* by Gary Soto)

That winter, snow fell on everything, turning the world a brilliant white.
(from *Each Kindness* by Jacqueline Woodson)

In the month of the Maple Sugar Moon, the snow's too wet for angel making, icicles rain from Grandpa's porch roof, and something is stirring in the woods. It's sugarbush spring.
(from *Sugarbush Spring* by Marsha Wilson Chall)

The snowflakes were resting after their twisting twirling dance through the crisp night air. Every twig in the forest wore a new coat of glimmering white.
(from *Stranger in the Woods* by Carl R. Sams II and Jean Stoick)

After studying a handful of weather beginnings, students are ready to try it out. We have found that starting with a shared experience and working through several different seasons helps students hold on to the strategy so they can use it when they work independently. We ask the students to choose a season and an activity they might be doing as the main character in a narrative. We remind the students to show, not tell, whenever possible. It's usually feasible to ask students to show, not tell the season and the character's feelings. Older students can also add what the character is thinking or feeling to create a good beginning. The following three examples were written as shared writing experiences in second-, fourth-, and fifth-grade classes:

A soft, cool wind blew through my hair as I pushed my new, shiny, royal-blue bike outside into the bright sunlight. Rust-colored leaves crunched under the tar-black wheels as I slowly walked my bike to the corner. My knees were knocking together, and a large lump rose in my throat. I swallowed hard. *I sure hope I don't fall off again on the hard cement,* I thought. It was the sixth time my dad was trying to teach me how to ride my two-wheeler bike that I had received on my birthday. That was two weeks ago, and I still couldn't do it.

Soft, puffy marshmallow clouds were piled high against a robin's-egg-blue blue sky. A balmy breeze tickled the leaves that were already beginning to turn shades of scarlet and gold. Earlier that morning, a light, cold drizzle had threatened to change my mother's mind about driving me to the stables. Now (thank goodness!) the sun was brightly shining on this warmer-than-usual Saturday afternoon. I bounded to the car and promptly rolled down the windows. *Wow!* I thought. *What a great day for my first riding lesson!* I leaned way out the window and yelled, "Hey, Mom, hurry up! I don't want to be late!"

Frosty puffs of breath hung in the air as I sighed deeply. I glanced up at the silvery mountain that was already filled with children and adults zigzagging down the slopes with ease. Following several steps behind my sister through the deep, dry, white snow I silently wished I was back home on the couch with a good book. We sat down on the hard, cold bench, and my sister removed her heavy gloves to strap my boots into the skis. I shivered even though I was wearing long underwear, heavy socks, a sweater, and a warm sea-green parka. *I will never learn to do this,* I thought to myself.

Choosing the Right Lead

The important thing about beginnings is that students have choice. There are many ways to craft a good beginning for narratives and informational pieces. Many of the strategies apply to all the modes of writing. Lynne often models with a narrative she has written that takes place in an amusement park. Her main characters are Billy and Lyddie. The problem is that Billy, who is usually brave, is afraid to ride the roller coaster but does not want to admit his fear to his sister and her friends. She returns to the story to demonstrate how she could craft many different leads for the same text. Revising the lead, or beginning of a piece, can be a powerful revision strategy. Students can make better sense of the different kinds of leads when each is written in the context of one setting. The following examples show the possibilities for Lynne's story:

Onomatopoeia: Clickety, clickety, clickety, clickety. The roller coaster slowly pulled along up the steep hill.

Snapshot Setting: It was hard to walk through the throngs of people—women pushing carriages, kids running and bumping into each other, older couples strolling along arm in arm—as bits of notes floated in between from the merry-go-round, my favorite ride.

Snapshot Character: Billy was not a coward. He just didn't like the twisty, turny rides, especially the ones that turned you upside down. For an eight-year-old, he was usually pretty bold. He even didn't mind sleeping in his own bedroom without a night-light.

Foreshadowing: If only Billy had known that he was tall enough to ride the Rolling Thunder. Why did he always talk before he thought things out?

Simile: The roller-coaster track twisted and turned like an enormous boa constrictor wrapped around the limb of an ancient tree of the rain forest.

Short, Choppy Statement: No. No. I'll never do that again!

Question: Is there any better way to spend a beautiful Saturday than at Great Adventure Amusement Park with your best friends?

Name Statement: I, Lyddie Jones, will never, ever take my younger brother to an amusement park with my best friends.

Action (Suspense): Higher and higher it climbed, until it almost disappeared into the billowing clouds, and all we could hear was the screaming.

Thoughtshot: *Why am I afraid to tell my sister how I feel?* Billy thought to himself.

Dialogue: "Come on, Billy! Hurry! If we run, we can ride in the front car!" Lyddie squealed with excitement.

Exclamation: "Look at how steep that hill in the roller-coaster track is . . . Why, it looks like it stretches to the sun!"

Metaphor: It was a beautiful day, but windy enough to send wispy cloudships sailing through the blue-ocean sky.

Personification: The old cars moaned and groaned as they were pulled up the wooden track by invisible hands.

Appeal to the Senses (other than sound): The sickeningly sweet scent of fear drifted to my nose as I stared at what seemed like miles of roller-coaster tracks. I glanced around me to see if anyone else caught a whiff. Salty beads of sweat had formed on my brow. I wiped them away with clammy hands.

Creepy Statement: The track rose up like a dark spirit across the blue sky, turning my insides to mush.

Weather: A soft rain spattered against the car windows as we drove down the New Jersey Turnpike. But there was a ray of hope, poking between dark clouds with golden spokes.

Quote (what people say): My mother always said that Lyddie should have been born the boy—Lyddie, who was always daring, courageous, and full of life.

Controversial Statement: Amusement parks! They should really be called torture chambers!

Taking a Reader into the Past: When Billy was only two, his grandpa swung him upside down and round and round. At first he giggled and laughed, but when he started sputtering and gagging and spitting up everywhere, he ran for his grandmother, burying his head in the folds of her skirt and crying his eyes out. Yes, that's when my brother must have started hating roller coasters.

A list such as this could be kept on a chart in the writing center or distributed as a handout for students' binders or stapled into the back of their writer's notebooks. As students explore mentor texts, they can label beginnings, add the examples to a chart such as the one above, and try to imitate them. Students should remember that descriptive language in a beginning acts as a hook to reel in the reader. It is worth spending time working and reworking the beginning of a text. Just as E. B. White did in *Charlotte's Web*, students should be given the opportunity to try out many leads to discover which one fits best.

Transitioning to the Middle

Many young writers are uncertain how to move into the middle of their narratives after drafting the lead paragraph. Often, they move to the event where the problem is solved or the most important thing happens, so their stories are over before they really get developed. We want them to have some strategies for creating a bridge—a way to ease into the part of the story where all the action is instead of leaping ahead. This bridge paragraph can be developed in several ways, depending on the author's stylistic purposes and interest for the target audience.

In *The Other Side* by Jacqueline Woodson, the author opens the story with a description of setting and a warning about the fence that separates the black and white communities. Her bridge paragraph is a description of one of the main characters, Annie. The other main character, Clover, is the narrator of the story and describes in this connecting paragraph what she sees from her side of the fence.

> That summer there was a girl who wore a pink sweater. Each morning she climbed up on the fence and stared over at our side. Sometimes I stared back.
>   She never sat on that fence with anybody, that girl didn't.

Her next paragraph begins the action of the middle, a jump-rope scene.

Picture books such as *Crab Moon* by Ruth Horowitz, *Something Beautiful* by Sharon Dennis Wyeth, *Roller Coaster* by Marla Frazee, *Widget* by Lyn Rossiter McFarland, and *Red Kite, Blue Kite* by Ji-li Jiang provide excellent examples of bridge paragraphs. You can ask students to work in pairs to discuss these transition paragraphs and how they work to tell the story. Share in whole group and record on an anchor chart with the students' explanations. For example, the bridge paragraph in *Crab Moon* is a rich description with appeal to the senses of sight, sound, and touch. In Wyeth's text, the author describes a classroom scene where the young girl records her definition of the word *beautiful* in her writer's notebook. This "bridge paragraph" is important.

The actions that follow are the little girl's search throughout the neighborhood for her "something beautiful." The bridge relates to the final actions in this story. Frazee's bridge in *Roller Coaster* helps the story transition by describing the roller coaster itself and the requirement of being tall enough to ride. She brings us to the point of the characters getting into the cars before the middle where the ride and all the action begins.

Creating a bridge paragraph will help our writers get ready to draft the events of the story without jumping ahead too quickly into the main events. As writers of story, we learn to keep our readers waiting and to build excitement and anticipation. The Your Turn lesson "Moving to the Middle" at the end of this chapter will help your students develop strategies for creating a bridge paragraph.

Endings

As with beginnings, there are many ways authors choose to end a story. Sometimes, as in the ending of *Widget, Lilly's Purple Plastic Purse, Fireflies!*, or *Night Tree*, we learn what the character is thinking and feeling. As in *Patches Lost and Found* or *Crab Moon*, sometimes there is a final action. Sometimes the characters learn a lesson as Stellaluna and her friends Pip, Flitter, and Flap do in *Stellaluna* by Janell Cannon, or linger on a memory as the young girl in Chall's *Up North at the Cabin* or the homeless boy in Eve Bunting's *Fly Away Home* do. The important thing is not only that the ending be connected to the story in some way and leave the reader satisfied but also that it be interesting and memorable. As Ralph Fletcher (1993) says, "It is the ending, after all, that will resonate in the ear of the reader when the piece of writing has been finished. If the ending fails, the work fails in its entirety" (92).

To move students beyond thinking that a story ends when they write "The End," we must show them the possibilities that exist for creating satisfying endings. In our classes, we usually begin by returning to the books the students are already familiar with—the mentor texts we have used as read-alouds, whose words and images have found their way into the hearts and minds of our students. We begin by examining them together as a group and then making a chart of types of endings and the books that are examples of each type. (See Figure 5.4.) Students are quick to find books (such as the ones mentioned before) where the author ends with a memory, a thought or feeling, a final action, or a lesson learned.

Depending on the books examined, students also may come up with many other interesting categories to add to the chart. In a second-grade class Rose was working with, one child offered a different category. "Look, Mrs. Cappelli," Timmy said. "In this book [*The Kissing Hand* by Audrey Penn], Chester's kiss is saying 'I love you' to his mother. Could that be a different kind of ending—where something speaks?"

Memory That Lingers	**Final Action**
Granddaddy's Turn by Michael S. Bandy and Eric Stein	*Crab Moon* by Ruth Horowitz
Up North at the Cabin by Marsha Wilson Chall	*Tomás and the Library Lady* by Pat Mora
Fly Away Home by Eve Bunting	*Patches Lost and Found* by Steven Kroll
Betty Doll by Patricia Polacco	*Something from Nothing* by Phoebe Gilman
Hope, Wish, Dream	**Lesson Learned/Decision Reached**
Crab Moon by Ruth Horowitz	*Shortcut* by Donald Crews
Henny by Elizabeth Rose Stanton	*Stellaluna* by Janell Cannon
Lilly's Purple Plastic Purse by Kevin Henkes	*Alejandro's Gift* by Richard E. Albert
The Other Side by Jacqueline Woodson	*Yard Sale* by Eve Bunting
Thoughts or Feelings	**Bookends**
Fireflies! by Julie Brinckloe	*Jessica* by Kevin Henkes
Mama's Nightingale by Edwidge Danticat	*The Sunsets of Miss Olivia Wiggins* by Lester Laminack
Night Tree by Eve Bunting	*One Tiny Turtle* by Nicola Davies
Widget by Lyn Rossiter McFarland	*Miz Berlin Walks* by Jane Yolen
Accomplishments/Discovery	**Starts All Over Again**
Nana in the City by Lauren Castillo	*Chester's Way* by Kevin Henkes
Something Beautiful by Sharon Dennis Wyeth	*Imogene's Antlers* by David Small
When I Was Five by Arthur Howard	*The Relatives Came* by Cynthia Rylant
The Memory String by Eve Bunting	*The Troublemaker* by Lauren Castillo
Amazing Grace by Mary Hoffman	

Figure 5.4
Example of a chart listing possibilities for endings.

"I suppose it could be," Rose answered. "Let's see if we can find that type of ending in any other book." Other students joined Timmy on the search for this unusual ending, and before long they had added *The Wednesday Surprise* and *Someday a Tree*, both by Eve Bunting, to the category labeled "Something Speaks," which they had added to their chart. Sometimes the categories that students create are simple ones such as "Happy Endings," "Funny Endings," or "Surprise Endings." Students should be encouraged to add their thinking to the chart as they make new discoveries. Charts do not have to be completed in one session. Work on them is ongoing in the unit of study—in this case, the study of endings.

As students continue to explore endings, they will discover that the endings of many books fit into more than one category. For example, although Daniel engages in several final actions in *Crab Moon*, he also expresses a wish for something in the future and does so by speaking:

> Slowly and grandly, the crab pulled herself forward. Stepping and pausing, Daniel's feet felt their way into the bay. He followed until she disappeared. Then he gave the water one last, long look and whispered to his horseshoe crab, "See you next summer."

Fireflies! also combines a series of final actions with the emotions of the main character:

> I flung off the covers.
> I went to the window, opened the jar, and aimed
> it at the stars . . .
> The moonlight and the fireflies swam in my tears,
> but I could feel myself smiling.

In *Muncha! Muncha! Muncha!* by Candace Fleming, Mr. McGreely is so happy to have finally outsmarted the bunnies that he picks the vegetables and places them in his basket (final action), only to discover that the bunnies were hiding inside. G. Brian Karas's final illustration shows Mr. McGreely munching the carrots with the bunnies—he has made a decision to share his vegetables. This same technique of using an illustration as part of an ending can also be found in *Click, Clack, Moo: Cows That Type* by Doreen Cronin (pictures by Betsy Lewin), and *An Angel for Solomon Singer* by Cynthia Rylant (pictures by Peter Catalanotto). Both of these books combine a decision with a final action. (See the Your Turn lesson at the end of this chapter on how to use final illustrations to help students create satisfying endings.)

For older students, this categorizing can be expanded to their individual notebooks. Students may actually copy several lines, label the type(s) of endings involved, and give the source (title, author, and page number when appropriate). When students have the opportunity to revisit charts and notebooks, their learning becomes more powerful because it is ongoing. Learning about endings is not a finite process; it continues to develop as the writer develops.

Although we can certainly introduce books that illustrate a variety of types of endings that we think our writers can imitate, it is important to let students explore and discover endings on their own. Using books from library, home, and classroom collections, students can work individually or in pairs to explore endings, adding to class charts or lists in their writer's notebooks. This process of self-discovery will open their minds to the possibilities of creating meaningful and satisfying endings.

We return once again to several favorite mentor texts when our students are ready to craft their own satisfying endings. An easy ending for students to compose is one that reveals the main character's feelings through thoughts or dialogue. In fact, almost all narratives seem to end by revealing the main character's emotions. Although this type of ending can stand by itself, it is also often used in combination with one or more types of endings.

We begin by asking students to retell the stories they have heard many times before. This helps them remember what they were feeling as the stories' endings resonated in their hearts and minds. By doing this, students realize the importance of an ending. The next step is to have students return to a previously written story and revisit the ending. We often ask them to see if there is a place for dialogue or the character's thoughts to help the reader know and understand what the character is feeling. Sometimes we might suggest that the students try to show the character's emotion with a physical description—a wide grin, teary eyes, or arms raised in triumph. Here is an opportunity to make reading and writing connections. Students understand that the most common response a reader makes to a text is a personal connection. It is in the ending that the reader gets the full effect of what has transpired in the story and how it has affected the character. Therefore, it is up to the writer not to lose writing stamina and quit before he or she delivers a satisfying ending.

After revisions are made, students share their endings in small response groups. We encourage the students to act as a writing community and continue to praise and polish. In whole group, the students reflect on how it worked for them—how their endings improved and why they think they did so.

Maggie, a second grader, is just beginning to understand the importance of endings. In the ending of the following piece about a trip to the zoo with her family, she combines her feelings with a wish for the future.

> The sun was shining. It was a wonderful day to go to the zoo. I ran downstairs and said, "Dad, let's go to the zoo!" Dad said OK. We went with Aunt Madeline, Libby, and Max. When we got to the zoo we first went in the monkey house. I smelled a rotten egg smell. I heard crazy ha-has. I felt like I was on a safari. When we got out of the monkey house we saw the penguins. They were black with sharp beaks. I heard them yap and yap as they waddled along then splashed in the water. When it was time to go we walked back to the car. I was TIRED! When I got home I laid on the couch and fell asleep. I can't wait to go back—maybe on the next sunny day.

Kyle, a third grader, effectively added dialogue to a final action to end his story about snowboarding. The explanation attached to the dialogue shows us that Kyle is happy.

> One snowy day when it was icy-cold outside, I put my winter clothes on and made a tunnel to my friend's house with my snowboard. We ran like graceful deer through the snowy grass to Cold Spring Elementary School. It had the best sledding hill ever!
>
> We built a ramp out of snow, packing it down with my snowboard. I tried out the ramp first. I did a 360! Then my friend Brandon used my board and wiped out. My snowboard flew into a tree. CRASH! So we made snowballs and threw them at the snowboard to try to get it loose, but it wouldn't budge.
>
> "We can't throw high enough," I said. Slowly, I tried to climb the ten-foot tree. It did not work. CRASH! I was covered in snow, lying on my back and looking up at the tree that still clutched my snowboard in its arms. But I did not want to give up. "I have a plan!" I shouted.

We dashed home to get basketballs, and to our surprise, when we got back to Cold Spring's hill, the snowboard was on the ground! "How did that happen?" I asked. I picked up my snowboard and looked at the tall spruce tree. "Thanks," I said with a grin. Then I jumped on my snowboard and rocketed off the ramp.

Once students understand the importance of the ending, they can begin to experiment with other types, possibly using them in combination with the thoughts and feelings of the main character(s). It is not enough just to show students a type of ending and assign them to use it. Students need to be able to choose from a variety of endings so that they are sure to use the kind that fits best with the story they are writing. They can learn to recognize that the ending of the story is tied very closely to its beginning.

Writers often plant a seed of their ending in the beginning of their story. We see an example of this in *Shortcut* by Donald Crews. Twice in the opening pages of the book, the narrator tells the reader, "We should have taken the road." The second time he says it, the reader is starting to wonder why that is so. By the end of the story, we realize an important lesson was learned: they should always take the road. In *Alejandro's Gift* by Richard E. Albert, the main character's loneliness is evident from the first page. The reader understands that the resolution will need to deal with the character's emotions. In the end, Alejandro discovers that the gift he has given to the animals is an even greater gift to himself, because he will never be lonely again. In Eve Bunting's *The Wednesday Surprise*, the main character, Anna, helps us understand that a big surprise will be revealed by the end of the story. Bunting has our attention from the start and leaves us thinking about what the best surprise of all could be for Anna's father's birthday.

Students can return to their stories to see whether they have planted the seed of their ending in their beginning and share with a partner or small response group. They should be encouraged to find more examples of stories that clearly connect the beginning to the end and record them in their notebooks. Sometimes students can add one telling detail that will create this effect in their story. In Maggie's original piece about the trip to the zoo with her family, she ended by simply saying, "I can't wait to go back." After a class discussion about endings relating to beginnings and conferencing with her teacher, Maggie decided to add the last part—"maybe on the next sunny day"—to relate it to her beginning.

In Kelly's piece, "The Wave," the beginning clearly contains the seed of the ending. Her story is about plucking up her courage to jump the ocean waves. Kelly's ending is filled with self-discovery and a sense of accomplishment.

Beginning:
On a cool, crisp summer day, I had to face my biggest fear of all. I gulped as I walked with my dad to the dreaded ocean I feared most. I felt that feeling

you get when you know something is very wrong, but mine was a much worse feeling. I put my bare foot on the damp sand and the cool tidewater raced across it. I looked out at the never-ending ocean. I was ready (unless I didn't jump the wave).

Ending:
As soon as I jumped, all the butterflies burst out of my stomach. There I was floating in the freezing water with so much joy and happiness. I knew I could do it if I put my mind to it! I had finally conquered my biggest fear.

Sometimes authors plant the seed of the ending in the title of their story. The reader doesn't realize the significance of the title until the very end. Judy Schachner does this in her book *The Grannyman*: "So it was with the greatest respect that they gave their dear old cat a brand-new name. They called him the Grannyman."

In *A Taste of Blackberries* by Doris Buchanan Smith, we learn the significance of the title in the very last chapter: "'Do you remember,' I asked Jamie in my mind, 'the taste of blackberries?'"

Lynne uses her own example from her story "One Quarter Too Many" when working with her students. Originally, Lynne had titled the story "Darren's Lost Tooth." She wasn't happy with the title and asked her students for revision help. "Sometimes an interesting title is enough to make a reader read on, and sometimes a boring title makes a reader decide not to read the story at all." Her fourth graders read the story and came up with some new titles. When Curtis suggested "One Quarter Too Many," the entire class knew it was the right one. Lynne decided to insert the phrase into her final paragraph. That one revision made the ending more satisfying and provided the link she needed between the beginning and the ending of the story. Several students tried it out right away. In Ashley's story, she describes taking care of her uncle's cat, Meowlie, who is furious at having been left in her care. Her title "Gaining Her Trust" plants the seed of what will eventually transpire:

A jolt of surprise filled me suddenly, and I couldn't believe what I was hearing . . . purring! Her small throat rumbled with pleasure, and I was shocked to find that happen. Stroking her, I was happy—so happy that I felt like dancing and singing. She finally had let me pet her. I had gained her trust. It was an incredibly warm feeling that spread inside me and filled my heart. Meowlie and I were friends.

In Sarah's piece, "Sunday Surprise," about finding a litter of kittens in her garage, we find the title in the very last words. Sarah had been struggling to find a way to close her piece in a meaningful way. When she finally found the right title, she remembered *A Taste of Blackberries* and decided to use the title in the ending. As soon as she made that decision, the words spilled out of her.

That night we called the S.P.C.A. "What happened, Mommy? What happened?" I asked in excitement. Mom explained that the kittens were nursing from a cat that loved them. My mom was wearing a grin. I felt a grin spread across my face, too. I closed my eyes and almost cried with joy. My family had worked together to save the two little angelic kittens we had found in our garage, our Sunday surprise.

Building a Narrative

As we share our writing with our students, we always begin with our thinking. That's what prewriting is—thinking before you write. In one fourth-grade classroom, Lynne returned to *Up North at the Cabin* by Marsha Wilson Chall, a book built on small moments during a special summer spent with grandparents. Next, she showed the students a notebook entry where she had made a two-column chart of important people in her life and some activities and events she connects with those people.

Grandpa and Me	Mom and Me
Long walks in the Poconos	Coloring pictures at card table in the living room when I was sick and had to stay home from school
Swimming at Sailor's Lake and learning how to float	Walking to the library on Wadsworth Avenue
On the Ferris wheel at Dorney Park	Buying clothes for college at the Cameo Shop and Gimbels
Driving around and looking at horses	Eating cheeseburgers and milk shakes at Barson's restaurant as a special treat
Ice-skating on the "pond" Grandpa created for me on the lawn in Coopersburg	"Teaching" me how to drive

Then she shared a notebook entry that came directly from her thinking on the chart. Lynne thinks Chall's book certainly provided the model she needed for the following notebook entry about learning to drive with her mom. In turn, her model may have helped other students in the class. It's a chain reaction. The combination of children's authors and writing teachers as authors is very powerful. After Lynne modeled, her students discussed her piece (as they often do) and her use of proper nouns, color words, present tense, and dialogue in this example:

I slide behind the wheel of the big, sea-green Impala and my mom slides into the passenger seat. She glances at me as I insert the key and turn on the ignition. "Hold on one minute," she says. "Don't be in such a hurry." After a (what seems like forever) review of the brake, gas pedal, and mirrors we are ready.

I pull away from the curb smoothly and drive down Durham Street between parked cars on either side. No problem. We stop at Thouron, and I put on my right blinker and look both ways, pulling out onto the main road. Same thing on Mt. Pleasant, and again on Woolston Avenue.

Finally, we are back on Durham. I pull up beside my father's new, midnight-blue Rambler, and back into the empty spot in front of my house. "There!" I say. My mother is openmouthed. When the words finally come she demands a little too sharply, "Have you ever done this before?"

"Of course not, Mom!" I answer.

We try to model these notebook entries—small units of time that can be expanded into an entire narrative during a writing workshop period—as often as we can. First, we firmly believe that we need to be trusted members of our students' writing community, not just someone who assigns writing as a spectator but never a participant. Second, we need to demonstrate that writers write about what they know. They don't need Disney World vacations or white-water rafting trips to be able to write well. They can write about catching fireflies in their backyards on a warm June night with their friends as Julie Brinckloe describes in *Fireflies!* If they include the juicy details, we can imagine it, too, making connections about our own backyards and warm summer evenings.

Remember Frank's notebook entry, a small moment about fishing with his uncle that we discussed in Chapter 4? When Frank returned to find a possible topic for a complete narrative, he recognized the possibility for this piece. He had already found a spot to explode a moment in time. Now he needed to engage in some self-reflection:

- What is my point, or "so what"?
- What is my purpose for writing this piece?
- Who is my audience?
- If I have already written about the most important event in my story, where should I begin without getting too far away from this event?
- How can I write a satisfying ending? What do my readers (my target audience) need to know and feel to be satisfied?

Since reflection is built into the Your Turn lessons, our students are used to thinking about their writing and how what they have attempted to do helps them become better writers. This self-reflection is one of the most important steps in helping writers of any age continue to move forward.

Frank decided he could use this notebook entry to write a narrative, but he needed a new beginning. He wanted his readers to understand the special relationship he had with his uncle and why this was such a special moment in his life. He thought his ending was a good one—just a splash of dialogue that helped his readers understand what he and his uncle were thinking and feeling. In a conference with Frank, Lynne agreed and added that another reason she enjoyed the ending was that she could infer that Frank was going to throw the fish back because of its size. Readers like to be good detectives when they read.

Fishing with My Uncle Frank
by Frank

My bedroom is still dark as my mom shakes me awake. "Your uncle is on the way," she whispers into my ear as I try to pull the covers closer. Then I remember. Today is my first fishing trip ever, and the best thing about it—I get to spend an entire day with Uncle Frank (my namesake) without my two younger sisters. I leap from the bed like a young dolphin showing off for his friends. Two hours later I am at the seashore, breathing in the salt air.

I am wearing my Scooby-Doo life jacket. "Hold on!" my uncle says as we leave the spring-boarded dock. As we start to pull away, the old gas motor smells like a thunderstorm that has just finished. I throw my grass-green and Crayola-purple jig into the water.

All of a sudden . . . PLOP! My rod dips into the water like an Oreo when you dunk it into cotton-white milk. My uncle and I watch our lines and the water. My hands are wet and clammy with anticipation. *If only I can bring home a fish today,* I think to myself. Hours pass . . . nothing. Then I feel a little tug. I wait. Yes, there it is again. Or is it just my imagination?

Yes! There it is again! The line is bowed and I feel the tension as the fish (It must be a fish?) pulls hard to get away. I struggle to lift him up out of the water. I feel salty sweat stinging my eyes, but there is no hand free to brush the sweat away. My toes are smashed against the side of the boat and causing me great pain. Why did I take my sneakers off? I concentrate on the task at hand, my heart beat, beat, beating in my chest with excitement. All of a sudden, I yank the rod, and my prize is dangling in the air. The battle that takes me a long five minutes is definitely worth it!

"Fifteen-and-a-half-inch flounder," I yell. So close, I think, but I'm proud about my first flounder that smells like a skunk's spray.

"Half an inch and he is almost a keeper!" my uncle yells back.

Sometimes we share before we ask the students to write in their notebooks. Other times, we share with a student during a writing conference. Additionally, we share bits and pieces of our writing when we join a peer response group on a particular day. It is important to show students that writing is much more interesting when we develop a few high-quality ideas rather than write in list fashion. We are careful to model with events that our students can relate to and enjoy. We want them to find everyday moments that can be expanded by details, dialogue, appeal to the senses, thoughtshots, and anecdotes as well as by adding powerful beginnings and satisfying endings. We want them to understand the importance of writing for a target audience. We want them to understand the importance of all the story elements and how they work together to create a narrative. Most important of all, we want our students to learn how to slow down and write small to write big. By slowing down the writing, they will be able to add the content that develops their ideas. It will make their writing as big as life.

The Importance of a Road Map

Mentor texts provide road maps for students to follow. It is important that students almost have the text in its entirety in their heads before they try to imitate it. They don't need every detail, but they do need a story map. Noting powerful beginnings and satisfying endings through read-alouds, literature circle discussions, and conference time will help students internalize the strategies authors use to create a text worth reading. Francisco, an English language learner, wrote the following story as a fifth grader. It was his first year in the United States. The influence of the mentor texts *Fireflies!* and *Crab Moon* is evident. Francisco also tried several different leads before he settled on using a name statement. But as you can see, it is quickly followed by a description of setting and character.

A Bird Called Pipo
by Francisco

It was afternoon and I, Francisco Goncalves, was studying my Portuguese vocabulary. I was in my house, a yellow building with a gigantic palm-tree rounded by rocks on its front, with my grandma Beatriz. She has gray hair and green eyes and is not a very tall person. I already towered above her by almost a head.

It was hot and I was sweaty, so I decided to take a shower to cool off. After I took my shower, I was surprised to see something falling from the window—something black and small. I ran to the door.

"A bird!" I exclaimed. "Surely he broke his wing if he fell from the palm tree. It is like diving to the death!" The palm tree towered over everything else—even the house. It was gigantic. I gently picked him up. The bird seemed to know I was trying to help. "He needs a name if I'm going to keep him. Aaaa . . . Pipo! Yah! Great name! Hi, Pipo!"

When I brought him home, I explained to everybody what had happened. After that, I put a bandage on Pipo's wing. Later that evening, I grabbed a box and make some holes on it so that Pipo could breathe. I put a one-inch cup of water and a cup with food (bread and grains) so that Pipo could eat and drink.

"Dinner!" Mom yelled.

After dinner, I brushed my teeth and went to bed. It was hard to get to sleep because I kept wanting to check on my new feathered friend. Finally, I could not keep my eyes open.

"Good night, Pipo," I whispered softly. Pipo whistled. He seemed to understand.

When I woke up, Mom and I had a talk about Pipo's presence at home. "He's mine!" I yelled. "I gave him a name . . . a home!"

"Son, you have to understand that nature is his home, not here, and he is already cured," Mom replied.

I thought, and thought and finally arrived to a conclusion . . . She was right. I hated her at this moment . . . but she was right. This was not his place. I grabbed the box and now that we were outside, I opened the box and freed him.

With a jump he flew and flew until he disappeared. "Good-bye, Pipo. Good luck!" I called after him. I waved my hand and grinned even though my eyes were filled with salty tears.

Think About It—Talk About It—Write About It

- How do you help your students learn how to develop the setting in their narratives?
- What kinds of leads do your students most often use? What kinds of leads do you think they are ready to learn?
- What lessons do you use to help your students create a satisfying ending to a narrative? How do you help them understand which type of ending works best for a specific piece?
- What read-alouds do you already use in your classroom that would make wonderful models for story structure?
- Find a small moment in your writer's notebook (or write one) and try expanding it into a complete narrative with a beginning, a middle, and an end.

Your Turn Lesson 1

Creating a Physical Description of a Character Using Roald Dahl

Roald Dahl's character descriptions are wonderful models of how an author brings readers into a book by helping them visualize the character and experience the mood created by the description. Often, snapshots of a character are sprinkled throughout a book, but many books begin with a snapshot of a setting or a character, and many times, it is a combination of both. A snapshot is a photograph in words. It is useful in informational and persuasive modes of writing as well as narrative. We chose to use Dahl as a mentor author because his characters are bigger than life and seem to walk right off the page.

Hook: Read excerpts of Roald Dahl's *Matilda*, using the physical description from the chapter titled "The Trunchbull." Display the description and read it several times. Continue to share descriptions of characters from other Dahl books such as *James and the Giant Peach* or *The BFG*. See the examples included here.

> *The giant took off his black cloak and hung it against the wall. Sophie saw that under the cloak he was wearing a sort of collarless shirt and a dirty old leather waistcoat that didn't seem to have any buttons. His trousers were faded green and were far too short for his legs. On his bare feet he was wearing a pair of ridiculous sandals that for some reason had holes cut along each side, with a large hole at the end where his toes stuck out.*
> —*The BFG* by Roald Dahl

> *That face of hers was the most frightful and frightening thing I have ever seen. Just looking at it gave me the shakes all over. It was so crumpled and wizened, so shrunken and shriveled, it looked as though it had been pickled in vinegar. It was a fearsome and ghastly sight. There was something terribly wrong with it, something foul and putrid and decayed. It seemed quite literally to be rotting away at the edges, and in the middle of the face around the mouth and cheeks, I could see the skin all cankered and worm-eaten, as though maggots were working away in there.*
> —*The Witches* by Roald Dahl

After sharing many of Dahl's books as read-alouds, explore other favorites to find snapshots of characters. Options: *Charlotte's Web* by E. B. White, *Stone Fox* by John Reynolds Gardiner, *Olivia Saves the Circus* by Ian Falconer, *My Ol' Man* by Patricia Polacco, and *A Bike Like Sergio's* by Maribeth Boelts.

Purpose: *One important strategy to build a narrative is to create descriptions for the characters and settings. As you can see, Dahl chooses to create a vivid painting in our minds of each of his characters. He describes what they look like, even telling us what they are wearing, and they become very real to us. Today we are going to write some snapshots of people who may have appeared or who will appear in our personal narratives and memoirs. We can use this strategy when we create essays about famous people or as a way to open a research report around a historical event by using a snapshot of one or more key players in that event.*

Brainstorm: Ask students to turn and talk with a partner or small group about characters they are familiar with in real-world experiences or ones they can vividly recall from books. Have them jot down ideas for characters in their notebooks and, in whole group, share some of their thinking.

Model: The paragraph below is intended as a model for upper elementary and middle school children.

> *I am going to use Roald Dahl's descriptions to write my own lead paragraph about my riding instructor. It is important to choose a character who is familiar to me. As I write, I am going to think about the feelings that I associate with that person and the specific times or events that I remember. It will help me when I decide to create an entire draft during writing workshop.*

> *His long nose unevenly divided a face that was strong, noble, and weather-beaten. The china-blue eyes spelled mischief as well as cynicism, and the long (much too long) gray-blond locks lazily curled this way and that. On the right side, he often tucked them behind his one good earlobe. The other lobe, half removed after a mishap with the Jeep and a telephone pole on a whiskey-soaked summer evening, would not hold back the wealth of hair, so he often raised a large hand to brush away the hair from his face. He towered above all of us, his enormous frame filling the doorway. We were crazy about him, thrilled by his British accent and willing to obey every command if he so much as smiled in our direction.*

Shared/Guided Writing: Ask students to choose something from the class list of characters or something else they think of and write a lead paragraph that describes their main character. Make sure that all the students have examples from various books or samples from Dahl's books. Display the sample model on the board or chart paper, making sure it is visible to the class. Students can share their drafts with a partner and talk about what they have revealed about their character through their description. Ask struggling or younger writers to orally write first by talking about their ideas with a partner. The teacher can model this technique with another student. Another helpful strategy is to get the students to draw a picture of their character before they begin to write.

Independent Writing: Ask students to revisit a draft or a finished portfolio piece. Revise the lead paragraph to include a vivid snapshot of a character. If they are ready, students can begin a new draft for a narrative. Furthermore, students can use this strategy to begin an informational essay or research piece with a snapshot of a character where it is applicable. For example, informational reports about the Civil War could begin with a description of Robert E. Lee or Ulysses S. Grant or both (in a comparison format). It is always a good idea to have young writers share their writing with a partner, with a small response group, or in the general sharing session of writing workshop.

Reflection: Students can turn and talk with a partner about their lead paragraphs.

How did the description of character help your readers (peer response group/teacher) visualize him or her?

How did your snapshot of the character help create a certain mood for the story or essay?

What strategies did you use to create a strong, clear description of the character?

How can you use "show, don't tell" strategy here?

Where would you use this strategy—a snapshot of a character in the lead paragraph or scattered throughout your draft—again?

Your Turn Lesson 2

Crafting a Lead Sentence

Many young writers are still developing their understanding of more complex language structures. Sometimes we can assist in this development by borrowing the syntax of the authors of our mentor texts. Students can then play around with word substitutions as they internalize the structure and make it part of their schema.

Hook: The first sentence of *Too Many Tamales* by Gary Soto provides an excellent model of a beginning that describes the setting. Other books with openings that work well with this type of activity are *Owl Moon* by Jane Yolen and *Nana in the City* by Lauren Castillo.

Purpose: *Writers, today I'm going to show you how you can borrow an author's sentence structure to help you write an opening sentence. We've talked about the different ways that authors begin their stories. Today we're going to practice writing an opening sentence that helps the reader visualize the setting.*

Brainstorm: Write the first line of *Too Many Tamales* on the board or overhead with three important words underlined:

> <u>Snow drifted</u> through the streets and now that it was <u>dusk</u>, Christmas trees glittered in the windows.

Ask students to brainstorm other nouns that could be used in place of *snow*. These could be weather related or seasonal. Begin a new column, and list verbs that might be used with some of the nouns listed (they don't have to be lined up next to the noun they will be used with). Make a third column of words that could be used in place of *dusk*. These would relate to time. For example, a list might include the following:

rain	poured	morning
sunshine	pelted	dawn
hail	drizzled	twilight
wind	shone	evening
clouds	filtered	night
leaves	pounded	afternoon
flowers	blew	fall
pumpkins	scattered	autumn

Model: Use some of the words from the list to replace the underlined words in the original sentence. Revise the rest of the sentence as needed. Here are two examples:

Leaves scattered through the streets and now that it was autumn, jack-o'-lanterns glowed in the windows.

Flowers bloomed in the garden and now that it was summer, butterflies flew from bloom to bloom.

Shared/Guided Writing: Invite students to try creating new sentences just like you did. You may want to start with a shared experience, and then invite students to work in pairs or individually.

Independent Writing: Ask students to return to a notebook entry or a piece they already wrote that could be revised to begin with a sentence that describes the setting. The use of this structure does not necessarily have to be the opening sentence, but generally would be part of the beginning. Students could also be given the option of using a sentence they created to begin a new piece of their own.

Reflection: After students share their revisions or new beginnings, ask them to reflect on what they did.

How did using this sentence structure help you begin?

How did your piece improve by beginning with a description of setting?

How did the words you used help the reader visualize the setting?

Is the setting important to what you are writing about?

When could you use this again? Would you change anything?

Option: Students can post the sentences they composed in a writing center. Other students can borrow them as leads for new pieces.

Your Turn Lesson 3

Moving to the Middle

Lead paragraphs introduce the main character and establish the setting of a story. Sometimes they hint at the story's problem, but often the problem surfaces in the middle of the story. One way to show students how to move seamlessly from the beginning to the middle is through a bridge paragraph that describes the setting, a character, an object, or an event. The bridge paragraph acts as a link to move the story forward. For our youngest writers, this bridge could be one or two sentences.

Hook: A good mentor text for this lesson is *Crab Moon* by Ruth Horowitz. Return to this book and examine how Horowitz transitions from the end of the lead on the second page to the first event. She transitions by describing the mother and son's walk from the cabin to the ocean, appealing to several senses and painting a picture in the reader's mind.

> *That night, the fat, round face of the full moon wavered on the surface of the water.*
> *The path felt cool under Daniel's feet. As the beam of their flashlight swept the beach, he drew a sharp breath.*

Other books that could be used for this lesson are *Last Stop on Market Street* by Matt de la Peña, *A Bike Like Sergio's* by Maribeth Boelts, *Fireflies!* by Julie Brinckloe, *Widget* by Lyn Rossiter McFarland, and *Who Wants Broccoli?* by Val Jones.

Purpose: *Writers, today we will practice how to move from the beginning of a story into the middle with a few transition sentences, just like Ruth Horowitz does in* Crab Moon.

Brainstorm: Ask students to brainstorm some settings for a story, such as the school cafeteria, the school playground, a neighborhood park, a swim club, a sledding hill, a soccer field, or an amusement park. Then go back and attach some possible events or problems that could happen in each place. For example, for the school playground you might have a kickball tournament, not getting chosen for a game, losing your glasses, or not realizing your class has returned to the classroom.

Model: Choose an idea and write a lead paragraph. Then model how you will transition into the action of the plot using a bridge paragraph. An example for losing glasses on the playground might go like this:

Lead Paragraph
"Class, time to line up for recess," Mrs. Hall announced. I furiously scribbled the last sentence of my story before sliding it into my folder. The rest of the class had already lined up so I

grabbed my jacket, slipped it on, and got in line. I realized too late that I had forgotten to take off my new glasses and put them away, so I just slipped them into my coat pocket.

Bridge Paragraph

Kids were already spilling out onto the playground. Balls were bouncing on the blacktop or flying through the air into hoops. I ran across the blacktop to the soccer field where a game was about to begin. The air was so warm and humid that I was already roasting. I took off my jacket, threw it on the ground, and dashed to take my spot on the field.

Shared/Guided Writing: Ask students to return to the brainstormed list and choose a different setting and problem. Together, write a beginning to introduce the main character(s) and/or the setting of the story. Then create a bridge paragraph to move the story into the action. If students need more practice, have them work with a writing partner to create another example.

Independent Writing: Have students return to a narrative they are currently working on or have already published. Ask them to try out a bridge paragraph as a way to move into the action in the middle of their story. Alternatively, they can choose an idea from the brainstormed list and create the beginning and transition for a new story.

Reflection: *What strategies did you use to create your bridge (transition) paragraph?*

How did the use of a bridge paragraph help your story?

Was the crafting of a bridge paragraph easy or hard for you? Explain.

Do you think this technique is appropriate for all your narratives? Why or why not?

Can you find other examples of bridge paragraphs in class read-alouds, your independent reading, or stories shared in peer conferences?

Your Turn Lesson 4

Adding a Satisfying Ending

There are many ways in which authors end their stories. As we discussed in this chapter, the most satisfying endings relate to the story in some way. For young writers, understanding that endings often include what the main character is thinking or feeling, a final action or decision, a wish for the future, or a lesson learned provides enough choice for them to begin to craft their own endings.

Hook: Choose some of the mentor texts you have been using in the classroom and examine the endings closely with the students. Look for books that have the types of endings you think your students can imitate in their own stories such as thoughts and feelings, final actions, wishes for the future, lessons learned, or discoveries made. Many of the books listed in the Treasure Chest of Books for this chapter are good resources. If you write the endings out on chart paper, they can be posted in the classroom. You might try underlining the words that describe the feelings, final actions, or future wishes.

> Lilly <u>ran and skipped and hopped and flew</u> all the way home, she was so happy.
> (final action)
> And she <u>really did want to be a teacher when she grew up</u>.
> (future wish)

Purpose: *As we have been discussing, endings are very important to any piece of writing. Since the ending is the last thing you will leave your reader with, it must be memorable and satisfying. A story without a good ending is like eating cake without the icing—there is something missing. Today I will show you how you can write that kind of ending—one that satisfies the reader—in your own stories.*

Brainstorm: In this case, brainstorming is closely tied to the use of literature in the hook. As students examine books and discover different types of endings, they are actually engaging in a type of brainstorming.

Model: Either read a previous notebook entry of your own or compose a new entry in front of the students. Stop before the ending and think aloud about how you would incorporate the parts of a satisfying ending as you compose it. If it is a personal narrative, be sure to include your thoughts and feelings as the main character and perhaps combine it with a final action, a future wish, a lesson learned, or a memory.

Shared/Guided Writing: Ask students to return to a previous notebook entry or piece of writing and consider how the ending could be revised. Invite some students to offer their pieces for group revision, or hold a guided conversation in front of the group. For example, Angela, a second grader, wrote a short narrative about how she and her brothers had built a snowman. It ended with the sentence "And this is how we made the snowman." Through guided conversation, Rose learned that it was the first time the children had finished a snowman complete with accessories (eyes, nose, scarf, and hat), all of which was part of the description of the event. With a little more questioning and some help from the class, the ending was revised as follows:

> *My brothers and I were all exhausted by the time we finished!*
> *We sipped hot chocolate and thought about how working*
> *together made it happen. We hoped our snowman would last*
> *for a very long time.*

Rose guided the students to realize that this ending matched the story of Angela and her brothers working together to create the snowman.

Independent Writing: Ask students to continue revisions of previous pieces. Students may also wish to start new pieces and concentrate on a satisfying ending.

Reflection: After students have the opportunity to revise or write, ask them to share in whole group or small group. The following questions can help guide their thinking:

> *How did your ending change?*
>
> *How is it satisfying?*
>
> *Does the ending you wrote fit the story?*
>
> *Would a different ending be better?*
>
> *What kinds of things should you think about as you write an ending to a piece?*

Your Turn Lesson 5

Building an Ending Using the Final Illustration(s)

Hook: Choose some mentor texts that use pictures to show characters' emotions, thoughts, and/or final actions to add to the author's last words (or, in some cases, to become the text) to create a satisfying ending. One of our favorites to use is the last page in *Widget* by Lyn Rossiter McFarland. Find a mentor text that ends with a final illustration or one where the picture could be used to create the text for the ending (you will cover any text on the final page, as is the case with Widget, when you return to it as your model).

Options include *An Angel for Solomon Singer* by Cynthia Rylant; *Click, Clack, Moo: Cows That Type* by Doreen Cronin; *Bunny Cakes* by Rosemary Wells; *The Baby Sister* by Tomie dePaola; *The Troublemaker* by Lauren Castillo; and *Muncha! Muncha! Muncha!* by Candace Fleming.

Purpose: *Authors try to balance telling with showing. In picture books, illustrations can show emotions and actions—even relationships between characters. We can imagine what the characters are thinking. Writers, today we will use the emotions, thoughts, and actions that illustrators reveal through their pictures to help us describe them in words and practice writing a satisfying ending.*

Brainstorm: Return to the text that transitions to the ending of *Widget* and share:

> "I didn't know you had a dog," said a neighbor.
> "Oh yes," said Mrs. Diggs.
> "It's nice to have a dog. Right, girls?"

Then display the final illustration with a document imager or project it on a whiteboard. If there is any text on this final page, cover it in some way so that only the picture is showing. Ask students how the illustrator helped to convey the feelings and thoughts of the main characters when they look at the picture. What are the cats and Widget doing on the final page? List the responses on a chart or the board. In the example from *Widget*, illustrator Jim McFarland surrounds Widget with the six cats. Students' responses might sound like this (these are actual responses from Jen Kennedy's second-grade class):

> The cats are rubbing against Widget.
> They are probably purring.
> Widget knows he has a home forever.
> The girls are waving their tails to show how happy they feel to have a brother.
> They are looking at him with love in their eyes.
> It looks like they are smiling.
> Widget is happy to finally have a family of his own.
> They think he is their hero.

Model: Take the responses from the students in the brainstorming session and show them how you would use them to create the text or add to the existing text for the page. For Widget, you might write the following:

> *The girls gathered around Widget. They pressed against him, rubbing and arching their backs. Soft purring rhythms filled the air. The cats almost smiled, gazing at their hero with love in their eyes. They wanted Widget to stay. He would have a home forever!*

Discuss the strategies you used to create this ending such as final actions, a final decision, and what the main characters are thinking and feeling.

Shared/Guided Writing: Choose another final picture from a different text. In a whole-class shared writing experience, decide on the feeling(s), possible thinking, and final actions that have been created by the illustration, and chart responses that describe the picture in a show-don't-tell fashion. Then write your ending using the picture clues, the original problem presented in this story, and the strategies we have identified in the satisfying endings of our mentor texts. Repeat the process with a small group if writing satisfying endings is completely new to your young writers or if you have discovered that they have experienced difficulty with endings.

Independent Writing: Ask the students to return to a previous story where they may have made use of illustrations as well to show the ending. If the students do not have a final illustration for a story they'd like to work with, then ask them to sketch an ending for a story of their choice in their writer's notebook. Next, have them add details to their final picture to create a sense of feelings, characters' final thoughts, or final actions. Finally, ask them to add text that would match the illustration and create a satisfying ending.

Reflection: *Think how final illustrations help you find the words you need to express the feelings and actions of the characters. How did the final illustration in the mentor text help you think about the words you needed to write a satisfying ending?*

What strategies did we use in our shared experience to create a satisfying ending with words?

How did your sketch or final illustration help you create an ending for the story you chose to work on? What strategies did you use?

Why is it important to write a satisfying ending?

Chapter 6

Using Scaffolds to Organize Texts

How to make a text work together in interesting, efficient ways is a challenge all writers face . . . We try to oversimplify this aspect of writing, teaching students to write everything either as a story with a chronological beginning, middle, and end, or as an essay with three to five paragraphs . . . but I believe that for students to write well, they need a repertoire of structural understandings that go beyond these two basic forms.

—Katie Wood Ray, *Wondrous Words*

When Rose's daughter, Ann, was quite young, they went into Philadelphia to see a performance of *The Nutcracker*. As they were walking to the theater, they passed a construction site. Because it was a weekend, there were no workers about, but you could clearly see a building emerging behind the elaborate scaffolds that were assembled. Ann inquired about the reason for the boards and platforms, and Rose explained that it was a scaffold—a framework to support the workmen and their materials while they built the structure. "Look beyond the boards," she explained, "and try to envision what will soon be finished. Without the framework, the workers could not do their job."

So it is with young writers. They need a scaffold, a framework, to help them do their job. As with buildings, sometimes the scaffolds are temporary, providing the words necessary to help developing writers organize their thinking. These framing words can stay and become part of the structure, or they can be taken away, allowing the writing to stand on its own. Sometimes the scaffold is more permanent, providing an internal structure to help writers organize their ideas. Almost always, the scaffold becomes part of a writer's schema. It gets in the head and finds its place in the context of what a writer knows about writing. Katie Wood Ray (1999) tells us that by having our young writers study the work of well-loved authors, we can help them envision possibilities for ways to structure words and texts.

Organizational Scaffolds in Children's Literature

Children's literature provides our students with endless possibilities for imitating scaffolds that authors use to help organize their texts in interesting and meaningful ways. Sometimes the scaffolds are in the form of words. For example, Sarah L. Thomson uses a simple phrase to scaffold her creative thinking about the paintings of Rob Gonsalves in two picture books: *Imagine a Day* and *Imagine a Night*.

> imagine a day . . .
> . . . when everything you build touches the sky.
> (from *Imagine a Day*)

> imagine a night . . .
> . . . when candlelight rises on butterfly wings to greet the lonely stars.
> (from *Imagine a Night*)

Every page in both books begins with the phrase "imagine a day" or "imagine a night."

Sometimes authors use one internal structure such as questions to organize the whole book. The question structure in *Ask Me* by Bernard Waber helps us know the main character through the series of questions her father asks her as they walk through their neighborhood. Sometimes, the little girl prompts her father to ask her the questions: "Ask me if I like ice cream cones." At other times, the father questions her response. (It is interesting to note that the whole book is written in dialogue without traditional punctuation. The speakers are identified by the color of the print.)

Have You Heard the Nesting Bird? by Rita Gray is an interesting book with which to study organizational scaffolds. The scaffold that is most noticeable is the question "Have you heard the nesting bird?" Rita Gray also uses rhyming, onomatopoeia so that we hear the songs of all the other birds mentioned throughout the book, and the scaffold of time moving from early morning to the evening and into the next day. The question scaffold is also employed in the back matter, where the author conducts an interview with the nesting bird, a robin.

By introducing our young writers to the organizational scaffolds authors use, we can help them envision new possibilities for their writing. One way to accomplish this is to engage our students in writing text innovations, a technique in which teachers and students collaborate to compose parallel versions of books using the author's scaffold, but changing the topic or subject and perhaps sometimes varying the structure itself. *Brown Bear, Brown Bear, What Do You See?* by Bill Martin Jr., *I Went Walking* by Sue Williams, *I Know It's Autumn* by Eileen Spinelli, and *When I Was Little* by Jamie Lee Curtis provide easy scaffolds for shared writing lessons. Shared writing provides a context in which writers can try out a particular writing strategy or, in this case, experiment with a specific structure, by collaborating with their teacher and peers to compose text. A shared writing experience offers the model and practice necessary to writers who may not yet be ready to try something on their own. By helping to construct the text and participating in reading and rereading it, developing writers are better able to internalize the structure and will be more likely to use it independently. The following is a compare/contrast scaffold from *When I Was Little* by Jamie Lee Curtis:

> When I was little, I . . .
> Now I'm . . .

It could easily be changed or adapted for writers to talk about ages, grade levels, or even seasons:

> When it was winter . . .
> Now that it's spring . . .

In *When Spring Comes* by Kevin Henkes, two repeated refrains help the reader move through the book to experience the arrival of spring and all the treasures it brings us. The book begins at the end of winter, and Henkes shows us through words and illustrations what will happen when winter disappears:

Before Spring comes, the grass is brown.
But if you wait, Spring will turn it green and add little flowers.

When using this book as a mentor text for upper elementary or middle school students, you will want to point out how the scaffold changes within the book and at the very end. For example, Henkes describes spring weather and talks about all the rain. He stops to question and comment directly to the reader. Henkes changes the scaffold ever so slightly to bring closure to the book and let the reader know that even when spring is finally here, there will be more waiting—for the next season, summer. Sometimes the scaffold can become an innovation in itself.

Margaret Wise Brown does something similar to Henkes, but in a slightly different way. She uses a basic scaffold that bookends her text on each page of *The Important Book*. However, she varies the sentence structures within the scaffold to maintain a fresh, unique quality for each page.

When we point out to students how authors sometimes vary their own structures, we allow them to come up with unique text innovations that fit their particular needs and their writing voices. Here is one class's shared writing experience that borrows the bookend scaffold from *The Important Book* but varies the structure within:

The important thing about school is that it has books.
It is true that its halls are silent in summer,
But they are filled with voices from September to June.
It is a place to make new friends.
It has kind teachers.
But the important thing about school is that it is filled with books.

After a shared writing experience using the scaffold, students are ready to write their own pieces. William, a third-grade English language learner, wrote the following:

The important thing about shoes is that you wear them.
Shoes protect your feet from the hard sidewalk.
They come in different sizes.
You can buy them in all the colors of the rainbow.
They can help you run faster.
There is a multitude of different types of shoes.
Shoes are fun to wear because you can do a lot of stuff with them.
But the important thing about shoes is that you wear them.

The paragraph structure in *The Important Book* can be modified to create a more sophisticated scaffold for older students. It also can be adapted for use in writing informational or persuasive pieces. In a third-grade class, Lynne took the opportunity to use the scaffold from *The Important Book* to synthesize information the students had learned about the *Mayflower*. She wanted them to understand the value of oral writing to help them organize their thinking before composing independent drafts. Oral writing is a prewriting experience where students can get their ideas flowing without being intimidated by putting pencil to paper. Like shared writing, oral writing is a particularly useful strategy for reluctant writers or at-risk writers as well as ESL students, but everyone can benefit.

After reading and discussing many texts that described the *Mayflower* and its voyage across the Atlantic, Lynne asked the students to share with a partner some of the interesting and important facts they remembered without returning to the books. By relying on their memories only, the students were offering the ideas that really stuck in their heads, the ones that were important to them. The books could be revisited at a later time for clarification, if needed. In whole group, Lynne recorded their responses on the whiteboard. Using this information, she modeled how to orally write a paragraph using the scaffold that she had created. The students immediately recognized the similarity to *The Important Book*. Lynne scanned the board for each idea that she thought could be meaningfully placed in each sentence, with the following result:

> *The important thing about the* Mayflower *is that it carried the Pilgrims to the New World. It had several sails that filled with wind to move it across the water. Another interesting fact is that it had a poop deck. I also learned that it was really a cargo ship that mainly carried barrels of wine. Something that surprised me was that the* Mayflower *was a good-smelling ship for its day. Most of the ships smelled like rotten garbage. But the important thing about the* Mayflower *is that it carried the Pilgrims to the New World.*

Together, Lynne and the class used oral writing to create a new paragraph, still using facts from the board. Some of the information was repeated or moved to a new place (they loved talking about the poop deck!). Next, the students were invited to create oral paragraphs with a partner. Finally, they independently wrote their own paragraphs about the *Mayflower*. It is important to note that many students returned to this scaffold on their own later in the year to write about people, places, or events they had researched. Oral writing and shared writing are powerful teaching tools, used alone or together, to help broaden the boundaries of organization within a writer's schema. When we help students recognize the scaffolds that authors use to organize their ideas, they are freed from the limitations of using a structure such as *first, next, then, finally* over and over. Although this structure seems to work well if you are giving directions on how to bake a cake or build a snowman, it doesn't fit every writing scenario. Different genres and modes of writing require different thought processes and different formats. When we make our students aware of the many structures authors use, they have a better understanding of how to organize their writing in a logical and meaningful way.

The Seesaw Scaffold

One of the easiest scaffolds for young writers to discover and imitate is the see-saw scaffold. Books such as *Fortunately* by Remy Charlip or *That's Good! That's Bad!* by Margery Cuyler bring the up-and-down motion of a seesaw to the back-and-forth structure of words.

While Rose was in a second-grade classroom assisting with writing conferences one day, she had the opportunity to suggest this scaffold to a budding writer. Rose pulled her chair next to Amanda, who was obviously proud of the piece she had written about her new puppy. "Tell me about your work today, Amanda," Rose began.

"Oh! We just got this new puppy, and he's so funny and does all these crazy and sometimes bad things, but he's really good, too, and well . . . just listen," Amanda gushed.

Rose realized that Amanda wrote much like she talked, in a random-thought way that just spilled out onto the page. Her piece lacked organization, and Rose immediately thought of the seesaw structure as a way to help her. She gave Amanda several books with a seesaw scaffold and suggested that she think about how the authors had organized their thoughts. Rose helped Amanda identify the seesaw scaffold and then guided her into thinking about how her piece might look if it were written in this way. Together they separated all the good, cute, and lovable things the puppy did from the naughty and mischievous things. Amanda then decided which things went together best. She talked it out, first using oral writing—trying it on for size, so to speak. Katie Wood Ray (1999) reminds us that it doesn't help writers just to read and think about how authors structure their pieces; they must also envision it for themselves. Then they are more likely to internalize it and add it to their schema for organization.

Sometimes the seesaw scaffold is not found within the entire book but in certain short passages when an author wants to emphasize a specific point. In *Tough Boris* by Mem Fox, we are introduced to Boris von der Borch, a gruff pirate who, as it turns out, has a sensitive side. The author describes him using the following lines:

> He was tough.
> All pirates are tough.
> He was massive.
> All pirates are massive.

Students can imitate a partial seesaw scaffold for nonfiction writing as Martin Jenkins does in *Chameleons Are Cool*:

> Some lizards eat bananas—chameleons don't.
> Some lizards walk upside down on the ceiling—chameleons can't.

There's even a lizard that glides from tree to tree—a chameleon certainly wouldn't do that!

Duck! Rabbit! by Amy Krouse Rosenthal uses a seesaw scaffold to present arguments for two different points of view. The narrators use the illustrations (what they are actually seeing) to give evidence for their opinion. The scaffold changes at the end when they start to see things from the other's perspective. As an extra plus, the author makes use of a circular structure at the very end.

Kate Messner's books *Over and Under the Snow* and *Up in the Garden and Down in the Dirt* use extended seesaw structures to provide us with a close look at nature's winter world and garden activities in springtime. Through the conversations, thoughtshots, and actions of the characters, readers develop an understanding of what is happening above and below the ground.

Up in the garden, there's so much to eat! Ladybugs feast on aphids. Nana crunches green beans. I bite a ripe tomato, warm from the sun. Juice dribbles down my chin.
    Down in the dirt, a robin's beak finds a cricket, a beetle, a grub. Slugs are scrumptious, too.
(from *Up in the Garden and Down in the Dirt*)

An unusual and complex seesaw structure is offered in *Snappsy the Alligator (Did Not Ask to Be in This Book!)* by Julie Falatko. The story goes back and forth between the narrator telling the story and Snappsy interjecting his thoughts. Older students may enjoy trying out a seesaw where the main character often steps out of the story and talks to the narrator through speech bubbles. This type of seesaw structure offers a chance to insert humor as Snappsy complains and argues with the storyteller. The scaffold changes when the narrator begins to talk to the main character: "Well, you have to come out. The story is really boring now."

Knots on a Counting Rope by Bill Martin Jr. and John Archambault offers another variation of the seesaw scaffold. The book is a conversation between a Native American boy and his grandfather about the story of the boy's birth. The words of each character are positioned in a way that allows the reader to easily identify the speaker and follow the back-and-forth rhythm of the conversation. Young writers could use this technique as they begin to experiment with conversation, before they are skillful with the use of quotation marks. This book came to the rescue one summer when Rose was working in a program for young writers sponsored by the Pennsylvania Writing and Literature Project. The class comprised students who had just completed first grade, so the range of skill level was wide. Although all the students were interested in writing and viewed themselves as writers, not all of them had the ability to express their thoughts in a way that made sense to the reader. One student, Alex, had a particular interest in Scotland and the Loch Ness monster. That interest was often reflected in his writing. One afternoon Rose had a particularly difficult time understanding the story Alex was so confidently and earnestly working on. As she talked with him, it became clearer that the opening was actually the dialogue of a ship's captain interspersed with the sound effects from an underwater beast. But there was no punctuation to guide the reader, no character identification, no clue to how this little scene might be connected to a larger piece. Because it was the work of a first grader who was about to be a second grader, Rose understood that some of it might still be beyond Alex's skill level. Still, she tried to help.

"Alex, you have an exciting scene here, but it is difficult to understand," she said. "Authors don't write down dialogue without identifying the speaker and using quotation marks to let us know the words that were spoken. Since this might be hard for you to do, why don't you just describe the action." Alex tried to comply, but describing the scene was not what he had intended, and Rose could tell that the confidence he was demonstrating in himself as a writer was being compromised. That evening, she thought a lot about what had happened, knowing she needed to do something to help move Alex's writing forward in a way he was ready to handle. Finally, a title surfaced in her memory, and the next day she returned to Alex with a copy of *Knots on a Counting Rope*.

"Alex, I think I've found a book that can help you organize your piece about the beast," she said. "The whole book is a dialogue between a young boy and his grandfather. The authors, Bill Martin Jr. and John Archambault, let us know who is talking by the way the lines are arranged on the page." Together, Rose and Alex examined the structure of the book, and then Alex used what they had discovered to reorganize his work. He placed the words of the captain on one side of the page and the sound effects from the beast on the other side. This line placement was similar to a poem for two voices and provided enough structure to make sense of the scene he had created.

Global Structures Versus Substructures

Sometimes a piece of writing has a global or overall structure and one or more substructures within the piece. A good example is the nonfiction book *Arctic Lights, Arctic Nights* by Debbie S. Miller. The overall structure in this book is the passing of time in Alaska from one summer solstice to another. The substructures include a snapshot of setting and characters (wildlife) on each page. These snapshots describe what is happening on one particular day each month. Each snapshot includes an onomatopoeia lead. This book could perhaps provide an interesting way for a student to organize a science report about the changes that occur in a particular place or to a particular animal throughout the seasons.

In *Feathers: Not Just for Flying* by Melissa Stewart, the overall structure is to illustrate that feathers serve many different purposes, as implied by the title. These purposes are expressed through the use of similes that compare feathers to common objects and then explained further with specific examples and additional details. The global structure is found at the top of a two-page spread in larger print and always follows the same format: a simile, ellipses, and a connection to a new simile with the coordinating conjunction *or*:

> Feathers can dig holes like a backhoe . . . or carry building supplies like a forklift.
>
> Feathers can distract attackers like a bullfighter's cape . . . or hide a bird from predators like camouflage clothing.

The additional information is found in text boxes that are scattered among the illustrations. In the author's note in the back of the book, Stewart lets us in on her process. She reports that although she had done all the research, she just wasn't satisfied with the way the information was framed. After numerous drafts, it occurred to her that she could compare feathers to everyday objects, using similes to make her book engaging and unique. Sharing this information about process with our students helps them realize the importance of finding the right organization to fit the text. Writers are decision makers, and this is just one of the decisions they will make. Mentor texts can provide options for making wise decisions about organizational structures.

In *Everglades*, Jean Craighead George provides a unique organizational format by telling a story within a story. She uses italics to separate the conversation between the storyteller and the children who are listening to him from the actual story he tells about the Everglades. Lois Lowry uses a similar technique in *Gooney Bird Greene*. Gooney Bird's stories are printed in a larger size to separate them from the narration of the book. Books such as these can help students better understand how to incorporate anecdotes into any mode of writing. It is important to show students that anecdotes can even be used within a narrative. When students understand and are able to recognize that within any mode of writing authors often use more than one structure, they are free to do the same in their own writing.

Sometimes authors seem to be writing two different stories, but link them together at some point before the ending. We have noticed this type of structure not only in picture books but also in novels, plays, and movies. One book that could serve as a mentor text to try out this organization is *Big Night for Salamanders* by Sarah Marwil Lamstein. Instead of just writing a basic life-cycle book about salamanders, Lamstein sets the scene for salamanders to begin their migration from their burrows to vernal pools. As their story unfolds, the author tells Evan's story. Evan is a boy who knows a lot about salamanders and is waiting for this "big night." As we learn about the salamanders' activity, we also see Evan preparing to help the salamanders cross the road safely. Eventually, their stories converge and Evan is successful in his mission. By using this structure, the author was able to present information about salamanders in a very engaging way. The back matter of this book includes elements of nonfiction, such as a description of the life cycle of the spotted salamander, a glossary, an index, and additional resources. *The Dog Who Belonged to No One* by Amy Hest takes two fictional stories to help readers understand more about the two main characters—a stray dog and a lonely little girl named Lia. As the story progresses, we watch the characters engage in different daily activities and finally come together at the end as they escape a storm. As their stories become one, their loneliness dissolves in their newfound friendship.

In Chapter 2, "Digging for Treasure," we discuss how some books that are organized around objects, such as *Aunt Flossie's Hats* by Elizabeth Fitzgerald Howard or *Wilfrid Gordon McDonald Partridge* by Mem Fox, can be used to help students find writing topics. After the connection is made, after writers realize that they also have stories to tell just like Mem Fox and Elizabeth Fitzgerald Howard, they can begin to see other possibilities with these books. Students can examine the books with new eyes, turning their attention to how the author made the book instead of just what the author wrote. Sometimes the book revolves around one object as in *Betty Doll* by Patricia Polacco or *Hairs/Pelitos* (written in both Spanish and English) by Sandra Cisneros. An author could use a series of anecdotes or small stories that revolve around one place, as in *In My Momma's Kitchen* by Jerdine Nolan, *Up North at the Cabin* by Marsha Wilson Chall, or *All the Places to Love* by Patricia MacLachlan. Students can examine their writer's notebooks for evidence of stories that revolve around an object, a place, or perhaps a person. For instance, they might have lots of entries describing the details of their Saturday morning soccer games or the adventures they share with their best friend or special times at their grandparents' cottage. When it comes time to work on a larger project, we can help students realize the structural possibilities within their notebook entries by revisiting the books that have become part of the classroom community. Sharing books that are written around people, objects, places, or events can show students that they, too, might find common threads running through their notebooks that can be woven into a single extended text.

Structures That Complete a Circle

Books written in a circular structure end where they began. Laura Numeroff has written several such books, beginning with the popular *If You Give a Mouse a Cookie*. Sometimes students call this the "start all over again" structure. It can be very obvious, such as in the Numeroff books, or more subtle, as in Cynthia Rylant's *The Relatives Came* and *Blackout* by John Rocco. *Two Bad*

Ants by Chris Van Allsburg and *Where the Wild Things Are* by Maurice Sendak provide variations of the circular structure. In these books, the main characters are at home as the story begins, they set out on an adventure, and finally they find their way home again. Books with these structures can be particularly helpful scaffolds to students who are beginning to move away from personal narratives to simple fictional stories.

A variation of the circular structure can be found in books where the entire first line is repeated at the end, as in Libba Moore Gray's *My Mama Had a Dancing Heart* or Lester Laminack's *The Sunsets of Miss Olivia Wiggins*. These repeated lines act as bookends to the story told between them and are easy for young writers to identify, although they may or may not notice it on their own. However, once we make students aware of a particular structure, they will look for it in other books or pieces of writing. Through reflection and discussion that may be part of a Your Turn lesson, young writers can be led to the realization of why the author chose a particular structure, or why it worked in that piece of writing. Our teaching should always be purposeful, helping our students understand the "why" behind the "what." It is not enough to engage students in a writing activity simply because it is fun. Writers must understand how a strategy or technique can help them move forward in their own writing.

In some books, a line is not repeated just at the beginning and the end but, rather, throughout the text. Sometimes, these repeated words act as a scaffold to provide rhythm to the writing, sometimes writers purposefully repeat a word or phrase to emphasize an important idea, and sometimes the words do both. Cynthia Rylant uses this structure in many of her books such as *In November* and *When I Was Young in the Mountains*. The repeated phrases in each book, which are also the book titles, are used to set off small vignettes while providing a rhythm to the writing. Another book that uses a repeated phrase is *Up North at the Cabin* by Marcia Wilson Chall. Chall uses the title as the repeated phrase for her book as well. Each time she begins a page with "Up north at the cabin . . . ," she shares a tiny memory of the time she spent there. One memory captures the loons landing on the lake at sunset while the little girl sits with her grandparents on the same side of the table so they can all watch "the loons dance down the sun." By studying books with repeated refrains, young writers can perhaps envision a new way to organize a piece about a place or a time of the year. In one fifth-grade classroom, Lynne returned to *In November* to create a shared writing experience, imitating Rylant's organizational structure.

In December snow lazily floats on the crisp, cold air while flickering fires fill our fireplaces, lighting up rooms with a rosy, warm glow. We nestle among plush pillows and comfy cushions to sip foamy hot chocolate and share our sledding stories.

In December Santa comes to town, and adults are swarming to malls that are as busy as beehives. Houses are filled with the sweet scent of pine wreaths and trees. Parents hide presents away, and grandmas bake those wonderful butter cookies in the shapes of bells, angels, and reindeer. We dream about Christmas morning when we will awake and leap from our beds without the help of a single alarm clock or a parent's wake-up call.

In December it's a time for thinking about those hard-to-keep resolutions. It's a time for wishes, hopes, and dreams. It's a time for families to come together and celebrate the end of one year and the beginning of a brand new year. It's a time for making memories that last. It's December.

Your Turn Lesson 2 at the end of this chapter offers another option for using this type of organizational structure.

Borrowing scaffolds is not just limited to the work of student authors. We can find many familiar scaffolds in the work of published authors. Pamela Duncan Edwards used the cumulative text structure from the nursery rhyme "The House That Jack Built" to create the nonfiction text *Boston Tea Party*. Cumulative texts are no strangers to students. They have listened to stories and sung songs that have this type of structure since they were young. A cumulative text takes the first sentence and builds on it, repeating all the phrases or sentences that went before. The following excerpt from *Boston Tea Party* illustrates this structure:

> These are the leaves that grew on a bush in a far-off land and became part of the Boston Tea Party. This is the tea that was made from the leaves that grew on a bush in a far-off land and became part of the Boston Tea Party.

The Napping House by Audrey Wood also uses a cumulative text structure:

> This is the house, a napping house, where everyone is sleeping. And in that house there is a bed, a cozy bed in a napping house, where everyone is sleeping.

Anthony D. Fredericks gets readers to take a closer look at nature through the use of a cumulative structure that also imitates "The House That Jack Built" in his books *On One Flower: Butterflies, Ticks and a Few More Icks* and *Around One Log: Chipmunks, Spiders, and Creepy Insiders*. However, the organization found in these books offers much more! The beginning sets up a scene that places the reader in the setting as an observer. The scaffold is used to introduce more creatures into the scene. These books are good examples to students of how to imitate a scaffold but make it their own, too.

In a Village by the Sea by Muon Van tells the story of a fisherman and his family through text that is connected by an introductory line that is repeated and links the progression of the events in the story. To create a satisfying ending, the progression of events in the story changes to lead the fisherman home where his family waits for his return.

Students can borrow the cumulative text structure for narrative or informational writing. When used for report writing, this structure helps students know their topic thoroughly, understand a sequence of events, and be able to write about it in a unique way. Structures such as these can actually serve to motivate students to work longer and harder on a project that requires writing.

Alphabet, Numbers, Colors, and More!

Common scaffolds that can be used as models for student writing are books that are organized around the alphabet, numbers, colors, sounds, days of the week, and seasons. Students of all ages can use the alphabet structure to organize their thinking. Alphabet books range from the very simple, such as *Matthew A.B.C.* by Peter Catalanotto that has one statement per page and is used to entertain, to the more complex, such as *Capital! Washington D.C. from A to Z* by Laura Krauss Melmed. This book has elaborate text as well as nonfiction features such as captions, time lines, and labels to inform the reader. Jerry Pallotta has written many nonfiction alphabet books filled with information and written in an engaging and humorous way. In *Eyeball Alphabet Book*, he adds a new substructure to every letter: an idiom about the eye. For example, on his "A Is for Alligator" page he explains what it means to "Keep your eye on the ball." This addition adds another layer of meaning that can help struggling readers and English language learners better understand commonly used expressions.

Sleeping Bear Press publishes many alphabet books that cover a range of topics such as hobbies, occupations, history, sports, states, countries, and animals. Some of the books, such as *C Is for Ciao: An Italy Alphabet* by Elissa D. Grodin and Governor Mario Cuomo and *P Is for Piñata: A Mexico Alphabet* by Tony Johnston, can be used to introduce readers to aspects of the land, the culture, and the history of a foreign country.

The ABC structure can be studied as a genre, especially for older students, who can examine a wide range of alphabet book formats to choose an appropriate model for a piece of writing they are about to begin. In Lynne's fourth-grade class, the students chose an ABC format to reconstruct their research about Alaska and display it as a quilt. (See Figure 6.1.) Each student chose a letter and explored a host of possible topics for it, often consulting with peers or the librarian, as well as the teacher, to ensure that they made the most appropriate contribution to the total accumulated knowledge about Alaska. The students decided to display the final product as a quilt hung in the hall, instead of a book, so that it could be shared with more people. Once they had tried out the ABC format, some students chose to use it again for a book report on "The ABCs of Maniac Magee" or as an alphabet book about dinosaurs written for a first-grade audience. Once students become comfortable with this structure, the possibilities are endless. One third-grade class decided to surprise Lynne with a writing ABC that captured the spirit of the writing workshop time they shared together.

The A, B, C of Writing

Adjectives and adverbs don't take the place of strong nouns and verbs!

Begin your piece with an exciting lead.

Capitalization of proper nouns is checked during the edit.

Dig deep to find memories and stories that are important to you.

Every sentence should not begin the same way!

Find places to add rich details.

Give your writing your full attention by reading and rereading your words.

Happy, sad, angry, embarrassed—just appeal to the emotions.

Intelligent readers want you to show, not tell!

Just write it down in your writer's notebook before your ideas escape.

Kindness is okay when you confer, but honesty is important if you're going to help.

Let your voice be heard! You are unique!

Metaphors are great to use when they are appropriate.

Never be afraid to take a risk and try something new.

Open up your heart when you write and be passionate about the language!

Poetry is for everyone—free verse, haiku, limericks, tanka, acrostics, ballads.

Quit your whining when you write to persuade or no one will listen!

Revise, revise, revise, revise, revise, revise, revise, revise, revise . . .

Similes can be tired if you are always as slow as a snail or as fast as a cheetah.

Take time to appeal to the senses with sounds, smells, and tastes.

Unusual ways of seeing everyday things—that's what a writer does!

Vivid word choice and voice make up your very own style.

When you have time, use the thesaurus and dictionary to help you.

Xtra, extra . . . read all about it: writing workshop is extra special because we have a voice.

Your character is revealed through actions, thoughts, talk, and physical descriptions.

Zany and crazy are allowed. It's okay to be different in writing workshop.

Books that are organized around numbers are another inviting scaffold for students to use. Like alphabet books they can be simple, as in *Daisy 1, 2, 3* by Peter Catalonotto, or more complex as in *Soccer Counts!* by Barbara Barbieri McGrath and Peter Alderman. In this book, a rhyming couplet introduces the number. Italicized text gives the reader a more complete explanation. *Birdsongs* by Betsy Franco is a beautifully illustrated book that uses both numbers and the sounds that birds make to create a text. Another substructure of this book is the passing of time from sunrise to sunset. The number scaffold in this book starts

Figure 6.1
This Alaska ABC quilt was created by a fourth-grade class.

with ten and works down to one. The bird sounds that are described are represented in different point sizes and are repeated to match the number with the text. Sounds are also used to scaffold *City Street Beat* by Nancy Viau. The author takes her readers on a journey through the city from morning to night and organizes the trip through the various city sounds—doorbells, shutters, fountains, trains, and so on.

Anita Lobel's *One Lighthouse, One Moon* presents three different stories that make use of three different scaffolds: color and days of the week, months of the year with use of strong verbs, and numbers with exact nouns.

One organizational scaffold to help young writers create a biography is to use a phrase or a sentence, sometimes slightly varied and scattered throughout the text, to emphasize an important character trait that defines a person. For example, in *The Tree Lady: The True Story of How One Tree-Loving Woman Changed a City Forever*, H. Joseph Hopkins emphasizes Kate's determination and willingness to think outside the box:

> From elms and oaks to eucalyptuses and palms, by the turn of the century, young trees from Kate's nursery were growing in every part of San Diego.

Most people didn't think a desert town could sustain so many trees. But Kate did.

The author varies this idea of "but Kate did" by sometimes writing "but not Kate" or "but she did" or "but now she did." The echo of this phrase stays with readers and allows them to contemplate each action in Kate's life through this character trait. We see it again in *Miss Moore Thought Otherwise: How Anne Carroll Moore Created Libraries for Children* by Jan Pinborough with the phrase "but Miss Moore thought otherwise" and in *Take a Hike, Teddy Roosevelt!* by Frank Murphy, who uses the phrase "so he did." As young writers conduct research for biographies, they can think of a character trait that defines their subject and that will pull the reader through the text with a simple statement and perhaps some variations on it. By reflecting on the person's character and choosing an important thread to link selective events that illustrate a particular trait, students can write a biography in a unique fashion and will most likely avoid the pitfalls of plagiarism.

Inside a Character's Head: Letters and Journals

Letters and journals are real-world structures that appeal to writers of all ages. Sometimes they have a serious tone, such as *Dear Levi: Letters from the Overland Trail* by Elvira Woodruff or *One Day in the Tropical Rain Forest* by Jean Craighead George. Sometimes they are more humorous, such as *Diary of a Worm* by Doreen Cronin or *First Year Letters* by Julie Danneberg. This structure allows students to organize information about people, places, and events in a familiar format while allowing them to practice the conventions of letter or journal writing. When Lynne was a fourth-grade teacher, her class was studying Harriet Tubman and the Underground Railroad. Together they examined books with journal entries to understand what a journal format looked like, as well as the type of information it contained. Lynne's students then created journals and wrote in the voice of Harriet Tubman to record memories—descriptions, thoughts, and feelings—that they thought she would have written in a journal if she had been literate.

Perhaps students could write a persuasive piece using a friendly letter format as Karen Kaufman Orloff does in *I Wanna Iguana* and *I Wanna New Room*. Letters go back and forth between Alex and his mother or father (depending on the book) in a seesaw manner. Close to the end, the scaffold changes, and Alex and his parents speak directly to one another. Sometimes when they use a back-and-forth seesaw scaffold, it is hard for students to come to closure. Both of these books demonstrate how a change in this type of scaffold can signal the ending. Another way to use a scaffold such as this is to write letters from two different locations (such as New Orleans or the rocky coast of

Maine) and offer insights into unique aspects of each place. *City Dog, Country Frog* by Mo Willems, a book organized across the seasons, offers us two different perspectives of city fun and country fun through the eyes of the characters.

Writing in the voice of another person, animal, or thing is an organizational structure all its own. We can find many examples, including *My Light* by Molly Bang, *Atlantic* by G. Brian Karas, *Sierra* by Diane Siebert, and *Look to the North: A Wolf Pup Diary* by Jean Craighead George. This structure helps students write from a point of view other than their own. This is the necessary practice they need to get better at persuasive writing. By using this scaffold, they have the opportunity to think from another's perspective—to walk around in someone else's skin—and to understand what it feels like, looks like, or sounds like. In other words, it prepares students to view the world not only through their eyes but also through the eyes of another individual or group. This scaffold helps them think outside the box. It promotes writing as thinking in a creative way.

By helping students see structures in literature that they might not see themselves—to walk alongside them and point things out—is the job of both teacher and mentor text. Students need to read a variety of texts and internalize the structures they present. Once they understand how those representations help readers make sense of text, they can use them as scaffolds for their own writing. Teaching students to use a variety of scaffolds adds another layer to helping them become more strategic writers.

Think About It—Talk About It—Write About It

- What organizational scaffolds do you and your students return to most often? Why are they helpful in organizing different types of writing?
- Have you found some favorite mentor texts that can support the scaffolds you use most often with your students? Share them with a colleague. If you do not have any favorites, talk with the school and local librarian for suggestions.
- Return to some of your favorite read-alouds and look for possible organizational structures that you can use in teaching writing.
- Return to your writer's notebook or pieces of writing you have used in class, published on a blog, and so on. Try rewriting the piece using one of the organizational structures discussed in this chapter, or create a new one that fits your genre and message.

Using a Seesaw Structure to Organize Writing

Hook: Return to familiar books that are written in a seesaw structure. These might include *Fortunately* by Remy Charlip, *That's Good! That's Bad!* by Margery Cuyler, or *Tough Boris* by Mem Fox. With your students, identify the scaffold and its characteristics. For instance, the same words are used back and forth, over and over (*Fortunately . . . Unfortunately . . . That's good! That's bad!*); the books begin and end with a positive statement.

Purpose: *Writers, sometimes authors organize their ideas by using a seesaw structure. Today, I will show you how to do that and you will have a chance to try it out in your own writing.*

Brainstorm: Ask students to think of situations they have experienced that might have a good side and a bad side. Some possibilities are playing a sport, having a little brother or sister, having a pet, or raining on the day of a picnic. You might want to get the class started by sharing a few ideas of your own. Search your memory or look through your notebook for things that might fit, such as hiring a babysitter for an evening out, taking a long plane ride, or snowing in April. Record the ideas on the board or on chart paper.

Model: Using one of your own ideas, relate the story or experience and write it up using the scaffold from one of the books previously presented. Here's an example:

> *I was looking through my notebook, and I noticed an entry where I wrote about it snowing in the beginning of April when the trees were already blossoming. There are good things and bad things about snow in April, so if I borrowed Margery Cuyler's scaffold, I could write the following:*
> *It's spring and the trees are beginning to blossom.*
> *The birds are returning to build their nests. That's good!*
> *A light snow has started to fall. That's bad!*
> *The trees look beautiful. That's good!*
> *The snow is hiding the branches and berries. That's bad!*
> *The sun is coming out! That's good!*

Shared/Guided Writing: Return to the list of brainstormed ideas. Pick a few and discuss some of the good things and bad things about each. Invite students to try out the scaffold by choosing one of the ideas and writing a few lines. This lesson also works well as a collaborative effort. If students are not ready to work on their own, consider constructing a text through whole-class share writing. Students can also work in partnerships to begin a short piece.

Independent Writing: Ask students to return to their notebooks and search for some ideas or previous entries that might work well using the seesaw scaffold. If they have difficulty identifying something from their notebooks, they can choose one of the brainstormed ideas or continue the piece started during guided writing.

Reflection: After sharing some pieces, ask students to reflect on how this scaffold worked.

> *How did the scaffold help you organize your thoughts?*
> *When could the seesaw structure be effectively used?*

For students who rewrote an existing notebook entry:

> *Did the use of the scaffold improve the writing?*
> *Would the writing work better in a different format?*

This is also a good time to explain to students that the words of the scaffold (the good thing, the bad thing, and so on) don't always have to be included. The idea is to use the comparing and contrasting of ideas as an organizational strategy. Through discussion, help students identify additional situations where the structure could be effective, such as comparing or contrasting two characters.

Your Turn Lesson 2

Using a Repeated Refrain as a Scaffold to Create Paragraphs

Hook: *In November* by Cynthia Rylant gives students a chance to see how an author uses a repeated phrase to organize the information presented in the text. The book is a collection of small descriptions that help the reader visualize and remember November. Each description begins with the words "In November . . ." and is organized around a different topic. Reread the book and chart with the students the topics and details Rylant uses to develop her ideas. Other books with this same type of scaffold are *Up North at the Cabin* by Marsha Wilson Chall, *If You're Not from the Prairie . . .* by David Bouchard, and *When I Was Young in the Mountains* by Cynthia Rylant.

Purpose: *Writers, today we are going to use the same structure Cynthia Rylant used, a repeated refrain, to organize information in paragraphs about your favorite months. Like Rylant, we will have to make a decision about the big ideas we want to develop. (Refer to the chart you created listing topics and details about them.) For example, see how Rylant talks about the trees, the birds, the food, and the special holiday that takes place in November. Each time she talks about a new idea, she starts with the phrase "In November . . ." I'm going to show you how you can do the same thing.*

Brainstorm: With your students, choose a month they might like to try out together. Brainstorm big ideas that relate to that month. For example, if you chose October, your list might include football, Halloween, leaves changing color, and weather. Develop ideas under these big categories as well. For instance, under Halloween you might have pumpkins, jack-o'-lanterns, trick-or-treating, costumes, haunted houses, or scarecrows. Brainstorm lots of ideas so you have lots to choose from. It's always a good idea to have more than you will actually use.

Model: Using the ideas listed, write one or two paragraphs around each topic. Think aloud as you write, demonstrating how you are building a paragraph around one central idea. For example, you might write the following:

> *In October, fat, heavy pumpkins dot the farmers' fields. A scarecrow stuffed with bright oat straw stands nearby, watching parents and children scurry to find the perfect one to take home. After scooping out the guts, parents help carve a scary face and place a candle inside. The golden light flickers as the jack-o'-lantern flashes a toothy smile at the trick-or-treaters on Halloween night.*

Shared/Guided Writing: Ask the students to work with a partner or in groups of three to choose another month and to brainstorm big, or main, ideas. Working together, they come up with details to support each main idea. As you circulate, encourage the students to think about holidays, sports, and weather and add appeal to the senses as part of the detail work. Next, have each pair or group report their thinking. Students in other groups can offer suggestions either aloud or on sticky notes (for older students). This greatly enriches the possibilities for everyone's success. Now they can begin to draft a paragraph or two beginning with the refrain "In [month] . . ." Students should think about how they are going to place their details in a meaningful way. Younger students can write their ideas on sentence strips so that they can more easily manipulate the order. Students can volunteer to share first-draft writing.

Independent Writing: Before students try this out on their own, brainstorm things other than months that they could write about, using a similar organizational scaffold such as seasons, holidays, or days of the week ("On Monday . . ."). They could also do this with a place in mind ("In Grandma's garden . . ."). Remind them to plan or prewrite first, getting their big ideas and details sketched in their notebooks before trying to write the paragraph.

Reflection: Ask students to think about how the repeated phrase helped them scaffold and focus their thinking as they created their paragraphs.

When could you use this again?

Are there drafts in your notebook that could be organized in this way?

Could it work for informational or persuasive writing?

How could it be used to create an advertisement, a song, or a poem?

Option: If all the students are writing about a different holiday, month, or state, you could create a quilt around that particular theme.

Writing in the Persona of Another

This type of writing ties in easily with science or social studies topics. It is a different way for students to demonstrate what they have learned and is a fresh alternative to report writing. For example, after you have studied a particular topic such as the rain forest, ask students to take on the persona of an animal, plant, or the biome itself to write about the things they learned. For younger students, this can be done as a shared project. In some classrooms, teachers have incubators and hatch baby chicks. Students could write their daily observations in the persona of a baby chick.

Hook: *Atlantic* by G. Brian Karas is written in the persona of the Atlantic Ocean. Return to this text and ask students to think about how the author used the voice of the ocean, writing in the first person, to give us information about it. Other books that use persona writing are *My Light* by Molly Bang, *Sierra* by Diane Siebert, and *Voices from the Oregon Trail* by Kay Winters.

Purpose: *When authors write in the first person as if they are something else—an animal, an object, a place, or even another person—it is called persona writing. Today I'm going to show you how you can organize information by using the voice of someone or something else just like G. Brian Karas did.*

Brainstorm: Choose a place that is familiar to students, such as a backyard or the school playground, and brainstorm a list of things they might be comfortable writing about. One class chose their backyards and created a list that included the following: sandbox, patio, trees, robin's nest, squirrels, rabbits, groundhogs, rosebush, mosquitoes, hammock, picnic table, sprinkler, garden hose, and barbecue grill. Record the ideas on a chart or board.

Model: Choose one and show students how to create a chart to organize and stretch their thinking. Think aloud as you write. The example below charts the thinking about a crab-apple tree. The categories could be different, depending on your purposes. For example, you might use a category for actions (G. Brian Karas describes many actions of the ocean), or you could use a category for changes (if you are taking on the persona of a caterpillar or a tadpole).

Description	Feelings/Thoughts	Observations
Tall	Eager for spring rain	Squirrels are leaping from limb to limb.
Standing in center of yard	Waiting for the boy to come and climb me	Robins yank worms out of the lawn.
Milk chocolate bark	Thrilled by the little girl's laughter as she pulls through the air to move the tire swing	Sparrows are starting to build their nests again.
Arms reaching into nearby maples		
Rough and sturdy		Today my blossoms fall like pink rain.
Bend under weight of snow		People are reading poetry about me.
Yield to strong north wind	Feeling rather pretty with all my new leaves sprouting	The little girl holds Shel Silverstein's *The Giving Tree* in her lap.
Tiny pink blossoms		
Limbs pointing in every direction that a compass points	Ouch! That pesky woodpecker just keeps hammering away.	

Using the model, create a beginning, perhaps starting with a snapshot using the ideas under description.

> *I am standing, tall and sturdy, in the very center of a large backyard. The winter snows have melted, and my milk chocolate bark no longer wears a coat of white. I stretch toward the sun, warming my numb limbs that have felt cold all winter long. Now my new green leaves are sprouting everywhere. I am becoming beautiful once more.*

Shared/Guided Writing: Have students work with a partner or small group to develop a chart of ideas about an object from the brainstormed list. Encourage the students to draw sketches if they need to. These can be placed around the chart like a border and could also contain some labeling. As you circulate around the classroom, don't be afraid to jump-start their thinking by offering a few ideas or asking some questions to help them visualize themselves in that persona. Share their thinking in whole group so that others can offer suggestions or layer the thinking. When enough ideas have been gathered, have them try to write a few paragraphs. In the above example, the feelings and thoughts column could lend itself to several paragraphs—the boy coming to climb, the girl coming to swing, and the woodpecker coming to find a tasty meal. The observations column could lend itself to individual paragraphs. You may want to model this over several days to give students lots of options.

Independent Writing: Students could return to the shared chart and try out one of the ideas they didn't use in partnership. After writing, encourage them to have an ear conference with a partner to make sure they are writing in the first person, staying in the persona of what they are writing about. (An ear conference focuses on revision, not editing.)

Reflection: Have students reflect on how this strategy worked. The following questions can help guide their thinking (choose according to what you think is appropriate for your grade level):

> *How did this work for you?*
> *Was it enjoyable?*
> *Was it easy or difficult?*
> *How did it help you organize your thinking?*
> *When could you use this again?*
> *Could you suggest a different prewriting strategy to help organize your thinking?*
> *How does writing in the first person affect point of view and the tone of the text?*

Option: Students can rewrite their piece using a friendly or business letter format while still maintaining the first-person voice.

Your Turn Lesson 4

Using an Adjective Scaffold

Author Dianna Hutts Aston and illustrator Sylvia Long have a series of informational books that introduce us to topics using specific adjectives to describe them. These big ideas are developed through an informational paragraph that follows. For our students, this scaffold is another interesting way to organize text for our readers and can be used across writing types. We suggest that you try something new here. Gather a collection of Aston's and Long's books from the school and local library. Ask students to preview each book—do a picture walk—and on a sticky note, give a reason why a particular book should be chosen as the read-aloud that will be used as the mentor text for this workshop lesson. Right away your students will be more engaged because they have had a choice in the process from the very beginning. Read the chosen book, allowing students time to examine the pictures and reflect on the structure. The following lesson is based on *A Butterfly Is Patient*.

Hook: As you return to the mentor text, ask students to notice the adjectives that describe the butterfly and how the idea each simple sentence presents is developed in a small paragraph.

Purpose: *Writers, today we are going to imitate the structure that Aston created to talk about butterflies in our writing. Like this author, we will need to think of specific adjectives to describe our topic. For today we are going to concentrate on topics we already know a lot about so that research will not be necessary.*

Brainstorm: With the students, list a number of topics they know a good deal about, such as school, soccer, baseball, dogs, cats, flowers, video games, brothers, sisters, grandparents, and so on. Choose one and do another quick brainstorming session for adjectives around the chosen topic as a model for what you will ask them to do in small groups or with a partner. For example, adjectives associated with dogs could be *lovable, loyal, protective, funny, entertaining, fierce, noisy, shy, silly, sleepy, energetic, smart, furry,* and *soft*. Ask students to choose a topic and work in partnerships or small groups to brainstorm accompanying adjectives. This brainstorming could be recorded on charts placed around the room. Students can then visit the charts of other groups and add additional adjectives. Carousel activities such as this build the collective thinking of the writing community.

Model: Return to the topic you chose and your brainstormed list of adjectives to create a statement and a paragraph that extends and develops that idea. Here is an example:

> *A dog is protective.*
> Dogs are very quick to learn who their family is—who feeds them, gives them a place to sleep, takes them on walks, and

gives them lots of love. They know who strangers are, too. Often they will bark, and sometimes they will growl if they feel their family is in danger or being threatened.

A dog is entertaining.
Many dogs will leap into the air to catch a Frisbee, play tug-of-war with a toy, or retrieve a ball. It is debatable whether they are entertaining their humans or they feel their humans are entertaining them. Many families delight in teaching their dogs tricks like rolling over, shaking hands, or playing dead so that they can perform for guests. Some dogs find their tails to be an object worth chasing and will entertain any onlookers by running in circles until they are exhausted.

Shared/Guided Writing: Return to the brainstormed list of topics and adjectives, and ask students to volunteer one topic for a shared writing experience. Together with the class compose a sentence using one of the adjectives for the topic. Then compose a short paragraph that explains the big idea. Repeat this process if you think your students need more practice, or have them work in partnerships or small groups.

Independent Writing: Ask students to use the lists created from the carousel activity to create their own big-idea sentences and paragraphs. Students may also return to their writer's notebooks to find other topics and brainstorm a new list of adjectives. Some students may want to create an entire book around their chosen topic. Others may want to explore a new topic they are interested in but need to know more about. These students may examine a text set around a topic and/or do more research to create their book.

Reflection: *Was this organizational scaffold easy or difficult for you to use? Explain.*

Where do you think you might be able to use this scaffold again?

How did the use of this scaffold help you focus your thinking?

Could this scaffold work for another form of writing such as a poem, an essay, or an opinion piece?

Options: By allowing students to imagine the possibilities, we build choice into our writing workshop and create an atmosphere of engagement. Another option is to invite students to use this scaffold in response to literature. They can take one or several characters from a book to create big-idea statements using character traits as the adjective. This lesson can be connected to reading workshop, where an anchor chart of character traits can be developed and defined. We also see possibilities for using it in an opinion piece or to scaffold a poem or essay.

Your Turn Lesson 5

Using Similes to Organize Text

Before this Your Turn lesson, it would be a good idea to investigate with your class what similes are and why authors would use them. The lesson will extend an understanding of similes and present this literary device as a way to organize a piece of writing.

Hook: *Feathers: Not Just for Flying* by Melissa Stewart gives students an understanding of how similes can be used to deepen our understanding of a text and even organize text. Share this book with your students and then return to it to examine the organizational format for the pages that include text. Students should notice the use of similes at the top of each page and the information and illustrations that explain the use of the simile. Here is an example from the text:

> *Feathers can warm like a blanket . . .*
> *On cold, damp days, a blue jay stays warm by fluffing up its feathers and trapping a layer of warm air next to its skin.*
>
> *or cushion like a pillow.*
> *A female wood duck likes her nest with feathers she plucks from her own body. These feathers cushion the duck's eggs and keep them warm.*

Be sure to share the author's note at the end of the book. Here, Stewart explains that she had collected lots of information about feathers but didn't know quite how to frame the book until she came up with the idea of using similes to compare feathers to everyday objects.

Purpose: *Writers, today we are going to use the same structure that Melissa Stewart used: two similes joined by the conjunction* or *and a few sentences that develop the idea behind the similes to organize information about a favorite topic.*

Brainstorm: With your students create a list of familiar topics to investigate. These might include family members (see *My Dog Is as Smelly as Dirty Socks and Other Funny Family Portraits* by Hanoch Piven—another mentor text for this lesson), specific areas of the school, rooms in a house, animals, vacation spots, food groups, flowers, methods of transportation, objects found in the classroom, occupations, and so on. Choose one of these broad topics and brainstorm again. For example, with classroom objects you could list pencil sharpener, pencil, desk, globe, chair, whiteboard, computer, books, paper, crayons, and others.

Model: Using the ideas listed on the brainstormed charts, write one or several similes and paragraphs around the similes. Think aloud as you create and encourage your students to help you if you get stuck. Here is our example:

A book can immerse you like a dive into a pool . . .
   When you read a book, you give it all your attention and
   you are drenched with words.

or can transport you to imaginary places like a magic carpet.
   Fantasy, science fiction, and fairy tales are genres that stir
   our imagination and let us leave the real world temporarily
   to experience a different world.

Shared/Guided Writing: Choose another item from the topic you modeled, and try it out again, with your students taking the lead. Provide gentle nudges if necessary. Repeat with as many examples as you think your class might need. When you think most of your students are ready, send them off to work with a partner or a small group to choose a topic and imitate this scaffold. Some students may still need to work in a small group with your guidance. After working, groups can share their thinking, which will serve as a quick check-in (formative assessment) to help you know whether everyone is on the right track. These writing pieces can be posted to serve as additional mentor texts.

Independent Writing: Students can continue using ideas brainstormed on the anchor charts or return to their writer's notebooks or reader response journals to find a new topic. Encourage them to refer to the models displayed in the classroom or reread Melissa Stewart's book. They may choose to create a book from their ideas, complete with sketches or photos. They may need to do additional research in the library or online.

Reflection: *Are there any drafts in your writer's notebook or portfolio of published pieces that could be reorganized or further developed using this scaffold?*

How did your work on this project deepen your understanding of similes?

How can you adapt this organizational scaffold for future use?

Was this work difficult or easy for you? Explain.

Chapter 7

Poetry:
Everybody Can Be a Writer

Poetry happens when people begin to look at the world differently. It is a way of uncovering the ordinary world: suddenly, in the hands of the poet, commonplace events take on new life and importance.

—Donald Graves, *A Fresh Look at Writing*

Chances are you shy away from reading, much less writing, poetry. Memories of high school and college come floating back to you, and you shudder. You remember reading the poetry of Donne, Yeats, and Tennyson and recall how the secret meanings of the poems they wrote seemed to remain a mystery to you. Only the poets themselves (and your esteemed English professors) understood what the poem was expressing. So why would you try to write poetry yourself or have your students write poems? Jean Little's character Kate in *Hey World, Here I Am!* talks about how Robert Frost's "Stopping by Woods on a Snowy Evening" had become an unpleasant experience for her:

> But today, the teacher told us what everything stood for.
> The woods, the horse, the miles to go, the sleep—
> They all have "hidden meanings."
>
> It's grown so complicated now that,
> Next time I drive by,
> I don't think I'll bother to stop.

Peter Elbow (1998) tells us that many people feel like they could be poets—that they could even write a good poem. He goes on to explain that they might not even have a topic, image, or feeling that they want to write about. And yet, they still feel poetic. Unfortunately, he laments, we learn to put those feelings away and instead search for something to write a poem about. Poetry becomes too hard and complex a task, and we abandon it. Like Kate, we no longer bother to stop, and in our writing workshops, poetry does not get the attention it deserves.

Many times we'll choose to read the poetry of Shel Silverstein and Jack Prelutsky because our students delight in the rhythm and humor of their work. We may also have our students write poetry, but we build poetry writing only around special holidays, such as creating cards for Mother's Day or Father's Day. The poetry might sound something like this:

> *Roses are red,*
> *Violets are blue.*
> *Chocolate is sweet,*
> *And so are you.*

This poetry sounds more like a greeting card—there is a general (mothers) rather than a specific (my mother) target audience, and it doesn't express the feelings of the writer. Although there is nothing wrong with creating poetry for special occasions, those poems should sing with emotion. Poems should express the unique thoughts and feelings of the writer. But poetry writing does not have to be reserved for special occasions. We can weave poetry into the writing workshop throughout the year and across genres. We can use poetry to introduce ourselves and build community in a classroom, compose a lead for an informational text, or playfully respond to a persuasive argument. Poetry creates pathways to songs, jingles, or entries in our writer's notebooks. Poetry offers a unique response to literature and makes the greatest gift of writing to those we love and care about when we express our true feelings.

We fill our classrooms with poetry that is fun to read and hear but may not always provide the best models for writing. When writing poetry, students should be allowed to concentrate on the feelings and images they wish to create through precise language rather than on rhyming patterns. You've probably received a poem like this from one of your students:

> *I went outside to play.*
> *It was a sunny day.*
> *Ships sailed on the bay.*
> *I have nothing more to say.*

This poem is an example of forced rhyme. The child, instead of concentrating on meaning, was concentrating on finding rhyming words, and the poem ends up not saying anything at all. This kind of wordplay is important in teaching phonological awareness to emergent readers and may help students develop an interest in language, but in writing workshop, the word choice must be more purposeful. This is not to say that students should be discouraged from using rhyme if they wish to do so, but it is to say that by filling our classrooms with mentor texts that provide many different models of poems that do not use rhyme, we can provide students with many more choices. We need to teach our students to look at poetry for specific word choice, economy of expression, voice, effective repetition, rhythm, use of an organizational scaffold, line breaks, and appeal to the senses as well as our emotions. An excellent resource for teachers is *A Kick in the Head: An Everyday Guide to Poetic Forms*. Paul Janeczko does a great job of introducing twenty-nine poetic forms, including a few that you may not have heard of such as the triolet, the roundel, and the villanelle. In *R Is for Rhyme: A Poetry Alphabet*, Judy Young provides many examples of literary devices, and poetic techniques and forms. *Baseball, Snakes, and Summer Squash: Poems About Growing Up* by Donald Graves is a wonderful book of unrhymed poetry. Students will make connections with these poems because they are filled with childhood experiences, laughter and tears, and wonderful words.

Seeing Poetry Everywhere

Children love poetry, and they can be successful poets if they have a host of mentors, a useful scaffold, and a lot of practice. The first step is to find poetry everywhere and to help students recognize that the best prose sounds like poetry. Powerful sentences often make use of the literary devices we so often find in a poem—alliteration, onomatopoeia, hyperbole, metaphor, simile, and personification. When children read books and find sentences that make them want to reread them and linger there, they have probably found prose that sounds like poetry. Consider the following examples from mentor texts:

The trees stood still
as giant statues.
And the moon was so bright
the sky seemed to shine.
—*Owl Moon* by Jane Yolen

Blinking on, blinking off,
dipping low, soaring high above my head,
making circles around the moon,
like stars dancing.
—*Fireflies!* by Julie Brinckloe

Sometimes you're lucky enough to stumble across a picture book that sounds like poetry from beginning to end and is appropriate for any grade level or level of readers. Ralph Fletcher's books *Twilight Comes Twice* and *Hello, Harvest Moon* are filled with beautiful prose created through the use of personification, strong nouns and verbs, metaphors, similes, and appeal to the senses. In *Twilight Comes Twice*, Fletcher writes:

In the summer, dusk
hisses on the sprinklers.
It flushes out millions of
mosquitoes
and armies of bats
to eat them.

Fireflies appear,
swimming through the air,
writing bright messages
in secret code.

When books such as these fill our classrooms, students begin to understand what beautiful language sounds like long before they can label it as a literary device such as simile or metaphor, or talk about the verb use in a particular context as unexpected or surprising.

Found Poetry

A natural segue into writing poetry is the use of found poetry. Found poems take existing texts and refashion them, reorder them, and present them as poems. Found poetry is much like a collage, often made from newspaper articles, street signs, graffiti, speeches, letters, or even other poems. A pure found poem consists exclusively of outside texts: the words of the poem remain as they were found, with few additions or omissions. Decisions of form, such as where to break a line, are left to the poet.

To create found poetry it's best to start with a short text with which you (the teacher) are very familiar and whose language you have already played around with. Begin by reading the piece silently and aloud. Poetry is meant to be read aloud, and often our ears will tell us what sounds like poetry. Start to make a list of words and phrases from the text. Place them on a page, line by line, in the form of a poem. After you are finished, you can do several things. You can read the poem just the way you wrote it down and leave it like that, or you can rearrange the lines, even deciding to use one or several lines as a repeating pattern, as effective repetition. You can decide where you need white space—for example, between couplets or quatrains—or that you don't need it at all. You can revise for word choice to create an alliterative phrase, add a color word, or substitute a more powerful verb. You can combine some thoughts or take something and find your own unique way to say it. In Lynne's classrooms, she asks the students to try to remain true to the content—in other words, not to change the content of the text or the feelings the original writer was trying to create—but often asks them to make the poem their own through revision efforts. When her students are finished and want to publish, Lynne asks that they include their source (author, title, publisher, and copyright), since their found poem started with someone else's words. Even the most reluctant writers will write found poetry since the words they start with are already written. No one suffers from writer's block.

Lynne wanted to introduce her third-grade class to found poetry. They reread excerpts from *Owl Moon* by Jane Yolen silently and aloud. Students examined lines and phrases that spoke to them and copied no more than six sentences or parts of sentences into their writer's notebook. They did not change the words in any way. Lynne modeled by showing one of her choices on the board and explaining reasons for her choices. She asked her students to choose their favorite line and discuss why they had chosen it. They copied their line onto an index card and stood to form a large circle. Lynne explained that they would "render" their line—speak it in the way they believed the author would have read it. She told them not to worry if they heard their sentence or phrase once or many times. Poets often use effective repetition.

Next, in small groups, she told them to arrange their cards and number them in a meaningful order. "You may add one 'wild card' phrase from the original text to improve your poem, but decide on the one phrase or sentence as a group. One line may be repeated as many times as you think would be effective. Then, you need to decide *who* is going to say *what* and *how* it will be said. We will type the poems on computers and copy them for everyone in the group. Practice the new found poem for your performance. Be sure to think about how you will introduce the performers and the poem. We will perform our poems for several third-grade audiences and explain how we created our found poems so other third graders can write found poetry, too."

For the next week, Lynne asked her third-grade writers to look for entries that had vivid images in them—words that sounded like poetry. She urged them to examine their portfolio's published pieces, too. Lynne read her notebook entry on her morning walk when she heard birds singing in the evergreens and demonstrated (modeled) how, using a personal experience, she created a found poem. She emphasized that this was not an entry where she was trying to write something poetic—she just found poetry material in it. After reading her entry to the class, she copied it onto chart paper and underlined the words and phrases she thought she could use to create her poem.

> <u>Birds come into the world singing</u>. *They sing when they're little chicks crowded in the nest.* <u>They sing at daybreak</u>—*almost as if they are* <u>welcoming the new day</u>. *I think they are so* <u>happy to see the sun rise</u> *in the eastern skies that they have to sing about it. It sounds* <u>like a church choir</u>, <u>singing in unison</u>. <u>The world is their cathedral</u>. *Every morning I look forward to that and* <u>eagerly await their morning hymn</u>.

> *Birds come into the world singing . . .*
> *Singing at daybreak,*
> *Welcoming the new day,*
> *Happy to see the sun rise.*
> *Singing in unison,*
> *Like a church choir,*
> *The world—their cathedral.*
> *Eagerly I await their morning hymn.*
> *Birds come into the world singing.*

Lynne mentioned that the students could use one of their own entries as a good place to start looking for found poems. She then gave her students the time they needed to see what they had in their entries that might be used for poetry drafts. An option was to find an article in a newspaper or magazine, an issue of *Weekly Reader* or *National Geographic* that had been delivered to the classroom, books for literature circle discussion, independent-reading books, poetry books, and their writer's notebooks to experiment with found poetry that they could draft, revise, edit, share, and even perform.

Shannon, a talented young poet in Lynne's classroom, made the decision to write all her responses to *The Midnight Fox* by Betsy Byars as found poetry. The students had been challenged to use a new form of written response for literature circle groups. Many students chose to write letters to each other and respond orally when they met in groups. Others had written first-person responses as journal entries in the voice of one of the main characters. Although Shannon adapted some lines and shortened them by omitting certain words, her response journal was a huge success (see Figures 7.1 and 7.2). She had taken in all the information and made this process her own. Other students began to use found poetry as a way to respond to literature.

① The Forest chase
Following the black Fox for a while
My facantion is wordless
The fox is a book I can't
                    put down
The fox is a game I can't
                    stop playing
Silents fills the air
Hearing the fox's cry
    Listening
            Listening
The fox returns

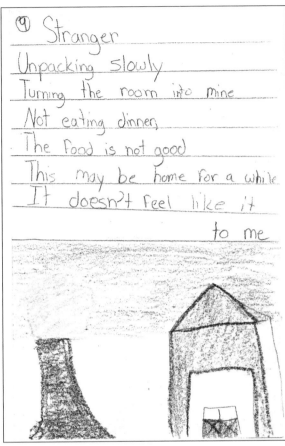

② Stranger
Unpacking slowly
Turning the room into mine
Not eating dinner,
The food is not good
This may be home for a while
It doesn't feel like it
                    to me

7.1 and 7.2
Shannon's found poems
from *The Midnight Fox*.

In Karen Drew's fourth-grade class, Lynne used a different entry from her notebook as a model to demonstrate to the students how they might write a found poem. She returned to *Looking at Lincoln* by Maira Kalman, a read-aloud Karen had shared with her students. She displayed each page on the document imager and asked the students to write down a line from each page that they thought belonged in a found poem they would write together about Lincoln. One line stayed with them: "I could look at him forever." After examining the first several pages, the students decided that they wanted to concentrate on his life as president of the United States. They all agreed that they would not include information about his stepmother, his wife, or his childhood. This is what all writers do. They decide what the focus of their writing will be.

After each page was viewed, Lynne asked for volunteers and recorded their words, lines, or sentences they had written down. After they finished, they read the lines aloud and eliminated some of them. Then they chose a line they wanted to repeat in several places, including the beginning and the end to serve as bookends. They shortened some sentences and phrases to create a list format within their poem. Karen, Lynne, and the fourth-grade writers read and reread their found poem many times, and after each read, they cut and cut. Here is their draft after several revisions:

I could look at him forever!
With his hat he was seven feet tall.
He wrote many notes and stuffed them inside his hat.
What was he thinking about?
Democracy.
The Constitution.
Freedom.
Doing good for mankind.
What did he love?
His dog Fido.
Apples: Winesap, White pippins, Benoni.
Music and Mozart.
Mostly he loved people.
What did he hate?
Slavery.
He freed millions of slaves.
Murdered by a wretched man,
People wept with grief.
A great man is never really gone.
At his memorial you can read the words
". . . with charity for all."
I could look at him forever.

Lynne and Karen encouraged the students to look for opportunities across their day to respond to literature, social studies and science texts, and current events by using found poetry but to make sure they gave credit to their source, where they "found" the words and ideas.

There are many picture books, like *Owl Moon* and other books previously mentioned, that serve as wonderful sources for found poetry. *Crab Moon* by Ruth Horowitz is also a good choice. Working in a second-grade classroom, Rose used *Crab Moon* to teach the students how to work in small groups to create a found poem. After reading the book aloud, Rose copied just the text onto chart paper. She told the students she wanted to think like a poet and identify the words that sounded like music to her. She started to read aloud, sharing her thinking about the phrases she liked best and why she liked them. "'The weekend of the full moon,'" she read. "I get a very clear picture in my mind when I hear those words. I'm going to underline that phrase. 'Coming ashore for hundreds of millions of years,'" she continued. "I like the way the words work together to create a perfect rhythm. I think I'll underline that phrase." She continued reading through the book and modeling what she was thinking until she thought the students were ready to offer their own suggestions. Together they collaborated to identify phrases such as "under the sandy shuffle of the surf," "little by little," "barnacles and slipper shells—like jewels on a crown," and "slowly and grandly." Some students just liked the way the phrases felt in their mouths when they said them; some identified powerful images or noticed the use of alliteration or simile. The next day Rose returned with the phrases listed on chart paper. She modeled how she could choose a few of her favorites, move them around, and then do some revising by adding, subtracting, or changing words. With some suggestions from the students, she created the following piece of found poetry from Ruth Horowitz's *Crab Moon*:

> *Horseshoe crabs*
> *Under the sandy shuffle of the surf*
> *Horseshoe crabs*
> *Like restless cobblestones*
> *Horseshoe crabs*
> *Pausing and pulling their shells through the sand*
> *Horseshoe crabs*
> *Quiet as queens*

Then it was the students' turn. Working in pairs or triads, they picked between four and six phrases they liked best and recorded them in their notebooks. Rose asked them to share their thinking with their partners about the sounds of the words and why they liked the particular phrase they chose. She wanted them to become more aware of how powerful the language of poetry can be. An alternative to writing the phrases in notebooks is to have the students write them on sentence strips. This makes it easier to move the phrases around. Next, Rose instructed them to work together to create a found poem with the phrases chosen from *Crab Moon*. As in the modeling she had done, the students could move things around and revise as needed. She also allowed them to use one "wild card" phrase if they wanted to—an additional one from the list or an original thought.

> ***Crab Moon***
> by Nissi and Ashley
> *On the night*
> *of the full moon in June,*
> *horseshoe crabs came ashore*
> *under the sandy shuffle of the surf.*
> *Slowly and grandly,*
> *little by little,*
> *horseshoe crabs*
> *floated to shore.*

Crab Moon
by Sean and Colin
Little by little,
The beam of the flashlight
shone on the crabs.
Crowding and pushing,
They looked like a cobblestone road.

Found poetry is a wonderful tool to use across the curriculum with works of fiction and nonfiction. Students can even create a found poem from another poem. Found poetry uses the four communication areas—reading, writing, speaking, and listening—and helps provide new audiences for the students' writing. It helps students better understand the powerful images and rhythmic sounds created by the language of poetry. In "Frost in the Woods" from *A Writing Kind of Day: Poems for Young Poets* by Ralph Fletcher, the author describes a walk through the woods with his uncle, who stops to recite a short poem by Robert Frost that the experience has called to mind:

When he's done the words keep echoing
in a quiet place that has opened inside me.
I ask him: Did you write that poem?
He says: I rented it from Robert Frost.

Found poetry is an opportunity to let the words of the authors of our mentor texts echo inside the hearts and minds of our young writers. In a sense, they "rent" the words to create works of their own. Your Turn Lesson 2 at the end of this chapter provides some additional examples.

Using Scaffolds for Writing Poetry

Another way to get young writers to spill poetry from their hearts and minds onto the pages of their notebooks is to use the idea of a scaffold. Peter Elbow (1998) talks about using a rule to help writers get started. He cautions us not to begin with the most obvious rule for poetry—regular meter and a rhyme scheme—because it can limit our language choice and does not let us capture our true feelings. He suggests that other rules can be more effective, helping writers gather ideas. Elbow suggests beginning each line the same way, such as "I wish . . . ," "Now . . . ," or "Once . . ." He talks about using poems of address, beginning each line with the name of a person the writer cares deeply about. Then he talks about taking away the rule and listening to the way it sounds without the imposed rule or structure. We refer to these rules as scaffolds and have found them to be very effective in our work with writers of all ages, including adults.

With a chance to try it out and reflection on how it can best be used, a scaffold can easily become part of your students' schema for poetry. As a matter of fact, students often carry around scaffolds they have tried out just like they carry around the multiplication tables in their heads. Once a scaffold has been practiced, it can be used again and again in many different contexts. Both Lynne and Rose have used Charlotte Otten's poem "February" from *January Rides the Wind* (see Your Turn Lesson 1 at the end of the chapter). Although this book is no longer in print, the poems created by their students using this scaffold have become mentor texts for new classes of writers. In Bruce Bloome's fourth-grade class, Lynne introduced Otten's poem. Several students chose to use the scaffold months later when they were composing rain poetry. They didn't ask permission, they didn't need a review, and they didn't need any direction from the teacher. They used the scaffold because it was as comfortable to use that structure as it is to walk around in a favorite pair of sneakers.

April
by Veronica
April turns everything drippy:
Drippy umbrellas, drippy cars, drippy roads.
Tiny birds get knocked to the ground,
smashing tiny ants in five drip-droppy raindrops.

Blue April
by Nichole
April turns everything blue:
blue raindrops, blue houses, blue streets.
Blue raindrops lock you inside
like a prisoner in a jail cell
drowning you in boredom.

Thunderstorms
by Sara
Thunderstorms turn everything loud:
loud skies, loud windows, loud sidewalks.
Loud rain thunders down onto rooftops
where children quietly stare
into the foggy loud darkness.

Poems of address are most effective when students write about someone they know very well. To stimulate your students' thinking before they begin writing, try reading books about grandmothers and grandfathers, mothers and dads, or brothers and sisters. *My Ol' Man* and *My Rotten Redheaded Older Brother* by Patricia Polacco, *Song and Dance Man* by Karen Ackerman, and

When Mama Comes Home Tonight by Eileen Spinelli are good mentor texts for an activity such as this. Although not works of poetry, these books celebrate the unique qualities of these special people and can serve as models for our young writers of how they might think about the everyday words and actions of the person they are writing to. They can begin each line with the person's name and follow it by saying something to that person. Here is an example:

> *Grandma, your arms wrap around me like a warm blanket*
> *keeping me safe.*
> *Grandma, your special blueberry pancakes are the best part*
> *of Sunday mornings.*

After writing four or more lines such as this, ask your students to reread the poem and decide if lines need to be moved, shortened, or omitted. Finally, have them read the poem without the scaffold—the name of the person—and see if they like it even better. Poems such as these make great gifts at any time of the year and have a specific, rather than general, target audience.

Following the scaffold of the Cree Indian naming poem "Quiet Until the Thaw" by Jacob Nibenegenasabe is another way that students can create poems about themselves or people they know and care about. They have great success here because, again, they are writing about what they know. They are the experts. The poem has a simple scaffold that can easily be imitated. Rose models the use of this scaffold with a poem she wrote about her daughter.

> **Does Not Taste Tomatoes**
> *Her name tells of how it is with her.*
> *The truth is, she despises tomatoes.*
> *Everyone learned not to give her a tomato,*
> *or pasta with tomato sauce, or pizza, or ketchup,*
> *once this was known about her.*
> *As a child she would not wear red clothes, or write*
> *with red pencils or pens.*
> *She did not even like to ride in red cars.*
> *But after a while she mellowed,*
> *and would allow the occasional red ribbon in her hair.*

You can use this scaffold in shared writing experiences with students by writing with them about their classroom teacher, principal, nurse, librarian, or gym teacher. Ask the students to first brainstorm a list of things that they think reveal a key interest, characteristic, or talent of the person. Together, choose one item from the list and use it as the focus of their collaborative poem. It is important to have this focus. Without it, students have no idea where to begin, what to include, and where to end. Once they choose a person for their poem, they begin with a similar process. When they have found their focus, they can brainstorm words and phrases that detail their ideas and help create images for their reader. Give students lots of opportunities to talk about their ideas and add to their thinking. The more planning they do, the better their first drafts will be. Remember, emotions are at the heart of poetry. If the writer is writing a poem and feeling nothing, then the reader will also feel nothing.

In the following example, Veronica, a fourth grader, focused on her dad as a sports fan. Through her words, we feel his intensity and enthusiasm for sports. By the end of the poem, with tongue in cheek, we understand how the rest of the family is feeling.

Fan
His name tells of how
it is with him. The truth is he has
March Madness all month long.
He never takes his eyes off the
screen,
hypnotized by the players,
screaming to the T.V.—
Go! Team! Go! Go!
Any sport . . . football, basketball, soccer,
lacrosse or skating . . .
He is on the list.
He buys tickets and goes screaming for his
team.
Coming for the weekend,
Can't get his attention
when the game is on.
Now it is April and
March is over, but . . .
BASEBALL SEASON is here.
Every year we have to suffer.
His name is Fan.
His name is Dad.

Whereas Veronica's voice is light and humorous, the following poem Monica wrote about her dad takes on a more tender and serious tone.

His Name
His name tells of how
it is with him.
The truth is
he loves music.
He has his own band
which takes a lot of his time.
But he always finds time to teach

me to play piano.
He doesn't get up and
leave when I make
a mistake;
instead he tells me what I did wrong.
He's always there at my recitals
with a smile on his face that seems to say . . .
"That's my daughter!" His name is Teacher.
His name is Dad.

Young writers can easily imitate the scaffold of Judith Viorst's "If I Were in Charge of the World." After reading the poem together in class, Lynne and her fifth-grade students discussed things such as humor, line breaks, use of punctuation, unexpected rhyme, and effective repetition. They read and reread the poem, getting a feel for the rhythm and the words created. In Sydney's example below, the poem follows Viorst's syntax more precisely. Taylor, on the other hand, chose to adapt the scaffold to suit her writing process.

If I Were in Charge of the World
by Sydney

If I were in charge of the world
There'd be five months of summer,
More time in the day,
And lots of fun places.

If I were in charge of the world
I'd cancel shots,
Shooting animals,
Boring dinners,
Cleaning your room,
And picture day.

If I were in charge of the world
You wouldn't have nervous,
You wouldn't have Brussels sprouts,
You wouldn't have to wear dresses,
Or "go do your homework" . . .
You wouldn't even have homework!

If I were in charge of the world
Tests would be a lot easier,
Vegetables would taste as good as fruits,
War would be over,
And a person who is sometimes in a rush,
And sometimes forgets to brush,
Could still be In charge of the world!

If I Were in Charge of the World
by Taylor
If I were in charge of the world,
School would always be fun,
PSSAs wouldn't exist,
And no homework would come your way.

If I were in charge of the world,
Every boy on Earth would be on their best behavior ALL of the time,
Little brothers wouldn't bother you,
Or do anything you'd make them regret.

If I were in charge of the world,
Dads would let their 11-year-olds go to Fall Out Boy concerts,
No bad news would come your way,
No cavities would rot your teeth,
And a person who sometimes forgot to wake-up,
And sometimes forgot to shut-up,
Would still be allowed to be
In charge of the world.

One spring Rose was working in a first-grade classroom where the students were trying out different types of poems. Since she knew they were already familiar with question words, she decided to introduce them to question poems. Rose chose "Wind" from *Outside Your Window: A First Book of Nature* by Nicola Davies as her mentor poem. After reading the poem aloud to the students and then displaying it, she asked them what they noticed about it. They noticed right away that, except for the last line, the poem is written entirely as a series of questions, all beginning with "what." They also noticed that the poem is about all the things the wind does since no one can actually see it. Rose explained that question poems can ask questions about how something looks, feels, and sounds as well as what it does. It's like a riddle or guessing game, but instead of tricking the reader, the poem should describe the subject so well that you know right away what it is about. She modeled with her own question poem about the sun.

Sun
What greets the day each morning?
What warms the earth each day?
What smiles on us with shining rays?
What could it be?
The sun!

Since the students had already created an anchor chart of spring vocabulary to use in their poetry unit, Rose chose a word and together they created a question poem about mud. As the students offered responses, she noticed that many did not seem sure how to describe something with a question. They seemed to want to use the word in a statement like "Mud makes my toes feel squishy" instead of "What makes my toes feel squishy?" Often, she had to guide them into turning the statement into a question. She felt they would need more guidance. "Let's try it again," she said, and just as she was about to start a new poem, Charlie said, "I think I get it. The title of the poem is the answer to all the questions, and you don't say it again until the end."

"Yes, that's right," said Rose as she noticed heads nodding and heard audible "Ohhh"s. She smiled as she was reminded that sometimes when things aren't going quite as expected, students can find the perfect way to help. In a community of writers, everyone can be a teacher. Rose then asked the students to choose a word from the chart or something they knew a lot about and think about some questions they could use in a question poem about that thing. She conducted guided conversations with several students in front of the whole group and then asked them to share orally with a partner. (See the Your Turn lesson at the end of the chapter for more about writing question poems.) Read Charlie's poem "Baseball" in Figure 7.3.

Figure 7.3
Charlie's poem

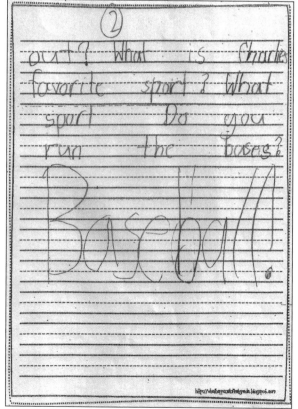

Creating Your Own Scaffolds

After studying a wide variety of scaffolds, students can begin to create their own. Lynne used "Come to the _____ . . . come!" to structure a poem about the Philippines and a poem about the stables. The first poem was written after doing a lot of reading; the second poem was created from personal experiences.

Islands of Beauty

Come to the Philippines . . . come!
Mountainous islands with volcanoes
Tops of coral reefs ringed by white beaches
Spectacular reefs meeting an azure sea
Come to the Philippines . . . come!
Rice terraces surrounding towns and villages
Beautiful, old Spanish churches
Tropical country with monsoon weather
Come to the Philippines . . . come!
Palms, rattan, vines, and ferns
Tiny striped clown fish flitting through the water
Dolphins, whales, sharks, and barracuda
Come to the Philippines . . . come!

My Special Place

Come to the stables . . . come!
Sweet-smelling alfalfa hay stacked in lofts
Crisp, pale wheat straw fluffed in box stalls
Oats, cracked corn, and sweet feed in bins.
Come to the stables . . . come!
Thoroughbreds snorting and pawing in pastures
Ponies rolling in warm, squishy mud
Riders going 'round and 'round the sandy rings
Come to the stables . . . come!
Bridles, saddles, halters, and lead shanks
Tack room smelling of Lexol and saddle soap
Tack trunks filled with brushes and blankets
Come to the stables . . . come!

After modeling with her poems, Lynne asked the students to list favorite places and events in their writer's notebooks. They shared these lists in small groups before making a big list on the board. As a class, they used shared writing to create a poem about the playground. Lynne took the opportunity to point out some of the craft techniques that were used, such as effective repetition and onomatopoeia. (See Figure 7.4.)

Figure 7.4
Shared writing, grade four.

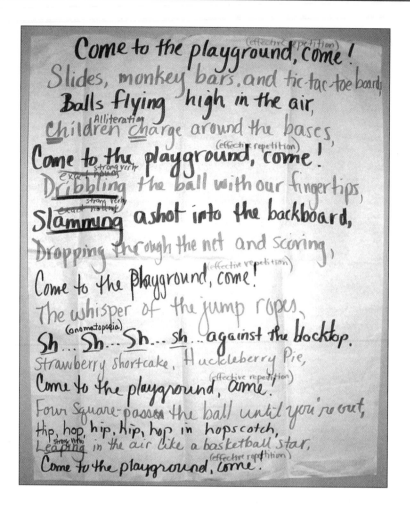

When the students were ready to write on their own, Lynne suggested they begin with the scaffold and repeat it as many times as they thought was necessary. She also pointed out certain lines of her models that were simply lists of things: plants, fish, objects found in tack rooms. She told them that listing could be effective if it was not overdone. Brandon asked if he was allowed to use rhyme. "Of course," Lynne replied, "so long as you concentrate on your ideas and feelings more than the rhyming." That was the information Brandon needed to make this scaffold work for him.

> Come to the seashore . . . come!!
> Come to the seashore where the ocean rises,
> Come to the seashore where there are many cool surprises. Come
> to the seashore . . . come!!
> Come to the seashore where dolphins flip in the air,
> Come to the seashore where I bet you will stare.
> Come to the seashore . . . come!!
> Come to the seashore where you can almost taste the briny air,

Come to the seashore where the wind will swipe your hair.
Come to the seashore . . . come!!
Come to the seashore where you say bye to the shore
And bye to the dolphins who flip in the air,
"See you next summer . . . Take care, take care."

Peter also wrote about the seashore. He didn't need Lynne's permission to change her scaffold; he just did it. The class loved hearing the unexpected rhythm and use of personification at the end of the poem. They also noticed that his poem showed the passing of time of a day at the beach.

Come to the beaches . . . come!
Endless views of water, restless and wild.
Waves come from far to flop on the beach.
Sand castles are built, containing crabs and shells.
Going into the water, shells brush against your feet.
Come to the beaches . . . come!
You feel the waves crashing over your head.
The water is cooling, so you lie and dry in the sun.
The sand is spanning everywhere.
Night crawls in.

Tytiana's poem provides us with tiny snapshots of the home she left behind. Her title "My Home Sweet Home" immediately tells the reader how she feels about Georgia. (See Figure 7.5.)

One fourth-grade class was immersed in a unit of study about poetry. They had been reading the works of Byrd Baylor to stimulate their thinking about nature. On a gray, rainy April morning, Lynne decided to read "April Rain Song" by Langston Hughes (from his book *The Dream Keeper and Other Poems*) and "Rain" by Robert Lewis Stevenson (from National Geographic's *Book of Nature Poetry*) to get students thinking about how they feel about the rain.

Lynne asked the students to write about rain in their writer's notebooks. "How do you feel about the rain? Can you explain what it is that makes you feel that way?" After a few minutes, she asked the students to talk about their feelings. Lynne returned to a favorite book of poetry, *Winter Bees & Other Poems of the Cold* by Joyce Sidman to read the poem "What Do the Trees Know?" After reading it aloud, she displayed it for a choral reading. Next, she asked

Figure 7.5

Tytiana's poem uses the "Come to the . . ." scaffold.

the students to turn and talk about what they noticed. The students discovered that this two-stanza poem begins with the question that also serves as the title for this poem. Lynne suggested that perhaps they could use a similar scaffold to write about rain. She wrote, "What does the rain _____?" and asked the students to talk about the different types of questions the rain might ask. Lynne recorded their words on chart paper.

What does the rain _____?

think	smell	sigh	write	sketch
do	taste	sing	dream	paint
spell	feel	speak	imagine	hiss
teach	cry	enjoy	build	love
share	learn	hoard	see	whisper
whine	save	play	celebrate	roar
hear	grow	say	hide	scream
chill	warm	wish	make	whimper
imagine	create	complain about	illuminate	steal
melt	ponder	spin	shelter	leave
save	cure	sing	protect	call
draw	plunk	hum	fear	pray
read	cause	eat	give	dance

Lynne reread the poem one more time. Then she shared "What the Waves Say" from *Water Sings Blue: Ocean Poems* by Kate Coombs as another example. "Today in writing workshop, you might consider writing about the rain. After listening to these poems, what kind of scaffold could you use to create your poem?"

Chelsea offered her suggestion. "We could pick one verb from the chart and use it three or four times in the question. Then we could come up with different answers."

Lynne nodded. "That's effective repetition. Exactly what Joyce Sidman used to create her text. Are there any other ideas?" Jack thought he might choose a different verb to place in the question each time and then answer the questions. Michael thought he wanted to work on sounds of rain to answer questions about how the rain would speak—in a whimper, a whine, a shout, a hiss, and a cry. Shelby wanted to know if the poem could rhyme. "Of course," Lynne responded. "But don't let the rhyme control your poem. It's the feeling that you have about rain—that's what should come through. Rhyme is great if it doesn't get in the way of expressing your true feelings and thoughts." Jessica thought she wanted to create a book of questions about rain with watercolor illustrations. "These are all good ideas," Lynne said. "Sometimes you need to draw a quick sketch and write down words and phrases that make you think of rain. Or you could start with your writer's notebook entry about rain. I've also brought some other books about rain for you to read. Let's write for the rest of the week and be ready to share our pieces on Friday. Remember, you can use scaffolds you've tried out for other poems, reports, or stories again for your rain poetry. Change the scaffold in a way that makes it work for you. Or use the scaffold to create the poem, and then take it away. Sometimes the poem stands up by itself without the scaffold. Read your poems aloud many times and let your ear tell you which way it sounds best. Remember, poems are written to be read aloud."

That Friday morning, which happened to be rainy, the students were ready to share their drafts. They had used peer and self-conferences to do some revising and editing. Although they weren't ready to publish, they were ready to share in whole group. They gathered on the rug and in comfy chairs. Lynne opened the windows and asked everyone to get very quiet. "Listen to the sound of the rain as I read some rain poems." After she was finished reading, Lynne whispered, "Who would like to share?" and a host of hands waved in the air. Chelsea shared her poem "What Does the Rain Sing?"

What does the rain sing?
The rain sings
a powerful song
that will shock you
like petrifying lightning.

What does the rain sing?
The rain sings
a steady song
that will guide you
through a pleasant day
with wonderful events.

What does the rain sing?
The rain sings
a soft, silent song
that will cradle you to sleep
like a sweet, sweet lullaby.
That's what the rain sings.

Madeline chose to use a question to frame her poem as well, but she added onomatopoeia. Her thinking was influenced by *Listen to the Rain* by Bill Martin Jr. and John Archambault, one of the mentor texts Lynne made available to the students to explore.

What does the rain put away?
Tip-tap, drip-drop, pitter-patter.
That is the alarm for animals,
telling them it's going to rain.

What does the rain put away?
Dewy bunnies that hop across wet grass,
rain-dropped tips of blades

Clip-clap, clip-clap, clip-clap.
What does the rain put away?
Puffed squirrels with flattened tails
crawl up the soggy bark of tree
to get inside their home.

Patter-patter, pitter-pitter.
What does the rain put away?
The slippery-slick birds
glide through drip-down leaves
to get to their soft nests
hidden high in the branches.

Pitter-patter, drip-drop, tip-tap.
The rain has stopped
and the sun puts everything back
that the rain put away.

Sarah imitated the same mentor text but decided to frame her poem with three different questions. She found a way to connect the questions in the conclusion of her poem:

What Does the Rain . . . ?
What does the rain grasp?
The rain grasps the little children,
pulls them outside and then . . .
SPLISH! SPLAT! Muddy children!
It's not the rain's fault.
What does the rain find?
The rain finds love.
Love that Earth needs to thrive forever!
What does the rain insist on?
Of course the rain insists on . . .
RAINING!
Everything would shrivel and die if it didn't.
So let the rain grasp the children,
Find the love,
And insist on raining!
It's for Earth . . .

Chelsea decided to take a second try at rain poetry. This time she let *Listen to the Rain* speak to her as a mentor text. You can see she used several strategies, including effective repetition, onomatopoeia, and the scaffold of the mentor text—the sequence of a rainstorm—to build her poem.

Listen

Drip-drop, drip-drop, drip-drop,
Listen . . .
the pitter patter of invisible dancers on our rooftops.
Listen . . .
the splash of mucky water as you hop into a puddle, then hop
back out like popcorn.
Listen . . .
the sad sky is crankily crying.
Listen . . .
the earth's delightful shower wipes away our fears.
Listen . . .
a watering can sprinkling the earth with a downpour of wetness.
Listen . . .
the precipitation slowly coming to an end.
Listen to the silence.
Listen to the rain.
Drip-drop, drip-drop.

Jacob created a completely different scaffold for his poem, but the influence of mentor texts is still apparent.

Split, splash, splish,
Rain's songs tuck the earth
with a silent splash.
Split, splash, splish.
Faster and faster
Then stops with a sudden halt.
All in yellow
a small boy comes trotting
like Paul Revere's horse
through murky, mucky mud.
In his mind he wonders,
"What will the rain sing next?"
No sooner does he ask
when the rain breaks out
in heavy metal rock.
Tip tip patter patter
tip tip patter patter
tip tip pat
tip tip patter patter

> *tip tip pat.*
> *What does the rain sing?*
> *What do these tips and taps*
> *and pitters and patters mean?*
> *Tip tip*
> *patter patter*
> *tip*
> *tip*
> *pat.*
> *The mystery goes on . . .*

Students can imitate the scaffolds they create and that you create as a teacher once they've had lots of practice. Lynne shared her poem about her grandfather's chair to demonstrate how she relied on a repeating line to get her thoughts down and organize them. She also showed them how she changed the structure to bring it to a close. (See Figure 7.6.)

She was surprised when one of her fifth graders came to her with a poem modeled after Lynne's poem. Compare Lynne's poem "Grandfather's Chair" with Searra's poem "Old, Old Baby Blanket." (See Figure 7.7.)

Figure 7.6 *(left)*
Lynne's sample poem "Grandfather's Chair."

Figure 7.7 *(right)*
Searra's poem "Old, Old Baby Blanket."

Grandfather's Chair
By Lynne R. Dorfman

Old, old chair
Mustard yellow cowhide
Sturdy and broad,
Arm rests worn burgundy
Where strong arms and hands
Once rested.
Cracked leather seat cushion
Gold metal tacks to hold the leather
Four strong, lion-clawed legs
To hold up its massive frame.

Old, old chair
Smelling of leather
Conjuring up faint whiffs of
Life Boy soap, Listerine
And Old Spice After Shave.
Warm, comfortable, and
Large enough to hold
A grandpa and his grandchild.

Old, old chair
Moved around a lot
Allentown to Emmaus
Emmaus to Coopersburg
Coopersburg to Quakertown
Then on to Telford
From Telford to Philadelphia
And finally to Dresher.

Old, old chair
A place to watch t.v. or read the paper
Snuggling in to listen to 45 records
Spinning out coal-mining songs
"I owe my soul to the company store…"
Or simple love songs -
"I give to you and you give to me,
True love, true love…"

Sometimes a lively polka
And then the chair would sit empty.
Grandpa would whirl/twirl us
Round and round and round
While we balanced on his stocking feet,
Laughing and throwing our heads back…
We didn't own a care in the world.

Old, old chair
A place to catch your breath
After the dancing's done
A place to sink down into comfort
Or nestle in a familiar lap
Seat cushion now cracked and split
Spilling stuffing outward
Great creases running like lifelines
Streaks of summer lightning

Lonely, old chair
Knows something's different
Something's missing
Even when it's filled
It's still empty
Poor, old chair
Everyone wrinkles a nose
Cries of "Throw it out!"
"Get rid of it!"
"Stop being so sentimental…
It's just a chair."

They call it junk
They call it trash
They call it an eyesore
They call it unattractive.
They don't see what I see…
A grand, old chair
Grandfather's chair
Mustard yellow cowhide
Sturdy and broad…

Comfortable
Familiar
Warmed with memories
Family treasure
Miss that old chair
Everyday

Old, Old Baby Blanket
By Searra

Old, old baby blanket
Grassy green, mustard yellow silk
Soft and warm
Framed in snowflake white
Hat-wearing ducks
Swim across its mossy pond.

Old, old baby blanket
Smelling of childhood
Cuddly as a teddy bear
Makes me feel safe
Makes me feel loved
Covering my bed

Old, old baby blanket
Takes away bad dreams
Brings good dreams
Moved around a lot
Hospital to Detroit, Michigan
Detroit, Michigan to Reading
Reading to West Chester
West Chester to Hatboro
Finally on my bed

Old, old baby blanket
Something to keep me warm
Something to keep me occupied when I'm alone
Cozy
Familiar
Walked-all-over-the-world traveler
Love that old baby blanket every day.

Exploring Color Through the Senses

Mary O'Neill takes us into the world of color in her book of poems *Hailstones and Halibut Bones*. In this book, she describes colors not only by the way they look but also through all the other senses and feelings they bring to mind. Other books such as *My Many Colored Days* by Dr. Seuss and *Color Me a Rhyme* by Jane Yolen also stimulate connections to colors and can be used to support the writing of color poems. These mentor texts can help writers begin to think about colors in new ways. We can then provide them with a scaffold for creating color poems that involves all of the senses.

When we use *Hailstones and Halibut Bones* with our classes, we begin by telling the students that we might think about colors not only through what we see but also through the smells, sounds, tastes, and feelings we connect with them. We tell them that this is just what Mary O'Neill does in her book of color poems. As we prepare to read aloud, we divide the class into groups or sections. We instruct each section to listen for the connections to a particular sense as we read. For example, one section might listen for the way O'Neill describes the smells of the color, and another might listen for the feelings that the color brings to mind. Giving students a specific purpose for listening helps them focus their attention on the read-aloud. After several poems are read and the responses are shared orally, the next step is to brainstorm a list of colors. It is always interesting to note how even the youngest writers can think beyond the rainbow. They often come up with responses such as aquamarine, chartreuse, or turquoise. The list is recorded on the board or on chart paper and placed in front of a list of phrases that recalls each of the five senses:

> looks like . . .
> sounds like . . .
> smells like . . .
> tastes like . . .
> feels like . . .

Together, we choose a color and brainstorm specific things associated with it. For example, the color yellow might get responses such as *the sun, honeysuckle, lemons, bumblebees, a dog's fur, canaries,* or *a school bus.* We also encourage students to connect with feelings, so responses to yellow might also include *warm* or *bright* or *cheery.*

Next, we use a shared writing format to begin composing a class poem using the scaffold. The students are instructed to name the color, pick a sense, and complete the thought. Through questioning, we assist students in extending their thinking to create a more complete image. In one first-grade class, Danny volunteered the following response for yellow: "Yellow looks like a sunflower."

"Close your eyes and think about the sunflower," Rose said. "Where is it? What part is yellow?"

"We have giant sunflowers with big yellow petals in our garden at home," Danny answered. "They grow so big they almost touch the sky."

With a little more probing and some help from the class, the line became, "Yellow looks like the petals of giant sunflowers in my garden, reaching for the sky." In our classes, the shared experience continues as ideas are extended, recorded, and revised. Finally, students use the scaffold to compose individual poems in their notebooks. Madeline, a first grader, composed the following:

> *Pink*
> *Pink feels like soft fur from a rabbit in the woods.*
> *Pink looks like a tulip that blossoms in the spring*
> *or the pink Valentine cards you get in the mail.*
> *Pink sounds like quiet ballroom dancing.*
> *Pink smells like beautiful flowers.*

There are many variations to this scaffold. Students can be given the option of writing about one color with all of the senses as in the example, sticking with one color and one sense, or describing many colors with one sense. Older students may veer away from the scaffold and be less structured in their thinking of how colors relate to senses. Consider this collaborative poem from a group of third-grade students:

> *What Is Purple?*
> *Purple is a violet singing a sweet, sleepy lullaby.*
> *It is the taste of grape jelly spread on warm wheat toast.*
> *The purple smell is the night sky on April Fool's Day.*
> *Medicine trickling down your throat is a purple feeling.*
> *Purple explodes in your mouth like Fourth of July fireworks.*
> *The full moon on a misty May night has a purple glow.*
> *Purple is a forgetful two-year-old with a mind of his own.*
> *It is the shy feeling that hides deep inside your heart.*

With lots of input and options we have found that all students can be successful writing poems about color. By guiding them in reflecting about how they created the images and why they were so effective, writers begin to internalize the language of description that eventually spills over into all their writing. You will find a Your Turn lesson with an additional color poem scaffold at the end of this chapter.

A Place for Poetry in Every Classroom

Reading and writing poetry should happen throughout the year, not just in April, designated as National Poetry Month. Ms. M., a character in Janiel Wagstaff's *Stella: Poet Extraordinaire*, offers sage advice as the teacher of Stella's second-grade class:

You know what, writers? Starting our year with poetry is perfect because it helps us learn to observe more closely, experiment with words freely, and discover how just a few words on the page can be powerful. Those are important things for writers to take to heart!

We believe that all students can be successful with poetry—that poetry levels the playing field. Even your most reluctant or challenged writers can find their voice through their poems. Because poems are often much shorter than essays and narratives, they are perfect for concentrating on revision strategies, especially emphasizing the importance of word choice. They offer a wealth of scaffolds, ranging from the very simple to the more complex, and provide students with both choice and challenge. Poetry as a genre serves us well when we begin with a feeling—a strong emotion about a person, a place, an object, or an event. Then we find the words that carry our emotions, creating vivid images to touch our readers' hearts.

Think About It—Talk About It—Write About It

- What poetry books do you use as read-alouds and mentor texts in your classroom? Do any of them contain free-verse poetry? Why do you think this is important?
- After reading this chapter, what kind of scaffold(s) would you like to try out with your young writers? Try it out in your writer's notebook first.
- How do you think reading and writing poetry across the year will help your students grow a reading and writing identity? Who are their favorite poets? Who are yours?
- Do you agree with us that poetry levels the playing field? Explain your thinking.
- Does your writer's notebook contain any poetry? Is there an entry in your notebook that you could rewrite as a poem, perhaps a found poem?
  Try it out.

Creating a Color Poem

Sometimes you can use student samples from your current class or previous classes as mentor texts with their permission. The scaffold for this lesson originally came from the poem "February" by Charlotte Otten that appears in *January Rides the Wind*. Since this book is no longer in print, we have turned to wonderful student samples that imitate her scaffold and even some that add a new twist.

Hook: Read excerpts from *Hailstones and Halibut Bones* by Mary O'Neill to get students thinking about color in terms of the different senses. Dr. Seuss's *My Many Colored Days* can help students associate colors with feelings. Then share some student samples that use the scaffold from "February."

Purpose: *Display some student samples on chart paper so that everyone can see it. Here are two you can use:*

<table>
<tr><td align="center">***August***
by Jack N.
August turns everything to yellow:
yellow skies, yellow grass, yellow roses.
Yellow bees buzz busily
searching for sweet nectar
among tall yellow sunflowers.</td><td align="center">***Blue April***
by Nichole
April turns everything blue:
blue raindrops, blue houses, blue streets.
Blue raindrops lock you inside
like a prisoner in a jail cell
drowning you in boredom.</td></tr>
</table>

Writers, let's look at the way these student authors put the words together and see if we can find the scaffold. (Lead students to identify the scaffold in the poem.)

> [Thing, feeling, holiday, etc.] turns everything to [color]:
> Color word that describes three things.
> Concluding sentence that begins with the color.

Today I will show you how to use this scaffold to write your own poems.

Brainstorm: Ask the class to brainstorm a list of colors. Pick some of the colors and have the class brainstorm things that could be that color. Encourage them to think about all the different senses as well as emotions. (See the books listed above for suggestions.) Examples:

> White—a blizzard, a pillow fight, a blinding light, a wedding, frosty air
> Black—a moonless night, Halloween cats, a bad mood, a loud boom
> Green—spring, St. Patrick's Day, an envious feeling, a grasshopper, April, a fresh breeze

Model: Return to the list of brainstormed ideas and use the scaffold to create a poem in front of your students. Think aloud as you compose so that students see how to go about choosing or changing words. Here is a poem from Rose's notebook:

> *A blizzard turns everything to white:*
> *white trees, white skies, white rooftops.*
> *White-tailed deer step gingerly,*
> *searching for a drink*
> *on white frozen lakes.*

Shared/Guided Writing: Create a poem as a whole-class shared activity, or invite students to work with partners to try out the scaffold. Take the opportunity to model the revision process as the class works together during shared writing.

Independent Writing: Invite students to continue to brainstorm ideas for other colors and to create their own poems using the scaffold.

Reflection: After sharing, ask students to reflect on how the scaffold helped them organize their thoughts. Here are some questions you might ask:

> *How did the scaffold help you use repetition effectively?*
>
> *Why was it effective?*
>
> *Could you envision using the structure of the first sentence from the scaffold as the lead in a piece of prose?*

Note: Through imitation of mentor texts, students often find ways to create something unique from the borrowed text. Many of our students had so much fun with this scaffold that they continued to adapt it to write about different topics other than color and months of the year. Here are some examples:

> Music makes every day a celebration:
> soft blues, country ballads, hard rock.
> People start toe-tapping their feet and
> clap, clap, clapping their hands while
> dancing to the beat—fast or slow.
> —Shared writing experience, grade five
>
> Popcorn makes every day a movie:
> happy endings, sad endings, terrifying endings.
> One buttery hand reaches for the bowl and
> the other wipes away the tears,
> then begins clap, clap, clapping!
> —Sarah M., grade five

Your Turn Lesson 2

Using the Endless Step Pantoum for Found Poetry

There are many ways in which poets choose to organize their words. Many times poems and song lyrics use effective repetition to create a sense of rhythm, to emphasize important words as an echo effect, and to place pictures firmly in the minds of the readers. Remember, a strategy is best modeled and practiced with a short text that is easily decodable for most or all of your students.

Hook: A picture book can be used. You may have already used *Owl Moon* (Jane Yolen), *Looking at Lincoln* (Maira Kalman), or *Fireflies!* (Julie Brinckloe) for found poetry. Mentor texts work well here because students are already familiar with the content; they can probably also easily identify with the teacher's choice of powerful phrases and/or sentences and understand the choice for a meaningful order.

Purpose: *As we have been discussing, found poetry is a wonderful way to create poems from books, newspapers, magazine articles, and even writer's notebook entries. One important strategy to help us organize our thoughts in poetry and create a rhythm without a particular rhyme scheme or meter is the use of effective repetition. Today we are going to write some poetry using a scaffold called "The Endless Step Pantoum." We can use this strategy when we create an introduction or summary about famous people or a historical event, or as a way of describing a place or a person. So this scaffold is very helpful in writing nonfiction poetry. The scaffold is created by the way the lines are repeated, so it is not one that we can remove or "take out" after the poem has been written. The scaffold holds the piece together.*

Brainstorm: Ask students to turn and talk with a partner or small group about the found poetry they have written and their sources for the found poetry. Students should look through their writing folders or portfolios and their writer's notebooks. In whole group, share some of their thinking.

Model: The paragraph below is intended as a model for upper elementary and middle school children.

> *I am going to use* Hello, Harvest Moon *by Ralph Fletcher to write a found poem using the endless step pantoum. I am giving each of you the structure of the pantoum so you can follow my thinking as I write a poem. The first thing I need to do is reread the book and pick out all the words and phrases that speak to me. I am going to list them on this chart paper.* [A partial list is included here.]
>
> stirring at the edge of the world
> round, ripe, and huge

hello, harvest moon
working its magic

*Now I'm going to write the pantoum. Here is the scaffold for this
kind of poem.*

Distribute a handout that looks like the one in this Your Turn lesson and
review with the students so they can see what lines will be repeated and
where.

*I have to think about where I'm going to place the words so the
poem makes sense and flows. I also see that the first line and
third line are repeated at the end of the structure, so I should
choose them carefully.*

Now write on the board or on chart paper. Try it out before you model in
front of your students if that will help you feel more comfortable.

Line 1_____
Line 2_____
Line 3_____
Line 4_____
Line 5_____ (repeats Line 2)
Line 6_____
Line 7_____ (repeats Line 4)
Line 8_____
Line 9_____ (repeats Line 6)
Line 10_____
Line 11_____ (repeats Line 8)
Line 12_____
Line 13_____ (repeats Line 10)
Line 14_____ (repeats Line 3 or 1)
Line 15_____ (repeats Line 12)
Line 16_____ (repeats Line 1 or 3)

Here is an example for the first two stanzas:

> *Stirring at the edge of the world,*
> *Round, ripe, and huge.*
> *Hello, harvest moon*
> *Working its magic!*
>
> *Round, ripe, and huge,*
> *A mixture of silver and shadow.*
> *Working its magic,*
> *Birch trees double-dipped in moonlight.*

As you can see, the phrases came from the chart where I did the brainstorming. Sometimes I just placed the phrases where I thought they would most logically go, and other times I shortened the phrase to maintain the rhythm.

Shared/Guided Writing: Now the students are ready to try it out with a partner or small group. You can take down the chart papers and use the book one more time, making a list of different phrases, or you could ask the students to choose another book and start with reading silently and aloud, then finding meaningful words, phrases, and sentences that sound like poetry or are very descriptive. Encourage students to examine photos or illustrations as well and to combine thoughts in interesting ways. Try out certain lines, and let the students revise by moving, removing, adding, and substituting until they are satisfied with the results. Students should be told to cite the source at the bottom of their drafts and include it in their final publication of pantoum poetry. Older children can use the pantoum to explore current events with newspapers and magazine articles.

Independent Writing: Students can certainly use another book, such as *Twilight Comes Twice* by Ralph Fletcher, or revisit a draft, a notebook entry, or a finished portfolio piece. Return to other mentor texts so students can comfortably begin here on their own. It is always a good idea to have young writers share their writing with a partner, with a small response group, or in the general sharing session of writing workshop.

Reflection: Students can turn and talk with a partner about their poems.

What revision strategies did you use?

Where did you have to move lines? Why did you do that?

How did the brainstorming of key phrases, words, and sentences help you write?

Did you find a different way to begin?

How can you use "effective repetition" in other writing you do?

Where would you use this strategy, the endless step pantoum, to organize your thoughts again?

Your Turn Lesson 3

Creating Haiku with Personification

There are many ways in which authors use personification to make their writing come alive and add their voice or the voice of someone or something else. As we discuss in this chapter, sometimes poets use a particular form or scaffold to create a poem. For young writers, understanding haiku as a form of poetry may help them use personification to write about nature and their feelings; however, it is important to remember not to emphasize too many poems that require a specific form such as limerick, cinquain, tanka, sonnet, or ballad. Often, introducing one of them during the course of a year is enough! Haiku includes what the poet is thinking or feeling about an action, a change, or an event in nature—sometimes a question or a wish for the future. Haiku examines a very small moment and tries to capture an experience in a fresh, intuitive way. Nature's flora and fauna, its weather, its changing seasons, night and day all provide our writers with enough choice for them to begin to craft their own haiku.

Hook: Choose some of the mentor texts you have been using in the classroom and examine several haiku closely with the students. Look for books that have haiku with personification, if that is what you are going to teach, or books where haiku appeal to the senses. Share *One Leaf Rides the Wind* by Celeste Davidson Mannis. Copy one or two examples on chart paper and display them.

Purpose: *As we have been discussing, personification can be an important part of any piece of writing. As we can see from the poems we talked about from our read-aloud, haiku poets often use personification, sometimes talking to waves, birds, trees, and oceans as if they could talk back—as if they have feelings like we do. Today I will show you how you can write that kind of haiku, that takes ordinary things and talks about them in extraordinary ways. That's what writers do. Our poems will satisfy our readers by appealing to the senses and helping us see things that are not people behave, feel, and think like people.*

Brainstorm: Ask the students to use their writer's notebooks to brainstorm a list of things that have to do with nature. You might take them on a nature walk with their notebooks if it is appropriate. Remind them to think of the seasons, day and night times, and their own backyards and familiar parks. Have them turn and share with a partner or small group, then report in whole group. Record their thinking on chart paper or the blackboard. If your students are giving you nonspecific words such as animals, birds, and flowers, remind them to be specific and talk about deer, sparrows, and daisies instead.

Model: Take one idea from the board and compose a poem. Make use of the senses and personification, if that is the skill you want them to imitate and practice. Here are some of Lynne's examples that use her students' suggestions of wind, Mother Nature, and blue jays:

> *Naughty Wind! You dare*
> *to turn umbrellas inside*
> *out and lift our skirts!*

> *Mother Nature sews*
> *shiny jewels into the*
> *midnight summer sky.*

> *Blue jay loudly scolds*
> *feasting squirrels that gather*
> *at his bird feeder.*

Shared/Guided Writing: Ask students to choose a topic from the board. After a topic has been chosen, get the students to sketch a scene. Have them turn and talk with a partner. What is happening in their scenes? Call on some students to explain their ideas. Start to create the haiku line by line or as an entire thought. For the first draft, don't worry about the five-seven-five syllable count—worry about the content instead. Next, work on word choice. Replace general words with specific words. Have you, with the students, personified an animal or inanimate object such as the moon? If not, how could you do that? Finally, play with the word choice and the number of words on each line until you achieve the syllable count. Don't sacrifice voice, word choice, and content for form. Repeat this process three or more times before releasing them to partner or small-group work. (Copy the haiku on chart paper and display it for future reference.) After students work with a partner or small group to create haiku, invite some groups of students to offer their pieces for group revision, or hold a guided conversation in front of the group.

Independent Writing: This part will probably take place the next day. Refer to the poems created during guided writing. First, ask students to continue revisions of their haiku from guided practice. Students may also wish to start new pieces and concentrate on using personification and appeal to the senses to create effective haiku.

Reflection: After students have the opportunity to revise or write, ask them to share in whole group or small group. The following questions can help guide their thinking:

How did your use of personification change the poem?

How is it satisfying to the reader?

Does your poem make us continue to wonder about something?

Would a different subject, season, or time of day work better?

What kinds of things should you think about as you write haiku?

When could you use haiku again?

When or where could you use personification again?

Your Turn Lesson 4

Creating a List Poem Focusing on Senses

Hook: Read "Song" from *Forest Has a Song* by Amy Ludwig VanDerwater. With your students, talk about how the poet organized her poem. The first stanza is an introduction; the second is a listing of sounds, or actions that suggest sounds. ("Squirrels chase.") The last line is the title of the book, and offers a scaffold that can be imitated. Discuss how the poet uses specific and rich vocabulary. A good companion text to use with this poem is *The Listening Walk* by Paul Showers.

Purpose: *Writers, today I will show you how you can use sounds to write a list poem just like Amy Ludwig VanDerwater did.*

Brainstorm: List places at school or at home where students could collect sounds. The list might include the playground, the cafeteria, the bus, walking home, a backyard, downtown, a park, the soccer field, a self-serve laundry, and so on. Choose a location that lends itself to taking a listening walk with your class. If you can't go somewhere, use the classroom. List as many ideas as you can, following the examples in "Song." For example, a listening walk on the playground might result in ideas such as children yell, kids squeal, cars honk, birds chirp, leaves rustle, swings creak, balls bounce, and others. Don't worry about rhyming unless it comes naturally.

Model: Using the ideas generated, begin a poem using "Song" as a scaffold—start with a general description and then list some of the things heard. Borrow a version of the last line as an ending. Here's an example:

> *Outside at recess*
> *I hear*
> *Fun and laughter*
> *Everywhere.*
>
> *Kids squeal.*
> *Balls bounce.*
> *Swings creak.*
> *Jump ropes slap.*
>
> *The playground has a song.*

Shared/Guided: Choose another location or use the same one, and write a poem together with the class. If students need more practice, they can work in partners to write additional poems.

Independent: Encourage students to choose a location and begin to gather sounds. Have them jot their ideas in their writer's notebook. This activity lends itself to a home assignment. When students are ready, perhaps the next day, they can share ideas with a partner before they write.

Reflection: *How well were you able to describe the sounds?*

Did you revise for better word choice?

How would this poem format work with a different sense, perhaps smells?

Your Turn Lesson 5

Creating a Question Poem with the Senses

There are many ways to create a question poem. Sometimes the poem is a series of questions, like a riddle. That is the kind used in the classroom snapshot described in this chapter. In this Your Turn lesson, we use questions and answers built around the senses like Nicola Davies does in "Baby Birds" found in *Outside Your Window: A First Book of Nature*.

Hook: Reread the poem "Baby Birds." Ask students what they notice. Guide them to noticing the questions built around the senses, in this case, sight and hearing.

Purpose: *Writers, today I will show you how to write a question poem using the senses just like Nicola Davies did in "Baby Birds."*

Brainstorm: For very young writers, be sure to review the five senses. Together with your class, create a list of nature-related words or things, places, and activities that are familiar to them, such as trees, butterflies, the moon, clouds, rain, baseball, soccer, flowers, dogs, deer, the park, the playground, and so on. You might also choose to create a chart such as the following for all or some of the words:

Object (place, activity)	See	Hear	Smell	Taste	Feel
Butterfly	Painted wings; bright colors; landing on flowers				
Rose	Pink, red, yellow thorns, leaves		sweet scent		velvet soft, sharp
Soccer	kids running, kids kicking ball	shouting, laughing, breathing hard		salty sweat on lips	out of breath
Rain	drops, dark clouds, puddles	plops, drips, splash, taps	dampness	wet, fresh, clean	sad, gloomy

Not all senses have to be filled in for each brainstormed object, place, or activity.

Model: Choose something from the brainstormed list to use for your question poem. Remember to think aloud as you write so that the students can better understand the process. Try to include at least two senses. Here's an example that uses a question/answer format:

Roses
Can you see them in the garden?
Pinks and reds in perfect groups.
What do you smell when you lean in?
A sweet and pleasant fragrance.
Beware—there's something sharp! What do you think it is?
A spiky thorn! It's dangerous.
Please be careful when you touch.

Shared/Guided Writing: Have the class help to choose something else from the brainstormed list. If you have not created a chart, brainstorm some things associated with the senses for the word chosen. Then together create a question poem on chart paper or a whiteboard so that all can see it.

Independent Writing: Ask students to create their own question poems. They can use the brainstormed list or find a topic in their notebook that they know a lot about.

Reflection: *How easily did you come up with a topic for your poem?*

Was it easy or hard to create questions?

Did you need to do any research for your poem?

Do you think you could use this format again? If so, would you change any part of the process?

Chapter 8

Choice, Voice, and All That Jazz

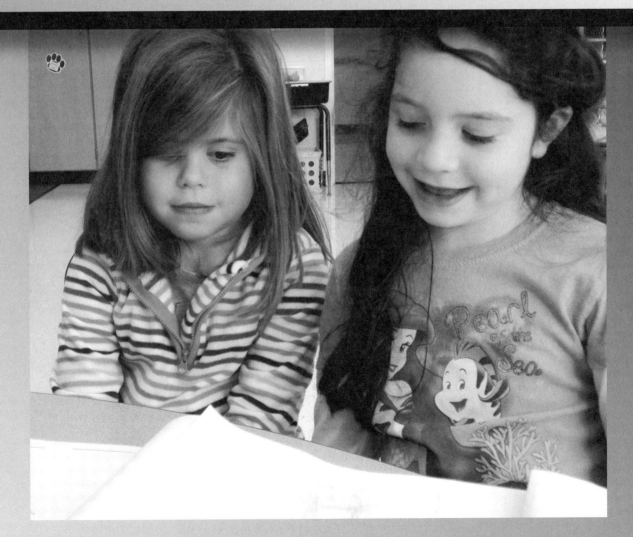

Writing teachers can do several things to help children revitalize the language in their writing. First, we need to attune the ears of young writers to magical language wherever they hear it—in books, poems, the writing of their peers, talk.

—Ralph Fletcher, *What a Writer Needs*

For some people, listening to a melancholy aria from an opera can make their heart soar. For others, it's the toe-tapping, knee-slapping rhythms of a country song, or the soulful strains of a saxophone singing the blues. Others are drawn to an electric guitar screaming the sounds of chaotic melodies. That's what style is all about—it's the atmosphere that's created by the artist that makes you want more, that delights your senses and carries you to a new heightened awareness of everything around you. In music, style is expressed in the arrangement of the notes. In writing, it's in the words. Style is all about the words an author chooses to carry his ideas. It's about the way he chooses to combine them, repeat them, eliminate them, use them to establish a point of view or stance, or a certain tone or mood. Style is choice, voice, and all that jazz!

In our work with teachers of kindergarten and grade one students, the question of style always comes up. Can we teach our earliest writers what style is? Is this even appropriate while they are still learning about letters and sounds and aren't writing much more than a sentence or two, maybe even just a few words? Style is an integral part of writing, so it is hard not to keep the "whole" in mind as we work with our students, even our youngest students, on a specific writing trait such as content or conventions. Without style, writing is dull and lifeless. There is nothing to delight the senses or interest the reader. If we want our students to grow into confident and capable writers, we must teach all aspects of writing from the start. Because style is all about word choice, even the youngest writers can use their expanding vocabularies to write with specificity and interest. The attention to precise language helps them learn at an early age to make every word count. Through modeling and reflection, we can show them that adding color words, number words, or size words adds detail to their writing and makes it more interesting to the reader.

In a kindergarten class one spring morning, Rose returned to a mentor text, *Bunny Cakes* by Rosemary Wells, to demonstrate the importance of using specific words as adjectives or as proper nouns. After rereading the first few pages of the book, Rose pointed out to the students how the author didn't just say that Max and Ruby each made Grandma a birthday cake, but that one was an "earthworm" birthday cake, and the other was an "angel surprise" cake with "raspberry-fluff" icing. She also pointed out that Max didn't want just any kind of candy for his cake, but rather a specific kind of candy: Red-Hot Marshmallow Squirters. "How do those words help the writing?" Rose asked the students.

"They tell you exactly what it was," Jack answered.

"It helps you get a better picture in your head," Alexis added.

"Yes," Rose explained, "Rosemary Wells used specific words, sometimes names of things, to make her writing clear and more interesting. Today I will show you how you can do that with your writing, too."

Rose understood that word choice begins with an awareness of words—making them a part of writers' speaking and listening vocabularies so that they eventually spill over into their writing vocabulary. To heighten this awareness with the students, she asked them all to stand in a circle. "Max wanted Red-Hot Marshmallow Squirters for his cake," Rose explained. "Think about a different kind of candy you might want if you were making that cake. Then we'll all go around the circle and share our thinking. Remember to be specific." One by one the students shared such things as M&M's, Hershey Kisses, Twizzlers, and Lifesavers. Children who couldn't think of something were encouraged to listen to others' responses and borrow a suggestion, which ensured 100 percent student participation. Rose next conducted the same activity with other categories. The students were asked to share such things as specific kinds of dogs, names of stores, boys' names, and girls' names. After modeling with her own writing, Rose asked the students to add the name of something in the writing they had done that day. Some of the students were able to apply the strategy immediately. For others, it came later as awareness of words became an integral part of the classroom experience—as students began pointing out names and other specific words in texts used for read-alouds and shared reading, as well as in their conversations. (See Figure 8.1.)

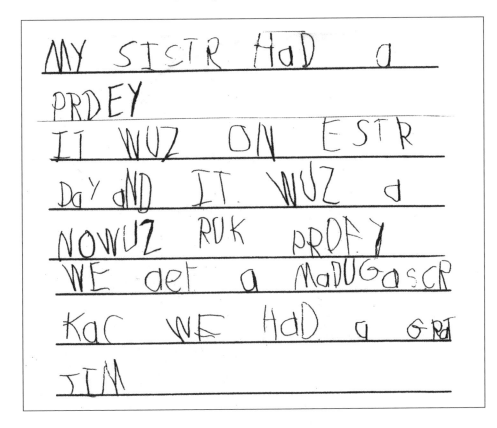

Figure 8.1
Jack, kindergarten: "My sister had a party. It was on Easter Day and it was a Noah's Ark party. We ate a Madagascar cake. We had a great time."

Making Use of Special Vocabularies

As an awareness of words grows, students develop special vocabularies that belong to topics in their writing territories. Many vocabularies revolve around sports such as basketball, football, and gymnastics. It is important that teachers help students become aware of the vocabularies they possess, and that they let students know they don't necessarily need to know how to spell all the words in their vocabularies before using them in their writing. Students should never abandon a perfect word because they are afraid they will misspell it. (At the same time, we are often amazed at the words students can spell when those words help them write about their keen interests. Take, for example, the first grader who can spell *tyrannosaurus rex* because he is passionate about dinosaurs.)

We need to point out the special vocabulary that authors use to achieve specificity and help the reader form mental images. In *Up North at the Cabin*, Marsha Wilson Chall uses the vocabulary of a fisherman with words such as *angler, spinners, leeches, bait, hook,* and *jig*. She names the trees—birch and pine—and names places—Lake Mille Lacs and Live Deer Park. Mentor texts such as these show students that they should be using specific, rather than generic, words. Proper nouns particularly deliver a powerful punch.

After Lynne made the fifth graders she was working with aware of the importance of special vocabularies, the students intuitively used them in their writing. For example, in a piece about performing in a club, Amanda used the vocabulary of musicians, such as *microphones, guitar, gig, high-pitched vocals,* and *on-key voices*. Megan, a fifth grader who is crazy about horses, wrote a narrative called "A New Horse in the Stables." She used words of the equine world, including *double vertical gymnastic, oxer, stallion, dandy brush, trot, saddle, salt block, hooves,* and *muzzle*. She wrote for her audience, other horse lovers, including Lynne, her writing teacher. Word choice is closely linked with an awareness of the target audience. For example, this book is written with teachers as the target audience. It would sound completely different if we wrote it for parents.

One-of-a-Kind Word Choice

Sometimes you may notice a particular craft involving word choice in an adult book you are reading. It might be used so much that it jumps right out at you, and you realize that it must be the author's fingerprint. Such is the case with Nick Hornby. *How to Be Good* is filled with wonderful adjectives created by stringing together a group of words with hyphens. The effect in Hornby's book is often to make the reader smile or even laugh out loud. After reading several of Hornby's books, Lynne started to notice the use of hyphenated words every-where, especially in books written for children. She pointed them out to the children in her class, noticing how they slowed the reader down and helped give a more vivid understanding of time and place, culture, or people. In *Talkin' About Bessie: The Story of Aviator Elizabeth Coleman*, author Nikki Grimes speaks in the voice of the schoolteacher and describes the school that Bessie attended as "the hot-in-summer, cold-in-winter, one-room Colored schoolhouse where I taught in Waxahachie." Sometimes the examples are more humorous, as in Don Graves's "no-thank-you helping" to describe the amount of summer squash his mother plops on his plate in *Baseball, Snakes, and Summer Squash.*

Lynne started to use hyphenated adjectives in her writer's notebook and noticed they began spilling into everything she wrote. Her students noticed it, too, and started finding examples in other texts, such as *Twilight Comes Twice* by Ralph Fletcher. (Also see *Butterfly Tree* and *Toad Weather* by Sandra Markle and *Mango, Abuela, and Me* by Meg Medina for examples.) Soon it appeared in their writing, too. Matthew had some fun in his story "That Day in the Sunshine State":

> I asked my dad for what had to be the umpteenth time on a hot and humid July 3rd, "How long will it take us to get to Florida?" He replied to me in a less-than-convincing tone. "We'll just be down there in the blink of an eye, and we'll get there before you know it." It appeared that I wasn't going to find out, so I just had to wait. I had to wait an oh-my-gosh-how-long-is-it-going-to-take wait. I had to wait an are-we-there-yet wait. The objects going by as seen through the car window blurred like fruit in a blender . . . we were on the turnpike.

Later on in this piece he talked about a "wet-your-pants scared" as well as "a side-splitting-roll-over-and-beat-the-ground-with-your-fist laugh."

Matt may have overused the technique, but he was trying it out, letting himself practice it. Eventually, he will hit his stride and be more selective. This time he was writing for an audience of fifth graders, who loved it.

Some students began to try this strategy in their writer's notebooks. Connor wrote this sentence: "Taking an Altoid out of the tin box, Andrew popped it into his mouth and made a fish-pucker look with a hint of tears." Kyle had several notebook entries on hyphenated adjectives, including "I was on the diving board with an I-am-going-to-die look on my face." What reader couldn't imagine those faces? (A try-out-the-fun-for-yourself Your Turn lesson on hyphenated adjectives can be found at the end of this chapter.)

Hyphenated adjectives can be found in informational writing as well. For example, in *Pink Is for Blobfish: Discovering the World's Perfectly Pink Animals* by Jess Keating, hyphenated adjectives abound—*finger-like projections, well-fed mole rats, cancer-free rodents,* and *food-filled hairs.* Our favorite hyphenated adjective describes the blobfish, what some people have called the ugliest animal in the world (according to Keating): "Luckily, blobfish don't use mirrors, so they aren't bothered by their less-than-cute faces."

Colorful Words

One of the easiest ways to help students develop word choice is through color, and there are many books written about just that. In the chapter on poetry, we demonstrate how books such as Mary O'Neill's *Hailstones and Halibut Bones* and Jane Yolen's *Color Me a Rhyme* can be used as scaffolds for writing poems about color. However, students can be introduced to other books about color in different ways. For example, we use *My Many Colored Days* by Dr. Seuss to have students write about their feelings on any particular day in their writer's notebooks. Students must understand that there is never a "right" answer here—it's about what they are thinking and feeling. Seuss writes, "Then all of a sudden I'm a circus seal! On my Orange Days that's how I feel." This mentor text has many things to offer. Another way to write from it is to ask students to create their own books for their many colored days. Sometimes Lynne uses a question to get the students thinking and writing. "Where would you look if you were trying to find brown? What would you see? Smell? Hear? Taste? How does brown make you feel inside? Choose a color and write about it in your notebook." This exercise helps students use color in their writing to describe their thoughts and show their feelings with unique combinations of words.

We often point out how authors use color. *Green Is a Chile Pepper: A Book of Colors* by Roseanne Greenfield Thong explores color using a variety of objects that can be found in a Hispanic community: "Brown is a *churro*, warm and sweet." Each color is listed in Spanish as well as in English. In *One Giant Leap*, Robert Burleigh describes the color of the moon through an astronaut's eyes: "It is gray, it is brown, it is blue-edged." Later on he describes the earth as "a big blue eyeball," and finally as "blue, white, light brown." Libba Moore Gray uses hyphenated adjectives to describe the color of snowflakes as "paper-white delicate" and talks about the "red-orange morning" in *My Mama Had a Dancing Heart*. Patricia MacLachlan does the same thing in *Painting the Wind* when she describes the "coffee-colored dog." Sometimes, as in the names of paints or crayons, colors are described very specifically—electric blue, eggshell, iron gray. Color names can also become proper nouns. In *Painting the Wind*, Patricia MacLachlan describes the tubes of red that the painter of flowers uses as Alizarin Crimson, Terracotta, Scarlet Lake, and Cadmium Red.

Students and teachers are quick to imitate. Barbara Wright, a fifth-grade teacher in Lynne's school, wrote in her journal about "Coconut brown leaves broken and tattered. Coffee-colored twigs ragged and lifeless." Lynne had modeled with her description of clothes flying on a clothesline as she talked about "buttercream skirts and tan trousers."

We often ask our students to think about where the authors of our mentor texts come up with their wonderful words. One place for color words might be a paint or fabric store. Making strips of paint samples available in your writer's workshop can help students add more precise words to their color vocabulary. Another strategy for more precise language is to ask students to think of the names of fruits and vegetables to use in their descriptions. Some examples from our students include strawberry sunsets, a cantaloupe moon, and avocado bedsheets. Even our youngest writers can be made aware of the importance of color. Alex, a sometimes-reluctant kindergarten writer, is beginning to develop an understanding that color increases the appeal of her writing to the reader (see Figure 8.2). Color can add a dimension of description to almost anything.

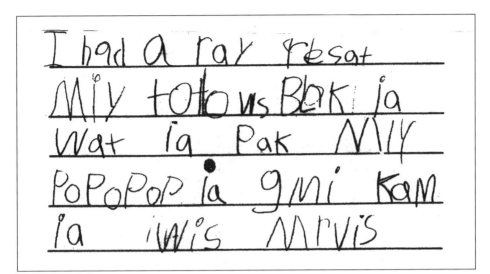

Figure 8.2
Alex's journal entry: "I had a real recital. My tutu was black and white and pink. My Poppop and Grammy came. It was marvelous."

Older students can explore the world of color by experimenting with hyphenated adjectives and words that are typically not color words. For example, in Jocelyn's story "A Dream Come True," which appears at the end of this chapter, she talks about the "firetruck-red kayak" and later on about "a sparkle of curiosity in her ocean eyes." Another fifth grader, Ashley, wrote "the splendid silver clouds rolled across the sky and confettied the earth with milk-white tears." Lydia wrote about a puppy named Sparky: "When I walked outside I saw nothing until, there it was . . . right in front of my face. It was a pearly-white wagging tail."

Applying Word Choice Strategies

Exploring word choice is exciting at any level. Writers fall in love with words, as do readers. In a third-grade classroom, Lynne's students were busily composing informational pieces to give the gift of writing for Mother's and Father's Day presents. Some students chose to write about a grandparent or a godfather. One student wanted to write about his favorite uncles, and another student wrote about a best friend. In writing workshop, it is important to give options, even when the students are writing about the same thing, usually to practice a mode of writing, a genre, or a certain organizational form. Of course, there are some weeks in the year when students have complete control over what they want to write. As always, Lynne encouraged students to write about someone they know well. "You should write about people, places, events, and ideas where you consider yourself an expert. Remember to revisit your 'Expert List' in your writer's notebook and add to it throughout the year."

In a previous Your Turn lesson, Lynne had used Dar Hosta's *I Love the Night* to discuss the use of hyphenated words. She returned to this mentor text to note an unusual fingerprint. Lynne pointed out the author's technique of taking the adjective each creature names to describe why the night is particularly special for him, then emphasizing the word with an adverb that is created by using that same word and adding *-ly*. Here are some examples from the book:

> "It is so beautifully beautiful for finding just the right leaf for my dainty and delicate eggs." (luna moth)
> "It is so gloriously glorious for agile aerobatics." (whip-poor-will)
> "It is so superbly superb for getting some wind under the wings." (owl)

Lynne asked her students what they thought about the strategy. "Why do you think the author used it?" she asked. "Do you like it as a reader? Do you like it as a writer?" Here are some responses from the third graders:

> "It makes you think about what each animal thinks is very important about the night. I started thinking that the night is important for us because it helps us grow." (as a reader)

> "It is kind of different. But you start to look for it every time she [the author] talks about a new animal. That's what writers do. Like in *Suddenly!* where something is gonna happen to the wolf so he won't get Preston Pig. You know 'cause the author says 'suddenly.'" (as a writer)

> "I think the author used it because she wanted to do something that would make her book special so kids would remember it. I never read a book that does the perfectly perfect thing." (reflection)

As Lynne modeled by writing a piece about her mom, she used the phrase *perfectly perfect* in her introductory paragraph and again in the closing paragraph. Lynne encouraged the third graders to embed this technique in their own writing as well. As the students drafted, Lynne and their classroom teacher walked around the room, commenting on their vivid details, their use of strong verbs and exact nouns, and their use of Hosta's craft. Every once in a while, Lynne would ask the writers to stop and listen to a student's sentence that used the "perfectly perfect" craft.

When the students returned to their pieces to engage in revision, they first turned their attention to Lynne's piece of writing. Each student had a copy at his or her seat, and Lynne's copy was displayed. One student observed that Lynne did not really use the "borrowed" phrase exactly the way the author did. "You didn't tell what your mom was perfectly perfect for," Alexandra said. "Like the tree frogs say the night is fabulously fabulous for calling to their friends. That was my favorite page." Lynne asked the students if they thought she should do some revision work where she used the phrase *perfectly perfect*.

It was unanimous! In front of the children, Lynne used a green transparency pen to draw a caret and added to her sentence "She's perfectly perfect" the words "for playing the piano and for making me feel loved." Then she looked at the closing paragraph and changed it to "She's perfectly perfect for the job of Mom." Again she revised: "She's perfectly perfect for making her daughter happy and for the hardest job in the entire world . . . being a mother."

The students reread Lynne's piece and were asked to reflect on the revision. Jamie liked the first change because she thought it sounded natural, like it belonged with the rest of the sentences. She also thought it sounded close to Dar Hosta's technique. "You gave me two good reasons, Jamie," Lynne said. "You always want your writing to come across to the reader as sincere and honest. It shouldn't be forced like trying to appeal to all five senses in a piece of writing when you don't really have a taste or a smell that works well in your description. It's the same thing."

Sam raised her hand. "I don't like the changes you made in the last paragraph." When Lynne asked her to be more specific, she answered that when she whisper-read the paragraph to herself, it sounded better the first way.

Lynne was thrilled. "Wow, Sammy, that's exactly what writers do. You know how we say that good revision comes from rereading your piece both silently and aloud? For me, my ear often tells me what isn't working in my piece."

Kevyn added his thoughts. "It sounds like you're trying too hard. Like when you hit a baseball—you can't hit anything when you get all stiff. You have to stay loose. Your writing sounds stiff there."

Lynne nodded in agreement. "Okay. I'm going to read the first paragraph aloud. Then we'll read it chorally. After we decide about my use of *perfectly perfect* in the introduction, we'll do the same thing for the closing paragraph and take a vote." The class was in full agreement with Jamie, Sam, and Kevyn. Lynne thanked her "response group" and reminded the third graders that as they held peer conferences, they should remember that suggestions can be used, adapted, or ignored. The writer has that right. She also reminded them that imitating an author's technique doesn't mean that a writer can't adapt it and make it his or her own. "The authors of our mentor texts help us learn how to be the best writers we can be by trying to imitate them and write like them. After some time, their fingerprints become your fingerprints. In fact, that's exactly what authors do. Authors are readers. They gather writing strategies as they read. Then they try it out in their writer's notebook—just like you. Maybe we'll find that Dar Hosta has actually borrowed this technique from another book she read. It's quite possible. Authors need mentor texts, too."

Attending to Our Nouns and Verbs

The most important parts of speech are nouns and verbs. They are often neglected in favor of adjectives and adverbs to add style to a piece of writing. Although there is certainly a place for words that describe nouns and verbs, style can be vastly improved if students reread their drafts to revise for stronger verbs and precise nouns. A good place to begin looking at powerful and unexpected verbs is *Six Dots: A Story of Young Louis Braille* by Jen Bryant. Look for verbs such as *announced, studied, repeated, bandaged, itched, teased,* and *traced.* Precise, vivid verbs such as these wake up one's writing. They appeal to the senses. Have your students note which ones make the reader feel, see, or taste. After working with some mentor texts, suggest that students read a few paragraphs from a piece they are currently working on, find the verbs, and try to replace vague verbs such as *do, make, put, get, go, have, run,* and *said* with more precise, vivid verbs.

When authors use personification, the verb is center stage. It is unexpected and surprising—it makes us want to linger there or even reread the sentence. In the beginning of *Journey*, a chapter book by Patricia MacLachlan, the main character is describing the time when his mother left, "before spring crashed onto our hillside with explosions of mountain laurel." Whoever thought that spring could "crash"! In *Through Grandpa's Eyes*, MacLachlan writes, "My waterfall fingers flow down his clay head, filling in the spaces beneath the eyes like little pools before they flow down over the cheeks." You can almost feel the clay sculpture, as if you are the one touching it. In *Fireflies!*, Julie Brinckloe writes, "And the fireflies poured out into the night." Often, it is not the fact that the verb is so unusual, but that the context in which it is used is unusual. Authors who write with style often use ordinary words in extraordinary ways. Ralph Fletcher's *Twilight Comes Twice* has many examples. For instance, he says that "Twice twilight slips through a crack." Fletcher also uses the verb *pours* and tells the reader, "Slowly dusk pours the syrup of darkness into the forest." His fireflies appear "swimming through the air." Strong verbs are everywhere—and they should be in your students' writing. Thesauruses may help, but students need to be on the lookout for precise and unexpected verbs when they read. They can keep track of them in their writer's notebooks or on charts hung in the room so that all students have access to them during writing workshop. Many writing gurus such as Lucy Calkins and Katie Wood Ray encourage teachers to make charts of their writerly discussions with children and post them to make the thinking visible and accessible.

During a writing conference with Kyle, a third grader, about a piece on snowboarding down Cold Spring's hill, he pointed to his best sentence: "I was covered in snow, lying on my back and looking up at the tree that still clutched my snowboard in its arms. But I did not want to give up." When Lynne asked Kyle why he chose that sentence, he knew right away. "It's my action word . . . you know, the verb. I changed it to *clutch* because it's a lot better than *held*. It's like when you really want something badly, and you're not going to give it up for anything." Lynne didn't even point out that Kyle had used arms to stand for the tree's branches. It wasn't important. This third grader was understanding how powerful verbs can be—how their specificity can lead to a deeper understanding and a clearer picture.

Nouns are important, too! They clearly capture the focus and message of a piece of writing. In *Take a Hike, Teddy Roosevelt!* Frank Murphy uses exact nouns that convey his purpose for writing about Teddy Roosevelt—his concern for the environment. Here we find nouns such as *sanctuaries, natural resources, national parks, frontier, wildlife, environment, bison, pollution,* and *extinct.* Chris Barton uses exact nouns, including many proper nouns in *Whoosh! Lonnie Johnson's Super-Soaking Stream of Inventions.* Nouns such as *Gallileo* (a probe), *Jet Propulsion Laboratory, Jupiter, workshop, walkie-talkie, transmitter,* and *prototype* give us a sense that the author is an authority on this subject. The nouns also help us understand what Lonnie Johnson accomplished.

Sometimes authors include foreign words, often nouns, in their text to lend an air of authenticity, illuminate a point, demonstrate tension or conflict, or give the reader a sense of setting. In *Thomas Jefferson's Feast* by Frank Murphy, we get a sense of Jefferson's stay in France through the way Murphy sprinkles French words into this part of the story:

> During his visit, Thomas saw a Frenchman eating a bright red fruit.
> It was called a *pomme d'amour*. (That means "love apple" in French.)

The central problem in *Mango, Abuela, and Me* by Meg Medina is emphasized through the grandmother's use of Spanish to try to communicate with her granddaughter, who speaks only English. Again, most of the Spanish words that appear in the text are nouns.

> Then, just before we turn out the light, she pulls out two things tucked inside the satin pocket of her suitcase.
> A feather—*una pluma*—from a wild parrot that roosted in her mango trees and a snapshot—*una fotografia*—of a young man with Papi's smile.
> *Tu abuelo*, she says, climbing into bed.

Words are perhaps the writer's most important tool. When we engage students in the meaningful study of words, they become more aware of their power and the responsibility they have as writers to make good choices.

Identifying the Person in the Writing: Voice

Sometimes you are reading a piece of student writing and without even looking at the name, you say something like, "This piece just sounds like Harry!" And when you look, you aren't surprised to find out that you are right. If you have ever written something that shouts, "It's me!" from beginning to end, and your peers, friends, and family members recognize your piece before they see your name, you were writing with voice. It is like a writer's own personal stamp.

When we conduct author studies, we often refer to the author's finger-prints—those aspects of an author's craft that seem to appear over and over in different works, such as Cynthia Rylant's use of parentheses in *An Angel for Solomon Singer, The Great Gracie Chase: Stop That Dog!*, or *Missing May* to name a few. Even Rylant's choice of topics lend themselves to her particular voice. If Rylant made a list of writing territories (see Chapter 3), at the top of her list would be family or relatives, pets such as cats and dogs, animals such as whales, home, and a love of the countryside and country living. When you feel that a writer is talking directly to you and understands his or her audience, that's voice, too.

Do you want to continue to read a story or a magazine article even when you have more important things that need to get done? Do you ever feel like you "just can't put it down" or that you need to share it with others almost as soon as you finish it? Did the writer seem to understand your needs and inter-ests? That's voice as well. Lynne often talks to her students and her teacher audiences about authors she reads, partly because she likes the genre in which they write, but most often because she feels the author understands her and is speaking directly to her. Elizabeth Berg is just such a writer. Lynne says she understands women her age and writes for them. For Lynne it is so magical that she is able to read an entire book in one or two evenings. Audience concern and audience awareness are definitely part of what voice is all about.

Ralph Fletcher talks about voice in his book *Live Writing: Breathing Life into Your Words* (1999):

> *Voice in writing sounds like a mysterious word, but it really isn't hard to understand. When I talk about voice in writing, all I mean is the sense of the author's personality that comes through the words on the paper.*
>
> *Writing with voice sounds honest and authentic. It has conviction and integrity.*
>
> *It has the quirks and rhythms of human speech. Writing with voice makes us feel as if we're listening to a real person.* (33–34)

One strategy to get students to recognize voice is to use some of their favorite authors who have written the mentor texts the class has been using. Lynne gives one group of students a set of index cards with several sentences and a paragraph on it from an unfamiliar book of a mentor text author. She gives four to eight other students a card with the name of an author on it. The cards are hole-punched with yarn strung through so the students can wear them around their necks. They also carry a mentor text by the same author. Everyone tries to find the mentor author they belong with and congregate in that area of the room. Students compare index cards, read the lines to each other, and listen for the "fingerprints" that are clues to an author's voice. Sometimes they will ask the "author" to read out of the mentor text he or she is holding. For exam-ple, one card may contain these lines:

> *You can get all hung up*
> *in a prickle-y perch.*
> *And your gang will fly on.*
> *You'll be left in a Lurch.*

Or

> *They kept paying money. They kept running through*
> *Until neither the Plain nor the Star-Bellies knew*
> *Whether this one was that one . . . or that one was this one*
> *Or which one was what one . . . or what one was who.*

Yes, you're right if you said, "That's Dr. Seuss!" There aren't many students who can't recognize his voice. An interesting thing to consider and share with students is the way that *Hooray for Diffendoofer Day* was written. Dr. Seuss died before he was able to complete this story, so Jack Prelutsky and Lane Smith wrote the book with the help of his notes and sketches. Prelutsky captured his voice so completely that it is almost impossible to believe Dr. Seuss did not write it word for word. And yet, if you reread the book again and again, there is a certain unique quality to it that must be the direct result of three voices blending into one—Prelutsky, Smith (the illustrator), and Seuss. Even if you don't want to consider using the book to teach voice, the explanation for how *Hooray for Diffendoofer Day* came to be is interesting, and it includes some wonderful pages showing Seuss's notes, including sketches and revisions.

One way to achieve a particular voice is to write in the persona of another. Doreen Cronin has had great fun doing this in her books *Diary of a Spider* and *Diary of a Worm*. Writing this way can be very freeing for children and is a great way to get them thinking outside the box, so to speak, and have fun at the same time. At a Celebrate Literacy Conference sponsored by the Pennsylvania Writing and Literature Project, one of the keynote speakers was James Howe, author of the Bunnicula series. Howe talked about writing as playing and how words can be funny. He noted that some students like to write comic strips, jokes, riddles, or stories that are funny. Often, Howe's stories make us smile or laugh. Even the idea that a sweet little bunny could be a vampire bunny that sucks all the juices out of vegetables, leaving them drained of color, is funny. Writing in the voice of an earthworm or spider, as Doreen Cronin does in her books *Diary of a Worm* and *Diary of a Spider*, could be funny as well.

Many wonderful books use this technique and are also good choices for mentor texts. One book we love to use for this purpose is *Stranger in the Woods* by Carl R. Sams II and Jean Stoick. You can actually hear the many animals talking. Not only is the book a great read-aloud, but it can be used for reader's theater and to teach students how to write vivid descriptions and good conversations. Listen to the voice in the following excerpts:

"Who-hoo's in the woods? Where? Where did the jays say? Where is
he?" (the owl)

Later . . .

"Coo-coo-could that be him?" (the mourning dove)

And later . . .

"I'm-m-m-m the smallest and I ca-ca-can scamper quickly." (the field
mouse)

Some books create conversation in a particular dialect to give us a sense
of setting and let us hear the unique voice of a character(s). Judy Schachner's
main character in *Dewey Bob* comes to life with his colorful language that gives
us a flavor for the setting of the story and the persona of Dewey Bob. She does
this through use of similes, dialect, and slang.

"Why, I'm as clean as the beans are green!" declared Dewey every time
he spun his little paws around a bar of soap.

"That's one heck of a moon," said the raccoon with a sigh. "And I'm
gonna save me some."

Patricia Polacco also uses dialect, slang, and similes to create voice for her characters in *Tucky Jo and Little Heart*. The narrator's voice is unique as he
(Johnnie) tells the readers about himself:

I grew up like any backcountry boy in Kentucky. Tougher than last
year's jerky and faster than a scared rabbit. I could whittle and carve just
about any kind of stick or wood and I could sneak up on just about
anything. Came right handy for huntin'. My pa taught me how to use a
shotgun when I was knee-high to a grasshopper.

Drew Daywalt uses another structure to create conversation between the
crayons in a box and Duncan, the boy who uses them, in *The Day the Crayons
Quit*. Through letters to Duncan, the various crayons' voices come to life. For
example, pink is feeling neglected and in a strong voice begins the note to
Duncan with:

Okay, LISTEN HERE, KID! You have not used me ONCE in the past
year. It's because you think I am a GIRLS' color, isn't it?"

It is important to note that authors sometimes use conventions to add voice to
the writing as Daywalt does here with capitals and underlining.

Most often, conversations are between characters, but sometimes authors choose to talk directly to the audience. Mo Willems, in the Pigeon book series, makes his characters come alive through monologues directed at the reader. The conversational tone brings out the humor of the Pigeon's remarks.

Hey, I've got an idea. Let's play "Drive the Bus"! I'll go first!

Snappsy the Alligator (Did Not Ask to Be in This Book!) by Julie Falatko is unique in that Snappsy sometimes talks directly to the narrator and sometimes talks to the audience through the use of speech bubbles. The narrator also occasionally talks to Snappsy through a speech bubble.

Why is this rude narrator trying to make it seem like I need a nap? (directed to the reader)

You're an awful narrator. You're just describing what you see in the illustrations. (to the narrator)

Oh gosh. Me?! The humble narrator? (narrator to Snappsy)

Sometimes the conversation includes parentheses that create a sense of intimacy with the reader. As we said before, this is a fingerprint of Cynthia Rylant, but other authors use it, too. Arthur Howard uses this technique in *When I Was Five* to indicate that something is a secret. Here, the parentheses are almost a signal to the reader to whisper. Maira Kalman uses parentheses a little differently in *Looking at Lincoln*. In this book, they are used to add additional information. In *The Great Gracie Chase: Stop That Dog!* Rylant uses parentheses to add a touch of humor. Parentheses can be used for many different reasons to help authors create voice. Young writers are often curious about techniques such as this, and once they begin to notice it, they want to try it, too. But as we have said before, it is important to discuss the "why" behind the "what." By doing this, we can help students use techniques purposefully to create voice in their writing. Kyle, a fifth grader, used parentheses to supply confidential information to his reader in "A Magically Magical Christmas Day": "Then Grandmom stops by and gives us a few presents. (We do not always like the presents—they are usually clothes—but hey, it is my grandmom!)" In the following example, Kristy, a second grader, experimented with parentheses. The sentences could have been written without the parentheses, but notice the kind of intimacy she creates with her audience as she chooses to share additional information as an aside.

My Poppop
by Kristy
My favorite ancestor is my Poppop. Poppop is my dad's dad. Poppop gives
us candy. (He is always happy to share!) My Poppop loves candy. Kathy got

a sweet tooth because of him. My Poppop is big. (The round kind.) When I was little he read me every story that we could find. (Except the scary kind.) My Poppop gives very big hugs. He calls them bear hugs. His favorite color is blue. My Poppop wears glasses only when he reads. My favorite part about my Poppop is his laugh. My Poppop likes to play chess, marbles, dominoes and tick-tack-toe. My Poppop lives in Pennsylvania but he migrates to Florida with my Grandmom for the winter.

I love my Poppop!

Sentence Fluency: The Ebb and Flow of Language

Once students begin to develop an understanding of what voice is, it's time to show them how the authors they love are able to create it. Writers achieve voice in many ways. Sometimes they vary the sentence structure as well as sentence length. Students must become aware that their writing sometimes lacks voice because they use the same structures over and over. A good example of an unusual sentence structure can be found in Rylant's *In November*. She offers this description of trees in late fall: "Without their leaves, how lovely they are, spreading their arms like dancers." This structure makes the language sound more like poetry than prose. Patricia MacLachlan also uses some unusual sentence structures in *Sarah, Plain and Tall*:

> I looked at the long dirt road that crawled across the plains, remembering the morning that Mama had died, cruel and sunny.

> She came through green grass fields that bloomed with Indian paintbrush, red and orange, and blue-eyed grass.

In the above examples, the adjectives come after the noun, not before it as in the more traditional way. Even the title of MacLachlan's work (*Sarah, Plain and Tall*) uses this unusual placement of adjectives. Other examples of this structure can be found in Fletcher's *Twilight Comes Twice* and MacLachlan's *Skylark*:

> "Trains bring people home, hungry and tired from work."
> (from *Twilight Comes Twice*)
> "Splashes of color in the sky, red, and silver, and green."
> (from *Skylark*)

In examining how authors vary sentence length, consider the following example from *John Henry* by Julius Lester:

> John Henry sang and he hammered and the air danced and the rainbow shimmered and the earth shook and rolled from the blows of the hammer. Finally it was quiet. Slowly the dust cleared.

Lester uses one long sentence followed by two short sentences. This gives the reader the feeling that a great deal of activity is going on and then it suddenly stops. Roald Dahl uses almost this same technique in *James and the Giant Peach* when he talks about the peach breaking free and rolling toward the aunts as they scramble to get out of the way. You can almost feel the peach gaining momentum as the aunts become more and more frantic. Then suddenly it stops. After reading these examples to students, we try to get them to feel the way authors vary their sentences by having them imitate this structure. They can brainstorm situations where there is a lot of activity or commotion going on that suddenly, for some reason, stops, such as the playground right before the whistle signals that recess is over or animals scurrying about in search of food right before the first clap of thunder is heard. Then they can try writing a long sentence followed by two short ones to describe the situation in their writer's notebooks or as a shared writing experience. Remember, it's not enough for students just to notice what authors do; they also need to think about why and try it out for themselves.

Sometimes authors create unusual sentence structures by breaking grammatical rules and writing fragments or run-ons. It is important for students to understand that writers do this purposefully, not because they don't understand how to write sentences correctly. Don Tate uses fragments to create powerful images and cause feelings to bubble up inside us in *Poet: The Remarkable Story of George Moses Horton*:

> But that didn't stop George from admiring the language that was all around him: Inspirational words read from the Bible. Hopeful words delivered in a sermon.
> Lively words sung in songs.

The unusual construction—creating a list with a colon followed by three fragments—can lead to a writerly conversation with your students. Why did the author choose to create three fragments instead of using traditional commas and the conjunction *and* to separate items in a list? Try writing the passage the traditional way, and then have your students read both versions aloud several times and comment about which one plays to the ear, not just the eye. Sentence fluency is all about hearing the sounds of language.

At times, an author chooses to repeat words or phrases to draw out one moment in time so the reader can have the same experience as the character in the story or feel the same things the author is feeling. Laurie Halse Anderson makes her readers fill the heat of an August day, the stillness in the air, in her book *Fever 1793*:

> It was going to be another hot August day. Another long, hot August day. Another long, hot, boring, wretched August day.

Anderson uses effective repetition here, building each time on what came before as well as using sentence fragments to help us experience what her character, Matilda, is thinking and feeling. We can already feel a day that seems to go on without end because there is nothing exciting to do and because the weather is not cooperating either. Connections such as these are powerful (See the Your Turn lesson on effective repetition at the end of this chapter.)

Avoiding Clichés: Creating Unique Figurative Language

When young writers begin to imitate the writing in mentor texts, they often choose to work with similes and metaphors. Perhaps they do it because figurative language (another technique writers use to create voice) is discussed in both reading and writing workshop, and because comparisons are something we tend to do naturally. The hardest thing about creating a simile or metaphor, however, is coming up with something fresh and interesting *and* appropriate to the text the student is creating. In Chapter 1, we talked about some first graders Rose was working with who began to notice that the similes and metaphors author Linda Oatman High uses in *Barn Savers* match her topic. Another source that demonstrates the use of words that match the topic is *Chrysanthemum* by Kevin Henkes. In this book, Chrysanthemum is getting used to her unusual flower name. When he describes her feelings, Henkes uses topic-related verbs: "She wilted." "She bloomed."

One way to develop unique comparisons, starting with similes and eventually challenging students to write metaphors, is to ask questions to elicit lists. We often use *Owl Moon* by Jane Yolen where she compares the whiteness of the snow to the milk in a cereal bowl and the fading voices to the quietness of a dream. Then we ask the students to think of the whitest, or quietest, or saddest, and so on things they know. Their responses are placed on anchor charts for future reference and inspiration. One fifth-grade student offered "an inchworm tunneling through the garden" as a response to the quietest thing he knew. Another suggested "the surface of the moon." Encouraging students to brainstorm before settling on the first thing that comes to mind will help them add voice to their writing.

During Lynne's work as a writing coach, she began to notice the same similes across grade levels and content: *as fast as a cheetah* (a favorite among third, fourth, and fifth graders) or *as deep as the ocean* or *as sweet as candy*. Students were creating comparisons that seemed to be inserted only for the purpose of having a simile or metaphor in their piece, not because it would enhance the writing in any way. It was almost as if the student had considered revision work to "add some style" to his or her writing and had plucked a simile or metaphor out of thin air, inserting it without any consideration of topic, theme, or appropriateness.

Lynne decided to return to a favorite mentor text to help students understand how similes and metaphors help create vivid pictures in the readers'
minds and anchor images and information there as well. Before reading, she
asked the students to help her make a list of all the tired, overworked comparisons that they sometimes resorted to just to be able to add a simile. Their list
included *as slow as a turtle, as red as a rose, as big as a blue whale, as hungry
as a horse, as quick as a bullet, as sly as a fox.* There were many more. Lynne
talked about how clichés are simply overworked, overused expressions. They
don't lend anything to the writing. Readers don't linger there, because they've
already heard it—over and over and over. Lynne told her students that they
could use a cliché to "hold the spot" until they thought of a better simile, and
that a good technique would be to draw a line under the phrase with a pencil
or highlighter to help them remember to go back and do some revision.

Lynne knew the students needed a great model. It was easy: *Amber on the
Mountain.* After she read Tony Johnston's beautiful story, Lynne asked the students to listen to it again, this time jotting down any similes or metaphors they
heard. Next, the class shared their notes while Lynne recorded the similes on
the board. She checked with the text so she could add or change a word to
match Johnston's exact language. Then she distributed paper and colored pencils. She asked her students to choose one of the sentences on the board, copy
it onto their paper, and illustrate it as they imagined it. When they were finished, they backed their drawings on colorful squares of construction paper and
glued the squares to bulletin-board backing paper to design a quilt. Lynne
wanted the class to be able to see the words and images for several weeks before
she revisited this lesson.

Three weeks later, Lynne returned to *Amber on the Mountain.* She asked
the students to describe the setting of the story and the story's topic and point.
Then they looked at the figurative language and discussed how it fit this story.
Amber lived high on a mountain. She was surrounded by natural beauty every
day and spent a great deal of time outside. The similes fit the text well.

Lynne also used this opportunity to demonstrate how other authors delib-
erately create figurative language with words that fit the topic of the story.

At this point, the students were asked to look at other mentor texts that
have wonderful figurative language. Working in pairs or small groups, they
searched for similes and metaphors and copied some into their writer's notebooks, jotting down their thinking about why the author used the literary
device, how it seemed to fit with the text, and how it helped the reader. Some
good choices are *Twilight Comes Twice* and *Hello, Harvest Moon* by Ralph
Fletcher, *One Tiny Turtle* and *Bat Loves the Night* by Nicola Davies, *Owl
Moon* by Jane Yolen, *Fireflies!* by Julie Brinckloe, and *Crab Moon* by Ruth
Horowitz. *Up North at the Cabin* by Marsha Wilson Chall is particularly good
for both similes and metaphors.

Then the students were ready to try it out for themselves. They looked
through pieces they had already written to exchange a tired or inappropriate

metaphor or simile for a better one or looked for a place to try out their new-found knowledge.

Nick was writing about a canoe trip down a river. After he'd written about ending up in the water and struggling to reach the shore, he added a sentence to show how he was feeling as he walked through the woods: "The pain began to rush through my body from being whipped around in the rapids like a rag doll." Lynne nodded. It was a good addition. She could close her eyes and see Nick in the water, arms and legs flailing like the loose limbs on her Raggedy Ann doll. Nick liked the alliteration as well.

Sarah had added a metaphor to describe the setting for her story. It was simple, and it worked. "The April Sunday was warm and cloudy." Sarah added this line to follow her lead: "The trees were all in bloom, standing tall and silent in a curving arc, wearing their white dresses for their outdoor prayer meeting. We, on the other hand, were dressed in comfy, faded jeans, oversized T-shirts, and well worn sneakers—ready to enjoy one of spring's first warm days." Lynne loved the picture and contrast it created in her mind—the trees dressed in their Sunday best and the people in casual work-or-play clothes.

Amanda balanced her description of a snowy night by adding this sentence to her thumbnail of the setting for a story she was working on: "As the pale moonlight shined a spotlight on tourists wearing fleece-lined jackets while slowly trudging through the heavy-coated street, our Caddy came to a sudden stop." Lynne talked with her about the way she showed that the streets were filled with snow and about her use of the word *spotlight* to describe the moon-beams—so appropriate for a story about performing in a club with her dad.

A student in another fifth-grade classroom was also working on trying out similes and metaphors. Jocelyn had returned to an entry in her writer's note-book. This piece eventually gave birth to a wonderful narrative. It was about her trip to North Carolina with her dad and her best friend, Rachel. Jocelyn had basically written a good lead paragraph. It was nestled in her writer's notebook, all safe and warm and blue, like a tiny robin's egg just waiting to be hatched. It began, "Clear, cool waves crash down onto the sandy beaches in Corolla, North Carolina. My best friend Rachel and I dive through the freeze-blue waves, collecting sand and shells in our dripping hair." Here Jocelyn added, "We wrap ourselves in our warm, sea-green towels with our lips as blue as the ocean—two tiny mermaids gazing out into the water as gray dolphins ride by." A perfect fit. She read her revision to the class, and heads began nodding. Vanessa said she knew Jocelyn had to be talking about the big beach towels that cover you from your shoulders to your feet. She said the towels, the sand and shells clinging to their hair, and the waves crashing all made the mermaid metaphor an excellent choice. (In her final revision that appears at the end of this chapter, Jocelyn decided to rewrite the story in the third person naming her-self "Sammi" and eliminating Rachel as a character.) Creating similes and metaphors is not easy, but if students study the craft of the mentor authors, have discussions about how it works and what effect it has, and find other examples in their independent reading, they can abandon the clichés and begin to experiment with surprising comparisons.

Discovering Our Writing Voices

Classroom communities are exciting places when they are filled with rich, writerly conversations, especially when those conversations center on style. In *Follow the Moon* by Sarah Weeks, we read the story of a baby sea turtle that hatches at the right time on the night of the full moon. For some reason, he doesn't hear the instinctive voice in his head telling him to follow the moon into the ocean. Sadly, he is left behind. But a young boy finds him, protects him, encourages him, and, at just the right moment, teaches him how to find the voice inside his head. At the end of the book, we see the little sea turtle swimming off, confident and independent in his new ocean home. Like that young boy, with the help of mentor texts, we can show our students how to discover the writing voices inside their heads. We can encourage them to write with confidence, choosing perfect words and arranging them in ways that will reveal their true selves to the reader. When we read their writing, we will hear it. Listen:

The Paleontologist
by Tristyn, grade two

One school morning before lunch a paleontologist named Mrs. Gittis came into our classroom. "Hi everyone, how are you doing," she asked. "Good," answered my class. Mrs. Gittis had a big heavy cart she had to pull around. The big cart had fossils in it. The fossils were as gray as an old man's hair. First she took out a triceratop's nose horn. Some people were thinking that the fossil was a plate on a stegosaurus back, but then I, the one and only Tristyn, raised my hand and yelled out, "It's a nose horn from a triceratops!" "Yes," said Mrs. Gittis, "I'm so glad you know what that fossil is!" she exclaimed. "Ya, I know. Aren't I smart!" I said, puffing my hair. Mrs. Gittis passed the fossils around including the triceratops horn. Before we knew it, it was time for Mrs. Gittis to leave. I wish Mrs. Gittis could come again. I had such a good time.

A Dream Come True
by Jocelyn, grade five

Dolphins, gray dolphins, gliding, gleaming gray dolphins swam through the clear-blue ocean. Sammi's eyes started to burn as she strained to see the mysterious creatures from her spot on the shore. Wrapped in an enormous blue-green towel with tangled hair holding small seashells, she looked like a beached mermaid. Sammi wished she was out there on a kayak, so close to them that she could feel them breathe. Little did she know that the thing she dreamed about all her life was about to come true.

"Yo!" Sammi's dad bellowed from behind her, giving her a stampede of chills running down her spine.

"Hi," Sammi whispered, still startled from the surprising appearance of her dad. Sammi looked down at the grainy-soft sand. Her eyes opened as wide as a shark's mouth that is ready to attack. She saw something that was a part of her dream—a kayak.

Sammi's dad carried the firetruck-red kayak down near the ocean to give it a test run. After he pushed it into the water, he pushed off the ocean floor and slid into the boat. Then he sat down on the black cushion and started to paddle deeper, deeper, and deeper into the ocean when it was wave-free. Waves started to come and the sturdy kayak just drifted over them. About ten minutes later, he came out of the ocean with a you-should-try-this smile on his face.

As soon as Sammi's dad had paddled off, Sammi had been anxious to go out on that kayak. She needed no encouragement. "Daddy, may I go out on the kayak with you?" Sammi asked in a wave of words and a sparkle of curiosity in her ocean eyes.

"Sure, I mean it was the best part of this vacation so far," her dad quickly replied. Sammi's heart lifted up with joy. She felt part of her dream come true . . . kayaking.

Together they lifted the heavy kayak off the white sand and headed towards the ocean. Sammi snapped the life jacket closed and plopped onto her dad's lap. She gripped the sides of the kayak and felt the excitement of holding her dream in her grip. Her dad started to paddle farther and farther into the deep ocean.

He stopped the kayak right where the dolphins swam one hour before. Sammi stared out into an ocean of empty blue. Thump! Something bumped into the kayak. Thump!

Sammi shut her eyes and felt her heart start to tremble. What if it was a shark? Surely nothing bad would happen on this short kayak trip! (How could anything interfere with her most passionate dream?)

"Look!" Sammi's dad whispered in a tone filled with raw excitement. When she opened her eyes, she rubbed them so she could see clearly. She looked all around the kayak, twisting her body to take it all in. Then she saw them. Sammi saw her dream. Dolphins, gray dolphins, gliding, gleaming gray dolphins swimming right next to the kayak.

She smiled like she never smiled before. Her heart beat as fast as a tsunami wave rolling to shore. She was so close to the dolphins that she could feel them breathe. Sammi thought to herself, "Dreams really can come true!" She continued watching the dolphins until at last, they left her and disappeared into the ocean mist. Then she fixed them in her mind, turned back to her dad, and smiled. They would remember this trip forever.

Think About It—Talk About It—Write About It

- How do you promote a love of language in your writing workshop and across the day?
- What are your favorite mentor texts to help students understand what voice is all about?
- What strategies in this chapter are you already using? What strategies would you like to try for the first time?
- What did you notice about style—word choice, voice, and sentence fluency in the student samples at the end of this chapter, "The Paleontologist" and "A Dream Come True"? Can you see the tracks of the teaching?
- Return to your writer's notebook. Find an entry to revise by trying out a strategy from this chapter. Can you add a hyphenated word? Can you create a purposeful rhythm by varying the length of your sentences? Can you add a simile that matches your content? Have fun!

Adding Hyphens to Stylize Your Writing

Hook: Janice Harrington's *Going North* provides an excellent model of the importance of adding hyphens to writing. For this lesson to be effective, this
book should be first used as a read-aloud. Return to it and show a few
pages on chart paper or an overhead transparency where hyphenated
words have been used to create wonderful adjectives, adverbs, and verbs.
Examine the use of *ink-black, soot-black, skillet-black night, going-north
day, knife-scrape, tickle-twirled, puppy-tight,* and *sniffle-sighs*. By this time,
students should be noticing that interesting words are created by joining
two words with a hyphen. Ask students what questions they have about
how these words are created. Options: *Baseball, Snakes, and Summer
Squash* by Donald Graves; *Talkin' About Bessie: The Story of Aviator
Elizabeth Coleman* by Nikki Grimes; *Twilight Comes Twice* by Ralph
Fletcher; *Up North at the Cabin* by Marsha Wilson Chall

Purpose: *Writing without details is boring. But often, we use average adjectives to
describe our nouns. If we use adjectives at all, they should be powerful,
purposeful, fresh, and interesting. Today I will show you how to create
unusual adjectives using the hyphen as you write. Asking questions such as
which nouns need more help will guide your thinking about the details you
need to add to your writing so that it is clear to the reader. If a hyphenated
word can add a precise description, a strong feeling, or a bit of humor to
the writing, you might consider using one or more hyphenated words
and/or phrases.*

Brainstorm: Ask students to think about a place they are familiar with, or something
they recently did, or a person they know very well. Ask them to write these
ideas in their notebooks, jotting down some adjectives that would
describe the place, event, or person. Have them share orally and record
some ideas on the board.

Model: Share some of your ideas about the places, people, or events that are
important to you. Add the adjectives. Begin to write a paragraph around
that place, person, or event. Revise by finding some places that could use
an adjective or two. Try to stretch your thinking by finding a place where
you could insert a hyphenated word. A variation is to take a piece from
your writing portfolio or writer's notebook and revise for hyphenated
adjectives. Here is Lynne's example:

> *I am standing on the beach and curling my toes into the warm,
> grainy sand. My grandparents stand on each side of me and
> each hold a hand tightly. They know I want to run toward the
> water. I close my eyes and breathe the salty air into my lungs.
> When I gaze out onto the blue-meets-blue horizon, I catch a
> glimpse of a gull floating high above me. I think to myself,* I wish

I could be that gull and never leave here. *The waves roll in and out, in and out, a pulsating rhythm that beats like my heart. It reminds me of life itself. I watch the water stain the sand a dark beige color. The foamy-fingered waves waltz out again to continue their dance from the sea to the shore. My grandparents smile at me, and I cry out to them and the whole world, "It's so beautiful . . . it's so very beautiful!" I catch my breath as the wonder of it all wraps around me like a warm blanket.*

Shared/Guided Writing: Ask students to choose one person, place, or event from their brainstormed list. Next, have them write several sentences about their choice in their notebooks and then revise for hyphenated adjectives. Invite one or two students to the front of the room for a guided conversation. Ask them to share their sentences. Write their examples on the board or chart paper. Continue to add to the list as more children share and/or ask children to create more examples from the brainstormed list the two volunteers have shared. Tell them that when they are writing by themselves, they can ask their own questions: What do they think readers would want to know that would help make their writing clearer, that perhaps could be added as a hyphenated adjective? What would add humor? Another feeling? Ask students to examine their independent reading and/or literature circle books for more examples. Hold an open discussion. What do these adjectives do for the reader? Do any examples jump out at you? Why?

Independent Writing: Have students return to their seats and add some adjectives using hyphens to the piece they began until their writing becomes as clear as possible. They can then share again with their partner and receive feedback.

Reflection: Ask writers to reflect on how the strategy worked for them. As a group, discuss how the writing became crisper as their new words were added.

How could you use this strategy during independent writing time?

Could it be used during partner share?

Could you use this strategy in another type of piece, such as a poem or informational report?

For their writer's notebooks, encourage students to collect examples of hyphenated words from books, magazines, newspapers, and other sources, including the work of their teacher and fellow classmates.

Your Turn Lesson 2

Developing an Understanding of Metaphor

For this lesson to work well, students will need to have some understanding of what a simile is and how to write one. (Refer to the section in this chapter on avoiding clichés for a simple and effective strategy.)

Hook: Return to *Trouper* by Meg Kearney and examine the following sentence: "My heart was a cold, starless night—until your face shone through the bars like a mini sun." Ask students to compare the part of the sentence before the dash with the part after the dash. They will most likely recognize that the second half is a simile, but they may not have a name for the first part. Explain that when two unlike things are compared without using *like* or *as*, it is called a metaphor. Demonstrate how you can rewrite the second part of the sentence as a metaphor—*until your face was a mini sun shining through the bars*. Try rewriting other similes found in this mentor text as metaphors. Options: *Tuck Everlasting* by Natalie Babbitt.

Purpose: *We have been talking about ways to add style to our writing through figurative language. You are familiar with similes. Now we are going to explore metaphors, a stronger way to make a comparison. Metaphors, like similes, help to anchor images in the reader's mind.*

Brainstorm: Create an anchor chart of lists to compare a time of day, a season, a place, or a holiday with something that is completely different. It may help students to think in terms of similes. For example, "The night is like a . . ." or "The night is as quiet as . . ." Record the responses as metaphors. Here are some examples for *night*.

> Night is . . . a mysterious stranger
> a blanket
> a canvas for the stars
> a witch's hat
> a sleepy child
> an invisible cloak

Model: Choose one metaphor and brainstorm details that support the metaphor. For example, if the night is a sleepy child, you might think of getting ready to go to bed, stretching, yawning, and dreaming. Then write a short paragraph using the details you listed.

> *The night is a sleepy child. It stretches and yawns, ready to lower the window shade and turn out the light. It climbs into its soft, dark bed and dreams of silvery moons and jewel-speckled skies.*

Shared/Guided Writing: Choose another metaphor from the list, brainstorm some details, and write a paragraph in a shared writing experience. Encourage students to try writing another paragraph around a metaphor of their choice with a partner. They can choose another from the list, or make up their own. For example, they might use "The night is a magician," or "Autumn is an artist," "a party girl," "a masquerader," or "a harvest queen." Circulate around the room, listening in and asking questions that will help students make their metaphors come to life. Share a few examples in whole group and display some around the room or in a writing center for future reference.

Independent Writing: Have the students return to a piece of writing they are working on, or a previously published portfolio piece, and reread the writing to find a spot or two where a metaphor might be appropriate. Have them use their writer's notebooks to brainstorm a simple metaphor and then think of details that might extend it and continue drafting. Or, they can create a new metaphor based on one of the classroom suggestions.

Reflection: Ask students to reflect on how using a metaphor adds style to their writing.

> *When is it appropriate to use a metaphor?*

> *Where might you try using a metaphor again?*

> *How can you take a simile and change it into a metaphor?*

> *What do you think is more powerful—a metaphor or a simile? Explain your thinking.*

> *How can you use a noun as an adjective to create a metaphor (for example, describing a dragonfly as a helicopter insect because it pauses to eat its food in the air)?*

Your Turn Lesson 3

Using Word Pairs to Create Rhythm

Hook: Some authors include word pairs in their descriptions of objects or actions. You can find examples in *Crab Moon* by Ruth Horowitz (*slowly and grandly . . . stepping and pausing*) and *Fireflies!* by Julie Brinckloe (*blinking on, blinking off . . . dipping low, soaring high*). An excellent mentor text to use for word pairs is *Georgia's Bones* by Jen Bryant. There are more than fifteen examples of word pairs in this book. As you reread the book, ask students to listen for the word pairs. Older students can jot them down in a notebook or on a thinking pad.

Purpose: *Writers, sometimes authors use words as pairs. Today we are going to look carefully at that technique and think about why authors might choose to use it. Then I'll give you a chance to try it out for yourself.*

Brainstorm: Ask students to share the word pairs they heard or jotted down as you read *Georgia's Bones* (or a similar mentor text). These can be listed on the board or on chart paper. Return to portions of the text and read sections where the word pairs are used (you could also copy part of the text on chart paper or display it with a document camera). For contrast, reread the sections as a list, without the word pairs. Ask students to brainstorm reasons the author might have chosen to use the words in pairs. Students might respond that it "sounds better" that way. Encourage them to think more deeply by asking why it sounds better. This thinking should lead to a discussion of rhythm and its importance as part of style. Then consider how the author did this (use of the word *and*, matching numbers of syllables, and so on). Ask them to consider other words that might go together and add them to the list.

Model: Compose a short piece in front of the class using some word pair examples. Try listing, then combining, as you think aloud about which way adds to the rhythm of what you are writing. You can also return to a previous notebook entry and revise. Here's an example from Rose's journal:

> *The other day I was driving along and I started to notice wildflowers growing by the side of the road. They were all different colors—blue, white, pink. They looked so cheery just blowing in the breeze. I knew the names of some of them and started to make a list in my head so I could write about it. I could write, "The other day I noticed strawflowers, Queen Anne's lace, red clover, and yarrow growing along the road." Or, I could use word pairs: "The other day I noticed some wildflowers growing along the road: strawflowers and Queen Anne's lace, red clover and yarrow, waving and nodding in the wind."*

Shared/Guided Writing: You could try this technique with the class in at least two ways. One way might be to compose a shared writing. Once a topic is decided on, students could pair up to think of word pairs (nouns, adjectives, verbs, or adverbs) that might be included. This initial brainstorming is a way to make sure all students are involved. Then you could compose the piece together. Alternatively, you could ask students to search their notebooks for pieces that could be revised by adding word pairs. You could then hold a guided conversation with a volunteer in front of the class.

Independent Writing: Ask students to try it out as they go about their work for the day. If some students are already working on a piece, they can try adding some word pairs. Others might revisit a notebook entry for revision or begin something new. If students have difficulty coming up with a topic, encourage them to revisit their heart maps or territories, or to do a quick memory chain—any technique you have already demonstrated to help them discover topics for writing.

Reflection: Ask students to reflect on this technique in pairs, small groups, or whole group. The following questions can help guide their thinking:

How did the use of word pairs help your piece?

How did it change your piece?

When is using word pairs effective?

Is this technique appropriate to use all the time?

Your Turn Lesson 4

Just the Right Rhythm: Using the Power of Three

Many writing gurus mention the power of three (sometimes referred to as the rule of three) in helping students add details to their writing. Although there is nothing magical about this number, for some authors adding details in groups of threes seems to provide just the right rhythm for the text. One of our favorite authors to use as a model for writing in threes is Kevin Henkes, but for this lesson, we decided to use a new favorite text, *Sophie's Squash* by Pat Zeitlow Miller. A fun activity for your class either before or after this lesson might be to send them on a scavenger hunt— have them examine books in the classroom library and student work posted in the halls for examples of objects, actions, feelings, or other details listed in threes. Older students can examine primary source documents (for example, "life, liberty, and the pursuit of happiness" in the Declaration of Independence). List the examples on an anchor chart for easy reference and be sure to add comments on how this strategy affected the text.

Hook: Return to *Sophie's Squash* and point out examples where the author used the power of three. Here are two examples:

> *Every night, Sophie gave Bernice a bottle, a hug, and a kiss.*

> *She made a bed of soft soil, tucked Bernice in, and kissed her good night.*

Create an anchor chart with examples from this book and/or other books so that students have a reference.

Purpose: *Writers, today I will show you how you can use the power of three to add details and create rhythm in your writing just like Pat Zeitlow Miller did. For this lesson, we'll focus on using our senses.*

Brainstorm: Together with the class, brainstorm some common activities or places the students know, and list some sensory details associated with them. Here's an example:

> Movie theater—the smell of popcorn, watching people find their seats, hearing excited conversations, hearing crackling paper while opening a candy bar, viewing previews of coming attractions, the sweet taste of soda, laughter.

Other places could be the soccer field, the school cafeteria, the school playground, a park, a walking trail, a grocery store, a school bus, and so on.

Model: Choose something from the list and write a short descriptive paragraph using three sensory details. You can focus on one sense or many different senses. Here are two examples from Rose's notebook:

> *This morning the trail was a flurry of activity as Cyrus and I took our walk. We passed twin spaniels jogging with their owner, a team of cross-country runners getting in shape, and several bicyclists enjoying a cool morning ride.*

> *An early morning walk on the trail is a great way to start the day. Birds welcome the day with song, the sweet smell of honeysuckle fills the air, and fellow walkers wave hello.*

Shared/Guided Writing: Choose another example from the brainstormed list and write a short paragraph with your students.

Independent Writing: Invite students to choose a different activity or place from the brainstormed list and try describing it with three sensory details. Or, you could invite them to return to a draft or published piece and find a place where they could add a series of three consecutive actions, sensory details, and so on. Students who have some experience with peer conferencing could trade drafts they are working on and have a partner suggest a place where a power-of-three revision would be effective.

Reflection: Invite students to reflect on the use of this strategy. The following questions can guide their thinking:

> *Why might authors use the power of three in their writing?*

> *If you have found examples from other authors, were there differences in how the strategy was used?*

> *Was it easy or difficult for you to apply this strategy to your own writing?*

> *Could you extend the paragraph you wrote into a complete story? Explain your thinking or try it out.*

> *How could this strategy be used in writing poetry, opinion pieces, or informational texts?*

Your Turn Lesson 5 — Using Effective Repetition to Emphasize How a Character Is Feeling

Authors use repetition for many different purposes. Sometimes, they use repetition to show characters' emotions or thoughts, or to reveal a character trait, as is the case in *Take a Hike, Teddy Roosevelt!* by Frank Murphy. Other times, authors use repetition to create rhythm, balance, and beauty, as Julie Brinckloe does in *Fireflies!* Other times, authors repeat a word or phrase to let readers know that what is repeated is important to the development of the story, such as the empty lot in *Happy Like Soccer* by Maribeth Boelts. Still other times, the repeated word or phrase links with the theme, as is the case with *Alexander and the Terrible, Horrible, No Good, Very Bad Day* by Judith Viorst. This lesson focuses on using repetition to emphasize how a character is feeling using *Chrysanthemum* by Kevin Henkes. Options: *Click, Clack, Moo: Cows That Type* by Doreen Cronin; *Ida, Always* by Caron Levis; and *The Tree Lady: The True Story of How One Tree-Loving Woman Changed a City Forever* by H. Joseph Hopkins.

Hook: Return to *Chrysanthemum* by Kevin Henkes. Show students the pages where the author uses these sentences:

> *Chrysanthemum wilted.*
> *She did not think her name was absolutely perfect.*
> *She thought it was absolutely dreadful.*

Discuss with students how the strong verb *wilted* is important to understanding how Chrysanthemum feels about her name.

Purpose: *Writers, today we will use effective repetition to help us describe how our main character is feeling, just like Kevin Henkes did.*

Brainstorm: Together with the class, brainstorm some situations and feeling words that could relate to the situation. For example, a situation could be that you are going to the lake for a picnic, but it starts to rain. Feelings that relate to that situation could be anger, disappointment, frustration, and sadness. Another situation could be that your birthday is next week. Feelings for that situation might be happy, elated, joyful, eager, impatient, hopeful.

Model: Choose a situation and compose a short piece in front of the class. Be sure to use effective repetition to emphasize the feeling you are attaching to the situation. Also see whether you can link a strong verb that would relate to the situation and emphasize the feeling. Think aloud as you write. Here's an example for the rainy picnic:

> *Today, we were going to the lake for a picnic. Today, it rained—no, it poured. I was drenched in disappointment. Today, I was going to fish with my grandfather. I was going to catch a big*

one! I was drenched in disappointment. We were going to play kickball and volleyball at the picnic. We were going to have fun. The rain would not stop. I was drenched in disappointment.

Shared/Guided Writing: Choose another situation from the brainstormed list and create a short paragraph with the class. If students need more practice, explore some other mentor texts that use effective repetition to emphasize how a character is feeling, or choose another situation and create another shared paragraph.

Independent Writing: Ask students to return to their writer's notebook, a previously published narrative, or a narrative they are currently working on to add effective repetition that will emphasize how their character is feeling.

Reflection: *How did the exploration of a mentor text or of mentor texts help you think about the words you needed to repeat to reveal something about the main character?*

What strategies did we use in our shared experience to create effective repetition that revealed how the character was feeling?

Why is it important to use effective repetition in our writing?

When could you use this strategy again?

Chapter 9

Walk Around in the Author's Syntax

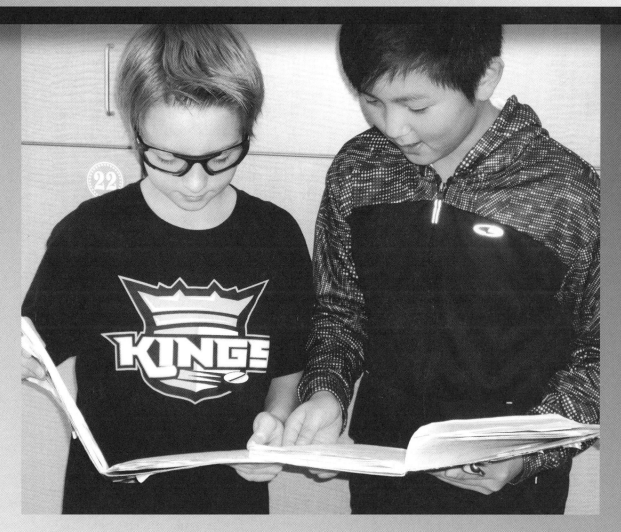

Instead of "drill and kill," instead of the mindless workbook pages, instead of the vapid test preparation materials, I use powerful literature and student writing to teach the rules of language.

—Jeff Anderson, *Mechanically Inclined*

251

Often, you need to examine your students' writing to know what a particular student or class really needs to be able to do. For instance, if your fourth graders are trying to use conversation in their narratives, but they don't use quotation marks and have no idea where to place end punctuation or that they should begin on a new line each time the speaker changes, then it's a good time to take a small group (or the whole group) and do some lessons on writing conversations. Many times these lessons can involve the use of mentor texts, providing far more interesting contexts than the pages of a grammar book or daily editing exercises. Grammar books are excellent references and can be useful during editing conferences with students. In addition, books such as Janet Angelillo's *A Fresh Approach to Teaching Punctuation*, Lynne Dorfman and Diane Dougherty's *Grammar Matters*, Barb Golub's *Infusing Grammar into the Writer's Workshop: A Guide for K–6 Teachers*, and Donna Topping and Sandra Hoffman's *Getting Grammar* will help you build the bridge between a traditional approach to the teaching of grammar (syntax and usage) and mechanics (conventions) and a user-friendly, meaningful workshop approach. Mechanics and grammar can be embedded in your daily teaching through the use of mentor texts so that students don't see it as a series of isolated exercises in a workbook but rather in the context of what real authors do.

Analyzing and Modeling Syntax from Mentor Texts

Word study work can include a look at a sentence or paragraph from a novel or picture book. Encourage the students to walk around in the author's shoes, in the syntax of another. It is hard to teach grammar and mechanics without talking about style. It's like reading and writing—they are linked in very specific ways. For example, take this passage from *Painting the Wind* by Patricia MacLachlan and Emily MacLachlan: "They came on the mail boat with their paints and easels and bags of books and favorite pots and pans." Notice that the authors chose to use the conjunction *and* instead of the traditional comma to separate items in a list. This strategy helps the writer give the sense that the amount of items coming off the boat is endless. Using commas would signal to the reader that everything had been named, whereas the repeated use of *and* signals that other items may not have been mentioned.

Kevin Henkes does the same thing in *Lilly's Purple Plastic Purse* but emphasizes verbs in his list: "When all of the students were buttoned and zipped and snapped and tied and ready to go home, Mr. Slinger strolled over to Lilly and gave her purple plastic purse back." Teachers and students alike can readily visualize a classroom scene at the end of the day where young students are getting ready to go home. The purposeful use of the conjunction *and* lets us feel the amount of preparation and activity that occurs at the close of the school day. In *Bunny Cakes*, Rosemary Wells writes, "She baked it and cooked it and iced it with raspberry-fluff frosting." Each action is emphasized because it is connected with the conjunction rather than with the comma. When passages such as these are read aloud, the reader is almost breathless, because there are not enough signals to pause. A way to embed this structure into your teaching is to have students copy these examples in their writer's notebooks and try it out—in other words, to walk around in the syntax of the author. Here are some examples from Rose's notebook:

> *The baby birds screeched and squirmed and opened their beaks wide for their dinner.*
> *The clouds dipped and drifted and danced across the setting sun.*

Very often it's best to use the mentor text, imitate it yourself, have your students participate in a shared writing where they imitate it, and then ask them to use it independently. After lots of sharing, go back and analyze exactly what the author did. Ask students what they noticed, and record their thinking on the board or on a chart. From *Lilly's Purple Plastic Purse* and *Bunny Cakes*, the students learned how to combine verbs to create a rhythm, decide on a logical and meaningful order for the three verbs they chose, and use the conjunction and to emphasize each item on the list and give the reader a sense of "more." This is a typical example of how the teaching of style and conventions can be blended. Of course, while you are engaging students in this rich conversation, you can help them develop the nomenclature of grammar and mechanics. With this specialized vocabulary, they will be able to talk about mentor sentences and passages in more meaningful ways, because everyone will be using the same language.

In a presentation to graduate students, we used the mentor text *Crab Moon* by Ruth Horowitz to provide practice with walking around in an author's syntax. We presented the following sentences:

> Everywhere they looked, horseshoe crabs crowded and pushed, like restless cobblestones. Under the sandy shuffle of the surf, he could hear the clack of the crabs' shielded backs bumping and scraping together.

First, the class analyzed the passage to see what exactly the author did, what syntax and punctuation she used. The first sentence starts with a phrase telling where, includes the subject (noun) and two verbs, and ends with a simile. The second sentence starts with a prepositional phrase telling where, uses an apostrophe to show ownership, and again includes two verbs in the rest of the sentence. After brainstorming some possible settings and actions, the class wrote the following passage using Horowitz's syntax:

> Everywhere they hiked, small animals scurried and hid like frightened children. In the freshwater stream, he could see the trout's silver fins, glistening and reflecting in the sun.

The teacher participants in this class could easily see that the same passage could be used in many different grade levels. What would differ would be the level of sophistication of the writer and the discussion of the grammar and conventions that would follow. For example, younger students could be practicing the rhythm of the sentences and starting sentences with phrases. Older students could be noticing where the subject-noun is and the tense of the verbs.

When students first begin to imitate authors' syntax, their imitation will match more closely. It might even sound very similar, but don't worry. The more you use mentor texts to help students understand language, the more they will move away from a copycat reproduction to make it their own. And it is this ownership that will bridge a writer's notebook playfulness to anything the student is writing—a narrative, an opinion essay, a poem, or a research piece. Teachers need to tuck in the teaching of mechanics and grammar on a daily basis. It won't take much time, but the rewards will be great.

Many times students get stuck on writing noun-verb or noun-verb-noun sentences, but this is not always bad. Donald Crews uses this sentence structure effectively in *Shortcut*:

> "I HEAR A TRAIN!"
> Everybody stopped.
> Everybody listened.

When you have students use this example to walk around in Crews's syntax, they are learning many things: how to write dialogue, how to use a variety of sentences with appropriate end punctuation, how to build on an emotion with the use of short sentences and effective repetition, and how to make use of print (all caps) to create a sense of urgency or emergency. Crews could have combined many of the short sentences and said, "'I hear a train!' Everybody stopped and listened when we heard the train whistle. We had to decide if we should run ahead to the path home or back to the cut-off." When students have the opportunity to read both versions—as a whisper reading and as a choral reading—they will soon recognize why Crews chose the sentence structures and the punctuation that he used. After a whole-group discussion in which students reflect on the passage, it is easy to move them to the next step: imitate the syntax and mechanics of the mentor text. The teacher can model first, and then the students can participate in a shared writing experience. Here are two examples of how a group of students imitated Crews's syntax:

> "I HEAR A WOLF!"
> Everybody gasped.
> Everybody cringed.
> We all heard the long, low howl.
> Should we run ahead through the thicket
> or back to the campsite?

"I SEE THE OCEAN!"
Everybody clapped.
Everybody smiled.
We all saw the waves rolling toward the shore.
Should we dash across the sand to the water's edge
or stand here to delight in the sunrise?

Sometimes students will begin to use the syntax of a mentor author independently, even combining the syntax of one author with the syntax of another. Hannah, a third grader, did exactly that after working with the lead paragraph from *Amber on the Mountain* by Tony Johnston to experiment with Johnston's syntax (see Your Turn Lesson 1 at the end of the chapter for a more complete explanation). Lynne was surprised to read Hannah's example, since she actually imitated E. B. White's opening paragraph in "Ames Crossing," a chapter in *Stuart Little*. Hannah used a series of dependent clauses to help her reader visualize the setting she created for her character:

Amber lived on a little island by Hawaii where the coconuts grew as big as small pumpkins, where the sea was so clear you could see all the way to the bottom, where the island people wore brightly colored clothing and the children played with Amber every day, where the golden bananas grew and the sweet scent of flowers lingered in the air. Amber loved it here, for she had so many friends.

At the beginning of the year, start a list of mechanical and grammatical concerns you think you will need to work on with your students. Talk with your grade-level partners. They may have some of the same needs and some different ones. Focus on what is necessary to move the writers forward, not on the individual pieces of writing. Look for examples in the mentor texts you are using that will provide practice in the skills that will give your students a more polished and individualized look to their writing. And please remember—writing cannot be taught in a year! As author George Ella Lyon (1999) so aptly says, "You see, writing is like any other discipline—like dancing, say, or playing a sport. To be good, you have to spend a lot of time practicing, learning the moves, gaining strength and agility" (89). Using a sentence or passages from mentor texts on a daily basis will give your students the strength and agility they need to convey their messages clearly and powerfully to their readers.

Developing a Sense of Sentence

When students are first beginning to write, one of their first needs is to understand where to put the end punctuation. Very young writers might put it at the end of every line, even if the thought continues. Or they might end up with one very long sentence that spans an entire page because they haven't put in any end marks at all. Students need to develop a sense of sentence, and one way to accomplish this is through the sense of hearing. By listening to the sentences of the authors they know well, students can begin to understand where the pauses and stops sound right.

To do this, you first need to find short passages from texts that your students can read fairly well, or that won't be too far beyond their reach through shared reading. The example from *Shortcut* shown above is a good choice for this exercise, as are passages from books such as *Widget* by Lyn Rossiter McFarland or *Crab Moon* by Ruth Horowitz. Display the passage and read it aloud with appropriate phrasing and expression, calling attention to the pauses and stops indicated by commas and periods. (In the beginning, you might want to use passages that contain just periods.) Next, read the passage chorally with the class several times until they can read it fluently. Distribute the passage to the students and instruct them to practice reading it for a few minutes every day. This can be done in pairs for peer support. At the end of the week, have the students work with a partner. While one student reads, the other student's job is to listen carefully and indicate the punctuation with an agreed-upon signal—perhaps a clap for a period, a snap for a comma, and two claps for an exclamation mark.

This activity can be adapted for any level. After students are familiar with this activity, you can vary it by forming two teams using two different passages. The partnerships formed at the end of the week have one student from each team. Each student hears a passage that is different from the one they practiced, so it raises the importance of reading and listening.

When students read and reread to develop a sense of sentence for writing, they are practicing reading fluency as well. Other activities that link writing and reading fluency are reader's theater, where students are reading directly from the mentor text, the choral reading of poetry, the performance of songs, and the recitation of riddles and jingles. Books such as *You Read to Me, I'll Read to You* by Mary Ann Hoberman, *I Am the Dog, I Am the Cat* by Donald Hall, or *We're Going on a Bear Hunt* by Michael Rosen are all good sources for reader's theater practice.

Word Splash: Building Descriptive Sentences

An interesting way to help your students develop an understanding of both sentence structure and parts of speech is by doing a "word splash" (similar to the idea splash explained in Chapter 4). We first learned about this technique from our friend and colleague Sue Mowery and liked it so much that we have used it extensively in our classrooms, adapting it and extending it to suit our needs and purposes. Begin by revisiting mentor texts to find illustrations of interesting characters. Some good books to use are *The Recess Queen* by Alexis O'Neill (illustrations by Laura Huliska-Beith), *Olivia* by Ian Falconer, *Mr. George Baker* by Amy Hest (illustrations by Jon J. Muth), *Big Pigs* by Leslie

Helakoski, and *Who Wants Broccoli?* by Val Jones. A word splash can also be used to introduce a new mentor text. In fact, sometimes you will get a greater variety of responses from students if the character you're working with is unfamiliar to them.

The procedure is simple. First, choose a picture and enlarge it to fill a page. Display it with a document camera or Smartboard; it is important that the picture be large enough to capture and sustain your students' attention. Create a three-column chart for adjectives, nouns, and verbs on the board. You can also use a separate piece of chart paper for each category.

Begin by asking students to brainstorm nouns that name the picture. For example, if it's a picture of a boy, someone in the class might say *friend*. You might ask if anyone knows a synonym for that word. Another student might say *buddy* or *pal*. Lynne was surprised when one of her students offered the word *chum*. Lynne asked her how she was familiar with that word since it is somewhat old-fashioned. She replied, "It was in a book I was reading, and I didn't know what it meant. My mom told me it meant 'friend.'" The next step is to brainstorm verbs. We like to use the *-ing* or *-ed* form when listing verbs, but you can use any form—it depends on what you want to teach. If you know your students need work on the past-tense form of irregular verbs, here is a chance to practice that skill (and get a little practice with spelling in, too). This list should be placed to the right of the list of nouns, since verbs typically follow nouns. One of the things you are trying to achieve here is a sense of sentence— a subject and a predicate.

Finally, add adjectives to the chart you are creating. To help students understand what an adjective is, they can test their responses in a short phrase. If it is a picture of a girl, the phrase would be "the _____ girl." Even very young students can easily determine whether the word they are choosing is an adjective if it fits in that frame. You can also add a column for adverbs, adverbial clauses, prepositional phrases, or any other part of speech, depending on grade level and what you expect your students to be able to do. If you are trying to teach sentence combining, you could include a list of conjunctions.

Here is an example of a chart created by second graders for a picture from *The Recess Queen* by Alexis O'Neill. (See Figure 9.1.)

Adjectives	Nouns	Verbs (*-ed* form)
nasty mean ugly mad crazy angry scary frightening furious rude bossy loud horrible terrible freaky red-faced	girl student classmate kid bully sister child teenager enemy meanie	shouted yakked screamed threatened yelled hissed ordered scared demanded barked commanded told bossed said growled

Once the chart is made, examine the list for opportunities to do word work. Sometimes you can ask students to find synonym pairs, antonyms, root

Figure 9.1
Illustration by Laura
Huliska-Beith from *The
Recess Queen* by Alexis
O'Neill.

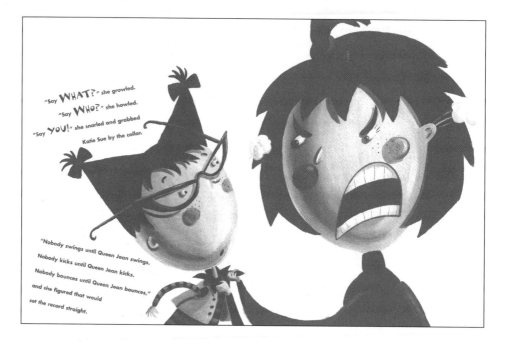

words, homophones, compound words, or words that have affixes. Now the children can write one or several sentences using the words from the chart to describe the character, where he or she is, or what he or she is doing. You can even challenge your most gifted students to use some words that are not on the chart. Here are two examples from a shared writing experience with second graders:

> The crazy girl screamed.
> The loud, angry bully yelled at a little girl and ordered her to leave the kickball game.

The first example can be used to teach students about simple adjective-noun-verb placement. The second sentence lends itself to teaching a compound verb structure. One word of caution: young students love to string adjectives together or try to use as many words as possible to create the longest sentence imaginable. This is where the importance of modeling comes in. Show your students that an effective sentence can be created with just a few words.

You can extend your teaching by having students imitate the basic noun-verb sentence structure as created in the first example but without the adjective. It is the most basic sentence pattern in our language and will help students develop a sense of sentence. Find mentor texts that use this pattern. Three good books to use are *Shortcut* by Donald Crews, *Roller Coaster* by Marla Frazee, and *Widget* by Lyn Rossiter McFarland. Ask students to create other noun-verb sentence patterns using the words from *The Recess Queen* chart and share them with a partner or whole group. Put some of these on sentence strips and post them so that students can have models for creating original sentences for any piece of writing. Students can open their notebooks and jot down a noun-verb sentence. This can be done in a matter of minutes (in fact, you can give students a race-the-clock time limit to challenge them) and can reinforce the grammar and principles you are teaching. If you like, you can pause here to chart precise nouns and powerful verbs, blending the teaching of grammar and mechanics with style.

You might return to this sentence on another day and ask the students to make it grow by adding an *-ly* word (adverb) that tells *how* the girl screamed. For example, the students might give you words such as *loudly, excitedly, happily, angrily,* or even *silently.* You can show them how these adverbs can be moved to different places in the sentence:

Angrily the girl screamed.
The girl screamed angrily.
The girl angrily screamed.

Here, it might be appropriate to use *Suddenly!* by Colin McNaughton or *Elsie's Bird* by Jane Yolen as a read-aloud and listen for the placement of adverbs. This knowledge of word placement is important for writing because it shows students how they can vary their sentence patterns.

Building from one simple activity, the teaching possibilities are endless. You can ask your students to tell *what* the girl screamed. This lesson would give practice in writing dialogue. Prepositional phrases could also be taught. Where was the girl when she screamed? Notice how the meaning of the sentence changes simply by changing the prepositional phrase:

In the library, the girl screamed.
At the ballpark, the girl screamed.
On the playground, the girl screamed.

Certainly it is appropriate to use a loud voice on the playground or at the ballpark, but we don't expect screaming in the library. Students can begin to understand and appreciate the power of words as well as how to make sentences grow with prepositional phrases.

Another lesson that illustrates the power of the single word is a look at adjectives. Changing the adjective in the sentence "The crazy girl screamed" gives students practice placing adjectives in a correct position in a sentence, but it also shows how one word can make a big difference. "The frightened girl screamed" is very different from "The crazy girl screamed."

We have found that once students are predisposed to the context of the mentor text, they give you only the words that the author used rather than stretching to use their own. Therefore, if you are doing a word splash, offer the mentor text as a read-aloud to your students at its conclusion. The students will listen with a heightened interest, eagerly waiting to hear which of the words they offered were used by the author. When you are finished, you can return to the original chart to add any nouns, verbs, and adjectives the students heard in the entire text. In *The Recess Queen* students might add *Mean Jean, Katie Sue, Queen Jean, growled, howled, snarled, quick, clean,* and *teeny*. Word splashes build vocabulary, develop syntax, and provide a way to investigate language on a weekly or monthly basis. They can also be conducted with pictures of scenes. This will help students build the vocabulary necessary to describe setting.

Improving Sentences with Participial Phrases

Elementary-grade writers often overuse the subject noun-verb way to begin each sentence. For our young writers, you might try to introduce present participles in their *-ing* form to begin a sentence. This will eliminate redundancy and improve the flow of the words in the sentence or paragraph. Participles are *-ing* and *-ed* verbs that can act as modifiers in a noun phrase. The participial phrase is often followed by a prepositional phrase or another modifier such as an adverb. These phrases can be found in various places in sentences. Here are three examples from *Elsie's Bird* by Jane Yolen.

> Timmy flew right out, winging through an open window.

> She ran across the farmyard, and into the tall prairie grass, crying the canary's name.

> Timmy Tune began to sing back, circling and circling overhead.

> In *Six Dots: A Story of Young Louis Braille*, Jen Bryant uses the *-ing* form of participles as well to add variety to her sentence patterns and show actions that are occurring simultaneously.

> I stumbled about the house, banging into the chairs, the walls, and the doors.

> Flipping my paper over, I moved my fingers from left to right, feeling the dots.

These mentor sentences are very similar in structure. The participial phrase is often followed by a prepositional phrase and is set off by a comma. Sometimes, an author pairs two participles as Bryant does in this sentence: "I sat in the front row, listening and memorizing." Mo Willems does the same thing in *The Story of Diva and Flea*: "Inside he saw Diva still sitting and smiling right next to the pair of feet and the broom."

In Karen Drew's fourth-grade classroom, Lynne read *Six Dots: The Story of Young Louis Braille* as a read-aloud. She returned to it the next day and posted five different sentences that used the –ing form of a verb at both the beginning and the end of a sentence. Then, Lynne asked students to brainstorm verbs in their –*ing* form. She asked them to think of all the activities they were involved in during and after the school day and on weekends. The anchor chart included *watching, running, working, reading, writing, visiting, hitting (a ball), kicking (karate moves), cooking, baking, tasting, devouring, sharing, talking, hugging, laughing, smiling, crying, screaming, yelling, picking (berries), licking (an ice cream cone), playing, resting, sleeping,* and *dreaming.*

Lynne wrote her examples on the board in front of the fourth graders to serve as models to imitate:

> *Running and shouting at the bus driver, Lynne desperately tried to get to the bus stop in time.*

> *Eating like a hungry hippo, Dad devoured my blueberry pancakes and asked for more.*

As Lynne wrote, she talked about her process, the punctuation she used, her choice of participles, and the words that followed the –*ing* participle(s). Then Lynne wrote another sentence on the board: "Talking about her writing process, Lynne wrote a sentence beginning with an –*ing* participle." Lynne asked the students to work with others at their table to try to use one or two –*ing* verbals (if the actions seemed to belong together) to write a sentence beginning with the –*ing* word(s). The students were encouraged to walk to other tables for revision help while Lynne and Karen circulated to observe and be available for questions. The students used the –*ing* verbs from the brainstormed list and wrote as many sentences as they could come up with in ten minutes. Here are two examples:

> Snorting and pawing, the wild Mustang let me know he did not want to be tamed.

> Dripping and glistening, the garden patch looked like a silver forest.

Once students seem comfortable with this sentence pattern, they can begin to experiment with the –*ed* participle form as a way to begin a sentence: "Clogged with dog hair, the bathtub pipe drained slowly." *Clogged with dog hair* modifies the noun *pipe*. Many times, authors begin a sentence with an –*ed* participle to introduce the emotion of the character first and what the character is doing second. It creates interest and is a fresh way to begin a sentence. A worthy example can be found in Lynda Mullaly Hunt's *Fish in a Tree*: "Embarrassed, I slide my drawings underneath my blank writing assignment." Beginning sentences with present participles will breathe new life into your students' writing.

Studying One Author's Use of Conventions

One of the best ways to study the use of conventions is through author study. By gathering the works of a particular author and examining the texts for different purposes, students can come to a deeper understanding of craft and conventions. Whose books do your students love to read? Whose works have you already examined for other purposes such as crafting a good beginning or studying the use of a repeated refrain? The authors whose words have found their way into the hearts and minds of your students are those you can return to for the study of conventions. One such author is Kevin Henkes, author of *Lilly's Purple Plastic Purse*, *Chrysanthemum*, *Chester's Way*, and *Wemberly Worried*, to name a few. His books can be used to study a variety of conventions, including end punctuation, dialogue, dashes, parentheses, use of italics, talking captions, capitalization, variation of print size, and ellipses.

One of Henkes's unique fingerprints as an author is what we refer to as "talking captions." His illustrations often contain the thoughts or words of the character, but they are not written in traditional speech bubbles, just simply printed next to or above the picture of the character, more like a caption. The first step in examining mentor texts for craft or conventions is to guide students to notice what the author is doing. As students begin studying Henkes's books, they may discover these talking captions themselves, or you can simply show several pages from his books and ask them what they notice. But as Katie Wood Ray (1999) reminds us, we must go beyond the noticing, helping our students develop a deeper understanding by questioning why a particular technique was used, and then guiding students to envision its use in their own writing.

If you were studying these talking captions, you might conduct a whole-class discussion about why Henkes added them to his illustrations. Have your students think about how they add to the story, and perhaps question why he chose not to use traditional speech bubbles. A class of first graders had the following ideas about why Henkes uses this technique in almost all of his books:

"I think he wants us to know what Lilly was thinking."
"Sometimes it adds more words that they said."
"It makes the story better because it adds more details."
"Maybe he doesn't like to draw bubbles."
"I think he wanted his books to look different."

If the technique you are studying has a name (such as ellipses or dashes), make sure you provide your students with the correct term. If it doesn't, work together to come up with a name the class will recognize and use. (The first graders coined the term *talking captions* to distinguish them from *speech bubbles*.) Finally, ask your students to think about how they might use the technique in their own writing. See Figure 9.2 for an example of one student trying it out. This would be an excellent time to build in some guided writing as suggested in the Your Turn lessons.

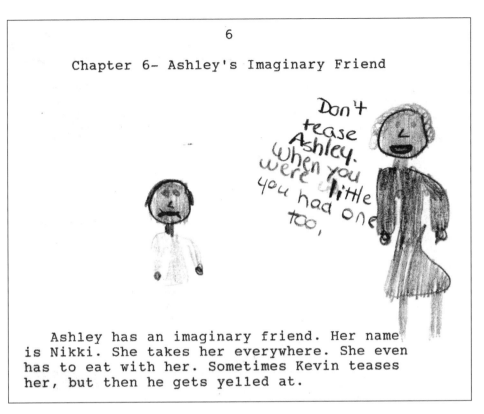

Figure 9.2
Annie experiments with talking captions.

Lucy Calkins (2003), Debbie Miller (2002), and Janet Angelillo (2002) remind us that charting the thinking that occurs in the classroom makes the work you do together permanent and visible. It allows the conversations to extend to other days and fosters connections to other areas of instruction. Charting, which can be conducted in the brainstorming part of the Your Turn lessons, helps students build their thinking gradually as new thoughts, ideas, and examples are added.

A chart developed for the thinking surrounding the talking captions and other conventions studied in the books of Kevin Henkes might look something like the one that follows. It was adapted from the work of Katie Wood Ray (1999) and Lucy Calkins (2003).

Of course there are some conventions, such as capitalizing names and using appropriate end marks, that we want students always to use. But other things, such as dashes, dialogue, or talking captions, require more thinking when considering appropriate use. You might find that students tend to over-use a particular technique when they first discover it. Through the reflections that take place at the end of the Your Turn lessons or during individual confer-ences, you can guide your students into thinking about when and how often the technique is appropriate to use. Reflection is a key ingredient in trying out any new skill. By making their thinking visible and getting feedback from the com-munity of writers, students can more deeply internalize the power of words and conventions.

| | | Conventions Ken Henkes Uses | | |
Books	What Did We Notice?	Why/When Is It Used?	It's Called . . .	Who Else Uses It?
Lilly's Purple Plastic Purse *Wemberly Worried* *Jessica Chester's Way*	There are words in the illustrations.	To add details. To tell what a character thinks. It adds more to what characters say.	Talking captions	
Chrysanthemum *Lilly's Purple Plastic Purse*	Names of people, some places, and some things begin with a capital letter.	Names begin with capitals. Places and things can have names just like people.	Capitalizing proper nouns.	
Lilly's Purple Plastic Purse *Kitten's First Full Moon* *Grandpa and Bo*	There are lines in the middle of a sentence and then more words.	Sometimes it's used before a list. It tells there are more words coming to explain something.	Dashes	

Colons and Epithets: Explorations of Style

The works of Linda Oatman High and other authors offer an interesting study in the use of the colon. In *Barn Savers*, there are many examples of the use of a colon followed by a listing:

> I shiver as I dress:
> soft flannel shirt,
> long johns,
> jeans,
> hard hat,
> boots,
> and scratchy leather gloves.
>
> Soon we see the barn:
> red paint peeling like sunburn,
> and old boards, splintered with cracks

Patricia and Emily MacLachlan use this same technique in *Painting the Wind*:

> And that is the way the painter paints the scene: the sand, a wave, and a little rainbow of water above a running dog.

Kyle, a fifth grader, had just finished looking at *Barn Savers*. He was in the middle of writing a piece about holiday traditions. His piece, titled "A Magically Magical Christmas Day . . ." did not originally include a list. After reading High's book, he revised it to include the following paragraph:

> Soon all my relatives (mostly children) are boasting about what awesome presents they were given. When the house gets quite quiet and bellies start to rumble, my grandmom fixes up a light snack before the three-course meal. When we finally sit down to eat, we can almost hear the table moan and groan with the weight of the Christmas feast:
>
> > salad drowned in ranch dressing,
> > mashed potatoes piled with gravy,
> > sweet cranberry sauce,
> > juicy honeyed ham,
> > roasted turkey with stuffing,
> > creamy, sweet corn,
> > yuck, slender asparagus,
> > soft, warm rolls,
> > a three-layer chocolate "moose" cake.
> > (It's big enough to satisfy a moose!)

Other examples of a colon followed by a list can be found in *Twilight Comes Twice* by Ralph Fletcher, *Up North at the Cabin* by Marsha Wilson Chall, and *Wallace's Lists* by Barbara Bottner and Gerald Kruglik. In *Painting the Wind*, the authors again use the colon, but this time what follows are the words on a sign that serve as a warning to store customers:

> A sign taped near the cake mixes reads: PLEASE DO NOT EAT FROSTING FROM THE CAN.

Some authors use the colon to indicate that what follows further explains their ideas. Examples of this kind of colon use can be found in *Mud* by Mary Lyn Ray, and *Arthur, For the Very First Time* by Patricia MacLachlan. Sometimes authors use the colon to set off dialogue as in *Wolf!* by Becky Bloom and *Six Dots: A Story of Young Louis Braille* by Jen Bryant. Bryant doesn't use the colon with all the examples of dialogue but reserves this punctuation to announce something important:

> On the day I was born, Papa announced me to the village: "Here is my son Loo-WEE!"

The important thing to remember is that we want to get students not only to notice a particular craft, or in this case, convention use, but also to consider why the author might have chosen to use it, and to examine its use across texts. This reflection will lead to a much deeper understanding and will help students consider many more opportunities for using it in their own writing.

In Chapter 8, we discuss the use of proper nouns as a way to help students add style to their writing. One way to further this discussion of noun specificity is to introduce the epithet. An epithet is a descriptive name or title used to enhance a description of a character. Sometimes it is humorous, as in *Olivia Saves the Circus* by Ian Falconer. Olivia describes herself as "Olivia the Tattooed Lady," "Olivia the Tight-rope Walker," the "Flying Olivia," and "Queen of the Trampoline," among others. Judy Schachner does the same thing in *Skippyjon Jones* when she has his mother refer to him as "Mr. Kitten Britches," "Mr. Fuzzy Pants," "Mr. Flutternutter," and "Mr. Cocopugs." During his imagined adventure, Skippyjon Jones refers to himself as "Skippito Friskito," and "El Skippito." Students can notice the use of capitalization here but also how the epithet breathes humor into the piece.

The use of the epithet is not limited to humor, however. In *Barefoot: Escape on the Underground Railroad*, Pamela Duncan Edwards uses epithets to show how the animals separate and describe the runaway slaves (the "Barefoot") from the slave catchers (the "Heavy Boots"). In *Stranger in the Woods*, Carl R. Sams II and Jean Stoick describe the Owl as the "Owl of Many Questions." This specific naming of a character helps the reader focus on a characteristic. In *The Recess Queen* by Alexis O'Neill, the personality of one of the main characters is appropriately summed up in her epithet "Mean Jean." Authors also use the epithets of historic figures in biographies. For example, Robert Burleigh refers to Babe Ruth as "the Babe" in his book *Home Run*. In another book, he and coauthor Ed Young use the epithet for the historical figure Tenzing Norgay as their title: *Tiger of the Snows*. They also give Mount Everest the epithet "Mother Goddess of the Earth." In *Snowflake Bentley*, a book about photographer Wilson Bentley, Jacqueline Briggs Martin uses "Snowflake Bentley" and "the Snowflake Man" when she refers to him. Jean Fritz teaches us in *Bully for You, Teddy Roosevelt* that "Teddy's Terrors" and "Roosevelt's Rough Riders" were epithets for Theodore Roosevelt's regiment. In *Painting the Wind*, the authors choose to refer to all the artists with epithets but do not capitalize the titles: *The painter of flowers, the painter of faces, the painter of still lifes,* and *the painter of landscapes.*

By studying the use of epithets across texts, students can gain a deeper understanding of the rules of capitalization. As they read books that use epithets, including historical texts, they realize exactly what an epithet is. They can easily see that if an epithet is used in place of a name, all the important words (just like a book title) are usually capitalized. In addition, they can discover another way to add style to their writing.

Hey! Study Those Interjections

Interjections are fun to explore with your students. They certainly have changed over time. In Ruth Heller's *Fantastic! Wow! And Unreal! A Book About Interjections and Conjunctions*, Heller shares interjections that were used by people who lived in the Middle Ages, such as "Alas!" and "Alack!" that we sometimes come across in the literature we read but never hear in our spoken language. Our grandmothers probably said things such as "Goodness gracious!" and "For goodness' sake!" or "Good grief!" as interjections. When we were growing up, we used "Cool!" and "Jive!" and "Wow!" or even "Groovy!" to declare how we felt about something. Students today often use "Awesome!" or "Gross!" as interjections. We use interjections to express emotions. Sometimes they show worry or concern: "Uh-oh" or "Whoa!" Other times, they express our delight: "Yeah!" They can also be used to show our contempt or disgust: "Yuck!" Sometimes, they are trying to draw attention to something: "Hey!" Many times, your students will use them to show surprise: "What!" or "Wow!" or "Awesome!" Interjections can stand alone, or commas can set them off. When they are strong, they are followed by an exclamation point. Mild interjections are followed by a comma.

There are many wonderful examples in children's picture books. A good place to start is Heller's book about interjections and conjunctions, perhaps as a read-aloud. The book has many colorful illustrations and can continue to serve as a resource for your students. (Ruth Heller has many books about parts of speech. Some are listed in Chapter 10, "A Treasure Chest of Books.") Return to a mentor text to explore the use of interjections. In *The Recess Queen* by Alexis O'Neill, several sentences use interjections. Sometimes, O'Neill uses capital letters to shout at the reader. Here are some examples from the text:

> "Oh! Katie Sue was one quick kid."
> "Say YOU!" she snarled and grabbed Katie Sue by the collar.
> "Well, Mean Jean bullied through the playground crowd."
> "Hey, Jeanie Beanie," said Katie Sue.
> "WELL—now when recess rolls around the playground's one great place."

The author ends her book with an interjection set apart from the rest of the text by its size, color, and position on the page. She helps the reader emphasize it even more by extending the sound of the word with the letter *s*. It's written in all capital letters: "YESSSSS!" It might be a good idea to display this page with a document camera and give the students time to talk about how the author emphasizes the interjection and how effective it is at the close of this particular story. You could simply ask your students what effect it has on the reader, what feelings they are left with.

There are so many great examples of the use of interjections that teachers of any grade level will be able to examine their use. In *Chrysanthemum* by Kevin Henkes, the interjections are fresh and appealing. They are also intended to be mild. "'Oh, pish,' said her mother. 'Your name is beautiful.'" "'Oh, pish,' said her mother. 'They're just jealous.'" Henkes also uses an interjection to express Chrysanthemum's joy on her first day of school: "'Hooray!' said Chrysanthemum. 'School!'"

Other fun examples include *We're Going on a Bear Hunt* by Michael Rosen, *Pigs in the Mud in the Middle of the Rud* by Lynn Plourde, and *Snappsy the Alligator (Did Not Ask to Be in This Book!)* by Julie Falatko. One of our favorite examples is in Pam Muñoz Ryan's *Mice and Beans*. It is written in Spanish and immediately translated into English so the reader will not misunderstand: "'¡Fíjate! Imagine that!' she said." She also uses an interjection that can stand for the thing she is talking about as well as serve as the familiar interjection "Rats!"

> But as Rosa María swept out the cupboard, she discovered the telltale signs of mice!
> "¡Ratones!" she cried. "Where are my mousetraps? I will set them all!"

Bravery Soup by Maryann Cocca-Leffler is another great book for students of all ages. It contains many interjections and opportunities to create skits for reader's theater so students can practice reading fluency to gain writing fluency. Print size and end punctuation will help the youngest readers understand exactly how the author intended the words to be spoken. In *Bravery Soup*, the use of interjections helps us understand exactly what the characters are feeling about facing their greatest fears. For our younger students, *Kitten's First Full Moon* by Kevin Henkes repeats the interjection "Poor Kitten!" several times to emphasize what a difficult night Kitten is having. At the end of the book the epithet changes to "Lucky Kitten!" to emphasize the satisfying ending.

Young writers enjoy experimenting with interjections and will have fun trying them out in narrative conversations. One word of caution: the overuse of interjections can give a piece of writing a nervous-and-jerky, breathless quality.

When you study parts of speech in an interesting way through the use of mentor texts, eventually it spills over into the students' own writing. Students become mentors for each other during peer conferences and shared readings. In Francisco's story, "It's Only a Dream," the fifth grader uses interjections to put his voice into the piece of writing:

> "Great!" I whispered to myself. "It seems I'm either being punked or I'm Harry in Harry Potter and the Secret Chamber." (Either way, could I explain the window thing? It restored itself? No way!)

Dylan, another fifth grader, inserts his voice by using interjections as well. He begins his piece about an experience at Disney World with an interjection that serves to pull the reader right in: "Whoa! This is incredibly awesome!" Later in the piece, he writes, "'Uh Oh!!' I heard a six-year-old say in a baby type of voice. That must be one tall six-year-old. Or maybe I'm just small . . . SHEESH!" Brielle, another student in this class, used an interjection to speak in the voice of her toddler sister: "'Ooooo . . . pretty colors!' we heard Jenna shout excitedly."

Embedding Grammar Study in Writing Work

We can teach grammar and mechanics in interesting, fun ways that will help students listen attentively, want to hear more, and try things out. Exercises that teach students the traditional rules of grammar are best learned within the context of real reading and writing so that students understand the "why" as well as the "how." We also know that students will learn something when they need it—when they are going to use it in their own writing. In this case, necessity is truly the mother of invention.

The best way to encourage students to take risks with grammar and mechanics, as well as develop an understanding of sentence, is to embed this teaching into daily practice. We are not speaking of the widespread use of a daily editing activity. Here, students are given sentences or passages with grammatical and/or mechanical errors to correct. Unfortunately, the students who can correct with ease are not challenged to take risks and try out new structures and conventions. The students who have difficulty with the daily edit are not growing either. After all, they are seeing things incorrectly, sometimes copying them down incorrectly, and then are expected to take this out-of-context experience and transfer it to their personal writing. From our observations, it doesn't happen that way. What we have found is that instruction in grammar and mechanics must be part of our everyday teaching. The easiest way to tuck in these skills is through the use of sentences or passages from mentor texts. This work will stretch students as writers through imitation, and eventually, through adaptation and playfulness with language; it will allow them to *own* these skills. However, on our bookshelves, we should have many grammar reference books that will help us understand how to analyze passages with students or work through grammar and mechanics issues during conferences. Some students will be able to consult these references independently, but it should be part of the work they are doing with real writing, not as isolated exercises.

According to Schuster (2003), teachers are often looking for simple formulas for correctness. He says we do this because teaching writing is perhaps the hardest thing we do. Then he tells us to remember to let the students break the "rules" if it leads them to better writing. Using passages or even just a sentence from mentor texts, students can study a variety of syntactic structures and punctuation rules. This practice will lead to an understanding of why the experts (the authors of the mentor texts) sometimes break the rules; it helps them bring their voices to the writing experience. Finally, it will help your students make their voices heard as well.

The teaching of grammar and mechanics is important. It is through these avenues that we teach our writers how to interact with their readers—their target audience—and make their message clear. Students will begin to understand that the rules for syntax and mechanics are the writer's tools for developing this relationship with the reader.

Think About It—Talk About It—Write About It

- What authors could you use to create a punctuation study with your students?
- What parts of speech and/or conventions will you study to move your students' writing to a new level of sophistication?
- What strategy did you read about that you will try with your students? How will you adapt it to the needs of your class?
- How can you embed the study of grammar and conventions into your writing workshop on a regular basis and even across the day?
- Look through your picture books to find inviting illustrations that can be used for word splash activities. Make a list in your writer's notebook.

Using the Syntax of an Author

Hook: *Amber on the Mountain* by Tony Johnston is a wonderful model of how an author brings readers into a book by helping them visualize the setting and experience the mood created by the description. By imitating the author's flow of language, or syntax, students can get a feel for how the author uses words. After sharing *Amber on the Mountain* as a read-aloud, reread the lead paragraph. Options: *Alejandro's Gift* by Richard E. Albert, *One Tiny Turtle* by Nicola Davies, and "Ames Crossing" in *Stuart Little* by E. B. White.

Purpose: *One important strategy to build content is to create descriptions for the setting and characters. Setting gives the reader a sense of place (where) and time (when) and helps create a mood. Today we will walk around in the shoes of Tony Johnston. We will use her syntax, or flow of language, to create interesting descriptions of setting while at the same time creating a mood.*

Brainstorm: Ask students to turn and talk with a partner or small group about settings they are familiar with in real life or ones they can vividly recall from books. Have them jot down ideas for settings in their notebooks. In whole group, record them on chart paper or on the board.

Model: I am going to use the lead paragraph from *Amber on the Mountain* to write my own lead paragraph, but I am going to choose a setting that is familiar to me and place Amber in it. As I write, I am going to think about what sensory experiences such as sights, sounds, and smells come to mind and the feelings I associate with that place.

> *Amber lived in a city so big it took hours to drive through traffic-snarled avenues from one side to the other. Skyscrapers loomed like granite mountains against a hazy blue sky. And the air made you sick— it was that thick and soured with pollutants. Still, for all that man-made ugliness, Amber was content. For city people had parks, museums, theaters, and libraries where she could be transported to other worlds.*

Shared/Guided Writing: Ask students to choose something from the class list of settings or something else they think of and write a lead paragraph that places Amber in a new setting. Make sure all the students can see the lead paragraph from *Amber on the Mountain*. Students can share their drafts with a partner and talk about how their sentences matched those of the mentor text and your model. Share a few in whole group using a document camera. Ask struggling or younger writers to first orally write by talking about their ideas with a partner. You can model this technique with another student.

Another helpful strategy is to get the students to draw their settings before they begin to write.

Independent Writing: Ask students to revisit a draft or a finished portfolio piece. Revise the lead paragraph to include a vivid snapshot of setting, using a favorite mentor text as a model. Students can also place Amber in a number of different settings as additional practice and post their lead paragraphs on the writing bulletin board. If they are ready, students can begin a new draft for a narrative. Furthermore, students can use this strategy to begin an informational essay or research piece with a snapshot of setting where it is applicable. For example, informational reports about endangered animals could begin with a description of the animal's disappearing habitat. It is always a good idea to have young writers share their writing with a partner, a small response group, or in the general sharing session of writing workshop.

Reflection: Students can turn and talk with a partner about their lead paragraph.

How did the language of the author help you write a better paragraph?

What strategies did the author use that you were able to imitate?

How did the language in the mentor text and your paragraph create a mood through setting?

How did the description of setting help your readers (peer response group/teacher) visualize it?

How can you use the show, don't tell strategy here?

When could you use this again?

Your Turn Lesson 2 — Using a Variety of End Punctuation

Once students have developed a sense of what a sentence is, it is time to help them understand the various types of sentences and the end punctuation that goes with each. It is also important for them to understand how meaning can be conveyed through various types of sentences.

Hook: *Yo! Yes?* by Chris Raschka comprises one- and two-word sentences through which two boys carry on a conversation. Meaning is conveyed through the use of periods, question marks, and exclamation points. This is a great mentor text to use for reader's theater. After your students are familiar with the content and have practiced how to use expression to convey the meaning indicated by the end punctuation, you can return to it to discuss end punctuation in more depth. You can also use short passages from other texts that contain a variety of sentence types. Good choices include *Kitten's First Full Moon* by Kevin Henkes, *Shortcut* by Donald Crews, and *Mr. George Baker* by Amy Hest.

Purpose: *Writers, we know it is important to use punctuation marks at the end of a sentence. We've seen how authors sometimes use a period, sometimes a question mark, and sometimes an exclamation point. Today we will practice writing a variety of different sentences with different end marks and talk about when it is appropriate to use each one.*

Brainstorm: Together with your students, think of some familiar situations or places that are familiar to them and record the list on the board or chart paper. This list could include things such as opening your lunch bag to see what Mom packed, picking teams at recess, arriving at a surprise birthday party, losing a tooth, or finally getting to your vacation destination.

Model: Pick one and, using a think-aloud, create some different types of sentences that might be associated with that situation. Make this thinking visible by jotting the sentences down on the board or in your notebook. For example, if you choose "opening up your lunch bag to see what Mom packed," the sentences could be

> "What's inside?" I wondered.
> Do you want to trade?
> It's peanut butter and jelly again!
> Time for lunch!
> I wondered what surprise my mom packed today.
> Slowly and carefully, I opened my lunch bag.

Then, in front of the students, put the sentences together in a way that might make sense, adding others as needed. Share your thinking as you write. Talk about why you are putting the sentences in the order you did and also why you used certain end marks. The sentences above might end up like this:

> *Finally, it was time for lunch! As I entered the cafeteria, I wondered what surprise my mom had packed today. My mouth watered as I thought of the possibilities. Could it be tuna fish? Could it be ham and cheese? Slowly and carefully, I opened my lunch bag. Ugh! It was peanut butter and jelly again! I looked over at my best friend.*
> *"Do you want to trade?" I asked hopefully.*

Shared/Guided Writing: Have students choose another situation from the brainstormed list and create different types of sentences that might be associated with that situation. This can be done in whole group as a shared writing, or students can work in pairs. Have them jot down at least two examples for each type of sentence, then use them in writing a small vignette.

Independent Writing: Students can return to a previous notebook entry or a piece they are currently working on to revise for appropriate end punctuation. They could also choose a different situation, brainstorm some sentences, and write another vignette. Yet another alternative could be to rewrite one of the models with different sentences that change the meaning. In other words, the example given could be rewritten so that peanut butter and jelly is a welcomed lunch.

Reflection: As students share their work, ask them to share their thinking about why they used periods, question marks, and exclamation points with certain sentences.

> *How does thinking about end punctuation help you convey the meaning you want?*

> *Would the meaning change if you used a different sentence type?*

> *Why is it important to vary your sentence types?*

Option: Students who understand basic sentence structure might return to the modeled example or the example they wrote and rewrite some of the sentences into fragments so that they sound more natural. (Tuna fish? Ham and cheese? Peanut butter and jelly again! Want to trade?) This would add another dimension to the writing. Students can reflect on which way sounds better and why.

Your Turn Lesson 3

Exploring Variations in Print

Hook: With your students, explore mentor texts for unusual print style. This could be the use of italics, bold print, underlining, variations in size, or use of all uppercase. Some good examples of print variations can be found in *Roller Coaster* by Marla Frazee, *Chameleons Are Cool* by Martin Jenkins, *The Recess Queen* by Alexis O'Neill, *Mice and Beans* by Pam Muñoz Ryan, and *Muncha! Muncha! Muncha!* by Candace Fleming.

Purpose: *Writers, we've been exploring the way authors sometimes write words in a different way. Today, we will think about the reasons why they make some words bigger or smaller, underline them, or make them stand out in some way. Then, we'll try out that technique for ourselves.*

Brainstorm: With your students, list the different types of variations in print that you noticed in the mentor texts you explored together. Remember to list specific examples. If you are working with younger students, you can limit the variations to one or two and perhaps just discuss writing some words bigger, or making the letters all uppercase. Ask students to consider the reasons they think the authors might have chosen to write the words as they did. An excellent way to do this is to create a chart that can be added to as students make new discoveries. Here's a short example:

Title and Author	Print Variation	Why did the author do this?	When could we use it?
Muncha! Muncha! Muncha! by Candace Fleming	*Furious* is all uppercase, bigger, and darker. *Happy* is bigger.	She wanted to show that Mr. McGreely was very angry; the reader should say the word loudly. To show that the word is important—his feelings finally changed.	If we want the reader to say the word loudly. For very important words that we want to stand out.

The categories of any chart can be changed to suit your purposes. You could also have a section for student examples.

Model: Return to a previous notebook entry or compose a short piece in front of the students. When you are finished, think aloud about how you could use some variation in print (take one word and make it bigger or smaller, underlined, and so on) and why you would do that. It is important for students to understand why certain words could be written differently and that if this technique is overused, it will lose its effectiveness.

Shared/Guided Writing: Ask students to return to a previous notebook entry and revise for print variation. As you circulate, conference with students about how and why they chose to make the revision. An alternative is to write a whole-class shared piece about a common experience (a recent class field trip, activity, or event) and decide together where it would be appropriate to vary the print in some way.

Independent Writing: Ask students to consider print variations as they work on individual pieces. They might also want to return to previous notebook entries or published pieces to revise for effective print variations.

Reflection: As students share their work, ask them to reflect on how this strategy worked for them.

What kind of print variations did you use?

How did this technique make your writing better?

What other variations in print could you use to accomplish the same thing?

What other variations would you like to try?

Your Turn Lesson 4

Writing Sentences with Compound Predicates

Many elementary and middle school writers often write sentences with compound subjects, but do not always consider using two or even three verbs in the same sentence. These writers are still tied to basic sentence patterns. Asking students to notice and write sentences with compound predicates presents an opportunity to teach them how to vary their sentence patterns and to engage in sentence combining.

Hook: Return to *Six Dots: A Story of Young Louis Braille* by Jen Bryant. Ask students to listen for the action words that describe what the subjects of this sentence are doing: "The older boys teased and stole." Explain to them that a simple sentence that uses more than one verb has a compound predicate. Emphasize that a verb is the word in the sentence that can show past, present, or future time. Options: *Snappsy the Alligator (Did Not Ask to Be in This Book!)* by Julie Falatko; *A Taste of Blackberries* by Doris Buchanan Smith; *Take a Hike, Teddy Roosevelt!* by Frank Murphy; *Crab Moon* by Ruth Horowitz; *In a Village by the Sea* by Muon Van; and *Chik Chak Shabbat* by Mara Rockliff.

Purpose: *Writers, today I'm going to show you how you can use more than one verb to describe what the subject of the sentence is doing to create sentence variety. Today we are going to concentrate on writing a sentence with two verbs by using the conjunctions* or, but, *or* and, *or combining two shorter sentences into one where it makes sense to do so.*

Brainstorm: Have students individually or with a partner generate a list of verbs that show action around an activity such as swimming in the past tense: *splashed, dove, jumped, flipped, sank, waded, propelled, paddled, catapulted, gulped (air), kicked, reached, swallowed (water), pushed, dipped, climber (into a raft), floated, bounced (on a diving board).* Have students turn and talk in small groups and add to their lists. Ask for examples of their activity linked with strong verbs that seem to go together, and create a two-column anchor chart labeled "Activity–Verbs." Place an activity on each new line and place two verbs next to each one in simple or past-tense form. These examples are from a third-grade class:

> swimming—kicked and splashed
> geese flying south—honked and flapped
> dancing—twirled and whirled
> football—charged and tackled
> baseball—hit and dashed
> getting ready for a birthday party—spread (the frosting) and placed (candles)
> getting ready for school—brushed (teeth) and washed (face and hands)
> gardening—pulling (weeds) and digging (small holes for plants)

Model: Create a paragraph around an activity or event or from the list on the anchor chart. If your first attempt does not include a sentence with a compound predicate, revise by combining sentences or add a new one. Talk through your process as you write or return to notice the verbs and sentences that have a compound predicate. Here is one example:

> *The twins* skipped *and* ran *toward the shimmering lake. When they got to the end of the pier, they* sat *down and* dangled *their legs to skim the water with their toes. Suddenly, Sam pushed Sara into the lake. Then he jumped in after her. When he surfaced, he* sputtered *and* laughed. *Sara* splashed *her brother and* called *for their two chocolate Labs to join them. Molly and Max did not need to be coaxed. The two dogs leaped into the cool water, too! Swimming in the lake was everyone's favorite thing to do on a hot August day!*

*Note: There are two sentences that could easily be combined to create a compound predicate. Ask students to find those sentences and combine them with a conjunction that seems to best fit. *Sam pushed Sara into the lake and jumped in after her.* Remind them that when they combine sentences, sometimes a word needs to be eliminated and other words need to be added.

Shared/Guided Writing: Use a document camera to display pages from the mentor text and other mentor texts to find sentences with compound predicates. *Crab Moon* is an excellent choice if it is available. Then, ask students to work in pairs and use their activity or an activity from the anchor chart to create a paragraph with a sentence or two that has a compound predicate. Experiment with the sentence by changing the conjunction or one of the verbs. Ask older students to read their paragraph and look for a place where two sentences could be combined into one if it makes sense to do so in order to create a sentence with a compound predicate. Share your sentences and/or paragraphs in whole-group discussion.

Independent Writing: Ask students to return to their writer's notebook or a piece of writing they are currently working on and find a few places where they could create a sentence with a compound predicate. Ask them to use one or two sentences with compound predicates to slightly change their sentence patterns. Older students can do some work here with sentence combining.

Reflection: Ask students to share some of their revisions using compound predicates. Reflect on one or two questions:

> *Was it easy or difficult to create sentences with compound predicates?*

> *What do you now know about sentences with a compound predicate?*

> *How did changing the placement of two or three verbs in one sentence affect the flow of your paragraph?*

> *When can you envision using this sentence pattern again?*

> *Did you try to combine sentences to create a sentence with a compound predicate? Did this help the flow of your paragraph or was it more effective as two separate sentences? Explain.*

Your Turn Lesson 5

Using Parentheses in Our Writing

Authors build content for their stories in many ways. Parentheses are used to set off information from the main text. Although this information can often be omitted, it adds interest and sometimes emotion and humor. One way to make use of parentheses is to reveal what the main character is thinking or feeling about his own actions or the actions of another character as a reflection or thoughtshot.

Hook: Choose some of the mentor texts you have been using in the classroom and examine the use of parentheses closely with your students. Here's an example from *Looking at Lincoln* by Maira Kalman.

> *Lincoln wore a very tall hat.*
> *(With his hat on he was seven feet tall.)*

Ask students what the information contained inside the parentheses makes us think. Ask students to debate: Is it necessary? Why or why not? Then, continue to find other examples in the mentor text and discuss them. What is the author's purpose each time she uses parentheses? Reread these parts of text with and without the information inside the parentheses. What does the reader gain from their use? What is lost without them?

Explain to your students that they might use parentheses to include material they want to deemphasize or that wouldn't normally fit into the flow of their text but want to include it to add voice, humor, or an aside. If the material within parentheses appears within a sentence, they do not use a capital letter or period to punctuate that material, even if it is a complete sentence. Options: *Roller Coaster* by Marla Frazee, *An Angel for Solomon Singer* by Cynthia Rylant, *Nothing to Do* by Douglas Wood, and *Missing May* by Cynthia Rylant.

Purpose: *As we have been discussing, the use of parentheses adds something unique and refreshing to a piece of writing. Since the kind of information contained inside parentheses is often very lightly sprinkled in a text, they should be purposeful and satisfying. Today I will show you how you can add parentheses to your writing to grow as a writer and add another convention use to your writer's toolbox.*

Brainstorm: In this case, *brainstorming* is closely tied to the use of literature in the *hook*. As students examine books and discover sentences that use parentheses, they are actually engaging in a type of brainstorming. While you copy examples on an anchor chart, the students can choose several examples to copy on a page in their writer's notebook. Mark the page(s) in the mentor texts with a sticky note for future reference. Allow students to add examples to the anchor chart as they find them in workshop or independent reading.

Model: Read a previous notebook entry of your own or compose a new entry in front of the students. Display your notebook entry or the writing you do so that everyone can see your use of parentheses. Talk about your process as you write. When you are finished, discuss why it would be important to include any of the comments inside the parentheses in this notebook entry. If it is a personal narrative, be sure to include comments inside the parentheses as your thoughts or perhaps a memory you recall. Here is Lynne's example:

> *My sister and I climbed on our bikes and pedaled for the lake. Diane complained about the heat (I was surprised it was not me), but she kept on pedaling. When we arrived, we spread our blanket and emptied our picnic lunch before us. We watched the ducks and tossed some bread crumbs into the water. The ducks dove for the scraps and entertained us for a long time. Then we lay down, closed our eyes, and napped (or at least, we pretended to nap—but it was hard to do).*

Shared/Guided Writing: If you think your students need more practice as a whole group, choose a classroom memory and record the events in a short paragraph. Return to the paragraph and have your students suggest revisions with sentences that contain explanations or asides in parentheses. Ask students to return to a previous notebook entry or published piece to consider adding a thought or two within parentheses. Invite students to offer their explanations to a partner or a small group while you circulate and listen in.

Independent Writing: Ask students to continue to revise their narratives or a notebook entry by adding a thought inside parentheses where it seems to fit best.

Reflection: The following questions can help guide their thinking.

> *How did your story change when you added thinking within parentheses?*
>
> *Does the text you added inside the parentheses reveal an emotion, a thought, or an explanation to your reader?*
>
> *Is it satisfying to the reader? How so?*
>
> *What kinds of things should you think about as you insert thoughts and feelings within a set of parentheses?*
>
> *Is writing to include parentheses easy or difficult for you? Explain.*

Chapter 10

A Treasure Chest of Books

Our goal now is to share our library with you. The books to which we referred, as well as some others we didn't mention, are organized around the chapters. You will notice that many books are listed more than once. These are our true mentor texts, the ones we go back to again and again and use for many different purposes. We have added brief annotations so that you will have some idea of what to look for or how the book can be used for a specific purpose. If you have already started your own library and have some of the titles mentioned, we hope you might look at them through new eyes and find additional ways to use them in your classroom. If you are just starting to build a library, start small and pick the books that you love and that can be used in many different ways. The treasure chest is not an exhaustive list by any means! There are always new discoveries to make, and we encourage you to make your own, to find your own mentors and keep growing.

Sometimes we need to find a new mentor. As we grow as writers and teachers of writing, our mentors can change. We are using the same skills and strategies; however, our level of sophistication and understanding changes. Some mentors will remain tried and true throughout your years as a teacher of writing. Others will serve as good friends who have perhaps moved away but with whom you still keep in touch from time to time. And then there are the new friends who come into your life who can teach you something you never even thought about before.

It is our hope that this book, along with the treasure chest of books we have provided in this chapter, will help you lay a strong foundation for your literacy house. Each year you will find new books, and perhaps you will need to build an additional room or two (we say that both figuratively and literally!) as you add books to your collection. Like all good literacy lessons, mentor texts should be revisited often. When you read them again as you grow as a writer, you make new discoveries that were there all along—you just weren't ready for them yet.

A Journey Through a Mentor Text

Teachers often ask how we discover a book as a mentor text. We first do what most people do. We are drawn to a book because of the title, author, book jacket, recommendation, or any number of other things. Then we read it for pleasure, reading like a reader, to gain a sense of what the book is about, its cadence and flow, its voice. After that, we start to look a little more closely at different passages or pages, slowing our process down to read like a writer. We engage in several close reads to discover the lessons that seem to jump off the page. We read through different lenses to help us examine the text for the qualities of writing—a clear focus, the development of ideas, a meaningful and logical organization, voice, word choice, sentence fluency, and conventions. We theorize and study the author's use of strategies to create powerful sentences, paragraphs, and story. This doesn't all happen in one sitting. We often return to a text weeks or maybe months later and discover something new. We share our thinking with colleagues as well as with students who also discover craft to study or point out things we might have missed. Come along with us as we journey through *Toad Weather* by Sandra Markle. This book tells the story of a young girl who has a rainy-day adventure with her mother and grandmother. The surprise her mother has promised is a toad migration. Together with neighbors and friends, Ally, her mother, and her grandmother help the toads cross the street to safety.

In *Toad Weather* we are delighted by a lead sentence that describes the weather and contains an unexpected rhyme—"In the gloomy-gray of a March day." Right away we know what Ally and her grandmother are thinking and feeling about a rainy day. Will these emotions change as we go through the story? What events will happen to make them feel differently about a rainy day? We notice that the book is written in the present tense, helping us to "be in the moment" with the characters. Before leaving the first page, we notice an example of the power of three. We page through the book to see if there are other examples of this strategy, and sure enough, there are. We notice that sometimes the threes are listed with commas, but sometimes they are fragments used with periods. Two examples of hyphenated adjectives jump out at us. Are there more? Yes! (Our favorite comes at the end—"after-the-toad-weather city"). The story is highly focused—everything takes place in the span of one evening.

As we look through the pages, we notice that powerful verbs are abundant: *press, bursts, slip, stomp, spy, splatter,* and many more. For older students, there are many sentences that use the –ing form of a verb to describe a noun, providing a great opportunity for a grammar lesson on participles.

We notice that the author uses dialogue effectively to move the story forward. Sometimes there is conversation between the three main characters. At other times, there is only one person speaking on a page. Some pages have no dialogue at all. These are all great examples for writers who shy away from using dialogue as well as for others who let it take over their story.

As we continue on our journey through *Toad Weather*, we notice figurative language, variation in print, effective repetition, and sentence variety. We recognize that these examples can be used with other texts when we are working with our writers on a particular strategy. We pay attention to the sounds of the words and the rhythms they create. We notice the short descriptions of what the characters are experiencing through their senses that help the reader travel with them through their neighborhood.

The ending of this story is a sharp contrast to the beginning. Everyone is feeling happy, and a sense of accomplishment is implied. We look at the carefully crafted final page that includes dialogue to reveal what the characters are thinking and feeling with a final action. A satisfying ending is often created by combining two or more strategies.

Markle's story is a great example for students who want to use their expertise about a topic of interest to write a story. She seamlessly embeds some facts about toad migration through the words of Ally's mother. In the author's note, Markle explains more about toad migration and when it occurs. Here's a perfect opportunity to teach students how to write an author's note to explain more about the facts they have scattered throughout their narrative. It gives our young writers, especially our more struggling writers, a chance to see how they can use their knowledge and expertise about an activity, event, or area of interest to create a story such as *Toad Weather*.

Chapter 2: Digging for Treasure: Discovering Personal Stories by Connecting with Literature

Connections to books can take many directions. The following books are rich stories for read-alouds that writers can easily relate to in some way. Although possible connections are listed, students might relate in a variety of other ways that lead to an awareness of the writing treasures in their lives.

Ackerman, Karen. 1992. *Song and Dance Man*. New York: Dragonfly Books.
Special time with grandfather.

Bean, Jonathan. 2013. *Building Our House*. New York: Farrar, Straus and Giroux Books for Young Readers.
An example of using photographs from an actual event to tell a story.

Boelts, Maribeth. 2014. *Happy Like Soccer*. Somerville, MA: Candlewick.
Can be used to demonstrate a "What if" story based in reality; connections to people and places.

Bradby, Marie. 1995. *More Than Anything Else*. New York: Orchard Books.
Connections to important things in your life.

Bram, Elizabeth. 2015. *Rufus the Writer*. New York: Schwartz and Wade.
Demonstrates how to find ideas for writing.

Brinckloe, Julie. 1986. *Fireflies!* New York: Aladdin Books.
Special times with friends; catching fireflies; conflicted feelings—feeling happy and sad at the same time.

Brunelle, Nicholas. 2005. *Snow Moon*. New York: Penguin Young Readers Group.
A "What if" story based on an event from the author's childhood.

Bunting, Eve. 1989. *The Wednesday Surprise*. Boston: Houghton Mifflin Harcourt Books for Young Readers.
Tells about a special time with grandmother who has learned how to read. Writers can connect to things that they have accomplished and how that accomplishment was shared with others.

———. 1994. *Night Tree*. Boston: Houghton Mifflin Harcourt Books for Young Readers.
Memories connected to holidays.

———. 1999. *Butterfly House.* New York: Scholastic.
Learning how to do something with grandfather's help; also connections to setting something free.

———. 2015. *The Memory String.* Boston: Houghton Mifflin Harcourt Books for Young Readers.
Using objects to spark memories.

———. 2015. *Yard Sale.* Somerville, MA: Candlewick.
Can lead students to ask questions and make connections as sparks for story ideas.

Capucilli, Alyssa Satin. 2015. *Tulip and Rex Write a Story.* New York: HarperCollins Children's Books.
Example of creating a story from a collection of words; example of oral rehearsal (the main character, Tulip, uses the words she collected on a walk to orally tell a story).

Castillo, Lauren. 2014. *Nana in the City.* New York: Clarion Books.
Connections to time spent with special person, in this case a grandmother.

Catalanotto, Peter. 2005. *Matthew A.B.C.* New York: Atheneum Books for Young Readers.
An example of "What if": What if all the students in a class had the same name?

———. 2006. *Emily's Art.* New York: Atheneum Books for Young Readers.
Connections to feelings, especially in illustrations.

———. 2015. *The Newbies.* New York: Atheneum Books for Young Readers.
An example of a "What if" story.

Cisneros, Sandra. 1991. *The House on Mango Street.* New York: Vintage Books.
This book is probably most appropriate for older students. The story is told in a series of vignettes that can be used to help students make connections to the stories in their own lives. A particularly useful vignette is "My Name," which can help students start thinking about their own names.

Cooper, Elisha. 2006. *Beach.* New York: Orchard Books.
Rich in thumbnail sketches that provide seeds of ideas.

Crews, Donald. 1996. *Shortcut.* New York: Greenwillow Books.
A close call—recalling a time of excitement and danger.

———. 1998. *Bigmama's.* New York: Greenwillow Books.
Memories built around places and objects.

Daywalt, Drew. 2013. *The Day the Crayons Quit.* New York: Philomel Books.
An example of a "What if" book. What would your crayons say if they could talk?

de la Peña, Matt. 2015. *Last Stop on Market Street*. New York: G. P. Putnam's Sons.
A boy on a bus ride across town with his grandmother learns how to appreciate the wonder and beauty in ordinary things.

Evans, Richard Paul. 1993. *The Christmas Box*. New York: Simon and Schuster.
Excerpts can be used to demonstrate how senses can trigger memories.

Fleischman, Paul. 2013. *The Matchbox Diary*. Somerville, MA: Candlewick.
A little girl visiting her grandfather finds a cigar box filled with matchboxes. Each small box holds a memento of the grandfather's childhood and journey to America. He uses the objects to tell her the stories. This book could spark stories around objects students have saved.

Fox, Mem. 1985. *Wilfrid Gordon McDonald Partridge*. New York: Kane/Miller.
Demonstrates how objects can spark memories.

Golenbock, Peter. 1992. *Teammates*. Boston: Houghton Mifflin Harcourt.
Uses photographs of real people and places to tell the story.

Hanlon, Abby. 2012. *Ralph Writes a Story*. New York: Two Lions.
Ralph is a reluctant writer and is a great model for helping young writers understand where they can find ideas for stories.

Henkes, Kevin. 1991. *Chrysanthemum*. New York: Greenwillow Books.
Writers can make connections to their names.

———. 2006. *Lilly's Purple Plastic Purse*. New York: Greenwillow Books.
Connections to special people or things, also "getting in trouble."

———. 2010. *Wemberly Worried*. New York: Greenwillow Books.
Young writers can relate to things they worry about; beginning suggestions for a "What if" list.

High, Linda Oatman. 2002. *Beekeepers*. Honesdale, PA: Boyds Mills.
Special time with grandfather who is teaching how to do something.

———. 2012. *Barn Savers*. Honesdale, PA: Boyds Mills.
Special time with dad; connections can also be made to souvenirs and how they help us remember special times or places.

Hills, Tad. 2012. *Rocket Writes a Story*. New York: Random House.
An example of creating a story from a collection of words and observing everyday things.

Hoberman, Mary Ann. 2002. *Right Outside My Window*. New York: MONDO.
Can be used to spark connections and writing ideas about things "right outside the window."

Hopkinson, Deborah. 2012. *Annie and Helen*. New York: Random House.
    Use of primary source documents—photos, letters, to tell a story.

Horowitz, Ruth. 2004. *Crab Moon*. Cambridge, MA: Candlewick.
    Connections to special places and events; can be used to dig up
    memories connected to feelings.

Houston, Gloria. 1992. *My Great Aunt Arizona*. New York: HarperCollins.
    Connections to special people in our lives.

Howard, Elizabeth Fitzgerald. 1995. *Aunt Flossie's Hats (and Crab Cakes
    Later)*. Boston: Houghton Mifflin Harcourt.
    Memories built around objects—in this case, hats.

Johnson, Angela. 1990. *Do Like Kyla*. New York: Orchard Books.
    Connections to trying to be like an older sister or brother; can lead to
    thinking about special things sisters or brothers do together.

Johnston, Tony. 1998. *Amber on the Mountain*. New York: Puffin Books.
    Can be used to connect to stories about friends or learning how to do
    something.

Joyce, William. 2003. *George Shrinks*. New York: Harper Collins.
    A "What if" story. Can be used to inspire more what-ifs.

Keats, Ezra Jack. 1976. *The Snowy Day*. New York: Puffin.
    A special time in the snow.

Kroll, Steven. 2005. *Patches Lost and Found*. New York: Two Lions.
    Connections to stories about pets; great demonstration of story mapping.

Laminack, Lester. 2004. *Saturdays and Teacakes*. Atlanta, GA: Peachtree.
    Spending time with grandmother.

Lee, Suzy. 2008. *Wave*. New York: Chronicle Books.
    A wordless book. Writers can connect with the range of emotions
    evoked through the illustrations and experiences depicted.

Lowry, Lois. 2009. *Crow Call*. New York: Scholastic.
    Writers can make connections to a special outing with a relative or to
    reconnecting with a relative who has been absent from their life for a
    time.

———. 2015. *Gooney Bird Greene*. Boston: Houghton Mifflin Harcourt.
    An excellent read-aloud to encourage students to tell the stories of their
    lives; helps students understand that ordinary events can be told and
    written in an extraordinary way.

MacLachlan, Patricia. 1993. *Journey*. New York: Yearling.
    Use of photographs for finding writing topics; connections can also be
    made to names.

———. 1994. *All the Places to Love*. New York: HarperCollins.
    Can be used to spark memories about special places.

Markle, Sandra. 2015. *Toad Weather*. Atlanta, GA: Peachtree.
A special family time to spark a memory for writing.

Mattick, Lindsay. 2015. *Finding Winnie: The True Story of the World's Most Famous Bear*. New York: Little, Brown.
Use of photos and artifacts to recount a story.

McKissack, Patricia C. 2001. *Goin' Someplace Special*. New York: Atheneum Books for Young Readers.
Connections to special places.

McLerran, Alice. 1991. *Roxaboxen*. New York: HarperCollins.
An imaginary place created during children's play; use to make connections to playtime adventures.

Messner, Kate. 2011. *Over and Under the Snow*. San Francisco: Chronicle Books.
A companion text to *Owl Moon*; recalls an outing with father that can spark connections for writers.

Moss, Marissa. 1995. *Regina's Big Mistake*. Boston: Houghton Mifflin Harcourt Books for Young Readers.
Young writers can relate to mistakes they have made and how those mistakes might have been fixed.

Nolen, Jerdine. 2001. *In My Momma's Kitchen*. New York: Amistad.
A collection of stories that occur in the same place; connections to memories about special places.

Polacco, Patricia. 1994. *My Rotten Redheaded Older Brother*. New York: Simon and Schuster.
Use of photographs—finding the story behind the picture; connections to special people.

———. 1999. *My Ol' Man*. New York: Puffin Books.
Use of photographs—finding the story behind the picture; connections to special people.

———. 2004. *Betty Doll*. New York: Puffin Books.
Using objects to spark memories.

Rappaport, Doreen, and Lyndall Callan. 2000. *Dirt on Their Skirts: The Story of the Young Women Who Won the World Championship*. New York: Dial Books for Young Readers.
Can be used as an example of starting with photographs to write a story.

Ray, Mary Lyn. 2001. *Mud*. Boston: Houghton Mifflin Harcourt Books for Young Readers.
Connections to things.

Ruurs, Margriet. 2016. *Stepping Stones: A Refugee Family's Journey*. Victoria, British Columbia: Orca Book.
A story to help young writers find the stories of their lives that show how we help one another, how we deal with change, and how important family is to all of us. The text is written in English and Arabic.

Ryan, Pam Muñoz. 2001. *Hello Ocean*. Watertown, MA: Charlesbridge.
Use of the senses to describe a special place; can be used to connect memories to a special place, particularly the seashore.

Rylant, Cynthia. 1991. *Night in the Country*. New York: Atheneum Books for Young Readers.
Use of sounds to spark memories; connections to places.

———. 1996. *An Angel for Solomon Singer*. New York: Scholastic.
Connections to special places and people as well as wishes and dreams.

———. 2001. *The Relatives Came*. New York: Atheneum Books for Young Readers.
Visits from relatives.

Schachner, Judith Byron. 2003. *The Grannyman*. New York: Puffin Books.
Connections to stories about pets.

Shannon, David. 2004. *A Bad Case of Stripes*. New York: Scholastic.
An example of a "What if" story.

Showers, Paul. 1993. *The Listening Walk*. New York: HarperCollins.
Can be used to encourage using the sense of hearing on a walk to stimulate story ideas.

Small, David. 1988. *Imogene's Antlers*. New York: Dragonfly Books.
A "What if" story. Can be used to inspire more what-ifs.

Stanton, Elizabeth Rose. 2014. *Henny*. New York: Simon and Schuster.
An example of a "What if" story.

Stead, Philip C. 2016. *Ideas Are All Around*. New York: Roaring Brook.
An example of taking a walk in your neighborhood to generate story ideas; use of photographs.

Thomson, Bill. 2010. *Chalk*. Las Vegas, NV: Amazon Children's Publishing.
A wordless book. Writers can connect to the emotions of the characters; can also be used to spark a "What if" story.

Van Allsburg, Chris. 1984. *The Mysteries of Harris Burdick*. New York: Houghton Mifflin.
The book is a collection of drawings, each accompanied by a title and a caption. Students can write the stories that go with the drawings.

Williams, Vera. 2007. *A Chair for My Mother*. New York: Greenwillow Books.
Connections can be made to times writers have saved money for something special.

Wood, Douglas. 2006. *Nothing to Do*. New York: Dutton Books for Young Readers.
: Brainstorming lists of things to do, which can be seeds of writing ideas.

Woodruff, Elvira. 2006. *Small Beauties*. New York: Alfred A. Knopf.
: A little girl saves objects from nature and her family's home in Ireland. An example of how objects can be used to spark memories.

Wong, Janet. 2000. *This Next New Year*. Princeton, NJ: Pomelo Books.
: Can spark connections to other cultural holidays or celebrations.

Wyeth, Sharon Dennis. 2002. *Something Beautiful*. New York: Dragonfly Books.
: Everyone has "something beautiful" in his or her life. What's yours?

Yolen, Jane. 1987. *Owl Moon*. New York: Philomel Books.
: Connections to special outings with father or other relative.

Chapter 3: What Are You Really Writing About? Discovering the Inside Story

Ackerman, Karen. 1992. *Song and Dance Man*. New York: Dragonfly Books.
: Can be used to stimulate thinking about territories, in this case relatives or grandfather.

Bang, Molly. 2004. *My Light*. New York: Blue Sky.
: First-person narrative written in the voice of the sun.

Baylor, Byrd. 1995. *I'm in Charge of Celebrations*. New York: Aladdin Books.
: Can be used to stimulate thinking about territories and then narrowing the territory to very specific things.

Bogan, Paulette. 2015. *Virgil and Owen*. New York: Bloomsbury.
: Makes a specific point about friendship.

Brinckloe, Julie. 1985. *Fireflies!* New York: Aladdin Books.
: Can provide a stimulus for connecting with emotions to find topics for writing—feelings of being happy and sad at the same time.

Browne, Anthony. 1998. *Voices in the Park*. New York: DK Publishing.
: Examples of different points of view.

Bunting, Eve. 1994. *Night Tree*. Boston: Houghton Mifflin Harcourt Books for Young Readers.
: Illustrates narrowing the topic—the book describes one holiday tradition, not the whole holiday.

Castillo, Lauren. 2014. *Nana in the City*. New York: Clarion Books.
: Can use as an example of walking through parts of a city to find places that suggest story ideas.

Crews, Donald. 1996. *Shortcut*. New York: Greenwillow Books.
 Can provide a stimulus for connecting with emotions to find topics for writing.

———. 1998. *Night at the Fair*. New York: Greenwillow Books.
 Can be used to stimulate thinking about territories, perhaps summer fun, then narrowing the territory to something more specific.

Curtis, Jamie Lee. 1993. *When I Was Little: A Four-Year-Old's Memoir of Her Youth*. New York: HarperCollins.
 Good stimulus for thinking about heart maps, especially for younger students.

Davies, Nicola. 2004. *Bat Loves the Night*. Cambridge, MA: Candlewick.
 Narrowing the topic (one specific kind of bat); information on the flap gives information about the author and indicates that the book came from personal experience.

———. 2005. *One Tiny Turtle*. Cambridge, MA: Candlewick.
 The introduction provides a wonderful example of narrowing the topic, especially for a nonfiction piece.

de la Peña, Matt. 2015. *Last Stop on Market Street*. New York: G. P. Putnam's Sons.
 Can use as an example of walking through parts of a city to find places that suggest story ideas.

Dotlich, Rebecca Kai. 2009. *Bella and Bean*. New York: Atheneum Books for Young Readers.
 Contains an example of collaborative writing.

Hanlon, Abby. 2012. *Ralph Tells a Story*. New York: Two Lions.
 Promotes developing a writer's identity, oral rehearsal of story, the importance of sharing, and the joy of being a writer.

Hooper, Meredith. 2015. *River Story*. Somerville, MA: Candlewick.
 Prologue to the story shows narrowing the topic to just one river.

Hoose, Phillip, and Hannah Hoose. 1998. *Hey, Little Ant*. Berkeley, CA: Tricycle.
 An excellent model for explaining point of view.

Horowitz, Ruth. 2004. *Crab Moon*. Cambridge, MA: Candlewick.
 Can provide a stimulus for connecting with emotions to find topics for writing—feelings of excitement, surprise, fear, or nervousness.

Howard, Arthur. 1999. *When I Was Five*. Boston: Houghton Mifflin Harcourt Books for Young Readers.
 A clear example of making a point—the point is stated in the last line.

Jenkins, Martin. 2001. *Chameleons Are Cool*. Cambridge, MA: Candlewick.
 The introduction is an example of narrowing the topic; the point is made in the title.

Karas, G. Brian. 2004. *Atlantic*. New York: Puffin.
First-person narrative written in the voice of the Atlantic Ocean.

Keating, Jess. 2016. *Pink Is for Blobfish: Discovering the World's Perfectly Pink Animals*. New York: Alfred A. Knopf.
Final statement at the end of the book reveals the point.

Kilborne, Sarah S. 1998. *Peach and Blue*. New York: Dragonfly Books.
A book about friendship that helps illustrate point of view.

Koehler, Fred. 2016. *Super Jumbo*. New York: Penguin.
Makes a specific point about friendship.

LaMarche, Jim. 2000. *The Raft*. New York: HarperCollins.
In the author's note, Jim LaMarche explains that the story comes from bits and pieces of his boyhood summers—time spent with his grandmother, a raft he found, the power of drawing. Young writers could examine their heart maps and combine bits and pieces to create a story.

Little, Jean. 1990. *Hey World, Here I Am!* New York: HarperCollins.
A collection of individual stories with common characters; can be used to stimulate emotions for hand maps.

Lowry, Lois. 2009. *Crow Call*. New York: Scholastic.
Contains an author's note where Lowry explains how the story originated. She also explains how it can serve as a connection to writers and readers on a broader scale.

Lyon, George Ella. 2003. *Mother to Tigers*. New York: Atheneum Books for Young Readers.
Contains an author's note that provides additional information and reveals the source of the idea for the book.

MacLachlan, Patricia. 1994. *All the Places to Love*. New York: HarperCollins.
Can be used as an example of taking a walk in a particular place to find story ideas.

Markle, Sandra. 2011. *Butterfly Tree*. Atlanta: Peachtree.
Author's note reveals that the inspiration for the book came from a personal experience; written in first person and present tense; includes additional information about monarchs.

McKissack, Patricia C. 2001. *Goin' Someplace Special*. New York: Atheneum Books for Young Readers.
A good stimulus for thinking about heart maps; contains an author's note that provides more information on the origin of the story.

Michelson, Richard. 2006. *Across the Alley*. New York: Penguin.
Makes a specific point that friends can teach each other.

Murphy, Frank. 2000. *The Legend of the Teddy Bear*. Chelsea, MI: Sleeping Bear.
Contains an author's note that provides more information and reveals the inspiration for the book.

Nolen, Jerdine. 2001. *In My Momma's Kitchen*. New York: Amistad.
Can be used as an example of places as territories for writing topics.

O'Neill, Alexis. *The Recess Queen*. 2002. New York: Scholastic.
Makes a specific point about friendship.

Orloff, Karen Kaufman. 2010. *I Wanna New Room*. New York: G. P. Putnam's Sons.
The title of the book states the point.

Pilutti, Deb. 2015. *Bear and Squirrel Are Friends*. New York: Simon and Schuster.
The title of the book states the point.

Rappaport, Doreen. 2016. *John's Secret Dreams: The Life of John Lennon*. New York: Disney-Hyperion.
Contains a note from the author as well as the illustrator (Bryan Collier) that explains the process, research, and thinking each went through to create the book.

Rocco, John. 2014. *Blizzard*. New York: Hyperion.
Contains a neighborhood map with labels.

Rosenthal, Amy Krouse. 2009. *Duck! Rabbit!* San Francisco: Chronicle Books.
Can be used to show different points of view.

———. 2009. *Spoon*. New York: Hyperion.
Can be used to show different points of view.

———. 2013. *Exclamation Mark*. Scholastic.
Can be used to show different points of view.

Rylant, Cynthia. 2002. *Best Wishes*. Katonah, NY: Richard C. Owen.
Helps identify the author's writing territories.

Schachner, Judy. 2002. *Yo, Vikings!* New York: Dutton Children's Books.
An example of a book that came from the author's experience.

Scieszka, Jon. 1996. *The True Story of the 3 Little Pigs!* New York: Puffin.
An example of telling a story from a different point of view.

Siebert, Diane. 1996. *Sierra*. New York: HarperCollins.
Written in first-person narrative from the point of view of the mountain.

———. 2015. *Heartland*. Boston: David R. Godine.
Written in first-person narrative from the point of view of the American Midwest.

Spinelli, Eileen. 2004. *I Know It's Autumn*. New York: HarperCollins.
Example of a book where the point is in the title.

———. 2008. *The Best Story*. New York: Penguin.
This book can be used to introduce heart maps.

Stead, Philip C. 2012. *Bear Has a Story to Tell*. New York: Roaring Brook.
An example of collaboration in telling a story.

Stewart, Melissa. 2014. *Feathers: Not Just for Flying*. Watertown, MA: Charlesbridge.
An example of a book where the point is in the title.

Stinson, Kathy. 2006. *Red Is Best*. Toronto, ON: Annick.
Can be used to show different points of view.

Swinburne, Stephen. 2002. *Safe, Warm, and Snug*. Boston: Houghton Mifflin Harcourt Books for Young Readers.
Uses rhyming couplets to explain how animals protect their young; the point is found in the title; contains explanations of each animal in the back.

Van, Muon. 2015. *In a Village by the Sea*. Berkeley, CA: Creston Books.
Includes an author's note that explains how the story was inspired by events in a village that have been repeated for centuries.

Wagstaff, Janiel. 2015. *Stella Tells Her Story*. Peterborough, NH: SDE Professional Development Resources.
Includes a great example of whole-class and partner sharing to find topics for writing.

Whitcomb, Mary E. 1998. *Odd Velvet*. San Francisco: Chronicle Books.
Can be used as an example of topic and point.

White, E. B. 1952. *Charlotte's Web*. New York: HarperCollins.
The first chapter can lead to a discussion of the emotions that are revealed. Connections made can be used in creating a hand map.

Willems, Mo. 2004. *Don't Let the Pigeon Drive the Bus!* New York: Hyperion.
This book and the other Pigeon books are examples of a book where the point is stated in the title.

———. 2014. *Waiting Is Not Easy!* New York: Hyperion.
This book and the other Elephant and Piggy books provide examples of books where the point is stated in the title.

The following books, all by Cynthia Rylant, can be used to explore some of her writing territories. This is just a sampling of Rylant's many books that help us know something about her and where she gets her writing ideas:

Henry and Mudge: The First Book. 1987. New York: Simon and Schuster.
This is the first in a series of books about the big dog Mudge. Rylant also wrote the Mr. Putter and Tabby series about the adventures of a cat and her owner.

Night in the Country. 1991. New York: Atheneum Books for Young Readers.
When I Was Young in the Mountains. 1993. New York: Puffin Books.
Dog Heaven. 1995. New York: Blue Sky.
Cat Heaven. 1997. New York: Blue Sky.

The Great Gracie Chase: Stop That Dog! 2001. New York: Blue Sky.
The Relatives Came. 2001. New York: Atheneum Books for Young Readers.
Gooseberry Park. 2007. Boston: Houghton Mifflin Harcourt.

The following books by Judy Schachner can be used to explore her territories of pets and family:

The Grannyman. 1999. New York: Dutton Books for Young Readers.
Mr. Emerson's Cook. 2002. Akron, PA: Reading Matters.
   This book contains an afterword that provides factual information about Ralph Waldo Emerson and also reveals some of Schachner's family history that inspired the book.
Yo, Vikings! 2002. New York: Dutton Children's Books.
   This book contains an author's note that explains how the story came from a personal experience.
Skippyjon Jones. 2005. New York: Puffin Books.
Skippyjon Jones in the Doghouse. 2007. New York: Puffin Books.
Bits and Pieces. 2013. New York: Dial Books.

Chapter 4: When Writers Use a Magnifying Lens

Arden, Carolyn. 2004. *Goose Moon.* Honesdale, PA: Boyds Mills.
   Examples of elaboration to further explain an idea.

Boelts, Maribeth. 2014. *Happy Like Soccer.* Somerville, MA: Candlewick.
   Splashes of dialogue used to bring characters to life.

Bottner, Barbara, and Gerald Kruglik. 2004. *Wallace's Lists.* New York: Katherine Tegan Books.
   Contains examples of thoughtshots.

Bram, Elizabeth. 2015. *Rufus the Writer.* New York: Schwartz and Wade.
   Picture frames across a two-page spread to show a step-by step process; dialogue; stories embedded within the text.

Brinckloe, Julie. 1986. *Fireflies!* New York: Aladdin Books.
   The whole book provides details surrounding a small moment in time.

Brown, Marc. 1990. *Arthur's Pet Business.* New York: Little, Brown.
   Additional story details can be found in the illustrations.

Bunting, Eve. 2006. *One Green Apple.* New York: Clarion Books.
   A sprinkling of dialogue, and rich descriptions of people, places, and objects.

———. 2015. *The Memory String.* Boston: Houghton Mifflin Harcourt Books for Young Readers.
   Examples of show, don't tell.

Burleigh, Robert. 1997. *Flight: The Journey of Charles Lindbergh*. New York: Puffin Books.
Contains an example of slowing down the action to add specific details that explode a small moment in time.

———. 2003. *Home Run*. Boston: Houghton Mifflin Harcourt.
Contains an example of slowing down the action to add specific details that explode a small moment in time.

———. 2009. *One Giant Leap*. New York: Philomel Books.
Examples of rich descriptions of setting and an object.

———. 2010. *Tiger of the Snows: Tenzing Norgay: The Boy Whose Dream Was Everest*. New York: Atheneum Books.
Contains examples of thoughtshots, sensory details, and exploding a moment in time.

Castillo, Lauren. 2014. *Nana in the City*. New York: Clarion Books.
Use of dialogue to focus on the most important part of the story and indicate when things are shifting.

Chall, Marsha Wilson. 1992. *Up North at the Cabin*. New York: HarperCollins.
Appeal to the senses to build content.

———. 2000. *Sugarbush Spring*. New York: HarperCollins.
Use of dialogue with description to build content.

Crews, Donald. 1996. *Shortcut*. New York: Greenwillow Books.
Dialogue used strategically to focus on the most important part of the story; additional story details can be found in the illustrations.

Dahl, Roald. 2007. *The Witches*. New York: Puffin Books.
Examples of snapshots of character; show, don't tell (the chapter "The Meeting" is especially good for "fear"). Note: Many of Roald Dahl's books (listed in the "Treasure Chest of Books" under Chapter 5) provide examples of snapshots of character.

Dotlich, Rebecca Kai. 2015. *One Day, The End*. Honesdale, PA; Boyds Mills.
Additional story details can be found in the illustrations.

Falatko, Julie. 2016. *Snappsy the Alligator (Did Not Ask to Be in This Book!)*. New York: Penguin Young Readers Group.
Includes an example of passage of time; opens with a rich description of character.

Falconer, Ian. 2000. *Olivia*. New York: Atheneum Books for Young Readers.
Examples of show, don't tell—we learn about Olivia by the things she says and does; this is also an example of snapshot of character.

Farris, Christine King. 2006. *My Brother Martin: A Sister Remembers Growing Up with the Rev. Dr. Martin Luther King Jr.* New York: Aladdin Books.
Contains examples of anecdotes to build interesting content.

Fletcher, Ralph. 1997. *Twilight Comes Twice.* New York: Clarion Books.
Appeal to the senses to build content.

Franco, Betsy. 2007. *Birdsongs.* New York: Simon and Schuster.
The whole book is a rich description of setting.

Gardiner, John Reynolds. 2010. *Stone Fox.* New York: HarperCollins.
Includes examples of character snapshots.

Giff, Patricia Reilly. 2004. *Pictures of Hollis Woods.* New York: Yearling.
Travels back and forth between time; examples of exploding a moment.

Gottesfeld, Jeff. 2016. *The Tree in the Courtyard: Looking Through Anne Frank's Window.* New York: Alfred A. Knopf.
Opens with a rich description of a character, in this case, a tree.

Grimes, Nikki. 2002. *Talkin' About Bessie: The Story of Aviator Elizabeth Coleman.* New York: Orchard Books.
Contains many examples of the use of anecdote to provide interesting information about a character and build content; snapshots of character and setting; some examples of exploding a moment.

Henkes, Kevin. 1991. *Chrysanthemum.* New York: Greenwillow Books.
Show, don't tell through use of illustration.

———. 2004. *Kitten's First Full Moon.* New York: Greenwillow Books.
Examples of actions in a series connected by and; phrases in a series separated by commas to show getting from here to there.

———. 2006. *Lilly's Purple Plastic Purse.* New York: Greenwillow Books.
Examples of adding content through the use of descriptions and details. Henkes's style is to use "the power of three" in his explanations, most often adding three details to elaborate on something; some examples of show, don't tell.

Hesse, Karen. 1999. *Come On, Rain!* New York: Scholastic.
Appeal to the senses to build content.

Hest, Amy. 2008. *The Dog Who Belonged to No One.* New York: Abrams Books for Young Readers.
Elaboration—additional sentences explain how the dog was helpful.

Hills, Tad. 2012. *Rocket Writes a Story.* New York: Random House.
An example of how to add content through questioning.

Hooper, Meredith. 2015. *River Story.* Somerville, MA: Candlewick.
Examples of description and elaboration.

Hopkins, H. Joseph. 2013. *The Tree Lady: The True Story of How One Tree-Loving Woman Changed a City Forever.* New York: Simon and Schuster.
Rich description of setting and character.

Hopkinson, Deborah. 2012. *Annie and Helen.* New York: Random House.
Examples of anecdotes and the power of three to add details.

Horowitz, Ruth. 2004. *Crab Moon*. Cambridge, MA: Candlewick.
Exploding a moment—slowing down the action and adding more detail; examples of show, don't tell; passage of time.

Howard, Elizabeth Fitzgerald. 1995. *Aunt Flossie's Hats (and Crab Cakes Later)*. Boston: Houghton Mifflin Harcourt.
Rich descriptions; appeal to the senses.

Johnston, Tony. 1998. *Amber on the Mountain*. New York: Puffin Books.
Vivid description to build content; examples of thoughtshots and dialogue.

Keating, Jess. 2016. *Pink Is for Blobfish: Discovering the World's Perfectly Pink Animals*. New York: Alfred A. Knopf.
A book rich in description; builds content with explanations and examples; contains examples of how to elaborate.

LaMarche, Jim. 2000. *The Raft*. New York: HarperCollins.
Example of exploding a moment as Nicky discovers a fawn in trouble and rescues her; splash of dialogue that serves to break up lengthy descriptions of events.

Laminack, Lester. 2004. *Saturdays and Teacakes*. Atlanta: Peachtree.
Use of dialogue to build content. The dialogue is written in italics.

Ludwig, Trudy. 2013. *The Invisible Boy*. New York: Alfred A. Knopf.
Short description of character; speech bubbles to extend content; thoughtshots; contains an example of letter writing.

Lyon, George Ella. 2003. *Mother to Tigers*. New York: Atheneum Books for Young Readers.
Use of anecdote to build content; use of explanations to elaborate and add details.

MacLachlan, Patricia. 1994. *All the Places to Love*. New York: HarperCollins.
Appeal to the senses to build content.

MacLachlan, Patricia, and Emily MacLachlan. *Painting the Wind*. New York: HarperCollins.
Descriptions of objects to build content; dialogue sprinkled throughout the story; use of listing to add details.

Markle, Sandra. 2011. *Butterfly Tree*. Atlanta: Peachtree.
Dialogue is written in italics and used to sustain interest. It is also used to create a satisfying ending.

———. 2015. *Toad Weather*. Atlanta: Peachtree.
Examples of listing with extended descriptions; use of dialogue to offer information or an explanation.

Mattick, Lindsay. 2015. *Finding Winnie: The True Story of the World's Most Famous Bear*. New York: Little, Brown.
Contains an example of how to craft passage of time.

McFarland, Lyn Rossiter. (Illustrated by Jim McFarland.) 2006. *Widget.* New York: Square Fish.
Snapshot of character in the beginning; often adds details in threes; example of show, don't tell through illustration.

Messner, Kate. 2011. *Over and Under the Snow.* San Francisco: Chronicle Books.
Use of dialogue to offer an explanation.

———. 2015. *Up in the Garden and Down in the Dirt.* San Francisco: Chronicle Books.
Use of dialogue to offer an explanation, give a direction, and express emotion.

Naylor, Phyllis Reynolds. 2000. *Shiloh.* New York: Atheneum Books.
Written in the first person, this book helps students understand what it means to "be in the moment," assisting them in visualizing the details.

Paulsen, Gary. 2001. *Canoe Days.* New York: Dragonfly Books.
Appeal to the senses to build content.

Pilutti, Deb. 2015. *Bear and Squirrel Are Friends.* New York: Simon and Schuster.
Passage of time as depicted in the words across pages and in the illustration (we see how long Squirrel waited for Bear by the length of the scarf he is knitting).

Pinborough, Jan. 2013. *Miss Moore Thought Otherwise: How Anne Carroll Moore Created Libraries for Children.* Boston: Houghton Mifflin Harcourt.
Begins with a thumbnail sketch of character; rich description of setting and time period; use of the power of three to describe actions.

Polacco, Patricia. 1997. *Thunder Cake.* New York: Puffin Books.
Includes examples of purposeful dialogue.

———. 2004. *Betty Doll.* New York: Puffin Books.
Use of anecdotes to build content; rich descriptions of objects and people; use of dialogue to reveal more about a character; passage of time.

Raschka, Chris. 2007. *Yo! Yes?* New York: Scholastic.
Use of show, don't tell through illustrations.

Rawlinson, Julia. 2006. *Fletcher and the Falling Leaves.* New York: HarperCollins.
Rich descriptions; thumbnail sketch of setting.

Rocco, John. 2011. *Blackout.* New York: Hyperion.
Information in pictures adds additional content.

Rotner, Shelley, and Ken Kreisler. 2014. *Nature Spy.* New York: Atheneum Books.
Provides examples of looking at things in nature to see all the details and patterns—like looking at something under a magnifying lens; this concept can be linked to writing.

Ryan, Pam Muñoz. 2001. *Hello Ocean*. Watertown, MA: Charlesbridge.
  Use of the senses to build content.

———. 2005. *Mice and Beans*. New York: Scholastic.
  Use of thoughtshots to add content.

Rylant, Cynthia. 1996. *An Angel for Solomon Singer*. New York: Scholastic.
  Rich descriptions; examples of thought shots; snapshots of setting and
  character.

———. 2001. *The Relatives Came*. New York: Atheneum Books for Young
  Readers.
  Rich descriptions; appeal to the senses; passage of time.

Schachner, Judith Byron. 1999. *The Grannyman*. New York: Dutton Books
  for Young Readers.
  Opens with a description of character.

Schertle, Alice. 2000. *Down the Road*. New York: Houghton Mifflin Harcourt.
  Examples of descriptions; getting from here to there with use of ellipses.

Sierra, Judy. 2010. *Thelonius Monster's Sky-High Fly Pie*. New York:
  Dragonfly Books.
  Includes a sprinkling of dialogue and lists to build content.

Smith, Doris Buchanan. 2004. *A Taste of Blackberries*. New York:
  HarperCollins.
  Slowing down the action to explode a small moment in time by adding
  specific details; contains snapshots of character.

Stanton, Elizabeth Rose. 2014. *Henny*. New York: Simon and Schuster.
  Examples of elaboration by adding sentences with details; power of three.

Talbott, Hudson. 2012. *It's All About Me-ow*. New York: Nancy Paulson Books.
  Examples of ways to build content in nonfiction—listing using ellipses,
  charting, time line, thoughtshots in the form of talking captions, "how-
  to" explanations.

Whitcomb, Mary E. 1998. *Odd Velvet*. San Francisco: Chronicle Books.
  Combines dialogue and descriptions to build content and provide
  information about the main character.

White, E. B. 2012. *Charlotte's Web*. New York: HarperCollins.
  Provides examples of snapshots of character; characters are revealed by
  what they say and do.

Willems, Mo. 2004. *Don't Let the Pigeon Drive the Bus!* New York:
  Hyperion.
  This book and other books by Mo Willems use dialogue exclusively to
  create a story.

Woodson, Jacqueline. 2012. *Each Kindness*. New York: Penguin.
  Includes some examples of the power of three—listing objects, three
  actions; use of transition words to show passage of time.

Wyeth, Sharon Dennis. 2002. *Something Beautiful*. New York: Dragonfly Books.
Use of dialogue to build content; appeal to the senses; rich descriptions.

Yamada, Kobi. 2016. *What Do You Do with a Problem?* Seattle, WA:
Compendium.
Effective listing using entire sentences; thoughtshot voiced as dialogue to
the reader and followed by more thinking aloud.

Yolen, Jane. 1987. *Owl Moon*. New York: Philomel Books.
Appeal to the senses to build content.

Young, Judy. 2011. *A Book for Black-Eyed Susan*. Ann Arbor, MI: Sleeping Bear.
Includes examples of snapshots of characters.

Chapter 5: Growing a Narrative from Beginning to End

Albert, Richard E. 1996. *Alejandro's Gift*. San Francisco: Chronicle Books.
Opens with a description of setting that creates the mood of loneliness;
the ending describes a decision reached and resolves the feeling of
loneliness planted in the beginning.

Arden, Carolyn. 2004. *Goose Moon*. Honesdale, PA: Boyds Mills.
The beginning and ending are almost bookends ("Winter is coming . . ."
"Summer is coming") and signify the passage of time.

Bandy, Michael S., and Eric Stein. 2015. *Granddaddy's Turn: A Journey to
the Ballot Box*. Somerville, MA: Candlewick.
Opens with a setting that introduces the main character. The ending is a
memory that lingers and a thoughtshot.

Boelts, Maribeth. 2007. *Those Shoes*. Cambridge, MA: Candlewick.
Provides a good example of a story map, especially a clear problem and
solution.

———. 2016. *A Bike Like Sergio's*. Somerville, MA: Candlewick.
Follows a traditional story map with a clear problem (moral dilemma)
and a plausible solution; examples of snapshot of character.

Bradby, Marie. 1995. *More Than Anything Else*. New York: Orchard Books.
Begins with a description of setting combined with action; ending
describes an accomplishment and self-discovery as it reflects the seed
planted in the beginning of the story—Booker's desire to learn to read.

Bram, Elizabeth. 2015. *Rufus the Writer*. New York: Schwartz and Wade.
Opens with dialogue as a thoughtshot; ends with a final action and what
the characters are thinking and feeling; internal structure (Rufus's stories).

Brinckloe, Julie. 1985. *Fireflies!* New York: Aladdin Books.
Helps writers understand time—the beginning is not too far away from
the main event; ends with a final action where the feelings of the main
character are revealed.

Bunting, Eve. 1989. *The Wednesday Surprise*. New York: Houghton Mifflin Harcourt Books for Young Readers.
The lead paragraph plants the seed of the ending; the book ends with someone speaking.

———. 1993. *Fly Away Home*. New York: Houghton Mifflin Harcourt Books for Young Readers.
The ending describes a memory that lingers.

———. 1994. *Night Tree*. New York: Houghton Mifflin Harcourt Books for Young Readers.
The ending describes what the main character is thinking.

———. 1996. *Someday a Tree*. New York: Houghton Mifflin Harcourt Books for Young Readers.
Begins and ends with dialogue; the ending dialogue is from an inanimate object.

———. 2015. *The Memory String*. New York: Houghton Mifflin Harcourt Books for Young Readers.
Ends with a self-discovery.

———. 2015. *Yard Sale*. Somerville, MA: Candlewick.
Opens with a description setting that introduces the main character and her feelings. Ends with the characters' thoughts presented through dialogue and a lesson learned.

Burleigh, Robert. 1997. *Flight: The Journey of Charles Lindbergh*. New York: Puffin Books.
The first and last lines are the same—an example of a bookend structure.

———. 2003. *Home Run*. New York: Houghton Mifflin Harcourt Books for Young Readers.
An example of bookends—the beginning and the end mirror each other.

Cannon, Janell. 1993. *Stellaluna*. New York: Houghton Mifflin Harcourt Books for Young Readers.
Ends with what the characters are thinking as they describe a lesson learned.

Capucilli, Alyssa Satin. 2015. *Tulip and Rex Write a Story*. New York: HarperCollins Children's Books.
Beginning combines setting with action; ending combines action with what the character is feeling; could use Tulip's unfinished story that she is telling to map story structure; students could come up with an ending; use of talking a story out before writing it.

Castillo, Lauren. 2014. *The Troublemaker*. New York: Clarion Books.
A good example of a story map with a clear problem and solution. The last three pages are illustrations and reveal the satisfying ending and the beginning of a new story.

Chall, Marsha Wilson. 1992. *Up North at the Cabin*. New York: HarperCollins.
The ending describes a memory that lingers.

———. 2000. *Sugarbush Spring*. New York: HarperCollins.
Opens with a description of weather.

Crews, Donald. 1996. *Shortcut*. New York: Greenwillow Books.
Provides an example of establishing a beginning, middle, and end with one small moment in time; the ending is a decision that reflects the problem revealed in the beginning.

———. 1998. *Night at the Fair*. New York: Greenwillow Books.
A nearly wordless book. Orally telling the story and mapping it can help young writers internalize story structure.

Cronin, Doreen. 2000. *Click, Clack, Moo: Cows That Type*. New York: Simon and Schuster Books for Young Readers.
The ending combines a decision with a final action. Part of the ending is revealed in the final illustration by Betsy Lewin.

Dahl, Roald. 2007. *The BFG*. New York: Puffin Books.
Physical descriptions of character.

———. 2007. *James and the Giant Peach*. New York: Puffin Books.
Physical descriptions of character.

———. 2007. *Matilda*. New York: Puffin Books.
Excellent examples of physical descriptions of character (note especially "The Trunchbull").

———. 2007. *The Witches*. New York: Puffin Books.
Physical descriptions of character.

Danticat, Edwidge. 2015. *Mama's Nightingale*. New York: Penguin.
Begins and ends with the thoughts and feelings of the main character.

Davies, Nicola. 2005. *One Tiny Turtle*. Cambridge, MA: Candlewick.
The beginning of this lyrical nonfiction book is a snapshot of setting. The words from the opening line appear again in the ending—an example of a bookends book.

———. 2013. *The Promise*. Somerville, MA: Candlewick.
Beginning is a snapshot of setting.

de la Peña, Matt. 2015. *Last Stop on Market Street*. New York: G. P. Putnam's Sons.
The beginning is a series of actions; the book ends with dialogue.

dePaola, Tomie. 1999. *The Baby Sister*. New York: Puffin.
Final illustration can be used to create a satisfying ending using words.

Dotlich, Rebecca Kai. 2009. *Bella and Bean*. New York: Atheneum Books.
Opens with a character sketch of Bella.

Duke, Kate. 1994. *Aunt Isabel Tells a Good One*. New York: Puffin Books.
As Aunt Isabel tells a story, she provides an example of how to craft a
beginning, a middle, and an end.

Fleming, Candace. 2002. *Muncha! Muncha! Muncha!* New York: Atheneum
Books for Young Readers.
The ending combines a decision with a final action and is shown in the
final illustration by G. Brian Karas.

Franco, Betsy. 2007. *Birdsongs*. New York: Simon and Schuster.
Beginning and ending act as bookends to frame the story.

Frazee, Marla. 2006. *Roller Coaster*. New York: Houghton Mifflin Harcourt
Books for Young Readers.
Contains an example of a bridge paragraph from the lead into the
middle of the story.

———. 2014. *The Farmer and the Clown*. New York: Simon and Schuster.
A wordless book. Orally telling the story and mapping it can help young
writers internalize story structure.

Gray, Libba Moore. 1999. *My Mama Had a Dancing Heart*. New York:
Scholastic.
An example of bookends—the last line of the book repeats the first line.

Henkes, Kevin. 1997. *Chester's Way*. New York: Greenwillow Books.
A here-we-go-again ending indicates that the events might start all over
again.

———. 1998. *Jessica*. New York: Greenwillow Books.
An example of a bookends book, in which the beginning and the end are
the same.

———. 2006. *Lilly's Purple Plastic Purse*. New York: Greenwillow Books.
Begins with a description of what the main character, Lilly, loves; the
ending shows how Lilly is feeling combined with an action.

Hest, Amy. 2007. *Mr. George Baker*. Cambridge, MA: Candlewick.
Beginning combines a description of character and setting. The book
ends with onomatopoeia.

Hoffman, Mary. 1991. *Amazing Grace*. New York: Dial Books for Young
Readers.
Begins with a description of the main character in the form of describing
what she loves.

Hopkins, H. Joseph. 2013. *The Tree Lady: The True Story of How One Tree-
Loving Woman Changed a City Forever*. New York: Simon and Schuster.
Transitional phrases (*soon, but for two years, after graduation*).

Horowitz, Ruth. 2004. *Crab Moon*. Cambridge, MA: Candlewick.
Helps writers understand how they can transition quickly between
events to get to the main focus of the story. The beginning is a snapshot

of setting that quickly sets the stage for the main event of finding the marooned horseshoe crab. The ending describes a final action and includes dialogue.

Howard, Arthur. 1999. *When I Was Five.* New York: Houghton Mifflin Harcourt Books for Young Readers.
    The ending (the last line) describes a discovery made.

Jiang, Ji-li. 2013. *Red Kite, Blue Kite.* New York: Disney Hyperion.
    Contains an example of a bridge paragraph from the lead to the middle of the story.

Johnston, Tony. 1998. *Amber on the Mountain.* New York: Puffin Books.
    This book begins with a snapshot of setting; the ending includes the thoughts and feelings of the main characters as well as the final action of writing the letter; an excellent example of planting the seed for the ending in the beginning—Amber's loneliness in the beginning is resolved at the end.

Jones, Val. 2015. *Who Wants Broccoli?* New York: HarperCollins.
    Bridge paragraph—tells more about Broccoli as a character after the beginning before starting on the story events.

Kearney, Meg. 2013. *Trouper.* New York: Scholastic.
    Beginning is a scaffold that takes the reader back in time and then names something unexpected.

Kroll, Steven. 2005. *Patches Lost and Found.* New York: Two Lions.
    Clear beginning, middle, and end; has a satisfying ending in the form of a final action; an excellent example of story mapping—using pictures to plan a story.

LaMarche, Jim. 2000. *The Raft.* New York: HarperCollins.
    Begins and ends with dialogue.

Laminack, Lester. 1998. *The Sunsets of Miss Olivia Wiggins.* Atlanta, GA: Peachtree.
    An example of a bookends book, in which the beginning and the end are the same.

Ludwig, Trudy. 2013. *The Invisible Boy.* New York: Alfred A. Knopf.
    Question lead addressed to the reader; ends with final actions and self-realization; problem is clear to the reader.

Lyon, George Ella. 2003. *Mother to Tigers.* New York: Atheneum Books for Young Readers.
    Illustrator Peter Catalanotto set up the beginning of this book as a prologue, much like you might find in a movie before the credits roll; there are two pages of text before the title page. The last line includes the title of the book.

Lyons, Kelly Starling. 2012. *Ellen's Broom.* New York: G. P. Putnam's Sons.
    Opens with a setting that introduces the main character. The ending includes dialogue and a final action.

MacLachlan, Patricia, and Emily MacLachlan. 2006. *Painting the Wind*. New York: HarperCollins.
Lead contains the seeds of the ending and is a list of the main character's accomplishments; ending is a combination of what the main character is thinking and feeling and a self-discovery; contains a bridge paragraph on the second and third page.

Markle, Sandra. 2011. *Butterfly Tree*. Atlanta, GA: Peachtree.
Begins with a description of setting and action; ending speaks to creating a memory that lingers; good example of a middle where there are several attempts to reach the goal.

———. 2015. *Toad Weather*. Atlanta, GA: Peachtree.
Opens with a description of weather; the ending combines what the characters are feeling with a final action.

Mayer, Mercer. 1967. *A Boy, a Dog, and a Frog*. New York: Penguin.
A wordless book. Orally telling the story and mapping it can help young writers internalize story structure.

McFarland, Lyn Rossiter. 2006. *Widget*. New York: Square Fish.
Written with a clear beginning, middle, and satisfying ending that are easily identified; beginning combines description of character and setting; ends with a description of what the character is thinking and feeling; an excellent example of how the ending is most often tied to the beginning; contains an example of a bridge paragraph.

McNaughton, Colin. 1998. *Suddenly!* New York: Houghton Mifflin Harcourt Books for Young Readers.
An example of a surprise ending.

Meng, Cece. 2016. *Always Remember*. New York: Penguin.
The beginning starts with the end of the main character's (Old Turtle's) life. The ending is a summary list and a discovery made by the other characters and the readers of the book. This is an opposites structure that students may want to try.

Miller, Debbie S. 2007. *Arctic Lights, Arctic Nights*. New York: Walker Children's.
This is a nonfiction book that describes a year in the Arctic region. Each page is written as a snapshot of setting, describing what is happening from month to month. Each snapshot also begins with onomatopoeia; includes an introduction and a glossary.

Miller, Kathy M. 2009. *Chippy Chipmunk Parties in the Garden*. New Ringgold, PA: Celtic Sunrise.
Use of photographs to tell a story.

Mora, Pat. 2007. *Tomás and the Library Lady*. New York: Dragonfly Books.
The beginning combines a description of setting with how the main character is feeling.

Nolen, Jerdine. 2001. *In My Momma's Kitchen*. New York: Amistad.
An example of bookended beginning and end—beginning and ending lines are the same.

O'Neill, Alexis. 2002. *The Recess Queen*. New York: Scholastic.
Beginning is a description of a trait of the main character.

Paulsen, Gary. 2001. *Canoe Days*. New York: Dragonfly Books.
The ending line reflects the title of the book.

Penn, Audrey. 1993. *The Kissing Hand*. New York: Scholastic.
Ends with dialogue from an inanimate object.

Pilutti, Deb. 2015. *Bear and Squirrel Are Friends*. New York: Simon and Schuster.
Beginning reveals something unexpected; ends with the main characters talking to the reader by way of speech bubbles.

Pinkney, Jerry. 2009. *The Lion and the Mouse*. New York: Little, Brown Books for Young Readers.
A wordless book. Orally telling the story and mapping it can help young writers internalize story structure.

Polacco, Patricia. 2004. *Betty Doll*. New York: Puffin Books.
Ends with a memory that lingers.

Ramsey, Calvin Alexander. 2010. *Ruth and the Green Book*. Minneapolis, MN: Carolrhoda Books.
Opens with an action combined with a description of an object and what the character is thinking and feeling; ends with self-realization and what the character is thinking and feeling.

Raschka, Chris. 2011. *A Ball for Daisy*. New York: Schwartz and Wade Books.
A wordless book. Orally telling the story and mapping it can help young writers internalize story structure.

Rawlinson, Julia. 2006. *Fletcher and the Falling Leaves*. New York: HarperCollins.
Beginning and ending describe the setting.

Rylant, Cynthia. 1996. *An Angel for Solomon Singer*. New York: Scholastic.
The ending combines a decision with a final action; final illustration by Peter Catalanotto enhances the ending.

———. 2001. *The Great Gracie Chase: Stop That Dog!* New York: Blue Sky.
The beginning combines a description of character and setting.

———. 2001. *The Relatives Came*. New York: Atheneum Books for Young Readers.
An example of a book where the ending indicates that things will start all over again (sometimes called a circular text). The first line of the book sets the stage for the story that happens in the summer. In the end,

the relatives are dreaming of the next summer, when things will start all over again.

Sams, Carl R., II, and Jean Stoick. 2000. *Stranger in the Woods: A Photographic Fantasy*. Milford, MI: Carl R. Sams II Photography.
This book begins with a description of weather.

Schachner, Judith Byron. 2003. *The Grannyman*. New York: Puffin Books.
Begins with a physical description of the main character; the last line of the ending includes the book title.

Small, David. 1988. *Imogene's Antlers*. New York: Dragonfly Books.
A here-we-go-again ending indicates that the story might start all over again.

Smith, Doris Buchanan. 2004. *A Taste of Blackberries*. New York: HarperCollins.
The title appears in the ending.

Soto, Gary. 1996. *Too Many Tamales*. New York: Puffin Books.
Interesting beginning sentence that describes the weather.

Spinelli, Jerry. 1999. *Maniac Magee*. 2nd ed. Boston: Little, Brown Books for Young Readers.
Begins with a description of the main character in the form of what other people say about him.

Stead, Philip C. 2012. *Bear Has a Story to Tell*. New York: Roaring Brook.
An example of bookended beginning and end—beginning and ending lines are the same.

Trimmer, Christian. 2015. *Simon's New Bed*. New York: Atheneum Books for Young Readers.
An example of a simple story structure that students could map; includes a "prelude" to set up the story before it begins.

Wagstaff, Janiel. 2015. *Stella Tells Her Story*. Peterborough, NH: Professional Development Resources.
Provides a good example of mapping out a story with a beginning, a middle, and an end with use of transition words.

Weisner, David. 2011. *Tuesday*. New York: Houghton Mifflin Harcourt Books for Young Readers.
A wordless book. Orally telling the story and mapping it can help young writers internalize story structure.

Wells, Rosemary. 2002. *Bunny Cakes*. New York: Puffin Books.
A good mentor text to demonstrate the beginning, middle, and end of a story to very young writers.

White, E. B. 2012. *Charlotte's Web*. New York: HarperCollins.
Begins with a question. Students might try a different beginning— snapshot of setting, character sketch, and so on—just as E. B. White did,

and then talk about why this was such a powerful beginning. The book ends with the thoughts and feelings of Wilbur as he remembers Charlotte.

Wood, Douglas. 2006. *Nothing to Do.* New York: Dutton Books for Young Readers.
  An example of a book where the seed of the ending can easily be found in the beginning.

Woodson, Jacqueline. 2001. *The Other Side.* New York: G. P. Putnam's Sons Books for Young Readers.
  Contains an example of a bridge paragraph that takes the reader from the lead into the middle of the story.

———. 2012. *Each Kindness.* New York: Penguin.
  Beginning is a description of weather; ending describes what the character is thinking and feeling.

Wyeth, Sharon Dennis. 2002. *Something Beautiful.* New York: Dragonfly Books.
  Begins with a description of setting; ends with a final action in which the character makes a self-discovery; contains an example of a bridge paragraph.

Yamada, Kobi. 2016. *What Do You Do with a Problem?* Seattle, WA: Compendium.
  Opens with self-reflection; closes with a lesson learned.

Yolen, Jane. 1987. *Owl Moon.* New York: Philomel Books.
  Opens with a snapshot of setting.

———. 2002. *Miz Berlin Walks.* New York: Puffin.
  An example of a bookends book, in which the beginning and the end are the same.

Young, Timothy. 2013. *I Hate Picture Books!* Atglen, PA: Schiffer.
  Tells a story through the voice of the main character; shows how a character in a narrative changes feelings from beginning to end.

Chapter 6: Using Scaffolds to Organize Texts

Aston, Dianna Hutts. 2011. *A Butterfly Is Patient.* San Francisco: Chronicle Books.
  Organization uses adjectives to describe a butterfly and includes additional explanatory information.

———. 2015. *A Nest Is Noisy.* San Francisco: Chronicle Books.
  Organization uses adjectives to describe different types of bird's nests and includes additional explanatory information.

———. 2016. *A Beetle Is Shy*. San Francisco: Chronicle Books.
Unique adjectives are used to describe beetles—*telegraphic, kaleidoscopic, armored*, and so on; includes additional explanatory information.

Bang, Molly. 2004. *My Light*. New York: Blue Sky.
First-person narrative written in the voice of the sun.

Baskwill, Jane. 1996. *Somewhere*. New York: MONDO.
Repeated refrain, moving through different places.

Bouchard, David. 1998. *If You're Not from the Prairie* . . . New York: Aladdin Books.
Use of the repeated refrain "If you're not from the prairie . . ."

Brown, Margaret Wise. 1999. *The Important Book*. New York: HarperCollins.
A useful scaffold for writing text innovations.

Catalanotto, Peter. 2001. *Emily's Art*. New York: Atheneum Books for Young Readers.
Organized around days of the week; the first few pages of the book appear before the title page, serving as a preface.

———. 2003. *Daisy 1, 2, 3*. New York: Atheneum Books for Young Readers.
Number scaffold.

———. 2005. *Matthew A.B.C.* New York: Atheneum Books for Young Readers.
ABC text structure.

Chall, Marcia Wilson. 1992. *Up North at the Cabin*. New York: Lothrop, Lee and Shepard Books.
Contains the repeated refrain "Up north at the cabin . . ." to open small vignettes. This technique can be adapted by students and used as a structure for similar pieces such as "Down at the seashore . . ." or "Up at the lake . . ."

Charlip, Remy. 1993. *Fortunately*. New York: Aladdin Books.
Whole-book seesaw scaffold: "Fortunately . . ."; "Unfortunately . . ."

Cisneros, Sandra. 1997. *Hairs/Pelitos*. New York: Dragonfly Books.
Written in English and Spanish; organized around descriptions of each family member's hair.

Cooper, Elisha. 2006. *Beach*. New York: Orchard Books.
Organized around a day at the beach from morning until sunset.

Cronin, Doreen. 2003. *Diary of a Worm*. New York: HarperCollins.
Diary format; an example of writing in the persona of another.

———. 2013. *Diary of a Fly*. New York: HarperCollins.
Diary format; an example of writing in the persona of another.

———. 2013. *Diary of a Spider.* New York: HarperCollins.
Diary format; an example of writing in the persona of another.

Curtis, Jamie Lee. 1993. *When I Was Little: A Four-Year-Old's Memoir of Her Youth.* New York: HarperCollins.
Seesaw scaffold; good for writing a text innovation: "When I was . . ." "Now I'm . . . ," or "When it was . . ." "Now it's . . ."

Cuyler, Margery. 1993. *That's Good! That's Bad!* New York: Henry Holt.
Seesaw scaffold.

Danneburg, Julie. 2003. *First Year Letters.* Watertown, MA: Charlesbridge.
The book is a series of letters from students to their teacher.

Edwards, Pamela Duncan. 2001. *Boston Tea Party.* New York: G. P. Putnam's Sons.
Cumulative text structure.

Falatko, Julie. 2016. *Snappsy the Alligator (Did Not Ask to Be in This Book!).* New York: Penguin Young Readers Group.
A seesaw scaffold in which the main character speaks and the narrator tells the story. When the narrator enters the story, they both speak.

Fox, Mem. 1985. *Wilfrid Gordon McDonald Partridge.* New York: Kane/Miller.
Text is organized around objects.

———. 1998. *Tough Boris.* New York: Houghton Mifflin Harcourt.
Seesaw scaffold.

Franco, Betsy. 2007. *Birdsongs.* New York: Simon and Schuster.
Uses numbers and sounds as a scaffold.

Fredericks, Anthony D. 2006. *On One Flower: Butterflies, Ticks and a Few More Icks.* Nevada City, CA: Dawn Publications.
Uses a cumulative text structure.

———. 2011. *Around One Log: Chipmunks, Spiders, and Creepy Insiders.* Nevada City, CA: Dawn Publications.
Uses a cumulative text structure.

George, Jean Craighead. 1995. *One Day in the Tropical Rain Forest.* New York: HarperCollins.
A series of short descriptions of the rain forest at different times throughout the day.

———. 1997. *Everglades.* New York: HarperCollins.
Story within a story; use of print to define the scaffold.

———. 1998. *Look to the North: A Wolf Pup Diary.* New York: HarperCollins.
This book is written as a diary detailing the growth of a litter of wolf pups at intervals from one day to ten and a half months; contains the repeated refrain "Look to the North . . ."

Gilman, Phoebe. 1992. *Something from Nothing*. New York: Scholastic.
Contains a parallel story in the illustrations; several repeated refrains.

Gonsalves, Rob. 2015. *Imagine a World*. New York: Simon and Schuster.
Use of repeated refrain "Imagine a world . . ."

Gray, Libba Moore. 1999. *My Mama Had a Dancing Heart*. New York: Scholastic.
Bookend structure, in which the first line of the book is repeated at the end.

Gray, Rita. 2014. *Have You Heard the Nesting Bird?* New York: Houghton Mifflin Harcourt.
A repeated question organizes the text as well as the use of rhyme and onomatopoeia for bird sounds. Back matter includes an interview with the robin to provide additional information about the bird.

Grodin, Elissa D., and Governor Mario Cuomo. 2009. *C Is for Ciao: An Italy Alphabet*. Chelsea, MI: Sleeping Bear.
An alphabet book celebrating the land and culture of Italy.

Hall, Donald. 1994. *I Am the Dog, I Am the Cat*. New York: Dial Books.
Seesaw scaffold used to express point of view of the dog and the cat; written in a play format.

Henkes, Kevin. 2016. *When Spring Comes*. New York: Greenwillow Books.
Uses two repeated refrains to move the reader through the book; slight change in the scaffold to bring the book to closure.

Hest, Amy. 2008. *The Dog Who Belonged to No One*. New York: Abrams Books for Young Readers.
A seesaw scaffold; information about the two main characters, the dog and Lia, are alternated in a compare/contrast or seesaw manner.

Hoose, Phillip, and Hannah Hoose. 1998. *Hey, Little Ant*. Berkeley, CA: Tricycle.
Written in play format in two different voices. At the end the narrator steps in and asks a question.

Hopkins, H. Joseph. 2013. *The Tree Lady: The True Story of How One Tree-Loving Woman Changed a City Forever*. New York: Simon and Schuster.
Uses a repeated phrase/sentence to emphasize a character trait.

Howard, Arthur. 1999. *When I Was Five*. New York: Houghton Mifflin Harcourt Books for Young Readers.
Seesaw scaffold: "When I was five . . ."; "Now I'm six . . ."

Howard, Elizabeth Fitzgerald. 1995. *Aunt Flossie's Hats (and Crab Cakes Later)*. New York: Houghton Mifflin Harcourt Books for Young Readers.
Organized around objects; includes small anecdotes about several different hats.

Janeczko, Paul B., ed. 2001. *Dirty Laundry Pile: Poems in Different Voices.* New York: HarperCollins.
A collection of poems by many authors written in the voice of objects or animals.

Jenkins, Martin. 2001. *Chameleons Are Cool.* Cambridge, MA: Candlewick.
Seesaw scaffold used in opening.

Johnston, Tony. 2008. *P Is for Piñata: A Mexico Alphabet.* Chelsea, MI: Sleeping Bear.
An alphabet book celebrating the land and culture of Mexico.

Karas, G. Brian. 2004. *Atlantic.* New York: Puffin.
First-person narrative written in the voice of the Atlantic Ocean.

Laminack, Lester. 1998. *The Sunsets of Miss Olivia Wiggins.* Atlanta, GA: Peachtree.
Bookend structure—the first line of the book is repeated at the end; moves back and forth across time.

Lamstein, Sarah Marwil. 2010. *Big Night for Salamanders.* Honesdale, PA: Boyds Mills.
A seesaw scaffold—information about the migration of the spotted salamander is juxtaposed with the story of a young boy who helps the salamanders cross a busy road; includes additional information, a glossary, and an index.

Lobel, Anita. 2002. *One Lighthouse, One Moon.* New York: Greenwillow Books.
A series of three stories using days of the week, months, and counting as organizational structures.

Lowry, Lois. 2015. *Gooney Bird Greene.* New York: Houghton Mifflin Harcourt.
Use of print to define the scaffold.

MacLachlan, Patricia. 1994. *All the Places to Love.* New York: HarperCollins.
The text is composed of a series of memories about the places on a farm.

MacLachlan, Patricia, and Emily MacLachlan. 2006. *Painting the Wind.* New York: HarperCollins.
Organized around the different types of painters.

Mannis, Celeste Davidson. 2005. *One Leaf Rides the Wind: Counting in a Japanese Garden.* New York: Puffin Books.
Examples of haiku inspired by a Japanese garden; organized like a counting book.

Martin, Bill, Jr. 1983. *Brown Bear, Brown Bear, What Do You See?* New York: Henry Holt.
Whole-book scaffold useful for writing text innovations.

Martin, Bill, Jr., and John Archambault. 1997. *Knots on a Counting Rope.* New York: Square Fish.
The entire book is written as a dialogue between the two main characters, which is shown in the way the words are placed on the page.

McFarland, Lyn Rossiter. 2006. *Widget.* New York: Square Fish.
Seesaw scaffold used in part of the text.

McGrath, Barbara Barbieri, and Peter Alderman. 2003. *Soccer Counts!* Watertown, MA: Charlesbridge.
Number scaffold.

Melmed, Laura Krauss. 2006. *Capital! Washington D.C. from A to Z.* New York: HarperCollins.
Nonfiction ABC text; contains nonfiction features such as time lines, captions, and labels.

Meng, Cece. 2016. *Always Remember.* New York: Penguin.
The book is based on a repeating phrase scaffold that frames each experience: "And the would always remember." A shift in the final scaffold signals that the end is coming.

Messner, Kate. 2011. *Over and Under the Snow.* San Francisco: Chronicle Books.
Use of an extended seesaw scaffold to compare and contrast.

———. 2015. *Up in the Garden and Down in the Dirt.* San Francisco: Chronicle Books.
Use of an extended seesaw scaffold to compare and contrast.

Miller, Debbie S. 2007. *Arctic Lights, Arctic Nights.* New York: Walker Children's.
Passing of time—describes what is happening in a certain place on a particular day of each month.

Murphy, Frank. 2015. *Take a Hike, Teddy Roosevelt!* New York: Random House Children's Books.
Uses a repeated phrase/sentence to emphasize a character trait.

Nolan, Jerdine. 2001. *In My Momma's Kitchen.* New York: Amistad.
A series of small chapters organized around events that happen in one particular place—the kitchen.

Numeroff, Laura. 2015. *If You Give a Mouse a Cookie.* New York: HarperCollins.
Circular text organization.

Orloff, Karen Kaufman. 2004. *I Wanna Iguana.* New York: G. P. Putnam's Sons.
Uses letter format in a seesaw structure between two characters.

———. 2010. *I Wanna New Room.* New York: G. P. Putnam's Sons.
Uses letter format in a seesaw structure between two characters.

Pallotta, Jerry. 2015. *Eyeball Alphabet Book*. Needham, MA: Zorilla.
An alphabet book that also contains idioms about the eye.

Pinborough, Jan. 2013. *Miss Moore Thought Otherwise: How Anne Carroll Moore Created Libraries for Children*. New York: Houghton Mifflin Harcourt.
Uses a repeated phrase/sentence to emphasize a character trait.

Piven, Hanoch. 2012. *My Dog Is as Smelly as Dirty Socks: And Other Funny Family Portraits*. New York: Dragonfly Books.
A unique organizational scaffold using similes to describe family members.

Polacco, Patricia. 2004. *Betty Doll*. New York: Puffin Books.
Organized around one object, the doll.

Rocco, John. 2011. *Blackout*. New York: Hyperion.
Text and pictures organized like a simple comic strip/graphic novel.

Rosenthal, Amy Krouse. 2009. *Duck! Rabbit!* San Francisco: Chronicle Books.
A seesaw structure that uses two narrators to express different points of view; a simple text delivered in a conversational manner.

Ryan, Pam Muñoz. 2005. *Mice and Beans*. New York: Scholastic.
Text is organized around days of the week.

Rylant, Cynthia. 1993. *When I Was Young in the Mountains*. New York: Puffin.
Repeated refrain used to link small vignettes.

———. 2001. *The Relatives Came*. New York: Atheneum Books.
Circular text.

———. 2008. *In November*. New York: Houghton Mifflin Harcourt Books for Young Readers.
Repeated refrain: "In November . . ."

Sendak, Maurice. 2012. *Where the Wild Things Are*. New York: HarperCollins.
Home-adventure-home structure.

Siebert, Diane. 1996. *Sierra*. New York: HarperCollins.
First-person narrative structure written in the voice of the mountain; a companion book by the same author, *Mojave*, is about the desert.

Sierra, Judy. 2010. *Thelonius Monster's Sky-High Fly Pie*. New York: Dragonfly Books.
Borrows a familiar scaffold ("There was an old lady who swallowed a fly . . .").

Spinelli, Eileen. 2004. *I Know It's Autumn*. New York: HarperCollins.
Organized around events from morning to night; uses the repeated phrase "I know it's autumn when . . ." as a scaffold.

Stewart, Melissa. 2014. *Feathers: Not Just for Flying*. Watertown, MA: Charlesbridge.
  Global structure is the use of similes to compare feathers to other objects; contains additional nonfiction information.

Thomson, Sarah L. 2003. *Imagine a Night*. New York: Atheneum Books for Young Readers.
  Repeated refrain "Imagine a night . . ." begins each page.

———. 2005. *Imagine a Day*. New York: Atheneum Books for Young Readers.
  Repeated refrain "Imagine a day . . ." begins each page.

———. 2008. *Imagine a Place*. New York: Atheneum Books for Young Readers.
  Repeated refrain "Imagine a place . . ." begins each page.

Ulmer, Wendy. 2008. *A Isn't for Fox: An Isn't Alphabet*. Chelsea, MI: Sleeping Bear.
  A twist to the traditional alphabet book; uses rhyming couplets to explain what each letter does and does not stand for.

Van, Muon. 2015. *In a Village by the Sea*. Berkeley, CA: Creston Books.
  A cumulative text structure that links the events of the story.

Van Allsburg, Chris. 1988. *Two Bad Ants*. New York: Houghton Mifflin Harcourt Books for Young Readers.
  Home-adventure-home structure.

Viau, Nancy. 2014. *City Street Beat*. Chicago: Albert Whitman.
  Uses scaffolds of sounds and rhyme to organize the text; sounds appear in threes.

Waber, Bernard. 2015. *Ask Me*. New York: Houghton Mifflin Harcourt.
  Uses questions as the scaffold to move the text forward. The entire book is written in two different colors of print without the use of quotation marks to identify the speakers.

Willems, Mo. 2010. *City Dog, Country Frog*. New York: Hyperion.
  This book is organized across the seasons; different perspectives from two different characters.

Williams, Sue. 1992. *I Went Walking*. New York: Houghton Mifflin Harcourt Books for Young Readers.
  Whole-book scaffold for writing text innovations.

Williams, Vera. 2007. *A Chair for My Mother*. New York: Greenwillow Books.
  Contains a flashback describing the fire in the middle of the story about acquiring the chair.

Winters, Kay. 2014. *Voices from the Oregon Trail*. New York: Dial Books for Young Readers.
  The book is told through the different voices of the characters, who are on their westward journey.

Wood, Audrey. 2009. *The Napping House*. New York: Houghton Mifflin
Harcourt Books for Young Readers.
Cumulative text structure.

Woodruff, Elvira. 1998. *Dear Levi: Letters from the Overland Trail*. York:
Yearling.
Letter format.

Chapter 7: Poetry: Everybody Can Be a Writer

Ackerman, Karen. 1992. *Song and Dance Man*. New York: Dragonfly Books.
This book is a character sketch of a grandfather; can be used to
stimulate thoughts about special people.

Baylor, Byrd. 1995. *I'm in Charge of Celebrations*. New York: Aladdin Books.
An example of prose that sounds and looks like poetry and reflects the
beauty of the Southwest.

Brinckloe, Julie. 1986. *Fireflies!* New York: Aladdin Books.
Prose that contains poetic language.

Byars, Betsy. 1981. *The Midnight Fox*. New York: Puffin Books.
An inspiration for found poetry.

Collins, Pat Lowery. 1992. *I Am an Artist*. Brookfield, CT: Millbrook.
Describes how artists observe the world in special ways; uses a repeated
refrain "I am an artist . . ." to create poetic prose.

Coombs, Kate. 2012. *Water Sings Blue*. San Francisco: Chronicle Books.
A collection of poems about the ocean.

Davies, Nicola. 2012. *Outside Your Window: A First Book of Nature*.
Somerville, MA: Candlewick.
The book is a collection of poems organized by seasons that inspires
readers to observe the world. "Wind" is an example of a question poem.

Dotlich, Rebecca Kai. 2009. *Bella and Bean*. New York: Atheneum Books.
A good example of collecting words to create poems; use of notebooks.

Fleming, Denise. 1998. *In the Small, Small Pond*. New York: Henry Holt.
Uses a word scaffold (verb-verb-noun-verb) to describe the activities of
the pond animals in rhyme.

Fletcher, Ralph. 1997. *Twilight Comes Twice*. New York: Clarion Books.
Poetic language; excellent for use with found poetry.

———. 2003. *Hello, Harvest Moon*. New York: Clarion Books.
Poetic language; excellent for use with found poetry.

———. 2005. *A Writing Kind of Day: Poems for Young Poets*. Honesdale,
PA: Boyds Mills.
A collection of poems that provide especially good models for students.

Florian, Douglas. 2012. *UnBEElievables: Honeybee Poems and Paintings*. New York: Beach Lane Books.
A collection of persona poems about bees. Each page contains additional factual information.

George, Christine O'Connell. 2005. *The Great Frog Race: And Other Poems*. New York: Houghton Mifflin Harcourt Books for Young Readers.
Rhymed and unrhymed about simple pleasures of country life.

Graham, Joan Bransfield. 2001. *Splish Splash*. New York: Houghton Mifflin Harcourt Books for Young Readers.
A collection of mostly unrhymed, concrete poems about water in its many forms.

Graves, Donald. 1996. *Baseball, Snakes, and Summer Squash: Poems About Growing Up*. Honesdale, PA: WordSong.
Unrhymed poetry that tells stories of childhood with heartfelt voice.

Heard, Georgia. 1997. *Creatures of Earth, Sea, and Sky*. Honesdale, PA: WordSong.
Poetry for two voices; examples of unrhymed poems.

Hopkins, Lee Bennett. 2010. *Sharing the Seasons: A Book of Poems*. New York: Simon and Schuster.
A collection of poems from different poets organized by seasons. Hopkins introduces each season with a poem of his that follows the same scaffold.

———, ed. 2015. *Jumping Off Library Shelves: A Book of Poems*. Honesdale, PA: Word Song.
A collection of poems from a variety of poets about the library.

Horowitz, Ruth. 2004. *Crab Moon*. Cambridge, MA: Candlewick.
Poetic language; excellent for use with found poetry.

Hughes, Langston. 1996. *The Dream Keeper and Other Poems*. New York: Knopf Books for Young Readers.
A collection of free-verse poems by the author.

———. 2015. *Sail Away: Poems by Langston Hughes*. New York: Atheneum Books for Young Readers.
A collection of poems by Langston Hughes.

Janeczko, Paul B., ed. 2001. *Dirty Laundry Pile: Poems in Different Voices*. New York: HarperCollins.
A collection of poems by many authors written in the voice of objects or animals.

———, ed. 2005. *A Kick in the Head: An Everyday Guide to Poetic Forms*. Cambridge, MA: Candlewick.
A collection of twenty-nine poems that illustrate different forms with explanations.

———, ed. 2014. *Firefly July: A Year of Very Short Poems*.
A collection of poems from various poets organized across the seasons.

Kalman, Maira. 2012. *Looking at Lincoln*. New York: Scholastic.
A picture book biography of Lincoln used as a resource for found poetry.

Lewis, J. Patrick, ed. 2012. *Book of Animal Poetry*. Washington, DC: National Geographic Society.
A collection of poems from a variety of poets compiled by J. Patrick Lewis about animals from around the world. Includes advice about how to write poems about animals.

———. 2013. *World Rat Day: Poems About Real Holidays You've Never Heard Of*. Somerville, MA: Candlewick.
A collection of humorous poems about wacky holidays to celebrate.

———, ed. 2015. *Book of Nature Poetry*. Washington, DC: National Geographic Society.
A collection of poems from a variety of poets compiled by J. Patrick Lewis all about nature around the world.

Lewis, J. Patrick, and Douglas Florian. 2014. *Poem-Mobiles: Crazy Car Poems*. New York: Schwartz and Wade Books.
Humorous poems about imaginative cars.

Little, Jean. 1990. *Hey World, Here I Am!* New York: HarperCollins.
A collection of poems and vignettes from a young girl's viewpoint.

London, Jonathan. 1999. *Puddles*. New York: Puffin Books.
A story about the day after a night rainstorm; written in poetic form with lyrical language; many examples of onomatopoeia.

MacLachlan, Patricia, and Emily MacLachlan Charest. 2010. *I Didn't Do It*. New York: HarperCollins.
Poems told in the voice of puppies about their adventures, what they do and don't do, and so on.

Mannis, Celeste Davidson. 2005. *One Leaf Rides the Wind: Counting in a Japanese Garden*. New York: Puffin Books.
Examples of haiku inspired by a Japanese garden; organized like a counting book; use of personification and appeal to the senses.

Martin, Bill, Jr., and John Archambault. 1988. *Listen to the Rain*. New York: Henry Holt.
Poetic language used to describe the progression of a rainstorm.

Muth, Jon. 2014. *Hi, Koo! A Year of Seasons*. New York: Scholastic.
A collection of twenty-six haiku about the four seasons. Some of the poems do not follow the traditional haiku syllable structure, but all capture a moment using sensory images. The author capitalizes a word in each poem to offer the reader a path through the alphabet.

Nibenegenasabe, Jacob. 2000. "Quiet Until the Thaw." In *Americans'
Favorite Poems*, ed. Robert Pinsky and Maggie Dietz. New York: W. W.
Norton.
Poetry scaffold.

O'Neill, Mary. 1990. *Hailstones and Halibut Bones: Adventures in Poetry
and Color*. New York: Doubleday Books for Young Readers.
A collection of poems about colors that invokes all of the senses.

Otten, Charlotte. 1997. *January Rides the Wind*. New York: William
Morrow. (This book is currently out of print.)
Short poems about each month; examples of personification, exact
nouns, and specific verbs.

Paolilli, Paul, and Dan Brewer. 2003. *Silver Seeds*. New York: Puffin Books.
Acrostic nature poetry that spans daybreak to night.

Polacco, Patricia. 1994. *My Rotten Redheaded Older Brother*. New York:
Simon and Schuster.
Can be used to stimulate thoughts about special people.

———. 1999. *My Ol' Man*. New York: Puffin Books.
Can be used to stimulate thoughts about special people.

Purdie, Laura Salas. 2011. *Book Speak! Poems About Books*. New York:
Clarion Books.
A collection of poems written in the voices of books and things related
to them—characters, pages, dust jackets, and more.

Seuss, Dr. 1996. *My Many Colored Days*. New York: Knopf Books for Young
Readers.
Rhyming text that links colors to feelings.

Sidman, Joyce. 2014. *Winter Bees & Other Poems of the Cold*. New York:
Houghton Mifflin Harcourt.
A collection of poems about animals and how they survive winter. An
informational paragraph accompanies each poem.

Singer, Marilyn. 2011. *A Full Moon Is Rising*. New York: Lee and Low Books.
Poems about how the full moon is celebrated around the world.

———. 2013. *Follow Follow: A Book of Reverso Poems*. New York: Penguin
Young Readers Group.
A collection of reverso poems that offer a different perspective to some
classic fairy tales. The poems are read from top to bottom and then from
bottom to top for a different point of view. This book is a follow-up to
Singer's *Mirror Mirror*.

Spinelli, Eileen. 1998. *When Mama Comes Home Tonight*. New York: Simon
and Schuster Books for Young Readers.
Rhythmic prose that sounds more like a poem; can be used to stimulate
thoughts about special people.

Swinburne, Stephen R. 2010. *Ocean Soup: Tide-Pool Poems*. Watertown, MA: Charlesbridge.
Poems about sea creatures that inhabit tide pools. Includes factual information about each creature.

Thong, Roseanne Greenfield. 2014. *Green Is a Chile Pepper*. San Francisco: Chronicle Books.
A rhyming quatrain on every page describes different colors; includes Latino cultural references and language.

VanDerwater, Amy Ludwig. 2013. *Forest Has a Song*. New York: Clarion Books.
A collection of poems that follow a child on a walk through the forest across the seasons.

———. 2016. *Every Day Birds*. New York: Orchard Books.
A poem in book format that celebrates birds. Includes additional factual information in the back about each bird.

Vardell, Sylvia, and Janet Wong. 2012. *The Poetry Friday Anthology: Poems for the School Year with Connections to the Common Core*. Princeton, NJ: Pomelo Books.
A collection of poems with accompanying activities for each week of the school year. There are K–5 and middle school editions as well as teacher editions for both levels.

———. 2015. *The Poetry Friday Anthology for Celebrations: Holiday Poems for the Whole Year in English and Spanish*. Princeton, NJ: Pomelo Books.
A collection of poems in English and Spanish by a variety of poets. More than 150 holidays and celebrations are featured.

Viorst, Judith. 1984. *If I Were in Charge of the World*. New York: Atheneum Books for Young Readers.
A collection of poems that can be used as scaffolds.

Wagstaff, Janiel. 2016. *Stella: Poet Extraordinaire*. Peterborough, NH: SDE Professional Development Resources.
A narrative about a class and how their teacher introduces them to poetry. A great resource for both teachers and students.

Yolen, Jane. 1987. *Owl Moon*. New York: Philomel Books.
Poetic language; excellent for use with found poetry.

———. 2003. *Color Me a Rhyme: Nature Poems for Young People*. Honesdale, PA: WordSong.
Poems about the colors in nature accompanied by photographs.

Young, Judy. 2005. *R Is for Rhyme: A Poetry Alphabet*. Chelsea, MI: Sleeping Bear.
A collection of poems to illustrate scaffolds and poetic literary devices; includes explanations of each device or form.

Chapter 8: Choice, Voice, and All That Jazz

Anderson, Laurie Halse. 2000. *Fever 1793*. New York: Simon and Schuster Books for Young Readers.
Contains an example of a rubber-band (stretchy, or taffy) sentence.

Aston, Diana Hutts. 2016. *A Beetle Is Shy*. San Francisco: Chronicle Books.
Includes examples of hyphenated adjectives such as *cocoon-like, marble-size, water-gliding,* and *protein-rich*.

Babbitt, Natalie. 2009. *Tuck Everlasting*. New York: Square Fish.
Contains examples of metaphors.

Barnett, Mac. 2016. *Rules of the House*. New York: Disney Hyperion.
Strong verbs; use of fragments to build suspense; important content contained in a sign hanging on the wall; interesting dialogue; sentence variety; effective repetition.

Barton, Chris. 2016. *Whoosh! Lonnie Johnson's Super-Soaking Stream of Inventions*. Watertown, MA: Charlesbridge.
Use of exact nouns for authenticity and character traits; strong verbs; hyphenated adjectives.

Boelts, Maribeth. 2007. *Those Shoes*. Cambridge, MA: Candlewick.
Use of fragments for description; variation in sentence length; hyphenated adjectives; effective repetition using a phrase to emphasize setting.

Brinckloe, Julie. 1986. *Fireflies!* New York: Aladdin Books.
Use of unexpected verbs; word pairs; effective repetition to create a rhythm.

Bryant, Jen. 2005. *Georgia's Bones*. Grand Rapids, MI: Eerdmans Books for Young Readers.
Use of word pairs to create rhythm.

———. 2016. *Six Dots: The Story of Young Louis Braille*. New York: Alfred A. Knopf.
Strong verbs, exact nouns, including proper nouns and French words; purposeful use of fragments.

Bunting, Eve. 2006. *One Green Apple*. New York: Clarion Books.
Appeal to the senses; use of onomatopoeia; effective repetition; strong verbs; hyphenated adjectives; variety of sentence length.

Burleigh, Robert. 2003. *Home Run: The Story of Babe Ruth*. New York: Houghton Mifflin Harcourt Books for Young Readers.
Use of fragments.

———. 2009. *One Giant Leap*. New York: Philomel Books.
Similes; strong verbs; use of precise color words; purposeful use of fragments.

————. 2010. *Tiger of the Snows: Tenzing Norgay: The Boy Whose Dream Was Everest*. New York: Atheneum Books.
Contains hyphenated adjectives, similes and metaphors, unexpected nouns and verbs, parentheses, and exact language.

Carle, Eric. 2007. *"Slowly, Slowly, Slowly," Said the Sloth*. New York: Puffin.
A great book to introduce word choice; contains a page of factual information on sloths.

Chall, Marsha Wilson. 1992. *Up North at the Cabin*. New York: Lothrop, Lee and Shepard Books.
Examples of specialized vocabulary, hyphenated adjectives, and strong verbs; figurative language; personification.

Cooper, Elisha. 2006. *Beach*. New York: Orchard Books.
Excellent word choice—strong verbs, exact nouns, and specific adjectives; use of metaphor and simile; appeal to the senses.

Crews, Donald. 1998. *Bigmama's*. New York: Greenwillow Books.
Variety of sentence length and beginnings; use of proper nouns.

Cronin, Doreen. 2000. *Click, Clack, Moo: Cows That Type*. New York: Simon and Schuster Books for Young Readers.
Effective repetition to emphasize a sound; communication in the form of "typed" notes to create voice; a splash of dialogue.

————. 2003. *Diary of a Worm*. New York: HarperCollins.
An example of writing in the persona of another to create voice.

————. 2013. Diary of a Spider. New York: HarperCollins.
An example of writing in the persona of another to create voice.

Dahl, Roald. 2007. *James and the Giant Peach*. New York: Puffin Books.
Variation of sentence length; rich language.

Davies, Nicola. 2004. *Bat Loves the Night*. Cambridge, MA: Candlewick.
An example of narrative nonfiction; use of figurative language; strong verbs and adjectives.

————. 2005. *One Tiny Turtle*. Cambridge, MA: Candlewick.
An example of narrative nonfiction; use of figurative language; strong verbs and adjectives.

————. 2013. *The Promise*. Somerville, MA: Candlewick.
Contains examples of similes, alliteration, strong verbs.

Daywalt, Drew. 2013. *The Day the Crayons Quit*. New York: Philomel Books.
Use of conversations in the form of letters from crayons to their owner; word choice and tone lets us in on the feelings of the crayons.

————. 2015. *The Day the Crayons Came Home*. New York: Philomel Books.
A collection of postcards from the crayons to their owner, Duncan, provides examples of creating voice through word choice.

de la Peña, Matt. 2015. *Last Stop on Market Street*. New York: G. P. Putnam's Sons.
Strong verbs; noun pairs.

Edwards, Pamela Duncan. 1998. *Some Smug Slug*. New York: Katherine Tegen Books.
Can be used to introduce alliteration.

Falatko, Julie. 2016. *Snappsy the Alligator (Did Not Ask to Be in This Book!)*. New York: Penguin Young Readers Group.
The main character, Snappsy, talks to the reader and also to the narrator (who happens to be a chicken); use of dialogue through speech bubbles brings the character to life; humor embedded in illustrations and text.

Fleming, Candace. 2002. *Muncha! Muncha! Muncha!* New York: Atheneum Books for Young Readers.
Use of hyphenated words; fragments; word choice.

Fletcher, Ralph. 1997. *Twilight Comes Twice*. New York: Clarion Books.
Use of hyphenated adjectives and unusual placement of adjectives; strong and unexpected verbs used to create powerful images; figurative language.

———. 2003. *Hello, Harvest Moon*. New York: Clarion Books.
Figurative language; word pairs; alliteration.

Fox, Mem. 1992. *Night Noises*. New York: Houghton Mifflin Harcourt Books for Young Readers.
Contains examples of similes and onomatopoeia; strong verbs; repeated refrain.

Franco, Betsy. 2007. *Birdsongs*. New York: Simon and Schuster.
Alliteration; strong verbs, onomatopoeia.

Frazee, Marla. 2006. *Roller Coaster*. New York: Houghton Mifflin Harcourt Books for Young Readers.
Use of parentheses.

Graves, Donald. 1996. *Baseball, Snakes, and Summer Squash: Poems About Growing Up*. Honesdale, PA: Boyds Mills.
Use of hyphenated adjectives; strong sense of voice.

Gray, Libba Moore. 1999. *My Mama Had a Dancing Heart*. New York: Scholastic.
Use of hyphenated adjectives and color words.

Gray, Rita. 2014. *Have You Heard the Nesting Bird?* New York: Houghton Mifflin Harcourt.
Similes; metaphors, alliteration; onomatopoeia.

Grimes, Nikki. 2002. *Talkin' About Bessie: The Story of Aviator Elizabeth Coleman*. New York: Orchard Books.
Contains examples of hyphenated adjectives; written in the voice of different characters; examples of use of dialect.

Hall, Donald. 1994. *I Am the Dog, I Am the Cat.* New York: Dial Books.
Use of dialogue to hear different voices.

Hanlon, Abby. 2012. *Ralph Tells a Story.* New York: Two Lions.
Use of dialogue sprinkled throughout to create voice.

Harrington, Janice. 2004. *Going North.* New York: Farrar, Straus and Giroux.
Use of hyphenated words to create unusual verbs, adverbs, and adjectives.

Helakoski, Leslie. 2014. *Big Pigs.* Honesdale, PA: Boyds Mills.
Strong verbs; alliteration; purposeful use of fragments; unexpected rhyme.

Henkes, Kevin. 1991. *Chrysanthemum.* New York: Greenwillow Books.
Use of unexpected verbs that match the topic, in this case, flowers; effective repetition to emphasize what a character is thinking or feeling; proper nouns.

———. 2004. *Kitten's First Full Moon.* New York: Greenwillow Books.
Use of repeated phrase and sentence.

———. 2006. *Lilly's Purple Plastic Purse.* New York: Greenwillow Books.
Use of strong verbs and adjectives; alliteration.

Hesse, Karen. 1999. *Come On, Rain!* New York: Scholastic.
Examples of unexpected verbs.

Hest, Amy. 2007. *Mr. George Baker.* Cambridge, MA: Candlewick.
This book is a wonderful example of voice created with word choice (some invented words) and by writing in a very conversational tone; some fragments.

———. 2008. *The Dog Who Belonged to No One.* New York: Abrams Books for Young Readers.
Whispering parentheses to add information; repeated words; use of fragments; variation in sentence length.

High, Linda Oatman. 2012. *Barn Savers.* Honesdale, PA: Boyds Mills.
Use of similes that match the topic.

Hoose, Phillip, and Hannah Hoose. 1998. *Hey, Little Ant.* Berkeley, CA: Tricycle.
Use of dialogue to hear different voices.

Hopkins, H. Joseph. 2013. *The Tree Lady: The True Story of How One Tree-Loving Woman Changed a City Forever.* New York: Simon and Schuster.
Use of proper nouns; variety of sentence length; effective repetition to emphasize a character trait.

Hornby, Nick. 2002. *How to Be Good.* New York: Riverhead Books.
A book written for adults that contains many examples of hyphenated adjectives.

Horowitz, Ruth. 2004. *Crab Moon*. Cambridge, MA: Candlewick.
Use of figurative language; examples of strong verbs, alliteration, and word pairs.

Hosta, Dar. 2003. *I Love the Night*. Flemington, NJ: Brown Dog Books.
"Adjective-ly adjective" structure—for example, "perfectly perfect."

Howard, Arthur. 1999. *When I Was Five*. New York: Houghton Mifflin Harcourt Books for Young Readers.
Use of parentheses to whisper a secret.

Janeczko, Paul B., ed. 2001. *Dirty Laundry Pile: Poems in Different Voices*. New York: HarperCollins.
A collection of poems by many authors written in the voice of objects or animals.

Jenkins, Martin. 2001. *Chameleons Are Cool*. Cambridge, MA: Candlewick.
An example of nonfiction writing with voice; strong verbs and adjectives; hyphenated adjectives.

Jenkins, Steve, and Robin Page. 2014. *Creature Features: 25 Animals Explain Why They Look the Way They Do*. New York: Houghton Mifflin Harcourt.
Each animal is asked a question about their appearance in the form of a letter. The answer is given in first person from the point of view of the animal. This book is a good example of an alternative way to report research findings and shows nonfiction with voice.

Johnston, Tony. 1998. *Amber on the Mountain*. New York: Puffin Books.
Powerful similes and metaphors; some use of dialect to create voice; examples of good word choice with vivid verbs and adjectives.

Jones, Val. 2015. *Who Wants Broccoli?* New York: HarperCollins.
Variation of print; alliteration; strong verbs.

Kalman, Maira. 2012. *Looking at Lincoln*. New York: Scholastic.
Use of parentheses to add additional information; interesting use of thoughtshots (shown in larger print) where the narrator/author shares her thinking.

Kearney, Meg. 2013. *Trouper*. New York: Scholastic.
Use of similes and metaphors; a great book to teach voice (written in the voice of the dog); strong verbs; proper nouns; parentheses.

Keating, Jess. 2016. *Pink Is for Blobfish: Discovering the World's Perfectly Pink Animals*. New York: Alfred A. Knopf.
A great example of writing nonfiction with voice—hyphenated adjectives, engaging subtitles ("Made Ya Look!"), cartoon-like drawings, alliteration, specific language (*nocturnal, naturalist*).

Krans, Kim. 2016. *ABC Dream*. New York: Random House.
   A wordless alphabet book that can be used to teach alliteration (see some examples on the book jacket); examples of exact nouns that are perfect for use with ESL students.

Kearney, Meg. 2013. *Trouper*. New York: Scholastic.
   Proper nouns; metaphor; simile; whispering parentheses.

LaMarche, Jim. 2000. *The Raft*. New York: HarperCollins.
   Examples of strong nouns that use the nomenclature of a fisherman and an artist (*snorkel, tackle box, bobber*, etc.); hyphenated adjectives and nouns (*half-finished, tug-of-war*); and strong verbs.

Laminack, Lester. 2004. *Saturdays and Teacakes*. Atlanta, GA: Peachtree.
   Use of repeated refrains and fragments; written in a conversational tone that adds voice; use of parentheses to add more information; use of proper nouns specific to a certain era.

Lamstein, Sarah Marwil. 2010. *Big Night for Salamanders*. Honesdale, PA: Boyds Mills.
   Strong verbs; alliteration; onomatopoeia; examples of highlighting a verb (*pum-pumming, tat-tatting*).

Leedy, Loreen, and Pat Street. 2003. *There's a Frog in My Throat! 440 Animal Sayings a Little Bird Told Me*. New York: Holiday House.
   A collection of similes, metaphors, idioms, and proverbs that relate to animals; meanings are explained.

Lester, Julius. 1999. *John Henry*. New York: Puffin.
   Variation of sentence length.

Levis, Caron. 2016. *Ida, Always*. New York: Atheneum Books for Young Readers.
   Effective repetition to emphasize a theme; strong verbs; dialogue to create voice; sentence variety.

Ludwig, Trudy. 2013. *The Invisible Boy*. New York: Alfred A. Knopf.
   Variety of sentence structures, including leading with a prepositional phrase; hyphens to stretch out a word; voice established through speech bubbles.

Lyon, George Ella. 2003. *Mother to Tigers*. New York: Atheneum Books for Young Readers.
   Alliteration; strong verbs and adjectives; word pairs.

MacLachlan, Patricia. 1983. *Through Grandpa's Eyes*. New York: HarperCollins.
   Use of personification; unexpected verbs.

———. 1993. *Journey*. New York: Yearling.
   Use of personification; unexpected verbs.

———. 2004. *Skylark*. New York: Harper Trophy.
Unusual placement of adjectives.

———. 2015. *Sarah, Plain and Tall*. New York: HarperCollins.
Unusual placement of adjectives.

MacLachlan, Patricia, and Emily MacLachlan. 2006. *Painting the Wind*. New York: HarperCollins.
Adjectives after the noun; variety of sentence patterns and lengths; exact nouns; use of epithets; strong verbs; power of three; hyphenated adjectives.

Markle, Sandra. 2011. *Butterfly Tree*. Atlanta, GA: Peachtree.
Hyphenated adjectives (*blimp-sized, wind-tattered, golden-orange*); similes; alliteration.

———. 2015. *Toad Weather*. Atlanta, GA: Peachtree.
Hyphenated adjectives; alliteration; onomatopoeia; strong verbs.

McFarland, Lyn Rossiter. 2006. *Widget*. New York: Square Fish.
Contains examples of vivid verbs.

Medina, Meg. 2015. *Mango, Abuela, and Me*. Somerville, MA: Candlewick.
Hyphenated adjectives; use of Spanish words to add authenticity and interest.

Messner, Kate. 2011. *Over and Under the Snow*. San Francisco: Chronicle Books.
Alliteration; onomatopoeia; use of purposeful fragments; use of adjective-noun pairs to create rhythm (for example, "drowsy bears and busy squirrels"); hyphenated adjectives.

Michelson, Richard. 2006. *Across the Alley*. New York: Penguin.
Examples of similes.

Miller, Debbie S. 2007. *Arctic Lights, Arctic Nights*. New York: Walker Children's.
An excellent example of voice in nonfiction text; onomatopoeia; word choice.

Miller, Kathy M. 2009. *Chippy Chipmunk Parties in the Garden*. New Ringgold, PA: Celtic Sunrise.
Strong verbs and nouns; voice created through dialogue.

Miller, Pat Zietlow. 2013. *Sophie's Squash*. New York: Random House Children's Books.
Examples of the power of three; dialogue to create voice.

Murphy, Frank. 2000. *The Legend of the Teddy Bear*. Chelsea, MI: Sleeping Bear.
Contains examples of word pairs and alliteration.

———. 2003. *Thomas Jefferson's Feast.* New York: Random House Children's Books.
A sprinkle of French words for authenticity that includes a pronunciation key; exact nouns and verbs throughout; use of parentheses to add voice.

———. 2015. *Take a Hike, Teddy Roosevelt!* New York: Random House Children's Books.
Use of specific nouns and verbs; effective repetition.

O'Neill, Alexis. 2002. *The Recess Queen.* New York: Scholastic.
Word choice; rhythm.

Pattou, Edith. 2001. *Mrs. Spitzer's Garden.* New York: Houghton Mifflin Harcourt Books for Young Readers.
Can be used with older students to explain metaphor—the book uses gardening as an extended metaphor for teaching.

Paulsen, Gary. 2001. *Canoe Days.* New York: Dragonfly Books.
Use of figurative language.

Polacco, Patricia. 2015. *Tucky Jo and Little Heart.* New York: Simon and Schuster Books for Young Readers.
Purposeful fragments; proper nouns for specificity; colorful language, including similes, dialect, and slang; epithets (Kentucky Kid, Little Heart).

Ramsey, Calvin Alexander. 2010. *Ruth and the Green Book.* Minneapolis, MN: Carolrhoda Books.
Exact nouns, including many proper nouns; variety of sentence structures; powerful voices of characters.

Rawlinson, Julia. 2006. *Fletcher and the Falling Leaves.* New York: HarperCollins.
Strong verbs; sentence variation; alliteration.

Rockliff, Mara. 2014. *Chik Chak Shabbat.* Somerville, MA: Candlewick.
Strong verbs; use of proper nouns; a splash of dialogue to create voice; simile; sentence variety.

Ruurs, Margriet. 2016. *Stepping Stones: A Refugee Family's Journey.* Victoria, British Columbia: Orca Book.
The power of three; effective repetition; sentence variety including beginning with prepositional phrases; strong adjectives.

Rylant, Cynthia. 1991. *Night in the Country.* New York: Atheneum Books.
Variation in sentence length; fragments; onomatopoeia.

———. 1996. *An Angel for Solomon Singer.* New York: Scholastic.
Use of parentheses to indicate wishes or dreams.

———. 2001. *The Great Gracie Chase: Stop That Dog!* New York: Blue Sky.
Use of parentheses to add humor.

———. 2004. *Missing May*. New York: Scholastic.
Use of parentheses.

———. 2008. *In November*. New York: Houghton Mifflin Harcourt.
Unusual sentence structures to make prose sound like poetry; figurative language.

Sams, Carl R., II, and Jean Stoick. 2000. *Stranger in the Woods: A Photographic Fantasy*. Milford, MI: Carl R. Sams II Photography.
An example of writing in the persona of another, in this case, the animals.

Schachner, Judy. 2015. *Dewey Bob*. New York: Dial Books for Young Readers.
Use of conversations that include similes, dialect, and slang.

Seuss, Dr. 1961. *The Sneetches*. New York: Random House.
An example of a distinctive voice.

———. 1990. *Oh, the Places You'll Go!* New York: Random House.
An example of a distinctive voice.

———. 1996. *My Many Colored Days*. New York: Knopf Books for Young Readers.
Descriptions of colors linked to feelings.

Seuss, Dr., with Jack Prelutsky and Lane Smith. 1998. *Hooray for Diffendoofer Day*. New York: Knopf Books for Young Readers.
Blending of the voices of Seuss, Prelutsky, and Smith; includes pages of original notes and sketches made by Theodore Geisel; shows revision process.

Sierra, Judy. 2010. *Thelonius Monster's Sky-High Fly Pie*. New York: Dragonfly Books.
Examples of powerful verbs, exact nouns, super (unexpected or unusual) and hyphenated adjectives; made-up words; parentheses.

Steinberg, Laya. 2005. *Thesaurus Rex*. Cambridge, MA: Barefoot Books.
Can be used as an introduction to word choice, especially synonyms.

Stewart, Melissa. 2014. *Feathers: Not Just for Flying*. Watertown, MA: Charlesbridge.
Examples of similes on almost every page.

Talbott, Hudson. 2012. *It's All About Me-ow*. New York: Nancy Paulson Books.
An example of nonfiction with voice (written in the voice of the cat); parentheses.

Tate, Don. 2015. *Poet: The Remarkable Story of George Moses Horton*. Atlanta, GA: Peachtree.
Use of fragments; power of three; strong verbs and nouns.

Thong, Roseanne Greenfield. 2014. *Green Is a Chile Pepper*. San Francisco: Chronicle Books.
Specific word choice, especially adjectives and nouns; adjectives out of order; use of Spanish words to establish an authentic voice.

Trimmer, Christian. 2015. *Simon's New Bed*. New York: Atheneum Books for Young Readers.
Strong verbs; includes a hyphenated adjective.

Viorst, Judith. 1987. *Alexander and the Terrible, Horrible, No Good, Very Bad Day*. New York: Atheneum Books for Young Readers.
Use of effective repetition.

Weeks, Sarah. 2003. *Follow the Moon*. New York: HarperCollins.
This book is an extended metaphor for teaching and learning. It can be used as an example to students of how finding the voice inside their heads allows them to add style to their writing.

Wells, Rosemary. 2002. *Bunny Cakes*. New York: Puffin Books.
Includes examples of specific word choice and proper nouns; especially good as a mentor text for emergent writers.

Willems, Mo. 2004. *Don't Let the Pigeon Drive the Bus!* New York: Hyperion.
Monologue presented in the form of speech bubbles—the bus driver and Pigeon talk to the reader.

———. 2010. *City Dog, Country Frog*. New York: Hyperion.
Examples of whispering parentheses for further explanation.

Wood, Douglas. 2006. *Nothing to Do*. New York: Dutton Books for Young Readers.
Use of parentheses to provide more information.

Yamada, Kobi. 2016. *What Do You Do with a Problem?* Seattle, WA: Compendium.
Strong verbs; a variety of sentence structures; personification (the problem).

Yolen, Jane. 1987. *Owl Moon*. New York: Philomel Books.
Use of figurative language and onomatopoeia.

Chapter 9: Walk Around in the Author's Syntax

Albert, Richard E. 1996. *Alejandro's Gift*. San Francisco: Chronicle Books.
The opening paragraph is a snapshot of setting. It can be used to help students create other snapshots of setting by borrowing the structure of the author.

Barnett, Mac. 2016. *Rules of the House*. New York: Disney Hyperion.
Use of parentheses; quotation marks for dialogue; dash to show a thought is not finished aloud; apostrophes; variation in print.

Bloom, Becky. 1999. *Wolf!* New York: Scholastic.
Use of the colon for explanations; variations in print type.

Boelts, Maribeth. 2007. *Those Shoes.* Cambridge, MA: Candlewick.
Use of hyphenated words; ellipses; dashes; apostrophes; quotation marks; comma uses; variation in print; capitalization of proper nouns; variation in end punctuation.

Bottner, Barbara, and Gerald Kruglik. 2004. *Wallace's Lists.* New York: Katherine Tegen Books.
Use of colon for listing; use of italics to emphasize a word.

Bram, Elizabeth. 2015. *Rufus the Writer.* New York: Schwartz and Wade.
Use of quotation marks; colons; interjections.

Bryant, Jen. 2005. *Georgia's Bones.* Grand Rapids, MI: Eerdmans Books for Young Readers.
Examples of dashes; use of colon followed by a list.

———. 2016. *Six Dots: The Story of Young Louis Braille.* New York: Alfred A. Knopf.
Use of colons; ellipses; participial phrases; a variety of end punctuation.

Burleigh, Robert. 1997. *Flight: The Journey of Charles Lindbergh.* New York: Puffin Books.
Use of colons for a variety of reasons; examples of dashes; use of epithets.

———. 2003. *Home Run: The Story of Babe Ruth.* New York: Houghton Mifflin Harcourt Books for Young Readers.
Use of italics; epithet, "the Babe."

———. 2010. *Tiger of the Snows: Tenzing Norgay: The Boy Whose Dream Was Everest.* New York: Atheneum Books for Young Readers.
Uses colons and dashes for various reasons; italics to signify thoughts; capitalization of myriad proper nouns; contains examples of epithets and a variety of sentence types.

Capucilli, Alyssa Satin. 2015. *Tulip and Rex Write a Story.* New York: HarperCollins Children's Books.
Use of dialogue, ellipses, semicolon, end punctuation.

Chall, Marsha Wilson. 1992. *Up North at the Cabin.* New York: HarperCollins.
Examples of dashes, ellipses, and use of colon followed by a list.

Cocca-Leffler, Maryann. 2002. *Bravery Soup.* Morton Grove, IL: Albert Whitman.
A good text to use for reader's theater; includes interjections, different types of sentences, and a variety of conventions.

Crews, Donald. 1996. *Shortcut.* New York: Greenwillow Books.
Simple noun-verb sentence structures for sentence sense and punctuation for dialogue; use of all caps to indicate shouting.

———. 1998. *Bigmama's*. New York: Greenwillow Books.
Variation of print size; use of all caps to indicate shouting; dashes and ellipses; punctuation for dialogue.

Davies, Nicola. 2004. *Bat Loves the Night*. Cambridge, MA: Candlewick.
Examples of dashes and ellipses.

———. 2005. *One Tiny Turtle*. Cambridge, MA: Candlewick.
The beginning of this lyrical nonfiction book is a snapshot of setting. It can be used to help students create other snapshots of setting by borrowing the author's structure.

———. 2013. *The Promise*. Somerville, MA: Candlewick.
Examples of ellipses and use of a comma to separate words in a series.

Edwards, Pamela Duncan. 1998. *Barefoot: Escape on the Underground Railroad*. New York: Katherine Tegen Books.
Use of epithets; includes an author's note about the Underground Railroad.

Falatko, Julie. 2016. *Snappsy the Alligator (Did Not Ask to Be in This Book!)*. New York: Penguin Young Readers Group.
Variation in sentence types and print; interjections; use of double end punctuation; fragments; speech bubbles for conversation; commas; apostrophes.

Falconer, Ian. 2000. *Olivia*. New York: Atheneum Books for Young Readers.
Short sentences that can be used to develop sentence sense; use of illustrations for word splash.

———. 2001. *Olivia Saves the Circus*. New York: Atheneum Books for Young Readers.
Use of epithets; variation in print size.

Fleming, Candace. 2002. *Muncha! Muncha! Muncha!* New York: Atheneum Books for Young Readers.
Variation in print size; interjections.

Fletcher, Ralph. 1997. *Twilight Comes Twice*. New York: Clarion Books.
Contains examples of the use of a colon followed by a list.

———. 2003. *Hello, Harvest Moon*. New York: Clarion Books.
Use of italics, dashes, ellipses, and colon.

Fox, Mem. 1992. *Night Noises*. New York: Houghton Mifflin Harcourt Books for Young Readers.
Contains examples of ellipses and speech bubbles; variation of print style and size.

Frazee, Marla. 2006. *Roller Coaster*. New York: Houghton Mifflin Harcourt Books for Young Readers.
Simple noun-verb sentence; varying print type and size.

Fritz, Jean. 1997. *Bully for You, Teddy Roosevelt*. New York: Puffin.
Contains the use of epithets, parentheses, and commentary dashes.

Hall, Donald. 1994. *I Am the Dog, I Am the Cat*. New York: Dial Books.
Written in play format, this book easily lends itself to reader's theater.

Hanlon, Abby. 2012. *Ralph Tells a Story*. New York: Two Lions.
Variation in print; variety of end punctuation; use of speech bubbles; ellipses; quotation marks; apostrophes.

Helakoski, Leslie. 2014. *Big Pigs*. Honesdale, PA: Boyds Mills.
Compound predicates; illustrations for word splash; use of quotation marks; use of the apostrophe for slang; ellipses; variation in print.

Heller, Ruth. 1998. *A Cache of Jewels and Other Collective Nouns*. New York: Puffin.
Excellent examples of different types of nouns accompanied by rich illustrations.

———. 1998. *Many Luscious Lollipops: A Book About Adjectives*. New York: Puffin.
Many examples of the use of adjectives combined with rich illustrations.

———. 2000. *Fantastic! Wow! And Unreal! A Book About Interjections and Conjunctions*. New York: Puffin.
Contains many examples of interjections and the different kinds of conjunctions in context as well as in lists; beautiful illustrations are appealing to students.

Henkes, Kevin. 1991. *Chrysanthemum*. New York: Greenwillow Books.
Use of mild interjections; simple noun-verb sentences; capitalization of proper nouns; use of varying print size and italics.

The following Kevin Henkes books can be used to study a variety of conventions, including end punctuation, dialogue, dashes, parentheses, use of italics, talking captions, capitalization of proper nouns, variety of print size, and ellipses.

Chester's Way. 1997. New York: Greenwillow Books.
Jessica. 1998. New York: Greenwillow Books.
Grandpa and Bo. 2002. New York: Greenwillow Books.
Kitten's First Full Moon. 2004. New York: Greenwillow Books.
This book also uses an epithet.

Lilly's Purple Plastic Purse. 2006. New York: Greenwillow Books.
This book can also be used to show the use of and to replace commas.

Wemberly Worried. 2010. New York: Greenwillow Books.

Hest, Amy. 2007. *Mr. George Baker*. Cambridge, MA: Candlewick.
Use of dashes and semicolons; illustrations by Jon J. Muth can be used for a word splash.

———. 2008. *The Dog Who Belonged to No One*. New York: Abrams Books for Young Readers.
Use of ellipses.

High, Linda Oatman. 2012. *Barn Savers*. Honesdale, PA: Boyds Mills.
Use of the colon followed by a list.

Hoberman, Mary Ann. 2001. *You Read to Me, I'll Read to You: Very Short Stories to Read Together*. New York: Little, Brown.
Short poems written for two voices—can be used for reader's theater. This is part of a series of books that include fairy tales, fables, and Mother Goose rhymes.

Hopkinson, Deborah. 2012. *Annie and Helen*. New York: Random House.
Examples of dashes, variation in end punctuation, use of italics.

Horowitz, Ruth. 2004. *Crab Moon*. Cambridge, MA: Candlewick.
Short passages lend themselves to trying out the author's syntax.

Hunt, Linda Mullaly. 2015. *Fish in a Tree*. New York: Penguin.
Use of *–ed* participles to begin a sentence.

Jenkins, Martin. 2001. *Chameleons Are Cool*. Cambridge, MA: Candlewick.
Use of ellipses and dashes; variation in print size.

Johnston, Tony. 1994. *Amber on the Mountain*. New York: Penguin Putnam.
The opening paragraph is a snapshot of setting. It can be used to help students create other snapshots of setting by borrowing the structure of the author.

Jones, Val. 2015. *Who Wants Broccoli?* New York: HarperCollins.
Different uses of ellipses—one page has a period plus ellipses; use of quotation marks; end punctuation; illustrations for word splash.

Kearney, Meg. 2013. *Trouper*. New York: Scholastic.
Dashes; semicolon; end punctuation.

Keating, Jess. 2016. *Pink Is for Blobfish: Discovering the World's Perfectly Pink Animals*. New York: Alfred A. Knopf.
Boldface print; parentheses; use of hyphens; italics; variation in print; exclamation points; variety of sentence patterns; apostrophe use; use of commas.

LaMarche, Jim. 2000. *The Raft*. New York: HarperCollins.
Dashes; use of quotation marks; comma use.

Laminack, Lester. 1998. *The Sunsets of Miss Olivia Wiggins*. Atlanta, GA: Peachtree.
Uses italics to distinguish Miss Olivia Wiggins's memories from the present-day dialogue.

———. 2004. *Saturdays and Teacakes*. Atlanta: Peachtree.
Dialogue written in italics without quotation marks; examples of dashes and ellipses.

Lamstein, Sarah Marwil. 2010. *Big Night for Salamanders*. Honesdale, PA: Boyds Mills.
Variety of sentence types; dialogue; use of italics to separate information from the story.

Lowry, Lois. 2009. *Crow Call*. New York: Scholastic.
Examples of variation in sentence length; use of semicolon; alliteration.

Ludwig, Trudy. 2013. *The Invisible Boy*. New York: Alfred A. Knopf.
Ellipses; use of the dash; italics; commas for appositional phrases; apostrophes; quotation marks used to give a special name to something; participles.

Lyon, George Ella. 2003. *Mother to Tigers*. New York: Atheneum Books for Young Readers.
Use of dashes and ellipses; colon followed by a list as well as use of colon to further explain.

MacLachlan, Patricia. 2007. *Arthur, For the Very First Time*. New York: HarperCollins.
Use of colon to offer explanation or definition; use of bold print to indicate writing in a journal; use of italics to indicate the character's thinking.

———. 1994. *All the Places to Love*. New York: HarperCollins.
Use of the colon followed by a list; also contains examples of semicolons and dashes.

MacLachlan, Patricia and Emily MacLachlan. 2006. *Painting the Wind*. New York: HarperCollins.
Use of *and* to connect a series of nouns—items in a list; epithets; use of colons; dashes; semicolons; commas; capitalizing proper nouns.

Markle, Sandra. 2011. *Butterfly Tree*. Atlanta, GA: Peachtree.
Use of italics to show dialogue.

———. 2015. *Toad Weather*. Atlanta: Peachtree.
Dialogue; commas, dashes, end punctuation.

Martin, Jacqueline Briggs. 2009. *Snowflake Bentley*. New York: Houghton Mifflin Harcourt Books for Young Readers.
Use of epithets.

McFarland, Lyn Rossiter. 2006. *Widget*. New York: Square Fish.
Simple noun-verb sentence structures for developing sentence sense and punctuation for dialogue; ellipses.

McNaughton, Colin. 1998. *Suddenly!* New York: Houghton Mifflin Harcourt Books for Young Readers.
Variation of print size and style; use of word placement; variety of sentence types; use of speech bubbles.

Messner, Kate. 2011. *Over and Under the Snow*. San Francisco: Chronicle Books.
Variation in print; ellipses; dashes; use of commas; use of colon followed by a list.

Most, Bernard. 2003. *The Cow That Went Oink*. New York: Houghton Mifflin Harcourt Books for Young Readers.
Use of speech bubbles that are integral to an understanding of the text.

O'Neill, Alexis. 2002. *The Recess Queen*. New York: Scholastic.
Illustrations by Laura Huliska-Beith can be used for word splash; variation of print size; use of epithets.

Paulson, Gary. 2001. *Canoe Days*. New York: Dragonfly Books.
Interesting use of *and* to connect a series of objects without the use of a comma, like a rewind in the character's mind, recalling all the things he saw that day.

Pinborough, Jan. 2013. *Miss Moore Thought Otherwise: How Anne Carroll Moore Created Libraries for Children*. New York: Houghton Mifflin Harcourt.
Use of dashes; commas.

Plourde, Lynn. 2006. *Pigs in the Mud in the Middle of the Rud*. New York: Down East Books.
Simple noun-verb sentences; use of *and* to begin sentences for a list effect; use of ellipses; varying print size; conventions for conversation; interjections.

Pulver, Robin. 2003. *Punctuation Takes a Vacation*. New York: Holiday House.
Explains the importance of using punctuation marks in a very engaging way. Ellipses; use of different sizes and arrangement of print.

Ramsey, Calvin Alexander. 2010. *Ruth and the Green Book*. Minneapolis, MN: Carolrhoda Books.
Apostrophe use; comma after introductory clauses; quotation marks to designate a special name for something.

Rappaport, Doreen. 2016. *John's Secret Dreams: The Life of John Lennon*. New York: Disney-Hyperion.
Variations in print size and style.

Raschka, Chris. 2007. *Yo! Yes?* New York: Scholastic.
Can be used for examples of end punctuation.

Rawlinson, Julia. 2006. *Fletcher and the Falling Leaves*. New York: HarperCollins.
Different uses of commas; compound and complex sentences; ellipses; onomatopoeia.

Ray, Mary Lyn. 2001. *Mud*. New York: Houghton Mifflin Harcourt Books for Young Readers.
Use of colon to offer an explanation; simple noun-verb sentences.

Rocco, John. 2011. *Blackout*. New York: Hyperion.
Speech bubbles; ellipses; variation in print; exclamation points; fragments.

———. 2014. *Blizzard*. New York: Hyperion.
Examples of speech bubbles and labels.

Rockliff, Mara. 2014. *Chik Chak Shabbat*. Somerville, MA: Candlewick.
Compound predicates; use of quotation marks; ellipses; commas.

Rosen, Michael. 2003. *We're Going on a Bear Hunt*. New York: Aladdin Books.
A good text to use for reader's theater; includes interjections and variation of sentence types and print size.

Ruurs, Margriet. 2016. *Stepping Stones: A Refugee Family's Journey*. Victoria, British Columbia: Orca Book.
Use of commentary dashes; commas in a series; proper nouns; purposeful fragments; quotation marks for dialogue.

Ryan, Pam Muñoz. 2001. *Mice and Beans*. New York: Scholastic.
Use of variations in print style and size; ellipses; interjections.

Rylant, Cynthia. 1991. *Night in the Country*. New York: Atheneum Books for Young Readers.
Dashes; ellipses; use of colon.

———. 1993. *When I Was Young in the Mountains*. New York: Puffin Books.
Use of commas in compound sentences.

———. *An Angel for Solomon Singer*. New York: Scholastic.
Repeated use of parentheses to show what the main character is thinking.

Sams, Carl R., II, and Jean Stoick. 2000. *Stranger in the Woods: A Photographic Fantasy*. Milford, MI: Carl R. Sams II Photography.
Use of epithets.

Schachner, Judy. 2005. *Skippyjon Jones*. New York: Puffin.
Use of ellipses and variety of print size; examples of epithets.

Shapiro, Karen Jo. 2005. *Because I Could Not Stop My Bike and Other Poems*. Watertown, MA: Charlesbridge.
A collection of parodies written in the style of well-known poems; demonstrates how to use the syntax and mechanics of another author.

Stanton, Elizabeth Rose. 2014. *Henny*. New York: Simon and Schuster.
Ellipses; variation in print; end punctuation.

Steinberg, Laya. 2005. *Thesaurus Rex.* Cambridge, MA: Barefoot Books.
Use of colon followed by a list.

Trimmer, Christian. 2015. *Simon's New Bed.* New York: Atheneum Books for Young Readers.
Use of a different font to indicate dialogue; ellipses; end punctuation.

Truss, Lynne. 2006. *Eats, Shoots and Leaves: Why, Commas Really DO Make a Difference!* New York: G. P. Putnam's Sons.
A visual example of the use of commas; includes explanations written in simple language.

Walton, Rick. 2007. *Just Me and 6,000 Rats: A Tale of Conjunctions.* Layton, UT: Gibbs Smith.
Can be used to teach the purpose of conjunctions and the punctuation that goes with them.

Wells, Rosemary. 2002. *Bunny Cakes.* New York: Puffin Books.
An example of the use of *and* instead of commas to link actions.

Whitcomb, Mary E. 1998. *Odd Velvet.* San Francisco: Chronicle Books.
Variations in print.

White, E. B. 2005. *Stuart Little.* New York: Harper and Row.
Examples of a variety of sentence types; the opening to "Ames Crossing" is useful for trying out the author's syntax.

Willems, Mo. 2010. *City Dog, Country Frog.* New York: Hyperion.
Contains examples of the use of commas, ellipses, and dialogue.

———. 2015. *The Story of Diva and Flea.* New York: Disney-Hyperion Books.
Examples of parentheses; quotation marks for titles; participial phrases; variation in print.

Wood, Douglas. 2006. *Nothing to Do.* New York: Dutton Books for Young Readers.
Use of ellipses and commentary dashes; fragments as part of a list; variety of print size and type; use of italics.

Woodson, Jacqueline. 2012. *Each Kindness.* New York: Penguin.
Use of dashes; italics used for dialogue.

Yamada, Kobi. 2016. *What Do You Do with a Problem?* Seattle, WA: Compendium.
Opportunities to explore pronouns and their antecedents; purposeful use of fragments; ellipses; use of exclamation points; commas.

Yolen, Jane. 2010. *Elsie's Bird.* New York: Philomel Books.
Adverbs; commentary dash; quotation marks for song titles and dialogue; participial phrases.

Afterword

We continue to be inspired and grow as writers through the study of mentor texts and their authors. Our association with the many wonderful teachers we meet in graduate courses and conferences, as well as those with whom we work closely on a daily basis, is the extended writing community that sustains us and supports our work. When the classroom teacher reads aloud regularly to the students and becomes the model for writing along with the mentor texts, something quite magical happens in classrooms. Students express themselves as writers in extraordinary and unexpected ways. They develop a passion for writing and become mentors for their peers and even for their teachers. What happens, in fact, is that a writing community is built with a strong foundation of mentor texts that allows the teacher to start constructing the walls for many rooms using scaffolds from the mentor texts, adding windows, doors, and crown molding, like craft. At first the students are only apprentices, but eventually, they become master masons and carpenters. Just like Fred and Lulu, characters in *The Magic Toolbox* by Mie Araki, students can dream big and imagine something new if they have the right tools. The mentor texts and the teacher will provide them with just that—the tools they need to grow as writers.

There are many ways to stretch ourselves as writers. Shelley Harwayne (2005) has created writing lessons inspired by the children in the adult fiction she reads. Harwayne clearly demonstrates the importance of teacher-as-reader to do the job of teacher-as-writer. She encourages teachers to use the titles from her book *Novel Perspectives* for staff book clubs. In this way, teachers are reading like writers on two levels—with picture books and adult books as mentor texts. We find ourselves doing this all the time. Using mentor texts to help us live the writing journey with our students exemplifies what the reading-writing connection is all about. When you begin using mentor texts, the teaching possibilities are endless. You do not have to limit yourself to the mentor texts we have used here, but we invite you to start here with many of our favorites. We wish you good fortune as you embark on your writing journey.

References

Anderson, Jeff. 2005. *Mechanically Inclined: Building Grammar, Usage, and Style into Writer's Workshop*. Portland, ME: Stenhouse.

Angelillo, Janet. 2002. *A Fresh Approach to Teaching Punctuation*. New York: Scholastic.

Araki, Mie. 2003. *The Magic Toolbox*. San Francisco: Chronicle.

Atwell, Nancie. 1998. *In the Middle: New Understanding About Writing, Reading, and Learning*. Portsmouth, NH: Heinemann.

Bourque, Paula. 2016. *Close Writing: Developing Purposeful Writers in Grades 2–6*. Portland, ME: Stenhouse.

Boushey, Gail, and Joan Moser. 2009. *The CAFE Book: Engaging All Students in Daily Literacy Assessment and Instruction*. Portland, ME: Stenhouse.

Calkins, Lucy McCormick. 2001. *The Art of Teaching Reading*. New York: Addison-Wesley.

———. 2003. *Units of Study for Primary Writing: A Yearlong Curriculum, Grades K–2*. Portsmouth, NH: Heinemann.

Dorfman, Lynne, and Diane Dougherty. 2014. *Grammar Matters: Lessons, Tips, & Conversations Using Mentor Texts, K–6*. Portland, ME: Stenhouse.

Dunning, Stephen, and William Stafford. 1992. *Getting the Knack: 20 Poetry Writing Exercises*. Urbana, IL: NCTE.

Dweck, Carol S. 2008. *Mindset, the New Psychology of Success: How We Can Learn to Fulfill Our Potential*. New York: Ballantine Books.

Elbow, Peter. 1998. *Writing with Power: Teaching Techniques for Mastering the Writing Process*. New York: Oxford University Press.

Esbensen, Barbara Juster. 1995. *A Celebration of Bees: Helping Children Write Poetry*. New York: Henry Holt.

Fisher, Douglas, Nancy Frey, Heather L. Anderson, and Marisol C. Thayre. 2014. *Text-Dependent Questions, K–5: Pathways to Close and Critical Reading*. Thousand Oaks, CA: Corwin.

Fletcher, Ralph. 1993. *What a Writer Needs*. Portsmouth, NH: Heinemann.

———. 1999. *Live Writing: Breathing Life into Your Words*. New York: HarperCollins.

Fletcher, Ralph, and JoAnn Portalupi. 2001. *Writing Workshop: The Essential Guide*. Portsmouth, NH: Heinemann.

Gay, Carol. 1976. "Reading Aloud and Learning to Write." *The Elementary School Journal* 77:87–93.

Glover, Matt. 2014. "Vision and Choice in the K–3 Writing Workshop." In *Write Now! Empowering Writers in Today's K–6 Classroom*, ed. Kathy Ganske. Newark, DE: International Literacy Association.

Golub, Barb. 2015. *Infusing Grammar into the Writer's Workshop: A Guide for K–6 Teachers*. New York: Routledge.

Graves, Donald. 1994. *A Fresh Look at Writing*. Portsmouth, NH: Heinemann.

Harwayne, Shelley. 1992. *Lasting Impressions: Weaving Literature into the Writing Workshop*. Portsmouth, NH: Heinemann.

———. 2005. *Novel Perspectives: Writing Minilessons Inspired by the Children in Adult Fiction*. Portsmouth, NH: Heinemann.

Heard, Georgia. 2016. *Heart Maps: Helping Students Create and Craft Authentic Writing*. Portsmouth, NH: Heinemann.

Johnston, Peter. 2012. *Opening Minds: Using Language to Change Lives*. Portland, ME: Stenhouse.

Keene, Ellin, and Susan Zimmerman. 1997. *Mosaic of Thought: Teaching Comprehension in a Reader's Workshop*. Portsmouth, NH: Heinemann.

Lancia, Peter J. 1997. "Literary Borrowing: The Effects of Literature on Children's Writing." *The Reading Teacher* 50:470–475.

Lane, Barry. 2016. *After THE END: Teaching and Learning Creative Revision*. 2nd ed. Portsmouth, NH: Heinemann.

———. 1993. *Writing as a Road to Self-Discovery*. Shoreham, VT: Discover Writing Press.

Lehman, Christopher, and Kate Roberts. 2013. *Falling in Love with Close Reading: Lessons for Analyzing Texts—and Life*. Portsmouth, NH: Heinemann.

Lyon, George Ella. 1999. *Where I'm From, Where Poems Come From*. Spring, TX: Absey.

Marchetti, Allison, and Rebekah O'Dell. 2015. *Writing with Mentors: How to Reach Every Writer in the Room Using Current, Engaging Mentor Texts*. Portsmouth, NH: Heinemann.

Miller, Debbie. 2002. *Reading with Meaning: Teaching Comprehension in the Primary Grades*. Portland, ME: Stenhouse.

Morgan, Bruce. 2005. *Writing Through the Tween Years: Supporting Writers, Grades 3–6*. Portland, ME: Stenhouse.

Murphy, Pamela. 2003. "Discovering the Ending in the Beginning." *Language Arts* 80:461–469.

Oliver, Mary. 1994. *A Poetry Handbook: A Prose Guide to Understanding and Writing Poetry*. New York: Houghton Mifflin Harcourt.

Portalupi, JoAnn, and Ralph Fletcher. 2001. *Nonfiction Craft Lessons: Teaching Information Writing K–8*. Portland, ME: Stenhouse.

Ray, Katie Wood. 1999. *Wondrous Words: Writers and Writing in the Elementary Classroom*. Urbana, IL: NCTE.

———. 2002. *What You Know by Heart: How to Develop Curriculum for Your Writing Workshop*. Portsmouth, NH: Heinemann.

Ray, Katie Wood, with Lester Laminack. 2001. *The Writing Workshop: Working Through the Hard Parts (and They're All Hard Parts)*. Urbana, IL: NCTE.

Routman, Regie. 2005. *Writing Essentials*. Portsmouth, NH: Heinemann.

Schuster, Edgar H. 2003. *Breaking the Rules: Liberating Writers Through Innovative Grammar Instruction*. Portsmouth, NH: Heinemann.

Shanahan, Timothy. 2014. "Writing About Reading: Writing Instruction in the Age of the Common Core State Standards." In *Write Now! Empowering Writers in Today's K–6 Classroom*, ed. Kathy Ganske. Newark, DE: International Literacy Association.

Shubitz, Stacey. 2016. *Craft Moves: Lesson Sets for Teaching Writing with Mentor Texts*. Portsmouth, ME: Stenhouse.

Spandel, Vicki. 2005. *The 9 Rights of Every Writer*. Portsmouth, NH: Heinemann.

Topping, Donna, and Sandra Hoffman. 2006. *Getting Grammar: 150 New Ways to Teach an Old Subject*. Portsmouth, NH: Heinemann.

Vygotsky, L. S. 1978. *Mind in Society: The Development of Higher Psychological Processes*. Cambridge, MA: Harvard University Press.

Index

Page numbers followed by *f* indicate figures.